## DATE DUE

| | |
|---|---|
| | |
| | |
| | |
| | |
| | |
| | |
| | |
| | |
| | |
| | |
| | |
| | |
| | |
| | |
| | |

BRODART, CO.                                   Cat. No. 23-221

# THE COLLABORATION

BEN URWAND

# THE COLLABORATION

## HOLLYWOOD'S PACT WITH HITLER

THE BELKNAP PRESS OF HARVARD UNIVERSITY PRESS

CAMBRIDGE, MASSACHUSETTS & LONDON, ENGLAND ■ 2013

*Library of Congress Cataloging-in-Publication Data*

Urwand, Ben, 1977–
    The collaboration : Hollywood's pact with Hitler / Ben Urwand.
        pages   cm
        Includes bibliographical references and index.
        ISBN 978-0-674-72474-7 (hardcover : alk. paper)
    1. Motion pictures, American—Germany—History—20th century.   2. Motion picture industry—Germany—History—20th century.   3. Motion picture industry—United States—History—20th century.   4. Germany—Civilization—American influences.   5. National socialism and motion pictures.   I. Title.
    PN1993.5.G3U79 2013
    791.430973'0943—dc23          2013013576

# CONTENTS

THE COLLABORATION

# PROLOGUE

Eleven men were sitting in a screening room in Berlin. Only a few of them were Nazis. At the front of the room was Dr. Ernst Seeger, chief censor from long before Hitler came to power. Next to Seeger were his assistants: a producer, a philosopher, an architect, and a pastor. Farther back were the representatives of a film distribution company and two expert witnesses. The movie they were about to watch came all the way from America, and it was called *King Kong*.

When the projector began to whir, one of the representatives from the film company started to speak. He read out a script that emphasized the fictitious nature of the events on the screen. As he spoke, the others in the room watched the action unfold. They saw an enormous gorilla fall in love with a beautiful woman and then fall off the Empire State Building. One of the characters muttered something about beauty and the beast, and the movie came to an end.[1]

It was time to turn to the official proceedings. Dr. Seeger looked over at the first expert witness, Professor Zeiss from the German Health Office. "In your expert opinion," Seeger asked, "could this picture be expected to damage the health of normal spectators?"[2]

Zeiss was in no mood to cooperate. "First," he said, "I need to know whether the company trying to sell this film is German or American."

Seeger replied that it was a German distribution company.

Zeiss erupted. "I am astounded and shocked," he yelled, "that a *German* company would dare to seek permission for a film that can only be damaging to the health of its viewers. It is not merely incomprehensible but indeed an impertinence to show such a film, for this film is NOTHING LESS THAN AN ATTACK ON THE NERVES OF THE GERMAN PEOPLE!"[3]

There was a brief silence. Then Seeger requested that the expert not judge the motives of the company in this way but confine his statements to his own area of expertise.[4]

Zeiss returned to the original question. "It provokes our racial instincts," he said, "to show a blonde woman of the Germanic type in the hand of an ape. It harms the healthy racial feelings of the German people. The torture to which this woman is exposed, her mortal fear . . . and the other horrible things that one would only imagine in a drunken frenzy are harmful to German health.

"My judgment has nothing to do with the technical achievements of the film, which I recognize. Nor do I care what other countries think is good for *their* people. For the German people, this film is unbearable."[5]

Zeiss had argued his case with all the zeal of a good National Socialist. No one could fault his motives. In response, Dr. Schulte, assistant practitioner at a mental hospital in Berlin, defended the film company's position. Unlike Zeiss, he was calm and composed, and he denied all of the previous charges.

"In every instance that the film potentially seems dangerous," he said, "it is in fact merely ridiculous. We must not forget that we are dealing with an *American* film produced for American spectators, and that the German public is considerably more critical. Even if it is admitted that the kidnapping of the blonde woman by a legendary beast is a delicate matter, it still does not go beyond the borders of the permissible.

"Psychopaths or women," he added, "who could be thrown into a panic by the film, must not provide the criteria for this decision."[6]

The committee members were at an impasse. Both sides had advanced tenable arguments; no one was willing to pass judgment just yet. Six months earlier, all cultural institutions in Germany had been put under the jurisdiction of the Propaganda Ministry, and since then, no one really knew what was permissible and what was not. Certainly no one wanted to get on the bad side of the new propaganda minister, Joseph Goebbels. Seeger therefore requested the Ministry's position on the case, and he set up a second hearing for the following week.

There was just one more thing Seeger needed to do. He wrote to Zeiss and asked him to untangle his original statement. Was *King Kong* harmful to German health simply because it endangered the race instinct?

Four days later, Seeger received a reply. "It is untrue," Zeiss wrote, "that I said the film endangers the race instinct and is dangerous to one's health *for that reason*. Rather, my expert opinion is that the film is *in the first place* dangerous to one's health, and that it *additionally* endangers the race instinct, which is *another* reason it endangers one's health."[7]

Zeiss' letter may not have been entirely clear, but it certainly seemed as if he thought the film endangered one's health. The committee now just needed to hear from the Propaganda Ministry. A week passed without any hint of a reply, and then another. Seeger was forced to postpone the up-coming meeting. Finally, a letter arrived. After all the fuss, the Propaganda Ministry announced that *King Kong* did *not* harm the race instinct. Seeger quickly reconvened the committee.

Fewer people attended this time. The specialists had already testified, and the narrator was no longer needed. Instead of employing a voice-over, the distribution company wanted to retitle the film so that German viewers would recognize its value as pure entertainment. The company submitted a seventh attempt at a title—*The Fable of King Kong, an American Trick-and-Sensation Film*—and then the meeting got underway.

Seeger began by summarizing the plot of the film. "On an undiscov-ered island in the South Sea, animals from prehistoric times are still able to exist: a fifteen-meter-high gorilla, sea-snakes, dinosaurs of various kinds, a gigantic bird, and others. Outside this prehistoric empire, separated by a wall, live blacks who offer human sacrifices to the gorilla, 'King Kong.' The blacks kidnap the blonde star of a film expedition on the island and present her to King Kong instead of a woman of their own race. The ship's crew invades the gorilla's empire and has terrible battles with the prehistoric beasts in order to survive. They capture the gorilla by ren-dering him unconscious with a gas bomb, and they take him to New York. The gorilla breaks out during an exhibition, everyone flees in pan-icked horror, and an elevated commuter train is derailed. The gorilla then climbs up a skyscraper with his girl-doll in his hand, and airplanes bring about his downfall."[8]

Upon completing the reading, Seeger announced the big news. "Be-cause the specialist from the Propaganda Ministry stated that the film does not harm German racial feelings, the only thing left to determine is whether the film endangers the people's health."[9]

Seeger did not stop to point out that there was something very odd about the Propaganda Ministry's position. He himself had just said that the blacks in the film presented a white woman to King Kong "instead of

An American propaganda poster from the First World War. The gorilla, holding a club labeled "Kultur," represents a German soldier. Courtesy of Universal Images Group; Getty Images.

The promotional poster for the film *King Kong* (1933). Courtesy of Hulton Archive; Getty Images.

a woman of their own race." He was invoking Thomas Jefferson's claim from 150 years earlier that black men preferred white women "as uniformly as is the preference of the Oranootan for the black women over those of his own species."[10] In other words, he was bringing up an obvious racial problem with the film. This image did not seem to offend the Propaganda Ministry, however. In the Third Reich, it was perfectly acceptable to show an "Oranootan's" desire for "a blonde woman of the Germanic type."

It was acceptable even though this exact image had been used against Germany during the previous World War. In a massive propaganda campaign, the Americans and British had portrayed the Germans as savage gorillas who threatened the purity of innocent white women. The campaign had incensed many young Germans who went on to become Nazis, but it did not seem to be on anyone's mind anymore.

And so, instead of examining the obvious problems with *King Kong*, the committee simply returned to the original question of whether the film could be expected to damage the health of normal spectators. Zeiss had said that *King Kong* was "an attack on the nerves of the German people," and he had referred to particular images that he thought had a damaging effect. He had failed, however, to provide any justification for his view. The committee therefore rejected his testimony and found that "the overall effect of this typical American adventure film on the German spectator is merely to provide kitschy entertainment, so that no incurable or lasting effect on the health of the normal spectator can be expected." The film was simply too "unreal" and "fairy-tale like" to be believable. The committee then approved *King Kong* under the new title, *The Fable of King Kong, an American Trick-and-Sensation Film*.[11]

Still, Seeger was not entirely comfortable releasing the film in its current form. He decided not to show the close-ups of King Kong holding the screaming woman in his hand, for according to Zeiss they were particularly damaging to German health. He also did not show the derailing of the commuter train, for the scene "shakes the people's confidence in this important means of public transportation."[12]

On December 1, 1933, *King Kong* opened simultaneously in thirty first-run theaters throughout Germany.[13] The film received mixed reviews in the press. The main Nazi newspaper, *Völkischer Beobachter*, admired the technical achievement but criticized the cheapness of the plot. "It is unknown whether it was the Americans or the Germans who felt a need to call this a trick-and-sensation film," the paper reported. "It is thus unknown whether this was meant to be an excuse or a justification. All we know is that when we Germans hear the beautiful word 'fable,' we imagine something very different from this picture."[14]

Goebbels' personal newspaper, *Der Angriff*, began its review by posing the question of why *King Kong* enjoyed such incredible success in the United States. "We venture to say that it had little to do with technology and everything to do with the plot. This picture shows the terrific struggle of almighty nature—represented by King Kong and gigantic dinosaurs—against the civilized power of the highly developed white race. . . . Does civilization triumph in the end? Hardly! In truth King Kong is the tragic hero of this film."[15]

The discussion around *King Kong* went all the way up to the highest echelons of the Third Reich. According to the foreign press chief, "one of Hitler's favorite films was *King Kong*, the well-known story of a gigantic ape who falls in love with a woman no bigger than his hand. . . . Hitler was captivated by this atrocious story. He spoke of it often and had it screened several times."[16]

The Nazis' fascination with *King Kong* does not fit neatly into the accepted account of Hollywood in the 1930s. In the popular imagination, this was the "golden age" of American cinema, the great decade in which the studios produced such memorable films as *The Wizard of Oz, Gone with the Wind, Mr. Smith Goes to Washington*, and *It Happened One Night*. It was the decade in which Hollywood movies reached a level of perfection that previously had only been dreamed of. "One has the feeling," an eminent critic wrote of the year 1939, that "an art has found its perfect balance, its ideal form of expression. . . . Here are all the characteristics of the ripeness of a classical art."[17]

An important fact about Hollywood movies in this period, however, is that they were extremely popular in Nazi Germany. Between twenty and sixty new American titles hit the screens in Germany every year until the outbreak of the Second World War, and they infused all aspects of German culture.[18] A casual observer walking the streets of Berlin could see the evidence everywhere. There were lines of people outside the theaters, photographs of Hollywood stars on the covers of magazines, and glowing reviews of the latest movies in the newspapers. But for all the success and for all the hype, the American studios were forced to pay a terrible price.

This book reveals for the first time the complex web of interactions between the American studios and the German government in the 1930s.[19] It unearths a series of secret documents from archives in the United States and Germany to show that the studios came to a definite arrangement with the Nazis in this period. According to the terms of this arrangement, Hollywood movies could be shown in Germany, even potentially threatening ones like *King Kong*.

The idea for a book on Hollywood's dealings with Nazi Germany was sparked by a brief comment that the screenwriter and novelist Budd Schulberg made very late in his life. Schulberg said that in the 1930s, Louis B. Mayer, the head of MGM, screened films to the German consul in Los Angeles and cut out whatever the consul objected to.[20] The comment was shocking; if true, it seemed to shatter a common idea about Hollywood, one that has been recycled in dozens of books—namely that Hollywood was synonymous with anti-fascism during its golden age.[21]

The image of the most powerful man in Hollywood working together with a Nazi set off a nine-year-long investigation that resulted in this book.

The first research trip was not at all promising. The files of the Hollywood studios in the Los Angeles archives were scattered and incomplete, and they contained very few references to the activities of the German consul. The trade papers provided only superficial details of the studios' business dealings in Berlin. The 350 American movies that were permitted or banned by the Nazis (all of which were consulted) did not reveal much on their own. These materials in no way gave a complete sense of the relationship between Hollywood and the Third Reich.

The German archives were different. A quick examination of the files at the Bundesarchiv revealed not only Hitler's opinions of American movies but also a series of letters from the Berlin branches of MGM, Paramount, and Twentieth Century-Fox to Hitler's adjutants. These letters adopted a fawning tone, and one of them included the sign-off "Heil Hitler!"[22] That was not all: the Political Archive of the German Foreign Office also held detailed reports about the activities of the German consul in Los Angeles.

Visits to other archives then started to fill out the story. The scripts of various produced and unproduced films at the Margaret Herrick Library and the University of Southern California Cinematic Arts Library took on a new meaning in the context of the notes of the Los Angeles consul. The copyright records at the Library of Congress held the one remaining copy of the first-ever anti-Nazi film script, which the consul had prevented from being made. The files of various Jewish groups in Los Angeles contained the actual opinions of the heads of the Hollywood studios. The German censorship records were full of fascinating interpretations of American movies. And the Commerce and State Department materials at the National Archives revealed in great detail the business that the studios were doing in Germany.

Over the course of the investigation, one word kept reappearing in both the German and American records: "collaboration" (Zusammenarbeit). And gradually it became clear that this word accurately described the particular arrangement between the Hollywood studios and the German government in the 1930s. Like other American companies such as IBM and General Motors, the Hollywood studios put profit above principle in their decision to do business with the Nazis. They funneled money into the German economy in a variety of disturbing ways.[23] But, as the United States Department of Commerce recognized, the Hollywood studios were not simply distributors of goods; they were purveyors of ideas and culture.[24] They had the chance to show the world what was really happening in Germany. Here was where the term "collaboration" took on its full meaning.

The studio heads, who were mostly immigrant Jews, went to dramatic lengths to hold on to their investment in Germany.[25] Although few remarked on it at the time, these men followed the instructions of the German consul in Los Angeles, abandoning or changing a whole series of pictures that would have exposed the brutality of the Nazi regime.[26] This was the arrangement of the 1930s, and in coming to the end of a long search, it suddenly became clear why the evidence was scattered in so many places: it was because collaboration always involves the participation of more than one party. In this case, the collaboration involved not only the Hollywood studios and the German government but also a variety of other people and organizations in the United States. If this is a dark chapter in Hollywood history, then it is also a dark chapter in American history.

At the center of the collaboration was Hitler himself. Hitler was obsessed with movies, and he understood their power to shape public opinion. In December 1930, two years before becoming dictator of Germany, his party rioted against Universal Pictures' *All Quiet on the Western Front* in Berlin, leading to the first instances of collaboration with the American studios. For the remainder of the decade, he benefited immensely from an arrangement that was never discussed outside a few offices in Berlin, New York, and Los Angeles.

It is time to remove the layers that have hidden the collaboration for so long and to reveal the historical connection between the most important individual of the twentieth century and the movie capital of the world.

# ONE

# HITLER'S OBSESSION
# WITH FILM

Every night before going to bed Adolf Hitler watched a movie. He picked the title himself from a list presented to him at dinner, and then he led his guests to his private cinema in the Reich Chancellery (or, if he were on vacation, in the Berghof near Berchtesgaden). All the members of his household—his adjutants, his servants, even the chauffeurs of his guests—were permitted to join him. When everyone had taken a seat, the projection began.[1]

At this point, something quite strange happened: Hitler stopped talking. Earlier, at dinner, he had entertained or bored his guests with his monologues, and before that, he had dictated to his secretaries.[2] Now, suddenly, he was quiet. For this one brief period, which began somewhere between 8:00 and 9:00 PM and ran well into the night, he was absolutely captivated by the images on the screen.

After the movie, he started to talk again. He quickly gave his opinion of what he had seen. His adjutants noted down his opinions, which fell into three main categories. The first category was "good" (*gut*). He said that a movie was "good," "very good," "very nice and thrilling," or "excellent."[3] Often he admired something in particular: "the very good acting of Hans Moser," "the very good performance of

Hitler entertaining dinner guests at the Berghof near Berchtesgaden (1939).
Courtesy of Hugo Jaeger; Getty Images.

Zarah Leander."[4] Sometimes he even distinguished between the various aspects of a movie: "characters and shots: good; plot: not exciting enough."[5]

This led to the second category: "bad" (*schlecht*). He said that a movie was "bad," "very bad," "particularly bad," or "extraordinarily bad."[6] He used words like "repulsive" or expressions like "the most potent crap."[7] He singled out certain actors: "bad, particularly Gustaf Gründgens," "not enjoyed because of the bad performance of Gründgens."[8] On other occasions, he lamented the way a good actor's abilities were wasted: "Imperio Argentina: very good; directing: bad."[9]

Finally, there was always the possibility that Hitler would not watch a movie to the end. In such cases, the movie was "switched off" (*abgebrochen*): "switched off by order of the Führer," "switched off after the first hundred meters," "switched off after the first few minutes."[10] Sometimes, he switched off a movie simply because he did not like it. Other times, his reasons were more complicated. One night, for instance, he ordered the projectionist to switch off a movie about the World War, and then he gave his explanation: "The Führer is of the opinion that such issues should only be treated in huge productions."[11]

Nothing was ever allowed to interfere with Hitler's nightly screenings. When British Prime Minister Neville Chamberlain visited him on September 15, 1938, two weeks before the notorious conference in Munich, the schedule was as follows: from 5:30 to 8:10 PM, Hitler discussed the fate of Czechoslovakia with Chamberlain in his study; from 8:15 to 8:20, he reported the results of the discussion to his foreign minister Joachim von Ribbentrop; finally, after a quick dinner, he watched a German movie starring Ingrid Bergman. Even though his conversation with Chamberlain had gone well, he still made sure to give his honest opinion of the movie: he said that it was "not good."[12]

Over time, there was just one important change in Hitler's movie watching. His adjutants complained that there were 365 days in a year and not enough good German films to satisfy him. They therefore put in a request for more films from the United States. Hitler was pleased about this—he saw it as an opportunity to learn about American culture—and as usual, his opinions were noted down.[13] Here is a list of what he watched, mostly in June 1938:

*Way Out West* (Laurel and Hardy): good!
*Swiss Miss* (Laurel and Hardy): the Führer applauded the film
*Tarzan*: bad
*Bluebeard's Eighth Wife* (starring Gary Cooper, Claudette Colbert, directed by Ernst Lubitsch): switched off
*Shanghai* (starring Charles Boyer and Loretta Young): switched off
*Tip-Off Girls*: switched off[14]

It was a typical list. No matter what Hitler watched, his opinions always fit into the same three categories. His adjutants could sometimes even tell what his opinions would be in advance of the screenings. They knew, for example, that he was a big fan of Mickey Mouse cartoons.[15] In July 1937, he put in a request for five titles, including *Mickey's Fire Brigade* and *Mickey's Polo Team*.[16] The head of the Propaganda Ministry, Joseph Goebbels, took note of this and gave Hitler a surprise a few months later: "I present the Führer with 32 of the best films from the last 4 years and 12 Mickey Mouse films (including a wonderful art album) for Christmas.

He is very pleased and extremely happy for this treasure that will hopefully bring him much joy and relaxation."[17]

The members of Hitler's inner circle also knew that one of his favorite actresses was Greta Garbo. His reaction to *Camille* (recorded in Goebbels' diary) was particularly memorable: "Everything sinks in the presence of the great, isolated art of the divine woman. We are dazed and overcome in the deepest way. We don't wipe away our tears. Taylor is Garbo's ideal partner. The Führer is glowing. He thinks that bad casting of the male lead can often destroy the achievement of women. But in this film everything fits together perfectly."[18]

Not everyone knew about Hitler's movie preferences, however, and on a few unfortunate occasions, his tastes were criticized. After he watched a Laurel and Hardy slapstick comedy called *Block-Heads*, for example, he said that the film was good because it contained "a lot of very nice ideas and clever jokes."[19] The reviewer for the Nazi newspaper *Der Angriff*, on the other hand, did not appreciate this kind of humor at all: "Everything is so focused on the simplest slapstick comedy in the most primitive and exaggerated manner that you can predict just what will happen every time. . . . You can easily imagine the Americans throwing their arms up in the air with joy as the film unfolds. A nation that likes such a film must be deeply uncomplicated."[20] The German censors ended up banning this particular film, not for the humor but for the way it depicted the World War. They objected to the idea that Stan Laurel, who played a dim-witted American soldier, could have been guarding a trench from 1918 to 1938, and they disapproved of the thick-accented German aviator who told Laurel that he could go home.[21] Hitler reacted differently to the scene: in his view, it was just funny.

But these were minor disagreements in the scheme of things. Every now and then, Hitler reacted to a movie in a way that no one could have predicted. He was particularly keen to watch a Paramount film called *Tip-Off Girls* after some German criminals had carried out a series of holdups through the use of road blocks. He requested a copy of *Tip-Off Girls* from the Propaganda Ministry, along with a written translation of the dialogue.[22]

He was following very closely as he watched the opening scene: two men were driving a truck down a highway, and they came to a sudden stop when they saw a woman lying in the middle of the road.

"Are you hurt?" one man asked.

"Yeah, what's the matter, babe?" said the other.

"Oh, they threw me out of the car," she managed to reply.

Then, from behind the bushes, a gangster pointed a gun at the two drivers. "Alright, you guys, this is a stickup," he said. "I want your truck and everything in it. Come on, get moving."

As his men took over the truck, the gangster pulled the woman aside. "Nice work, Reena," he said. "Deegan will be pleased."

"That's my job, Marty—pleasing Deegan."[23]

It did not take long for Hitler to switch off the film.[24] *Tip-Off Girls* was definitely bad, but that was not why he stopped watching it. Rather, he realized he had something more important to do. Three days later, a law appeared that was personally written by the Führer. It was a peculiar law because it consisted of only one sentence: "Whoever sets up a road block with intent to commit a crime will be punished by death."[25]

This unusual episode hinted at the true motivation behind Hitler's nightly routine. Without any doubt, he derived a lot of pleasure from his movies. But he was also seduced by them. He believed that they contained a mysterious, almost magical power that somehow resembled his own abilities as an orator.[26] Out of a sense of awe and respect, therefore, he allowed himself to become a spectator. He stopped talking, he let the images unfold in front of him, and sometimes he was even overwhelmed by their power.

It is hard to pinpoint exactly when his obsession with the movies began. Perhaps it was nearly thirty years earlier, in 1910, when he was leading a very different life. Back then, he was boarding at a men's lodging home in Vienna, and one day he devised a promising business strategy with a man named Reinhold Hanisch. He would paint postcards of the city, Hanisch would sell the postcards at various pubs, and they would split the profits between them.[27]

Hanisch told the rest of the story: "At Easter we did well and had a little more money to spend, so Hitler went to the movies. I preferred to drink some wine, which Hitler despised. The next day I knew at once that he was planning a new project. He had seen *The Tunnel*, a picture made from a novel by Bernhard Kellermann, and he told me the story. An orator makes a speech in a tunnel and becomes a great popular tribune. Hitler was aflame with the idea that this was the way to found a new party. I laughed at him and didn't take him seriously. . . . He had more success with other people, however, for they were always ready for fun, and Hitler was a sort of amusement for them. There was continual debating; often the Home looked as if an election campaign were in progress."[28]

Hanisch's story is dubious in several respects. For a start, it is very unlikely that Hitler gave his first successful speeches or intended to found a political party this early in his life; according to most accounts, he discovered his political ambitions only after the World War. Furthermore, the film that Hanisch cited, which did contain a magnificent speech, was released not in 1910 but in 1915.[29] Still, it would be a mistake to write off Hanisch's story entirely. There were several popular movies about orators in 1910, and it is possible that Hitler saw one that convinced him of his true calling long before he officially discovered his talent.[30] This seems especially plausible in light of one final point: while Hitler was dictating a highly unusual chapter of *Mein Kampf*, he made the same connection himself.

The chapter, which Hitler called "The Significance of the Spoken Word," was a kind of meditation on his own oratorical abilities. He started out with a simple claim: books, he said, were worthless. A writer could never change the views of an ordinary man on the street. There was only one way to inspire change, Hitler said, and that was through the spoken word.[31]

He explained why this was the case. The first reason was that the vast majority of people were inherently lazy and unlikely to pick up a book if it went against what they believed to be true. There was a chance that they might glance at a leaflet or a poster advertising a contrary position, but they would never give it sufficient attention to change their views. Just as Hitler was dismissing the written word completely, however, he thought of a recent technological development that was much more promising:

> The picture in all its forms up to the film has greater possibilities. Here a man needs to use his brains even less; it suffices to look, or at most to read extremely brief texts, and thus many will more readily accept a *pictorial presentation* than *read* an *article* of any *length*. The picture brings them in a much briefer time, I might almost say at one stroke, the enlightenment which they obtain from written matter only after arduous reading.[32]

In this remarkable passage, Hitler was not merely revealing his fascination with film; he was actually imagining how film might one day rival the power of oratory. He was saying that the new technology might be able to transform the opinions of a large group of people quickly and without fuss. He stayed with the thought only for a moment, however, for he suddenly remembered his second great advantage as an orator: he stood directly in front of other people, and he brought them round to his side by picking up on and responding to their reactions. If he sensed that they did not understand him, he made his explanations simpler. If they did not follow him, he spoke more slowly and carefully. And if they were not convinced by the examples he gave, he simply offered different ones.[33]

In all of these ways, Hitler's powers as an orator were superior to those of the cinema. He could do something that an actor on the screen could never do: he could give a new performance every time. But just as he was about to dismiss "the picture in all its forms up to the film," he remembered something else: when people were gathered in groups at night, they frequently experienced an intoxicating effect that stirred the power of their convictions. Hitler had noticed that people were more likely to be convinced by his speeches after sundown. They were also more likely to be seduced by a piece of theater. "The same applies even to a movie," Hitler said, despite the fact that a movie lacked the dynamism of a live performance.[34] If movies were screened at around 9:00 PM—just when he and many other cinemagoers watched them—they could have a powerful effect.

These were just a few scattered remarks, of course. They were not meant to be interpreted as a coherent theory of film. Nevertheless, they were the first indication of an obsession that would remain with Hitler until his final days.

There is an interesting legend behind the genesis of *Mein Kampf*. While Hitler was serving a short sentence for the failed putsch attempt of 1923, he was in the habit of disturbing the various inmates of Landsberg Prison with his endless monologues, and someone suggested that he write his memoirs instead. He was taken with the idea, and he started dictating immediately to his chauffeur Emil Maurice and later to Rudolf Hess, both of whom had also been interned at Landsberg. The other prisoners were happy to get back to their usual activities, but soon the old habits set in, for every day Hitler insisted on reading his compositions to his captive audience.[35]

The pages Hitler dictated in those days were, for the most part, unoriginal and inaccurate. He was recycling arguments from speeches he had given countless times before and describing his own experiences in a way that showed little regard for the truth. Historians have been right to point out all the problems with his claims. But his embellishments were not only inaccurate; they were also the result of years of watching movies. His historical imagination had been deeply informed by film. The influence was particularly apparent in the way he recounted the single most important episode of his life, one that he would recite in many of his early speeches.

When he was young, Hitler said, he did not amount to much. He wished he had been born a hundred years earlier, during the Napoleonic Wars. He sat in a small room in Munich and read.[36] But, he added, "from the first hour I was convinced that in case of a war . . . I would at once leave my books."[37] With the outbreak of hostilities in August 1914, Hitler enlisted in the German army. And as he recalled his experience of the war a decade later in *Mein Kampf*, all of his years of movie-watching were discernible. He had turned his life into a film: "As though it were yesterday, image after image passes before my eyes. I see myself donning the uniform in the circle of my dear comrades, turning out for the first time, drilling, etc., until the day came for us to march off."[38] Then came sweeping long shots of the landscape as Hitler's regiment marched westward along the Rhine. A single thought plagued the men in those days: What if they reached the front too late? But they need not have worried. One damp, cold morning as they marched through Flanders in silence, they were attacked for the first time. The silence turned to a cracking and a roaring, and then to something else entirely: "From the distance the strains of a song reached our ears, coming closer and closer, leaping from company to company, and just as Death plunged a busy hand into our ranks, the song reached us too and we passed it along: '*Deutschland, Deutschland über Alles, über Alles in der Welt!*'"[39]

The song played loudly and the men fought boldly, and then, when the final notes had ended, the reality set in. The men in Hitler's regiment came to know the meaning of fear. Their laughter and rejoicing disappeared, and they started to question whether they should sacrifice their lives for the Fatherland. Every man heard a voice in his head telling him to abandon the struggle, and after many months, every man managed to overcome that voice. Eventually, the young volunteers became calm and determined old soldiers.[40]

The real menace, when it arrived, came in quite a different form. The enemy dropped leaflets from planes in the sky, and the troops read the following message: the German people were yearning for peace, but the Kaiser would not allow it. If the soldiers stopped fighting on the side of the Kaiser, then peace would be restored. Hitler admitted that he did not recognize the danger of these leaflets at the time. He and his comrades simply laughed at them, passed them on to their superiors, and went on fighting with the same courage as before.[41]

It was only when Hitler returned home for the first time that he witnessed the effects of this enemy propaganda. In Berlin, soldiers "were bragging about their own cowardice," and Munich was even worse: "Anger, discontent, cursing, wherever you went!"[42] Hitler chose his usual target: the Jews. He said that they occupied the main positions of authority in Germany because the bravest men were all fighting at the front, and, taking their cues from the enemy leaflets, they were creating division between the Bavarians and Prussians and sowing the seeds for a revolution. Hitler was disgusted by this state of affairs, and he returned to the battlefield where he felt more comfortable.[43]

This particular account of the war was, of course, deeply problematic. For a start, Hitler failed to mention that eleven days after his arrival at the front, he became a dispatch runner in the army—a dangerous job, to be sure, but one incomparable to that of a regular soldier.[44] He also did not mention that the Jews in his own regiment were especially brave, and that German Jews served in the army in equal proportion to the rest of the population.[45] But these details were beside the point. He was building up his story to a dramatic climax in order to lend credence to the most enduring lie of all.

Upon returning to the front, Hitler said, he found conditions a lot worse than before. His regiment was defending the same territory it had won years earlier, and the young replacements were worthless compared to the first volunteers. Despite these setbacks, however, his regiment held firm. It was still the same great "army of heroes." Then, on the night of

October 13, 1918, the English army used a new kind of gas whose effects were mostly unknown to the Germans, and Hitler was caught in the middle of the attack. "A few hours later, my eyes had turned into glowing coals," he said. "It had grown dark around me."[46] Fade out.

Hitler awoke in the hospital with immense pain in his eye sockets. He was unable to read the papers. His vision was coming back only gradually. And just when his eyesight was returning to normal, a local pastor visited the hospital and gave a short speech to the soldiers. The old man was shaking as he said that the war was over and that Germany had become a republic. He praised the boys for serving the Fatherland courageously, but now they had to put their faith in the victors. Hitler was distraught. After all the army's struggles, to be betrayed by a few cowards back home! This was the "stab-in-the-back" legend that Hitler would defend so vigorously later on, and as it sunk into his consciousness, the effect was overwhelming. "Again everything went black before my eyes," he said.[47] He quickly drew a moral from his experience: "There is no making pacts with Jews; there can only be the hard: either-or."[48] Then everything faded out completely, and his "film" ended.

But he had something more to say. He had an important analysis to make of the events he had just described. In a brief chapter of *Mein Kampf* entitled "War Propaganda," he outlined an interpretation of the conflict that would explain many of his later actions.

In Hitler's opinion, any struggle against an enemy had to be waged on two fronts. The first front was the physical battlefield, on which he believed that the German army had succeeded. The second front was the realm of propaganda, in which he insisted that the German government had failed. Hitler said that for four and a half years, German officials had produced materials that were completely useless in the struggle against the Allied forces. The Germans had suffered from the delusion that propaganda should be clever and entertaining on the one hand, and objective on the other. As a result, they had tried to make the enemy look ridiculous, when they should have made him look dangerous. Then, when the question of war guilt arose, German officials had accepted partial responsibility for the outbreak of hostilities. "It would have been correct," Hitler pointed out, "to load every bit of the blame on the shoulders of the enemy, even if this had not really corresponded to the true facts, as it actually did."[49]

The problem, Hitler said, was that the producers of this propaganda were fashioning their pamphlets, posters, and cartoons to the tastes of the bourgeoisie. Instead, they should have been thinking of the masses. And Hitler knew this group's psychology all too well. "The receptivity of the great masses is very limited, their intelligence is small, but their power of forgetting is enormous," he said.[50] Given these attributes, the authorities should have harped on about a few clear points until every last person was outraged. If the authorities had done this, their propaganda could have been as powerful as the weapons that soldiers used on the battlefield.[51]

In fact, it could have been more powerful. Hitler had kept an eye on the output of both sides throughout the World War, and he had noticed that what the Germans failed to do, the British and Americans did brilliantly. Even though the British and Americans were losing actual battles, their propaganda depicted the Germans as barbarians and Huns who were solely to blame for the outbreak of hostilities. This propaganda first spurred on their own soldiers, and then it actually started to eat away at the German people. And just when the great German army was about to declare victory on the battlefield, a few villains back home were able to take advantage of this situation and stab the army in the back.[52]

Hitler could barely restrain his admiration for the propaganda campaign of the British and the Americans during the war. If he had been in charge of propaganda in Germany, he said, he would have matched their efforts, and the outcome would have been quite different.[53] And yet in his account of the brilliance of the enemy's output, one detail was curiously absent. The propaganda that he was so impressed with did not solely take the form of leaflets falling from the sky. Some of the most potent images were contained in Hollywood films. The Americans used the new technology to contribute to the propaganda that in Hitler's opinion helped bring about the German defeat. In *To Hell with the Kaiser!*, the evil German leader carved up the world and gave America to his son; in *The Kaiser, the Beast of Berlin*, he committed a whole series of atrocities; and in *The Great Victory*, he ordered all unmarried women to submit to his soldiers so that he could repopulate the Reich. One particularly gruesome example, *Escaping the Hun*, even contained an optional scene in which German soldiers impaled a baby on their bayonets.[54]

Hitler did not mention any of these films in *Mein Kampf*, nor did he say anything about the "hate films" that the Americans continued to release after the war was over. These new films, like their predecessors, were full of images of aggression and brutality, and throughout the 1920s, they upset a large segment of the German population. One citizen had a particularly telling reaction when he watched MGM's *Mare Nostrum* (1926), in which German spies sunk an innocent passenger ship. "It is a repulsive, mean thing that this American film company has done, showing such things to the public eight years after the war ended," this viewer said. "The German characters are so exaggeratedly and poorly drawn that you feel yourself starting to choke in disgust . . . and you know that the rest of the world will start to dislike anything German as a result. America is always throwing around words like peace and reconciliation, but this film is a disgrace to the entire American film industry."[55]

*Mare Nostrum* was one of many silent movies about the World War that emerged in the 1920s. German public opinion was mounting against these Hollywood productions. Yet still Hitler did not speak out. Then, in November 1930, the German censors reviewed a new war movie that promised to be more successful than any other to date: Universal Pictures' *All Quiet on the Western Front* (*Im Westen nichts Neues*), based on Erich Maria Remarque's best-selling novel of the same title.[56] The censors made a few cuts to the print and then released it in Germany.[57]

From Hitler's perspective, this film was particularly threatening. Only the previous year, his associate Joseph Goebbels had watched *The Singing Fool* and had noted, "I was surprised at the already far advanced technology of the sound film."[58] Now, in 1930, a film had emerged that used the new technology of sound recording in an unprecedented way. Here was how *All Quiet on the Western Front* began:

It was the early days of the war in Germany, and a high school teacher was giving a speech to his students. He was staring at them intensely, waving his hands about in a theatrical manner, but no one could hear him—a parade for the soldiers was taking place outside, and the music was drowning him out. Suddenly, the band died down, and his words were clear. "My beloved class," he was saying, "this is what we must do. Strike with all our power. Give every ounce of strength to win victory before the end of the year." He clasped his hands together, apologized for what he was about to say, and started to roar: "You are the life of the Fatherland, you boys! You are the iron men of Germany! You are the gay heroes who will repulse the enemy when you are called upon to do so!"[59]

He was a good speaker, anyone could see that. As the scene continued, however, it became clear that this was not just an orator making a speech; this was a film using its own devices to show the power of oratory. And now it used one of those devices: it cut to a shot of a boy watching the teacher with uncertainty. "Perhaps," the teacher was saying, "some will say that you should not be allowed to go yet, that you are too young, that you have homes, mothers, fathers, that you should not be torn away." As the teacher was speaking, the film cut once again, this time to the thought process of the boy. He was arriving home in uniform for the first time, and his mother burst into tears when she saw him. Just then, he heard the orator in the background—"Are your fathers so forgetful of their Fatherland that they would let it perish rather than you?"—and suddenly his own father was looking at him with pride. The film cut from this dream sequence back to the boy sitting in the classroom, and he was obviously becoming convinced.

The orator gave voice to the doubts of the boys, and he kindled their hopes as well. "Is the honor of wearing a uniform something from which we should run?" he asked, as a different boy imagined himself in uniform, surrounded by a group of girls. "And if our young ladies glory in those who wear it, is that anything to be *ashamed* of?" he said, and the camera shifted back to this second boy, revealing that he was becoming convinced too.

**The high school teacher in *All Quiet on the Western Front* (1930) convinces his students to enlist in the German army.**

Now the orator was gaining momentum. The film cut more and more quickly between him and his audience, and when he was absolutely convinced of himself, he appeared in an extreme close-up, and he asked one of the boys what he was going to do. "I'll go," the boy replied. "I wanna go," said another. Soon everyone was agreeing to go, and the teacher was satisfied. "Follow me!" he screamed. "Enlist now!" "No more classes!" the boys yelled in response, and then everything turned into chaos.

"Nearly always," Hitler had written in *Mein Kampf*, "I faced an assemblage of people who believed the opposite of what I wanted to say, and wanted the opposite of what I believed. Then it was the work of two hours to lift two or three thousand people out of a previous conviction, blow by blow to shatter the foundation of their previous opinions, and finally . . . I had before me a surging mass full of the holiest indignation and boundless wrath."[60]

Hitler's description of his oratorical abilities in *Mein Kampf* corresponded exactly to what took place at the beginning of *All Quiet on the Western Front*. The opening scene not only revealed the power of oratory but also broke it up, analyzed it, and showed how it worked. The scene was like a movie version of Hitler's chapter on the spoken word. But after establishing the power of oratory, the film turned to its danger. Over the next two hours, *All Quiet on the Western Front* showed the effects of the boys' decision to join the German army. They began their training at the local barracks where their superior officer, Corporal Himmelstoss, drilled them ruthlessly and ordered them to crouch in mud, and when they arrived at the battlefield, they all wet their pants. During their first battle, one boy temporarily lost his sight, went hysterical, and ran into the enemy's line of fire; later, another boy did the same. They constantly went without food, they became wildly excited when they spotted some rats to eat, they shot hundreds of enemy soldiers from a distance and fought hundreds of others in the trenches, and if they were lucky enough to survive all these horrors, they often still had body parts amputated. From the moment they left the classroom, every image of the film argued against the orator's original claim that war was honorable, and showed instead that it was hell.

And then one of the few boys still alive, Paul Bäumer, was granted a week's leave to visit his family back home. As he walked through the town in a daze everything seemed different: the shops were closed, the streets were empty, there were no parades anymore. Occasionally he saw some horrific sight like a young boy sitting on the sidewalk playing with a bayonet, but he did not react; he just kept walking toward his house, and when his mother told him that he seemed different, he responded with the same blank expression. Later that day, he went to the local bar so his father could show him off to a group of friends, and he looked on in disbelief as they got out battle maps and told him what the army needed to do. He tried to argue with them, but they did not take him seriously, so he slipped away and wandered the streets some more. Soon he heard a voice he knew well: it was the high school teacher who had convinced him to go to war in the first place.

"Paul!" the teacher cried out. "How are you Paul?" The teacher had been giving a speech to a new batch of students and he was thrilled to have an actual soldier to support his argument. "Look at him," the teacher said—the film cutting from boy to boy, each one as impressed as the last—"sturdy and bronzed and clear-eyed, the kind of soldier every one of you should envy." He begged Paul to tell them how much they were needed at the front, and when Paul resisted, he begged him some more, saying that it would suffice to describe a single act of heroism or humility. Finally, Paul turned to address them.

But it was a disappointing speech. Unlike the teacher, who spoke with great enthusiasm, Paul slumped himself against the desk and said that for him the war was about trying not to get killed. The film cut to a shot of the boys murmuring in disbelief, and to the teacher who was trying to respond, and then, suddenly, Paul changed his tone. He looked into his teacher's eyes and said that it was not beautiful and sweet to die for the Fatherland; it was dirty and painful. When the teacher protested, Paul looked at the boys. "He tells you, *Go out and die*"—and then, turning back to the teacher—"Oh, but if you pardon me, it's easier to say 'Go out and die' than it is to do it!" Someone in the classroom branded Paul a coward, so Paul turned back to the boys one last time—"And it's easier to say it than to watch it happen!"

"It's easier to say it than to watch it happen." No line better captured the point of *All Quiet on the Western Front*. The film began with a speaker encouraging innocent boys to enlist and then forced the viewer to sit through the consequences: horrific images of death and destruction. From beginning to end, *All Quiet on the Western Front* was nothing less than film's declaration of war on the spoken word.

It was also something else. At the same time as *All Quiet on the Western Front* recognized the power of oratory in order to condemn it, the film provided an account of the World War that was directly at odds with Hitler's own embellished version. For him, the war had been a godsend; he had fantasized about it in a completely cinematic way in *Mein Kampf. All Quiet on the Western Front* contradicted everything he had imagined. Instead of the fond memory of drilling with "dear comrades," the early days at the military academy were humiliating for everyone. Instead of *Deutschland über Alles* playing over the first battle scene, the boys all wet their pants. Instead of becoming calm and determined old soldiers, they were constantly afraid. Instead of honor and courage, there was only defeat and despair. When Hitler and Paul Bäumer returned home, they both felt deeply disoriented, but Paul bragged "about [his] own cowardice" in just the way Hitler found so disgraceful. *All Quiet on the Western Front* was giving the very interpretation of the war that Hitler despised, and in a more compelling way than he ever could.

Finally, the film was even attacking Hitler's analysis of war propaganda. In a scene that was cut from the German version, a group of soldiers tried to work out who was responsible for the outbreak of the war.[61] The typical argument was given—some other country started it—and then one of Paul's friends came up with a different possibility.

"I think maybe the Kaiser wanted a war," he said.

"I don't see that," someone else replied. "The Kaiser's got everything he needs."

"Well he never had a war before. Every full-grown emperor needs one war to make him famous. Why, that's history!"

In other words: there were no enemy leaflets. The German soldiers independently arrived at the conclusion that the Kaiser was to blame for all of their pain and suffering.

And yet even though *All Quiet on the Western Front* argued that Germany had lost the war on the battlefield, that propaganda had played no part in the outcome, and that the spoken word was a dangerous weapon in the hands of a demagogue—in short, even though *All Quiet on the Western Front* argued against almost everything Hitler stood for—one final development was necessary before any action could be taken against the film. In the elections of September 1930, just a few months before *All Quiet on the Western Front* was released in Germany, the Nazis made landslide gains in the Reichstag, increasing their representation from 12 to 107 seats. Suddenly, Hitler had become a key political figure, and Joseph Goebbels was about to instigate what would become known as the "film war."[62]

On Friday, December 5, 1930, the first public performance of *All Quiet on the Western Front* in Germany was scheduled to take place at a cinema in Berlin called the Mozartsaal. The Nazis had purchased around three hundred tickets for the 7:00 PM showing, and many more party members were waiting outside. The trouble began almost immediately. As the teacher gave the speech encouraging the students to go to war, a few people in the audience started to shout. When the German troops were forced to retreat from the French, the shouting became more distinct: "German soldiers had courage. It's a disgrace that such an insulting film was made in America!" "Down with the hunger government which permits such a film!"[63] Because of the disruptions, the projectionist was

**Police stand guard outside the Mozartsaal in Berlin after the Nazi riots against** *All Quiet on the Western Front.* **Courtesy of Imagno; Getty Images.**

forced to switch off the film. The house lights went on, and Goebbels gave a speech from the front row of the balcony in which he claimed that the film was an attempt to destroy Germany's image. His comrades waited for him to finish and then threw stink bombs and released white mice into the crowd. Everyone rushed for the exits, and the theater was placed under guard.[64]

In the days that followed, the Nazis' actions met with significant popular approval. Everything seemed to go in their favor. Immediately after the riots, on Saturday, December 6, the matter was brought up in the Reichstag, and a representative of the German Nationalist Party sided with Hitler. On Sunday, *All Quiet on the Western Front* resumed at the Mozartsaal under heavy police protection, and on Monday, the Nazis responded with further demonstrations. On Tuesday, both the German Federation of Cinema Owners and the main student association of the University of Berlin spoke out against the film. On Wednesday, police president Albert Grzesinski of Berlin, who was a Social Democrat, pronounced a ban on all open-air demonstrations, and the main Nazi newspaper responded, "Grzesinski is protecting the Jewish film of shame!" Later that day, the members of the German cabinet watched *All Quiet on the Western Front* at the offices of the film board. Up to that point, the minister of the interior and the foreign minister had approved of the picture, and only the defense minister had objected to it.[65]

The situation came to a climax on Thursday, December 11. Prompted by the Nazis' actions, five states—Saxony, Braunschweig, Thuringia, Württemberg, and Bavaria—submitted petitions to ban *All Quiet on the Western Front*. At 10:00 AM that day, the highest censorship board in the country convened to determine the fate of the film. Twenty-eight people were present, far more than had attended one of these meetings before and more than would ever attend again. The board consisted of Dr. Ernst Seeger, chief German censor; Otto Schubert, a representative of the film industry; Dr. Paul Baecker, editor of an agrarian nationalist newspaper; Professor Hinderer, a theologian; and Miss Reinhardt, a schoolteacher and sister of the late general Walter Reinhardt. Also in attendance were representatives from the five protesting state governments and delegates from the Defense, Interior, and Foreign Ministries. The lawyer for Universal Pictures, Dr. Frankfurter, was accompanied by a retired major and two film directors.[66]

Everyone squeezed into the projection room, and for the second day in a row, *All Quiet on the Western Front* was screened. Seeger then asked the complainants from the state governments why they were opposed to the film. Each representative gave his own statement, and Seeger counted a total of three objections: the film harmed the German image; it endangered public order; and if it were permitted, then the rest of the world would think that Germany approved of the even more offensive version playing abroad.[67] These objections had been carefully tailored to the German film law, which prohibited pictures that "endangered public order, harmed religious feelings, provoked a threatening or immoral effect, or endangered the German image or Germany's relations with other nations."[68]

Seeger then turned to the delegate from the Defense Ministry, Naval Lieutenant von Baumbach, and asked him to comment on the first objection. Von Baumbach started by saying that in the aftermath of the war, the various nations of the world had been working hard to establish friendly relations with Germany. There was one area, however, that the spirit of the Locarno Treaty had failed to penetrate: "The area of film!" The Americans were continuing to make pictures that harmed the German image. Von Baumbach gave some examples from *All Quiet on the Western Front*: the German soldiers, he said, constantly wailed in fear, their faces were always distorted, they ate and drank like wild animals, and they only became lively when they beat a few rats to death. Such elaborate images might seem acceptable on the surface, but they were detrimental to Germany, and if Carl Laemmle of Universal Pictures did not like this opinion, then someone should ask him, "Why [do you] now produce yet another war film that cannot play in the same version in Germany as in the rest of the world?"[69]

The representative from the Interior Ministry, Dr. Hoche, then took the floor. He said that *All Quiet on the Western Front* contained so many images of death and defeat that it left German spectators feeling agonized and depressed. In calmer times, this might not have been a problem. But the fate of the film could not be determined in a vacuum. Obviously the German people were going through a moment of deep psychological distress and inner conflict. The economic crisis was mounting and there were still war debts to pay. The problem was not that a few extremist groups were artificially stirring up excitement; rather, *All Quiet on the*

# Muß sich ein Volk von Selbstachtung das gefallen lassen??

Vier Jahre lang hielt Deutschland der Welt stand —

A Nazi cartoon in which Polish, French, and Czech soldiers laugh at the German retreat in *All Quiet on the Western Front*. The caption reads: "Must a self-respecting people put up with this? For four years, Germany held out against the world."

*Western Front* had seized on the genuine anxiety of a large number of people. In order to preserve public order, the film should be taken out of circulation in Germany.[70]

All this was more than enough for Seeger. He had no desire to go through every objection against the film. If he could show that the film broke a single aspect of the law, then everyone could go home. He began his judgment by pointing out that *All Quiet on the Western Front* contained damaging German stereotypes. Sergeant Himmelstoss' mean action of dunking the boys in the mud represented untamed German aggression and gave the spectator the impression that Germany was responsible for the outbreak of hostilities. And whereas the French soldiers went to their deaths quietly and bravely, the Germans were constantly howling and shrieking with fear. Therefore *All Quiet on the Western Front* was not an honest representation of the war but a representation of German aggression and German defeat. Of course the public had reacted disapprovingly. Regardless of anyone's political affiliation, the picture offended a whole generation of German people who had suffered so terribly throughout the war. Seeger banned *All Quiet on the Western Front* on the grounds that it harmed the German image and said there was no need to consider the matter any further.[71]

And so, six days after the protests in Berlin, *All Quiet on the Western Front* was removed from screens in Germany. "Victory is ours!" Goebbels' newspaper proclaimed.[72] The Nazis had apparently won the film war. This was hardly surprising, for the members of the censorship board were all deeply conservative, and the whole affair had been carefully orchestrated from start to finish. The lawyer for Universal Pictures, Dr. Frankfurter, had even announced that he was pulling the film from circulation in Germany anyway. His company had consulted with the relevant government authorities, and the two groups had reached an agreement that they would stick to no matter what the censorship board decided.[73] And yet one last thing happened at the censorship meeting that turned out to have even more important consequences than the banning of the film.

Dr. Frankfurter had always assumed that the Foreign Office—the studios' best ally in Germany—would support the picture. When it was time for the representative, a man named Johannes Sievers, to give his report, however, he registered his disapproval in only a few sentences: "The Foreign Office's original position, which denied any problems with the film from a foreign-policy perspective, was based only on the materials available at the time. In the meantime, the Foreign Office has received communications from abroad that identify the film's detrimental effect on the German image. It has therefore come to the conclusion that the film must be seen as detrimental to the German image. The Foreign Office therefore recommends banning the film."[74]

Dr. Frankfurter was surprised. He had hardly said a word up to this point, but now he found that he could not hold back. He asked the minister what the "communications from abroad" were and when they had been received.[75]

"The communications were received in the time between the original inspection of the film and the one occurring today," Sievers replied. "They consist of official reports and private information that generally show how the reception of the film harms the German image."

"Am I right in assuming that these communications are concerned only with the foreign version of the film?" Dr. Frankfurter asked.

"Because the reports came from abroad, they can only be based on the version being shown there. However, the writers of the reports all emphasize that they are concerned not with particular moments but with the overall tendency of the film."

"What countries do these reports come from?"

"I cannot give particulars, since the Foreign Office is in touch with all European and foreign countries. The reports come mainly from America and England."

Dr. Frankfurter changed the subject. "Today's morning papers give the impression that the Foreign Minister has seen the current version of the film," he said.

"I know nothing about that," replied Sievers.

"Did the Foreign Office change its opinion of the film as a result of orders from higher up?"

Seeger interjected. The question was inadmissible because it concerned the internal workings of the Foreign Office.

Dr. Frankfurter tried a different approach. "When did the Foreign Office change its position on the film?" he asked.

"I refuse to answer that question."

"Is it that you don't want to answer it or that you can't answer it?"

"Both."

"Did the Foreign Office change its position after the first censorship meeting in Berlin?"

"Yes, after the meeting in Berlin."

Seeger interrupted again. He would allow no further questions in this direction.

"I have just one more question," said Dr. Frankfurter. "Something seems to be missing in the representative's statement, namely the opinion. When the Foreign Office changes its statement like this, then it might provide us with a reason."

But Sievers had understood that Seeger was on his side. "I have nothing further to say," he replied. And with that, the interrogation was complete.

As it turned out, Sievers' testimony had no actual bearing on the case. He had said that the communications from abroad were based on foreign versions of the film, and the law was primarily concerned with the version playing in Germany. Nevertheless, he had made a shocking admission. He had said that the scandal surrounding *All Quiet on the Western Front* had led the various German consulates and embassies around the world to investigate the impact of the film in their respective countries. In other words, the Foreign Office was doing something very intrusive: it was using its diplomatic privileges to determine whether *All Quiet on the Western Front* harmed the German image outside the German border. This was an unprecedented development, and it set into motion a new series of events.

Back in Hollywood, the president of Universal Pictures, Carl Laemmle, was troubled by the controversy surrounding his picture. He had been born in Germany, and he wanted *All Quiet on the Western Front* to be shown there. According to one representative, his company had "lost a fine potential business, for the film would have been a tremendous financial success in Germany if it could have run undisturbed."[76] Laemmle soon decided to send a telegram to William Randolph Hearst, the head of a massive media empire in the United States. "Would greatly appreciate your aid in support of my picture 'All Quiet On The Western Front' now threatened by Hitler party in Germany," he wrote. "If you feel you can conscientiously do so comment appearing over your signature in the Hearst press would be of immeasurable help."[77]

Hearst knew a good story when he saw one. On Friday, December 12, the day after *All Quiet on the Western Front* was banned in Germany, he released an editorial that appeared on the front page of all of his newspapers. He made sure to defend *All Quiet on the Western Front* as a pacifist film. But he went on to promote his own agenda. For years, he had been lashing out against France for the unfair terms of the Treaty of Versailles. Now he said that despite the treaty, Germany should still fight for peace. "France will want her last pound of flesh, of course. France will be supremely selfish. That is her nature," he wrote. Nevertheless, "Germany should not allow herself to be forced into war either by those without her boundaries who are hostile to her, or by those within her confines who mean well but think badly."[78]

The editorial did no good, of course. *All Quiet on the Western Front* still could not play in Germany. Laemmle was forced to adopt other measures. In June 1931, his company resubmitted the picture to the German censorship authorities, and it was approved for screening in front of war veterans' associations and world peace organizations.[79] Then, in August, Laemmle came up with a new, heavily edited version of *All Quiet on the Western Front* that he was convinced would not offend the Foreign Office. He made a trip to Europe to promote the new version, and he sent a copy of the print to Berlin. The Foreign Office soon agreed to support *All Quiet on the Western Front* for general screening in Germany under one condition: Laemmle would have to tell the branches of Universal Pictures in the rest of the world to make the same cuts to all copies of the film. On August 28, Laemmle informed his employees in Berlin that he was ready to cooperate with the request. His employees then wrote to the Foreign Office: "We expect that this obligingness on our part will provide a smooth pathway toward the unrestricted showing of the film in Germany."[80]

The approval of *All Quiet on the Western Front* went ahead without any difficulties, and in September, the film hit screens in Germany for a second time.[81] In early November, Laemmle went to Berlin and was pleased to discover that *All Quiet on the Western Front* was "doing good business."[82] The fate of the film abroad was another story. The Foreign Office wanted to make sure that Universal Pictures upheld the bargain, so it informed every German consulate and embassy of eight deletions that Laemmle had agreed to make. Some deletions were relatively minor: the dunking of the recruits in the mud, for example, was now to be shown only once. Other deletions were much more substantial, especially the ones numbered four through seven:

4. During the soldiers' conversation about the causes and development of the war, the remark that every emperor must have his war.

5. Paul Bäumer's address to his classmates at the end of the film: "It is dirty and painful to die for the Fatherland."

6. The whole story around this scene. The schoolboys and the teacher no longer appear in the second half of the film.

Carl Laemmle, founder and president of Universal Pictures. Copyright © John Springer Collection/Corbis.

7. Paul Bäumer's meeting in the bar with the old fighters during his holiday.

After outlining the changes that Carl Laemmle had agreed to make, the Foreign Office requested that an employee of every German consulate and embassy go out and see the film, and report back if anything was amiss.[83]

The first person to discover a problem was an employee of the German embassy in Paris. In mid-November this representative saw *All Quiet on the Western Front* at a cinema on the Avenue de la Grande Armée, and he noticed that both the offensive remarks about the Kaiser and the second classroom scene remained.[84] The Foreign Office then complained to Universal Pictures, and the company's employees were "extremely embarrassed": "We politely ask you—in the name of our president, Mr. Carl Laemmle—to accept our assurance that this up-to-now unexplained oversight is an isolated incident, and it will never happen again."[85]

This turned out to be wishful thinking, for the next month, consular officers in England and the United States watched the offensive version of *All Quiet on the Western Front* in their respective regions, and they quickly informed the German consul in Los Angeles, Dr. Gustav Struve.[86] Dr. Struve then wrote to his first point of contact in Los Angeles—not Universal Pictures, but the organization that represented the major Hollywood studios, the Motion Picture Producers and Distributors Association of America. This organization, popularly known as the Hays Office, was not a government agency but a private group that had been founded in 1922 to resist calls for government censorship. Its head, Will Hays, was a former postmaster general, and its foreign manager was a quick-tempered man named Frederick Herron.

Dr. Struve's letter to the Hays Office went as follows: "I am enclosing herewith a list of scenes which ought to be taken out of the film 'All Quiet On the Western Front,' according to the agreement between the Universal Pictures Corporation and the German Government last summer, in consequence of which the film above mentioned was admitted in Germany. The scenes, which have not been omitted at the performances in London and in San Francisco, according to the reports from these respective places, are the following: # 3, 5, 6 and 7."[87] This letter was immediately passed on to Frederick Herron, who dealt with all such matters. But Herron had no idea what Dr. Struve was talking about. He went through all his correspondence and found no reference to the eight scenes that should have been deleted. "The only record we have as to objectionable scenes," he wrote, "is relative to the school scene in which the teacher is urging his class to join the colors; the soapbox politician scene in which they discuss how the war should be conducted, and the Sergeant drilling the recruits in more or less of a severe manner. None of these do I consider legitimate objections and said so at the time. . . . I am rather curious to know just what Dr. Struve is objecting to in this picture at the present time. You might casually drop a remark to him that perhaps if the members of the German Government in Berlin would keep their promises to our representatives, and to the representatives of this office, instead of breaking such promises as they have done numerous times in the past, we would get along a little better."[88]

Herron was obviously angry, but his anger was misdirected, for Dr. Struve was totally right on this occasion: Universal Pictures had agreed to make the eight requested deletions. The real problem was that Carl Laemmle had gone over the heads of the Hays Office when he had made the deal in the first place. If he had consulted with Herron, he would have been told that *All Quiet on the Western Front* was unobjectionable in its original form and that under no circumstances should he cut the picture abroad just to assure its release in Germany. But while Herron wanted Universal Pictures to stand up to the Germans, Laemmle wanted to sell his picture, and if that meant cutting the scenes to which the Foreign Office objected, then the scenes had to be cut.

Laemmle had obviously made a terrible mistake. Over the next few months, he observed Hitler's rise to prominence, and he became increasingly nervous about the situation in Germany. In January 1932, he became so alarmed that he wrote once again to Hearst, this time on a much more important issue than the fate of his film. "I address you on a subject which I firmly believe is not only of great concern to my own race but also to millions of Gentiles, throughout the world," he wrote.

> Speaking as an individual, I have been greatly worried for some time about the members of my own family in Germany, so much so that I have already provided the means to enable them to leave the country on short notice and for their subsequent maintenance. My present concern, therefore, is not so much for those dear to me personally, as much as it is for those less fortunate members of my race who would necessarily be at the mercy of fierce racial hatreds.
>
> I might be wrong, and I pray to God that I am, but I am almost certain that Hitler's rise to power, because of his obvious militant attitude toward the Jews, would be the signal for a general physical onslaught on many thousands of defenseless Jewish men, women and children in Germany, and possibly in Central Europe as well, unless

something is done soon to definitely establish Hitler's personal responsibility in the eyes of the outside world.[89]

This time Hearst wrote no editorial. He did not even send a reply. He had become fascinated with Hitler, and he was not willing to take a stance just yet. Meanwhile, Laemmle continued to help Jews get out of Germany. He spent much of his time convincing American immigration officials that he could provide for the sustenance of individual Jews, and when the U.S. government started denying his requests, he approached other potential benefactors. By the time of his death, he had helped to get at least three hundred people out of Germany.[90]

And yet at precisely the moment that Carl Laemmle was embarking on this crusade, his employees at Universal Pictures were following the orders of the German government. In the first few months of 1932, the Foreign Office discovered that there were problems with versions of *All Quiet on the Western Front* playing in San Salvador and Spain. The company apologized with the assurance that "the movietone prints are being treated as requested."[91] Afterward there were only a few isolated complaints. Universal Pictures had made the requested cuts all around the world.

The Nazis' actions against *All Quiet on the Western Front* set off a chain of events that lasted over a decade. Not only Universal Pictures but all the Hollywood studios started making deep concessions to the German government, and when Hitler came to power in January 1933, the studios dealt with his representatives directly. In order to understand the result of these dealings—the great mark that Hitler left on American culture—it is necessary to turn to the situation in Hollywood. Before doing that, however, there is one final aspect of Hitler's obsession with film that needs to be considered.

Hitler adopted an unusual approach to the movies. First, he consumed them; indeed, he watched so many that his adjutants were worried he would exhaust the entire holdings of the Propaganda Ministry. Second, he took drastic action against a single film that opposed everything he stood for. There is a strange disparity here, and it is worth thinking about. Even when Hitler strongly disliked a movie at one of his nightly screenings, he did not usually become overly concerned. At most, he complained about an actor he disliked (usually Gustaf Gründgens), or he requested a copy of the latest Imperio Argentina film in Spanish because he thought the dubbed German version did not do this actress justice.[92] In the case of *All Quiet on the Western Front*, on the other hand, he provoked an outcry that was heard throughout the world.

The reason why Hitler gave such disproportionate attention to a single film is contained in a sentence from his chapter on war propaganda in *Mein Kampf*: "Where the destiny and existence of a people are at stake, all obligation toward beauty ceases."[93] This was trademark Hitler: even though he watched movies every night, even though his fascination with them connected deeply to his own experience as an orator, he did not imagine that the vast majority had anything whatsoever to do with propaganda. He would enjoy the screenings while he could, but if a movie emerged that threatened the existence of the German nation—a movie like *All Quiet on the Western Front*—then he was at war.

At the center of Hitler's understanding of film, therefore, lay a rigid distinction between art and propaganda, a belief that these two things had absolutely nothing to do with each other.[94] He applied this distinction to every aspect of what his party called the film war. In his encounters with American pictures, he targeted only the ones that he considered truly dangerous—a strategy that would have devastating implications as the decade wore on. And in his encounters with German pictures, he did something remarkable: he became a film producer himself.

Shortly after attaining power, Hitler commissioned the director Leni Riefenstahl to record the Nuremberg Rally of 1934, and the result was *Triumph of the Will*, the best-known Nazi propaganda movie. Naturally Hitler was the star. He gave a series of speeches to his followers, and in his first complete speech, he said, "Today you are not only being seen by the thousands in Nuremberg, but by *all* of Germany—which also sees you here for the first time today!" His meaning was clear: he was saying that thanks to the new motion picture technology, his speeches to the faithful members of his party could now be seen by everyone in Germany.[95]

The remark captured the essence of *Triumph of the Will*: this was a film about an orator's obsession with film. It was Hitler's opportunity to show off his oratorical abilities and, as the ending of the picture would make clear, to correct the damage inflicted on the orator by *All Quiet on the Western Front*.

In one sense, he succeeded. He certainly showed how skillfully he managed to captivate his audience's attention. All of his techniques were clearly visible. Here is how he started out his final speech: he spoke hesitantly, nervously, as if he thought he were about to fail. For a few uncomfortable moments, he looked as if he had nothing to say at all. He stared down at the podium, then back up at the audience, and finally he started mumbling that the ceremonies were coming to an end. His voice contained no emotion; his body remained still. Of course he was aware of the storm that was about to break. But he wanted to make his audience worry a little first. He was using a technique he had described in *Mein Kampf*—going through his audience's doubts one by one in order to convert them—only in this case, he was making them doubt his ability to finish the speech. It was a clever way of implicating them in his performance so that they would feel they were going though the journey with him.

Then came his next technique: he varied his voice and his body movements to enforce his arguments. He built up his audience's expectations by saying that once his enemies from other political parties used to purge the Nazi Party of its lesser elements. Then, after giving his audience time to digest this statement, he screamed that this same duty now fell to the Nazi Party itself. "Today, we must examine ourselves and remove from our midst the elements that have become bad, and therefore"— suddenly shaking his head and indicating his disapproval with his hand— "*do not belong with us.*"

As Hitler spoke, he cultivated a special relationship with his listeners: he showed them no respect whatsoever. He stood in front of them with a frown plastered on his face, and he refused to validate their excitement. He only changed his expression to serve his own argument. "Once, our enemies worried us and persecuted us," he said, smiling to indicate that his enemies did not worry him anymore. Then he resumed his normal pose, and when his listeners applauded, he only looked at them with indifference. Sometimes he acted as if their applause was interrupting him, and he held up his hands to cut it off. Other times—especially at the end, when he knew the most tumultuous applause was coming—he turned away, as if to say that he had no need for it at all.

These were the main techniques that Hitler employed, and he asked Leni Riefenstahl to record them for all to see. But Riefenstahl did more: she used a variety of techniques of her own to enhance their effect. She

varied close-ups of Hitler with extreme long shots of the crowd to emphasize his power over them. She made sure to cut from the intense final
moments of his sentences to the crowd going wild in response. And she
played music over his regular conversations so that his words were only
audible during his speeches.[96] She was striving for the same effect every
time: Hitler cultivated a mystical power over the masses, and she was
seeking to make him even more of an object of mystery.

Two years later, she did the opposite. She filmed the 1936 Olympic
Games in Berlin, and Hitler was present for many of the events. And in
the film that resulted, she portrayed Hitler as an ordinary spectator. She
even captured some of his usual reactions. When a German contender
made a winning hammer throw, she showed "good": Hitler applauding
and smiling with glee. When one of the German athletes dropped the
baton in a relay, she showed "bad": Hitler smashing his hand on his knee
and muttering some angry words. The only reaction she did not show was
"switched off."[97]

But in *Triumph of the Will*, Riefenstahl had a more ambitious agenda.
She was restoring the honor of the German nation by responding to the
movie that had caused so many problems four years earlier, *All Quiet on*

"Good": Hitler responds positively to a winning hammer throw by a
German athlete at the Berlin Olympic Games in 1936. Movie still
from Leni Riefenstahl's *Olympia* (1938).

*the Western Front.* The two films' final shots gave the connection away: *All Quiet on the Western Front* ended with German soldiers marching silently toward their graves; *Triumph of the Will* ended with Nazis marching forcefully toward the camera. And yet in one crucial sense, the American picture was actually more faithful to Hitler's arguments than the German one. Hitler had always said that the aim of the spoken word was to convert an audience of doubters into staunch believers. While that was just what had happened in the opening scene of *All Quiet on the Western Front*, in *Triumph of the Will* the crowds were already won over before the filming began. In one speech, Hitler went through the doubts of the SA, but he knew that they would never question his authority in the first place.[98] In another speech, he watched his listeners rise from their seats to show their support, but they were all committed Nazis already. Despite the sheer extravagance of *Triumph of the Will*, the film did not actually show the power of the spoken word. If anything, it only revealed the limits of Hitler's imagination.[99] He could have made any film he wanted, and he had merely asked someone to record his own speeches.[100]

But there was one type of film that was perfectly suited to Hitler's powers: the newsreel. Here was an opportunity for him to combine his oratorical abilities with a type of motion picture that was unburdened by art. In *Mein Kampf,* he had dreamed of being put in charge of propaganda; in the late 1930s, he had his chance. From the earliest signs of German aggression (which he recognized, since they were his own), he personally supervised the national propaganda effort.[101]

His first recorded interventions into the newsreel business took place in June 1938, just as he was preparing for a full-scale war with Czechoslovakia. One evening, he watched one of the Propaganda Ministry's proposed newsreels, and he had quite an intense reaction to it. He first objected to the depiction of the regular news: "I do not want these newsreels only to contain shots of myself. They should include more details of actual events. The newsreels must show the development of new buildings, mechanical inventions, and sporting events. The construction of the new congress hall in Nuremberg, for example, did not even appear *once.*" He then turned to the Czech situation: "The newsreel must be edited in a politically funnier way (*Die Wochenschau muss politisch witziger gestaltet werden*) so that, for example, you first see shots of the nervous Czech preparations. Then at the end you see one great shot of the German soldiers. Not a week should go by without the latest shots of the navy, the army, and the air force. Young people are chiefly interested in such things."[102]

Hitler had some strong ideas about how he wanted his newsreels to be made. In addition to his rules about content (fewer images of himself, more images of the army), he believed that the various shots needed to be organized in a more effective, captivating way. And from years of giving speeches, he knew exactly what needed to be done. Just as he always built his speeches to a forceful conclusion, he made sure to end his newsreels on a powerful note. He also understood that whereas the trick in oratory lay in tone and body movement, here it lay in editing. He therefore recommended that this particular newsreel begin with the fear of the enemy and then cut to a single image of German strength.

Hitler continued to supervise the propaganda effort when the real hostilities broke out. At least during the first year of the war, he made changes to newsreels before they went into circulation. His skills as an orator came in especially handy, for he edited the voice-overs that accompanied the images. But his changes involved few surprises. He continued to correct the Propaganda Ministry's tendency to boast whenever he was on the screen. He took a pen and struck out all the references to his military genius, leaving the sparest of statements, for example: "The Führer with his generals in military headquarters." He read the next sentence: "To the Führer's left is General Jodl, to his right is General von Brauchitsch." He noticed there was a mistake and switched the order.[103]

He also sometimes felt that the Propaganda Ministry tended to give too much detail, or the wrong kind of detail, about army maneuvers. A newsreel about the invasion of Narvik, for example, showed untrained German paratroopers triumphing over highly concentrated British forces. He made sure to eliminate the sentence about this lack of training.[104] By cutting out anything that undermined the natural conclusion of German victory, he maximized the payoff every time. And as usual, his most important edits came at the end. In a newsreel about the victory over France, he ended with the shots of the German army in Paris, and he crossed out the lines about the struggle to come.[105] In a newsreel about an English defeat at Trondheim, he cut the line "The general attack on England is imminent" and simply concluded with the victory.[106]

Only occasionally did Hitler break his normal rules. One newsreel about the German army's successful march through Belgium, for example, contained a short segment about prisoners of war. The narrator first gave the names of the captured generals who were appearing on the screen. Then came the regular prisoners: "Belgians, French, Negroes, Indians, whites, blacks, browns, and yellows . . . a colorful mess." Finally, in a speech that Hitler probably enjoyed, the narrator made fun of France's promise of protection: "Belgium! The French army is coming to help you!" All this remained in the final version, but Hitler added a new ending: "As in 1918 on the Rhine, these hordes were meant to be unleashed again on the German people, this time all over Germany, in the name of Western culture and civilization."[107]

And so, in a way, Hitler's dream of supervising the national propaganda effort came true. He edited German newsreels, and he did so methodically and even skillfully. He was undoubtedly very proud of this part of his contribution to the film war. His great victory, however, would take place on the other side of the globe.

# ENTER HOLLYWOOD

Long Arm of Hitler Extends to Hollywood Studio[1]

Hitler's relationship with Hollywood began with great turbulence. On December 5, 1930, a group of Nazis rioted against Universal Pictures' *All Quiet on the Western Front* in Berlin, and one week later, the film was banned in Germany. The Nazis' actions were instrumental in initiating an entirely new kind of arrangement with the Hollywood studios, one from which Hitler would benefit greatly as chancellor. Before examining his dealings with the studios, however, it is necessary to turn back slightly, to another event that in a much quieter way helped to contribute to the change.

Just two weeks before the Nazis protested *All Quiet on the Western Front*, a German director named E. A. Dupont watched a different American picture about the World War, entitled *Hell's Angels*. Dupont had little in common with the Nazis: he was a Jew, and his own latest picture had been criticized by German nationalists for portraying the beauty of a young Jewish girl. When he saw *Hell's Angels* at a theater in London, however, he was so appalled that he published a devastating review in a prominent German newspaper.[2]

He admitted that the picture was outstanding from a technical standpoint. An American millionaire named Howard Hughes had spent an unprecedented amount of time and money on it, and the results were apparent. The aviation scenes, especially the images of a British pilot flying head-on into a German zeppelin, were dazzling and convincing. As Dupont watched the German zeppelin plummet toward the ground, even he could not tell "where truth splits off from poetry."[3]

*Hell's Angels*, Dupont said, was one of the biggest, most expensive, most interesting, most successful films ever made, but it was also one of the most anti-German. During the World War, he explained, a Hollywood actor named Erich von Stroheim had become famous by originating the stereotype of the evil German officer. In picture after picture, von Stroheim had cursed and yelled in an exaggerated manner while committing all sorts of atrocities. The German characters in *Hell's Angels*, Dupont said, were like von Stroheim's illegitimate children. Whenever they spoke their lines in German, they deliberately distorted the language in a provocative way, and this practice could very easily have been avoided. In its current state, the film "showed much skill, many millions—no tact, no conscience."[4]

Dupont's review received considerable attention in the British press. "What Dupont objects to," one newspaper reported, "is the fact that every German is the caricature of a military type, and that where German is spoken it is a mixture of broken German and English. His argument is that when a film has cost so much, bona-fide Germans should have been engaged to play German parts, as the technical accuracy is so convincing that the average audience will go away in the belief that everything else about 'Hell's Angels' is accurate too."[5] In the days that followed the publication of the review, several important officials in the German Foreign Office took note of Dupont's argument.[6] There were rumors that the Foreign Office might urge Britain to ban the picture, and the question even came up in British Parliament.[7] In the end, however, something much more dramatic occurred: the Nazis rioted against *All Quiet on the Western Front*.

In the period that followed, two possible courses of action regarding Hollywood productions suggested themselves to the German authorities. The first was the agreement around *All Quiet on the Western Front*, which came to a swift conclusion. The second was the intense dispute around *Hell's Angels*, which managed to drag on for over two years. The dispute began at the highest level. In the last weekend of September 1931, French Prime Minister Pierre Laval and Foreign Minister Aristide Briand made an official trip to meet with German Chancellor Heinrich Brüning in Berlin. The trip was a tremendous success, apart from one detail. In the middle of the discussions, the German Foreign Office mentioned to the French prime minister that *Hell's Angels* was being screened at twenty theaters in Paris. The foreign manager of the Hays Office, Frederick Herron, could hardly believe it: "This was brought to the attention of Laval recently on his trip to Berlin, he being there three days supposedly to settle problems of a most important nature concerning the welfare of Germany and the world at large, and the German Foreign Office was small enough to inject this into the discussion and exact a promise from Laval that he would withdraw the permit for 'HELL'S ANGELS' upon his return to Paris. It is in my estimation one of the smallest and most absurd deals I have ever heard of. The French Foreign Minister gave his word on this matter, and of course, he was placed in a position where he could do little else. It is like a man visiting in a household and his host asking him to go home and fire his cook."[8]

*Hell's Angels* was immediately removed from screens in Paris. The distributor of the picture, United Artists, got in touch with the German Foreign Office and—given what had happened in the case of *All Quiet on the Western Front*—offered to cut anything objectionable. The Foreign Office refused and said that the whole picture had to be withdrawn. Frederick Herron was annoyed by this uncompromising attitude. "The Germans would do this sort of thing when the world is in a chaotic condition and really needs peace and not war," he wrote. "It is a rotten piece of business when Germany can tell France how she is to run her country."[9]

The German government's actions against *Hell's Angels* were very different from those against *All Quiet on the Western Front*, and the reason had to do with actual differences between the films themselves. Whereas *All Quiet on the Western Front* was a pacifist film that showed the horror of war, *Hell's Angels* had a questionable plot that existed merely to provide the thrills that followed. Dupont was right that the picture had no tact or conscience, and certainly most Germans would have found it unacceptable. Even the Hays Office had major problems with it: "The story of *Hell's Angels* is stupid, rotten, sordid, and cheap. It is like putting rundown, muddy shoes on a well-dressed woman. The whole idea is wrong—the girl is a plain little tart, the boys are a prig and a coward respectively, their conduct is out of the gutter."[10]

Still, the Hays Office was committed to representing *Hell's Angels* abroad, and Frederick Herron was the person responsible for appealing the German government's actions. In June 1932, after eight months of negotiations with all of his foreign contacts, Herron thought he had succeeded. "It is a darned shame that we have to give so much of our time fighting Howard Hughes' battles," he complained. "Without the help of this office his picture HELL'S ANGELS would have had hardly any circulation in any country in the world outside of England. It has been protested in fifteen or more countries and the only place that we have lost our battle against such protests has been in Spain."[11]

Herron was speaking too soon; the battle around *Hell's Angels* would continue for another few months. Although the Germans had failed to have the picture banned in most countries of the world, there was one place where they exerted total control: Germany itself. And this fact gave them an ingenious idea.

Ever since the World War, the German government had placed massive import restrictions on motion pictures. The government had put a wartime embargo on foreign films until May 1920 and then had regulated the footage of film that could be imported each year.[12] Finally, on January 1, 1925, the government had introduced the notorious quota system, which stipulated that one foreign film could be imported for every German film that had been produced in the previous year.[13] The new system had the desired effect, for the German film industry remained relatively strong in the 1920s, and the proportion of American movies in Germany shifted between 30 and 45 percent—a significant number, to be sure, but a huge drop from the period before the World War, when Germany had been Hollywood's second biggest export market. Other countries, which were flooded with American movies in this period, soon began following Germany's example by imposing quotas of their own.[14]

Every year, the German government added new restrictions to the quota system, and every year, the representatives of the American studios in Berlin contested the changes. In 1928, the government set specific limits to the number of films that could be imported, and then the government further complicated the system by creating three different types of import licenses.[15] On July 2, 1932—a few weeks after Frederick Herron had claimed victory in the *Hell's Angels* case—the government was expected to publish a new quota law that forced the American studios to produce pictures in Germany. After dealing with "absurd, ridiculous, and unfair" trade regulations for so many years, the American managers were seriously thinking of putting the situation to the test by quitting the German market.[16]

When the quota law of 1932 was published, the American managers began a particularly intense round of negotiations. They held meetings with senior government officials, they pointed out that they could leave the market at any moment, and in the end they reached an agreement on the question of forced production in Germany.[17] All these discussions seemed very important at the time, but buried in the new law was one addition that they did not contest and that would have a much deeper, more lasting impact. In a small section of the law, under the heading "Article Fifteen," appeared the following pronouncement:

> The allocation of permits may be refused for films, the producers of which, in spite of warnings issued by the competent German authorities, continue to distribute on the world market films, the tendency or effect of which is detrimental to German prestige.[18]

This sentence, which the German Foreign Office had slipped into the regulations, would influence Hollywood production for the remainder of the decade. Anyone with any power in the studio system would quickly become aware of its meaning. The point was not that the American companies could no longer make anti-German pictures; the German government could never have enforced such a law. Instead Article Fifteen merely stated that if a company distributed an anti-German picture anywhere in the world, then that company would no longer be granted import permits for the German market.

Article Fifteen would prove to be a very effective way of regulating the American film industry. The German Foreign Office, with its vast network of consulates and embassies, could easily detect whether an offensive picture was in circulation anywhere around the world. If one were discovered, the Foreign Office could then prevent the relevant studio from doing business in Germany.[19]

Since Article Fifteen was born out of the controversy surrounding *Hell's Angels*, it was fitting that the company responsible for the picture, United Artists, would be the law's first target. Before United Artists could be expelled from Germany, however, Article Fifteen stated that the company had to receive "warnings issued by the competent German authorities." In December 1932, the warnings were issued in a dramatic meeting in New York City. The official in charge of the proceedings was the German vice consul, Dr. Jordan, and representing United Artists were the sales manager, Al Lichtman, and the foreign manager, Arthur Kelly.[20]

In the opening remarks, Lichtman and Kelly said that the problem was essentially a financial one. United Artists had not produced *Hell's Angels* but had merely distributed it, and the company would lose approximately $1.5 million if the picture were withdrawn from circulation at this early stage.[21]

Dr. Jordan gave no reply to these excuses. He simply announced that the German government was invoking Article Fifteen of the quota regulations against United Artists. Lichtman responded by walking out of the meeting.[22]

Kelly started talking again. He said that United Artists had never been given the chance to receive and exchange suggestions about *Hell's Angels*. Furthermore, United Artists had recently distributed the German company Ufa's picture *The Congress Dances* in the United States at a considerable loss. If the Germans retaliated against United Artists, the Americans could easily retaliate against Ufa.[23]

Once again, Dr. Jordan said nothing in response. He just repeated his original warning. The German government was invoking Article Fifteen of the quota law against United Artists.

Kelly became agitated. He stiffened visibly. "This is of no importance to us, as we've got no business in Germany anyway," he said.

Dr. Jordan did not react. He repeated the warning one more time "to leave no doubt about the government's intentions." Kelly responded that he had fully understood the meaning of the warning.[24]

In the days that followed, Dr. Jordan was warned by Frederick Herron not to annoy United Artists too much. The company was extremely powerful and could easily adopt dangerous retaliatory measures. For example, the company could make an anti-German film with an all-star cast that would be much more difficult to "ban" than *Hell's Angels*.[25]

Ten months later, Arthur Kelly gave a quick interview in Berlin in which he said that United Artists pictures were "too attached to the American mentality" to do worthwhile business in Germany.[26] If he really meant that, he changed his mind very quickly, for the following year he submitted a series of films to the German censors.[27] Almost all were rejected instantly.[28] One year after the drama around *Hell's Angels*, United Artists had become the first casualty of Article Fifteen.

The creation of a law to regulate the production of hate films in Hollywood was a powerful move by the German government, but at almost the same time, a second, even more ambitious scheme was underway. In January 1932, six months before the introduction of Article Fifteen, a special agent of the German Foreign Office named Dr. Martin Freudenthal made a trip to the United States to study the American studio system. For an entire year, he dealt with some of "the biggest men in [the] industry," and by the end of his trip, he had worked out quite a different course of action for his government to follow.[29]

Other countries had organized similar missions in the late 1920s. Canada, Chile, China, and Mexico had all sent representatives to Hollywood to ensure that their cultures were portrayed accurately. The best-known example had been Baron Valentin Mandelstamm of France, who had insisted on payment for his services and who at one point had convinced the French government to place a temporary ban on Warner Brothers' product.[30] No representative, however, had been as enthusiastic as Martin Freudenthal. Whenever Freudenthal took the train, he engaged with passengers about various issues, "for example, the church, American women, etc." in an attempt to learn more about Americans. The first thing he noticed about these people was that they did not respond well to excessive formality; it simply made them put up their guard. He therefore decided to conduct all his interactions in a casual, informal, "free-and-easy" manner. So, for example, when Will Hays told him that he was not the first representative to come to Hollywood—that other countries were sensitive about their portrayals as well—he replied that Germany was a "special case." Germany's reputation had been systematically destroyed by the movies of the postwar years, and the studios needed to be "good sports" and fix the problem.[31]

He had a point. The representatives of other countries had generally been concerned with matters of accuracy or morality. Valentin Mandelstamm, for example, identified details in film scripts that were "incorrect" or contained "fundamental errors," and he objected to a scene in *All Quiet on the Western Front* in which a group of French women allowed themselves to be seduced too quickly.[32] Freudenthal, on the other hand, was concerned with the constant portrayal of the German defeat on the screen, and in the aftermath of the World War, this was a genuinely important matter.

Freudenthal quickly realized that his job was not going to be an easy one. Several major obstacles stood in his way. For a start, the film industry was changing every day. Given film's complicated relationship to art, to economics, to technology, and "last not least" to politics, it was no easy object of study. Furthermore, his own mission was very precarious. Up to this point, foreign representatives had only attempted to protest films still in production, not films that had already been completed. Freudenthal was protesting both types, and he had little to offer the studios in return.[33]

By far the biggest obstacle he encountered was the Hays Office. The employees of this organization, particularly Frederick Herron, saw themselves as the "field guards" of the industry, and they became agitated whenever Freudenthal interacted directly with the studios. At the beginning of his trip, Freudenthal had impressed several studio executives, and he had even been offered a position in Fox's production department. Very quickly, however, the employees of the Hays Office started to intervene, and Freudenthal was forced to enter into a "gentleman's agreement" with them: he promised not to deal with the studios directly as long as they consulted him on all cases relating to Germany.[34]

Freudenthal was able to make some gains under the new agreement. He convinced the Hays Office to use its influence to cancel a Paramount feature about the German sinking of the *Lusitania* during the World War. He also managed to bring about significant cuts to a Fox film called *Surrender* set in a German prison camp. Other negotiations were more difficult: when he objected to a new film by RKO called *The Lost Squadron*, the employees of the Hays Office did not take him very seriously.[35]

This particular film had an interesting backstory. Earlier, when *Hell's Angels* was being made, the producer, Howard Hughes, had offered a pilot named Dick Grace $250 to perform an extremely dangerous stunt involving the shooting down of a German Gotha bomber. Grace had refused, saying that he wanted $10,000—a fair price given the risk involved. Hughes ultimately paid someone else $1,000 for the job, and the terrible fate of the Gotha bomber was visible in the final cut of the film.[36]

The following year, Grace published his novel *The Lost Squadron* about a tyrannical movie producer, de Forst, who made aviation pictures independently in Hollywood. At the opening of the novel, de Forst was working on a new feature called *Hell's Free Acre*. At the end, he put acid on the wires of a plane so that it would crash and give him the footage he needed.[37] Dick Grace had good contacts in Hollywood, and he managed to convince David Selznick to turn *The Lost Squadron* into a feature for RKO. The movie was faithful to the book apart from a couple of details: Selznick changed the villain's name from "de Forst" to "von Furst," and he hired none other than Erich von Stroheim to play the part.[38]

And so by sheer coincidence, the movie that was intended as an attack on *Hell's Angels* ended up invoking its most damaging stereotype. The main character of the film, who was obviously meant to represent Howard Hughes, was now being played by Erich von Stroheim, the worst German villain on the screen. Although *The Lost Squadron* was not a hate film in the conventional sense—it was not degrading the German army—Freudenthal felt that any German who watched it would be deeply offended by von Stroheim's dialogue. Freudenthal was following E. A. Dupont's lead by saying that this deliberate distortion of the German language was the most damaging mockery of all.[39]

The American authorities did not speak German, however, so they could not understand Freudenthal's critique. Frederick Herron was particularly resistant. He met with Freudenthal about *The Lost Squadron* several times at the New York branch of the Hays Office, and he absolutely refused to cut the dialogue. Freudenthal then left for Los Angeles, and Herron warned his representatives there about the new visitor: "You will probably get frightfully fed up with this man, because he comes to stay ten minutes and stays two hours, but I don't see any way of getting around him as he is attached to the Embassy as a direct representative of the Ambassador."[40]

A few weeks later, Herron received a visit from the vice consul in New York, Dr. Jordan, who brought up the Americans' cooperation in *The Lost*

*Squadron* case. Herron was confused, so Dr. Jordan gave him proof: "He had a cable from the Foreign Office in Berlin saying that our new sob sister 'Freudenthal' had made a report on this, saying that he suggested that we cut out all the German language in the picture, and that I said I would do what I could." Herron looked at the cable in disbelief and, not for the first time, lost his temper: "I said I could not carry out my part of that sort of an agreement, that we had licked him in numerous places of the world and we were ready to take up this question whenever it came up and fight it out."[41]

In the end, Freudenthal managed to make some headway on *The Lost Squadron*. As a result of his actions, a portion of the German dialogue was cut.[42] He also learned an important lesson from the experience: the Americans were not deliberately trying to offend Germany. Their negative portrayals of German characters were, for the most part, unintentional.[43]

This realization affected Freudenthal's whole attitude toward his mission. When the German government published Article Fifteen of the film regulations, he was in the middle of his trip, and he was not exactly enthusiastic about the new development. Although he understood that the law might be necessary in certain cases, he mostly thought that it was a mistake. After meeting with powerful figures in the film industry, he had understood that very few of the offensive moments in American movies were deliberate. Consequently, a punitive legal measure like Article Fifteen made no sense. Freudenthal wanted instead to work hand in hand with the American studios to prevent future negative depictions of the German people.

Of course, Freudenthal was under no illusions about why the studios had been meeting with him in the first place. "The American companies' attitudes to my mission varied according to their immediate interest in the German market," he said.[44] In other words, the companies were following his recommendations only because they wanted to sell more of their films in Germany. Up to this point, Freudenthal had always replied to such demands by saying that "political questions of honor should not be connected to questions of economics."[45] With the publication of Article Fifteen, he probably found it much more difficult to use this excuse.

At the end of his year in the United States, Freudenthal returned to Germany to give a report on his experiences. The people who welcomed him back were entirely different from the ones who had sent him on his mission in the first place. On January 30, 1933, Hitler had become chancellor of Germany, and on March 5, the National Socialists had won 43.9 percent of the vote in the Reichstag elections, allowing them to form a coalition government with their nationalist allies. On March 31, just eight days after Hitler had assumed dictatorial powers, Freudenthal met with some of the most important political figures in Germany. The lessons that he had learned were of great interest to the Foreign Office, the Defense Ministry, the Interior Ministry, and especially to the newly formed Propaganda Ministry. Everyone listened as Freudenthal outlined a brand new plan to combat the hate film problem in the United States.[46]

He began by pointing out that the most successful moments of his trip had been his interactions with the heads of the Hollywood studios. He had received permission from the Hays Office to meet directly with Carl Laemmle of Universal Pictures, and as a result of their meetings, Laemmle had agreed to postpone the sequel to *All Quiet on the Western Front*, entitled *The Road Back*. Throughout the rest of the year, Freudenthal had met with Laemmle's son, Carl Laemmle Jr., and many more pictures were changed in Germany's favor. "Naturally," Freudenthal said, "Universal's interest in collaboration [*Zusammenarbeit*] is not platonic but is motivated by the company's concern for the well-being of its Berlin branch and for the German market."[47]

Other studio heads were just as obliging. An executive at RKO promised that whenever he made a film involving Germany he would work "in close collaboration" with the local consul general. An executive at Fox said that he would consult a German representative in all future cases as well. Even United Artists offered "the closest collaboration" (*engste Zusammenarbeit*) in return for some understanding in the *Hell's Angels* case. "Every time that this collaboration was achieved," Freudenthal said, "the parties involved found it to be both helpful and pleasant."[48]

In light of his experience, Freudenthal proposed that a permanent representative should be stationed in Los Angeles to work directly with the studios on all movies relating to Germany. The representative should be officially connected to the Los Angeles consulate, and he should put the bulk of his energy into "educating and training" the studios about

German national feeling. He should invoke Article Fifteen only as a last resort. "Prevention of disease is much better than treatment in a hospital," Freudenthal said. "To avoid the possibility of invoking Article Fifteen, friendly collaboration at the actual site of production is recommended."[49]

From the Nazis' perspective, Freudenthal's report could not have come at a better time. Hitler had only been in power for eight weeks; the Reichstag had only been dissolved for eight days; a fresh start was entirely possible. If Freudenthal had wanted the position he was describing for himself, however, he was disappointed by the end result. He was transferred to a legal division of the Foreign Office, and a German diplomat named Georg Gyssling, who had been a member of the Nazi Party since 1931, was sent to Los Angeles.[50] Whether Gyssling had much experience with film is unknown, but he plunged into his new work with great enthusiasm. His superiors in Berlin noted the results in two words: "Very efficient."[51]

At the time of Gyssling's arrival in Los Angeles, the most problematic picture underway was *Captured!*, a Warner Brothers feature set in a German prison camp during the World War.[52] Warner Brothers had promised to show the picture to a German official before distributing it, and on June 16, 1933, Gyssling was invited to give his opinion of an American movie for the first time.[53]

From the beginning of the meeting, it was obvious that Gyssling was a very different figure from Freudenthal. On the screen, a group of British soldiers were lining up for inspection, and the German camp commander, a cruel man, punched one of the soldiers on the chin. As the soldier fell to the ground, Gyssling was adamant in his response—this scene had to go. The camp commander then made a sneering remark about another soldier's Victoria Cross, and Gyssling said that this would have to be cut out too. A third soldier asked desperately for water, and Gyssling said that none of these images could appear in the final version of the film.[54]

As *Captured!* continued, it became clear that there was hardly anything to which Gyssling did not object. The soldiers were hauled into a massive room where they were forced to have a group shower—this, Gyssling said, made the camp look ridiculous. The soldiers revolted against the guards and were locked up as a result—this was too brutal. The German camp commander threw coffee in the face of his orderly, and the orderly reacted by killing the commander—by no means could this be shown. The list went on, and by the end of the film, Gyssling had requested a massive number of cuts.[55]

Two months after the meeting, *Captured!* was released at theaters across the United States—without Gyssling's cuts.[56] It is uncertain what happened at this point, but in all likelihood Gyssling sent one of his warnings to Warner Brothers. First he would have cited the text of Article Fifteen: "The allocation of permits may be refused for films, the producers of which, in spite of warnings issued by the competent German authorities, continue to distribute on the world market films, the tendency or effect of which is detrimental to German prestige." Then he would have added a sentence of his own: "As this letter has the character of a warning in the sense of said provision, I beg to ask you to let me know the decision which you will make regarding the distribution of 'Captured!'."[57]

Warner Brothers had a lot to lose. It had been selling pictures in Germany for years, and it employed dozens of people in a distribution office in Berlin. In March 1933, just when Hitler had come to power, its gritty crime drama *I Am a Fugitive from a Chain Gang* had created a sensation in Germany. In the film's first run, people had flocked to theaters for thirty-four days straight, and the reviews had been ecstatic.[58] "Thrill after thrill, image after image shoots past your eyes," the Nazi newspaper *Völkischer Beobachter* had reported. "Our directors can learn a lot from this American film."[59] *I Am a Fugitive from a Chain Gang* was the fifth most popular film in Germany in 1933, and Warner Brothers was hoping that its hit musical *42nd Street* would be an even greater success.

Warner Brothers soon consulted with Frederick Herron about the situation. Herron had more experience with this kind of thing than anyone else, for he had been the one person to question Martin Freudenthal's judgment in the previous year. Still, Herron's difficulties with Freudenthal did not even compare to what he thought of Gyssling. "You probably have gathered that this Consul out there is looking for trouble," Herron said. "I know just exactly what you are going to be up against; he is narrow minded and you will always find in any dealings you have with him that there will be trouble."[60] Herron encouraged Warner Brothers to make some but not all of Gyssling's cuts to *Captured!*, and then he arranged to show the new version to a different German consul named Gustav Müller. This man, at least, was not a Nazi.

The second official screening of *Captured!* took place on January 12, 1934, in Warner Brothers' offices in New York. Müller proved to be a much more accommodating guest than Gyssling. He watched the film calmly and patiently, he compared the edits in the new version to those requested by Gyssling seven months earlier, and he listened attentively to the clarifying remarks of Herron and the Warner Brothers representative. Overall, the session was very productive. When a British officer in the film appeared in front of a German war tribunal, Herron explained that Warner Brothers had removed a series of close-ups of the German judges because these created a very unfavorable impression. Müller expressed his approval of the new version and requested just a few more cuts. The Warner Brothers representative then promised to change all the prints of *Captured!* worldwide according to the German specifications. The American copies would be edited within one week; the others would take just a little longer than that.[61]

Both the Hays Office and Warner Brothers were pleased with the result. "This is just an example of what can be done if you deal with intelligent people, rather than with obstructionists of the type of Dr. Gyssling," Herron noted.[62] One week later, Herron worked with Müller again, this time on a Columbia picture entitled *Below the Sea*. Müller objected to the film's references to the U-170, a type of submarine that the Germans had used during the World War. He asked Columbia Pictures what it could do about the following line, which he remembered as: "Hey, Schlemmer, I thought may be you like to know Im standing right along side your old tub the U 170." The representative for Columbia Pictures said it would be extremely difficult to change the line at such a late stage but eventually agreed to blur out all references to the U-170 in the final cut of the film.[63]

News of the two cases quickly reached the trade papers in the United States. "American film companies are still afraid of offending the German government . . . preferring to continue business there in spite of current conditions," *Variety* reported. "Two companies, Warner Brothers and Columbia, made deep concessions last week rather than possibly get into trouble."[64] Just as this announcement was being printed, however, Warner Brothers got into trouble anyway. Gyssling must have noticed that the company had gone over his head in dealing with another consul, for at precisely the moment that *Captured!* was being edited in New York, more serious action was being taken in Berlin. The Propaganda Ministry sent out a letter to all German consulates and embassies worldwide to announce that *Captured!* was the worst hate film made since the World War and that Article Fifteen had been invoked against the company.[65] Warner Brothers' interests in Germany were doomed. *42nd Street* was rejected by the German censors for being "too leggy," and the company closed its office in Berlin in July 1934.[66]

For the remainder of the decade, the studios still doing business in Germany were very careful to remain on good terms with Georg Gyssling. Every time they embarked on a potentially threatening production, they received one of his letters reminding them of the terms of Article Fifteen. In response—as will be seen in a later chapter—they did not make the same mistake as Warner Brothers. They simply invited Gyssling to the studio lot to preview the film in question, and they made all the cuts that he requested. In an effort to keep the market open for their films, they were doing just what Gyssling's predecessor, Martin Freudenthal, had envisioned: they were collaborating with Nazi Germany.

All of the interactions between the German government and the American studios that have been considered up to this point were based on two primary concerns. The Germans were concerned with the question of national honor: they felt that the studios had been systematically destroying their reputation since the World War. The studios, on the other hand, were concerned with economics: they felt that the Germans had been placing unfair trade restrictions on their product. These two conflicting concerns were crystallized in Article Fifteen, and in a different time and place, the story might have ended here. But from the moment Hitler came to power, a third element was added to the equation, and the relationship between Hollywood and the German government became infinitely more complicated.

As has been noted, ever since the World War, the American studios had experienced tremendous financial difficulties in Germany. Before the war, Germany had been their second biggest export market; after the war,

Germany had dwindled to a small but important source of foreign revenue.[67] The Americans still continued to do much better business in Germany than other foreign studios, of course: only a handful of British films, for example, reached Germany in this period. Nevertheless, the Americans were constantly frustrated by the quota regulations that the German government had enacted to protect local film companies such as Ufa. In 1925, in an effort to respond to the mounting problems, the U.S. Department of Commerce had formed a separate motion picture division, and eventually the department had sent a trade commissioner, named George Canty, to Berlin.[68]

Canty was a shrewd businessman, and he had advised the American studios on how to respond to each new addition to the quota regulations. When the Germans had insisted that all dubbing be done locally, for example, he had not become overly concerned, but when they had imposed massive booking restrictions on foreign pictures, he had urged the American managers to threaten to quit the market.[69] On only a few occasions had Canty found himself at a loss about how to proceed. "I am working on a brief . . . to be submitted to the Bureau as soon as I can get it clear in my head," he had once written to his superiors in Washington after reading a draft of the new trade laws. "I am doing my level best to hurry up . . . before a too deep study of what is needed . . . to protect the domestic industry may result in a characteristically German set of regulations too full of complications to permit our successful operation under them."[70]

As Canty knew well, the Nazis had promised to simplify the quota system if they came to power. In July 1932, a senior film official had proclaimed that the Nazi Party was "absolutely in favor of international exchange and collaboration." Although the party would not tolerate such atrocities as *All Quiet on the Western Front* or *Hell's Angels*, American movies would always be welcome in Germany. Ideally, the quota would return to the original stipulation: one foreign film admitted for every German film produced. "But if it turns out that we can't make enough films ourselves to sustain the local market," the Nazi spokesman had added, "then we will definitely have to loosen the quota. We are not planning on sitting idly by while theater owners lose money just because Ufa is dictating our import policy!"[71]

Surprisingly, the Nazi spokesman seemed to be telling the truth. In the year after Hitler won the Reichstag elections, the American companies experienced fewer economic difficulties in Germany. George Canty met with Joseph Goebbels' film assistant, a man named Mutzenbecher, and he was told "that the Americans were needed along with the right kind of Germans to help the Party develop the film to its proper worth." This was just the opposite of the previous government's policies, and Canty was delighted. "I placed myself on record in pledging the American interests to a cooperation which would restore the German market to its proper worth," he reported.[72] A few weeks later, he had further "friendly contact" with Mutzenbecher and other prominent Nazis in the industry, and it was agreed "that a working arrangement with the American interests was absolutely necessary in order to break down film barriers abroad . . . and that collaboration with our office was about the only way these matters could properly be discussed."[73]

After years in Berlin, Canty was hoping that his efforts were finally paying off. He might obtain favorable business conditions for the American studios. He still had a few concerns, of course. He knew that Hitler's rise to power had created a variety of more general problems for foreign companies operating in Germany. Above all, he was worried about a new law that prevented foreign companies from taking their money out of the country.[74] The law, which was of great concern to many American businesses operating in Germany (including General Motors and IBM), did not immediately affect the studios, however, for the Nazis considered film a cultural product rather than a commodity.[75] In the early days of the Third Reich, George Canty found that the Nazis were unusually cooperative in all financial matters relating to film. The real problem, he soon discovered, lay elsewhere.

In the middle of March 1933, rumors started circulating that all Jewish film workers in Germany were about to lose their jobs.[76] Sure enough, in one hour on March 29, Ufa fired many of its best writers, directors, actors, and technical specialists.[77] The following week a small group within the Nazi Party—the Salesmen's Syndicate—sent a letter to the American film companies in Germany insisting that all Jewish employees be discharged. The letter caused considerable panic, because the American companies employed not only a large number of Jews but also a large number of Nazis, and the Nazis began terrorizing the Jews. In this chaotic situation, the company managers decided to send all Jewish personnel on temporary leave for their "mental preservation." Then Nazi labor organizations started forming within the individual companies, and a spokesman for the organization at Paramount announced that the Jewish employees could not come back.[78]

Canty decided to meet with his contacts in the Propaganda Ministry about the situation. He explained what was going on, and they told him to keep the Jewish employees out of the workplace while they gauged the feelings of the Salesmen's Syndicate. Canty wanted to follow this advice, but the American managers did not, and on April 20, the Jewish employees returned to work. The renewed business activities lasted exactly one day. The head of the Salesmen's Syndicate ordered exhibitors not to buy films from Jewish salesmen, and the Propaganda Ministry "became peeved" at the disobedient managers.[79]

At around this time, Max Friedland—the local manager of Universal Pictures and the favorite nephew of Carl Laemmle—was pulled out of his bed in Laupheim and taken to prison. He remained there for five hours without being told the charge.[80] The manager of Warner Brothers, Phil Kauffman, had his car stolen and was beaten up by thugs.[81] The manager of Columbia Pictures was next on the list, so Canty gave him identification papers and advised him to leave Germany. The manager of MGM, Frits Strengholt, was also getting ready to leave, but Canty told the authorities that he was a gentile and he was permitted to stay.[82]

After this show of strength, the remaining American managers pulled their Jewish salesmen off the job again while Canty resumed his discussions with the various branches of the German government. Back when the troubles had started, Canty had predicted the eventual outcome in a report to the Department of Commerce. "I presume some readjustments will have to be made in our company personnel as time goes on, inasmuch as they are indelibly stamped as Jewish companies," he had written. "But I don't mean by this that we are yet obliged to rid ourselves of all Jewish employees. I almost feel that we will eventuate by discharging the dispensable and keeping the indispensable, if there be nothing specific against any of these latter; but our company managers will need to have cool heads for the handling of numerous petty troubles meanwhile."[83]

Canty's prediction turned out to be absolutely correct. He presented lists of the most desirable Jewish salesmen to the Foreign Office, and he managed to obtain exemptions for them.[84] The rest had to go. In early May, the Hollywood studios announced their decision: "U.S. Film Units

Yield to Nazis on Race Issue." As *Variety* reported, "American attitude on the matter is that American companies cannot afford to lose the German market at this time no matter what the inconvenience of personnel shifts."[85]

Of course, the compromise affected both of the parties involved. At the same time as the studios were forced to fire many of their Jewish salesmen, the Nazis agreed to provide protection for the salesmen who remained. Canty was "definitely assured that if any resistance was shown by exhibitors to the orders of the Nazi body, [he] was merely to bring the individual cases to the attention of the Ministry whereupon police measures would be invoked to carry out the orders."[86] For the next three years, Jewish salesmen distributed American pictures in Germany. Only on January 1, 1936 did the Nazis pass a new law forbidding all Jews from working in the film distribution business.[87]

The reason for the compromise of 1933 was simple. There had been a big decline in German film production ever since the Nazis had dismissed all Jews from Ufa, and American movies were badly needed to make up the difference in the theaters.[88] The Hollywood studios had significant bargaining power in this situation, and one of their demands was to retain half of their Jewish personnel. They also managed to obtain much better conditions for the sale of their films in Germany: the first quota under the Nazi regime contained fewer restrictions than usual and remained in place for three years rather than for one.[89] The studios sold a total of sixty-five pictures in Germany in 1933, up from fifty-four in 1932.[90] "All in all," Canty reported, "we have very little to complain about."[91]

Still, the purging of the salesmen from the American companies operating in Germany introduced a new element to the relationship between the two groups. The Nazis, in complete consistency with their anti-Semitic policies, were insisting that all cultural workers in Germany be of Aryan descent. This would have been entirely unremarkable in the history of the Third Reich were it not for a single fact: the founders of the Hollywood studios, who were doing business with the Nazis, were mostly Jews themselves. As numerous commentators have pointed out, the men who created the studio system in Los Angeles were Jewish immigrants of Eastern European descent. These men included William Fox, who founded Fox; Louis B. Mayer, who ran MGM; Adolph Zukor, who ran Paramount; Harry Cohn, who ran Columbia Pictures; Carl Laemmle, who ran Universal Pictures; and Jack and Harry Warner, who ran Warner Brothers. "Of 85 names engaged in production," one study noted in the 1930s, "53 are Jews."[92]

Why did these powerful executives (with the exception of William Fox, who lost control of Fox in 1930) choose to do business with the most anti-Semitic regime in history? The excuse of ignorance can immediately be ruled out. One of the most persistent myths about the rise and fall of the Third Reich is that the outside world had no knowledge of the extent of the Nazis' brutality. In fact, events in Germany were always reported in American newspapers, although not necessarily on the front page. The Hollywood executives knew exactly what was going on in Germany, not only because they had been forced to fire their own Jewish salesmen but also because the persecution of the Jews was common knowledge at the time.[93]

The actions of the Hollywood executives look especially problematic when set against the early efforts of the largest Jewish organization in the United States, the American Jewish Congress. On March 27, 1933, just when the American companies were cooperating with the Nazis on the salesman issue, this organization put together a rally at Madison Square Garden to protest the treatment of Jews in Germany. The honorary president of the American Jewish Congress, Rabbi Stephen S. Wise, announced the reason for the gathering in no uncertain terms: "The time for caution and prudence is past. . . . What is happening in Germany today may happen tomorrow in any other land on earth unless it is challenged and rebuked. It is not the German Jews who are being attacked. It is the Jews. We must speak out. If that is unavailing, at least we shall have spoken."[94]

These were brave words, and the American Jewish Congress' next move was to call for a boycott on German goods. The idea was a contentious one at the time: two other important Jewish groups—the American Jewish Committee and the B'nai B'rith—consistently refused to support the boycott.[95] And in the 1930s, these were the groups that enjoyed the closest ties to the American studios. In the aftermath of the rally at Madison Square Garden, the studios ignored the boycott idea. Then, with the help of the Anti-Defamation League of the B'nai B'rith, the studios formulated one last policy that affected both their dealings with the Nazis and American culture generally.

In late May of 1933, a Hollywood screenwriter named Herman J. Mankiewicz—the man who would later write *Citizen Kane*—had a promising idea. He was aware of the treatment of the Jews in Germany and he thought, Why not put it on the screen? Very quickly, he penned a play entitled *The Mad Dog of Europe*, which he sent to his friend Sam Jaffe, a producer at RKO. Jaffe was so taken with the idea that he bought the production rights and quit his job.[96] This producer, who, like Mankiewicz, was Jewish, planned to assemble a great Hollywood cast and devote all his energies to a picture that would shake the entire world.

Nobody had ever made a movie about Hitler's persecution of the Jews before, and Jaffe was worried that somebody in Hollywood might steal his idea. He therefore took out a full-page advertisement in the *Hollywood Reporter* and announced his intentions in a letter addressed "To The Entire Motion Picture Industry." "Because I sincerely believe that in 'The Mad Dog of Europe' I have the most valuable motion picture property I have ever possessed," he wrote, "and because I wish to take sufficient time to prepare and film it with the infinite care that its subject merits, I hereby ask the motion picture industry kindly to respect my priority rights."[97]

Next, Jaffe needed to find someone to turn the play into a workable film script. He would have asked Mankiewicz to do the job, but Mankiewicz was under contract at MGM, so he was forced to find someone else instead.[98] He eventually hired an unknown screenwriter named Lynn Root, and he found that Root worked fast. After one month, Jaffe was in possession of the script.[99] He opened it to the first page. "This picture is produced in the interests of Democracy, an ideal which has inspired the noblest deeds of Man," he read. "Today the greater part of the civilized world has reached this stage of enlightenment."[100] This was a strong beginning; it set the stakes very high. Jaffe read on. As he read, the film came to life in his mind:

It was July 1915. The setting was the home of the Mendelssohns, a patriotic Jewish family living in Germany in the first year of the World War. The Mendelssohns had recently sent their oldest son off to the Western Front, and they were spending the afternoon with their best friends, the Schmidts. The fathers were enjoying a game of chess, the mothers were organizing a charity event, and the children were playing outside. Just then, a telegram arrived, and the Mendelssohns learned that their oldest son had been killed in battle.

The second Mendelssohn child, a boy of just sixteen, was determined to carry on his brother's legacy. He forged the date on his birth certificate so

Herman J. Mankiewicz, author of *The Mad Dog of Europe* and *Citizen Kane*. Copyright © John Springer Collection/ Corbis.

that he would appear to be eighteen, and he enlisted in the Imperial German Army Air Service. Soon he was regarded as a hero: he had shot down dozens of enemy planes, and people were saying that he was invincible. But one day, the Mendelssohns received a telegram announcing that their second son had been killed too.

The third boy to go off to war was the Schmidts' oldest son, Heinrich. Unlike the Mendelssohn boys, Heinrich was not killed in battle. He fought bravely until the end. When he returned home, however, he was a completely different person. He was angry and bitter, and he could not stop complaining about the bad treatment that Germany was receiving. "Taxes, war debts, reparations—everything is our fault," he said. "I'm sick of it. The German heart should be hard and strong and ruthless, to crush our enemies, inside and out."[101]

Heinrich, like so many others, was looking for a different kind of leader, and one day he met Adolf Hitler. He was seduced by Hitler's charm, and he overlooked everything else. He joined the National Socialist Party, he participated in the failed putsch of 1923, and he ended up sharing a prison cell with the great leader himself. The two men got along famously until someone from Heinrich's past came by for a visit. Hitler was shocked when he read the name on the visitor's card.

"Ilsa Mendelssohn," he said. "Who is she?"

"Why . . ." Heinrich began.

"Jewish!" Hitler yelled.

"Yes."

"You call yourself a Nazi—and you bring a Jew to my very door."[102]

Heinrich explained that he had proposed to Ilsa Mendelssohn, a family friend, just before he had left for the Western Front. Hitler was unrepentant. "If you're unworthy I must tear you out of my heart as I now command you to tear out that Jewish girl," he said. "Decide now. Are you a Nazi—or are you a Jew lover?"[103]

Sure enough, Heinrich did as Hitler asked. He met with Ilsa, and he told her how he felt about the Jewish people: "No Jew can be a German. They are enemies of Germany—parasites feeding on German blood." When Ilsa protested, Heinrich replied coldly, "I never want to see you again. I mean it. You and your Jewish family."[104]

At this point, the scene changed. The film reverted to a newsreel. Important historical events unfolded, one after the other: the Dawes Plan of 1924, the development of German-American relations, the visits of several important Americans to Berlin. Then, just as everything looked like it was improving, the stock market collapsed. Banks closed, people lost their jobs, optimism disappeared. In the ensuing chaos, President Hindenburg named Adolf Hitler chancellor of Germany, and soon afterward, Hitler assumed supreme power.

The setting was now Germany in the present day. As expected, Hitler was carrying out his campaign promises. Large numbers of people were being forced to walk down the streets carrying signs that read "I am a Jew." Mud and filth were being thrown at them. In the background were shops that had been closed down. "Don't buy here—Jew!" was scrawled on the doors. Stones had been thrown through the windows.[105]

Despite these horrors, the Mendelssohn father—a history professor at the local university—was determined to go to work as usual. When he entered his classroom, he was dismayed by what he saw. A student was standing against a wall wearing a cap that read "JEW." A pen was stuck in the student's shoulder and blood was dripping from the wound. Another student was writing "My teacher is a Jew" on the blackboard. Mendelssohn tried to restore calm, but the students were defiant. "We're not taking orders from Jews!" one of them yelled.[106] Finally, a different professor entered the classroom and told Mendelssohn that he could no longer work at the university. Mendelssohn took the Jewish boy by the hand and left the classroom for good.

The same day, an important event took place: Heinrich was appointed chief commissioner of his hometown. The first thing he learned upon his return was that his brother had married Ilsa Mendelssohn and that they had had a child together. "So you were carrying on while I was at the front," he told Ilsa. "What else would I expect from a Jew?" Then he turned to his brother and said, "You're through with her. With her and her Jewish brat."[107] A few days later, a new law appeared in the newspapers: "Hitler decrees all Aryans married to Jews must separate or be sent to prison camps."[108]

Everything was happening very quickly now. Professor Mendelssohn's last remaining son, a boy named Hans, was brutally murdered by Nazi thugs. Mendelssohn went to his old friend Schmidt for help, and Schmidt went to his son Heinrich. But Heinrich refused to do anything. "I'm not here to help the Jews," he said. "I'm here to drive them out. They're traitors to Germany. . . . We must get rid of the vermin."[109]

With no one to help him, Professor Mendelssohn went to the morgue alone to recover his son's body. He found that it had been branded with swastikas. In his fury, he yelled at a group of Nazis who were present: "We Jews are good enough to die on the battlefield but not good enough to live in the Fatherland." The Nazis shot him dead. Then Schmidt arrived and saw what had happened. "Stop this bloodshed . . . this persecution of the innocent," he screamed. The Nazis killed him too.[110]

When Heinrich found out about the deaths, he was shocked. He finally saw the error of his ways. He raced over to his brother and Ilsa. He gave them identification papers, and he told them to drive across the border. As they were leaving, a group of Nazis started shooting at them. Heinrich threw himself in front of the gunfire and died, and the car sped away to safety. On this curiously optimistic note, the picture came to an end.

Sam Jaffe put the screenplay down. A couple of things were immediately clear. For a start, *The Mad Dog of Europe* was not the greatest film script he had ever read. The pacing was erratic, the characters were shallow, and the writing was mediocre. The plot contained too many twists and turns, and it was difficult to keep track of all the events that had taken place. He would need to make a significant number of revisions if the picture were to be appealing to a mass audience.

Still, the news was not all bad. The subject matter was just as fresh and original as it had been from the start. Nothing like it had ever been filmed before. Also—and this was the most important point of all—nothing about it was that surprising either. The persecution of the Jews was common knowledge at the time, and all the events in the screenplay had already occurred or could easily be imagined. Jaffe had on his hands a subject that was on everyone's mind, and he was going to be the first person to address it. He decided to push ahead with the undertaking.

Of course, various forces had been put in place to prevent a picture like this from ever being made. First and foremost was Georg Gyssling, who was in charge of invoking Article Fifteen of the German film regulations. Up to this point, Gyssling had only ever used Article Fifteen against traditional hate pictures, that is, pictures that disparaged the German army during the World War. As anyone could tell, *The Mad Dog of Europe* was infinitely more threatening, for it did more than just bring up old wounds—it attacked the present German regime. Here was a film, "the tendency or effect of which [was] detrimental to German prestige."

Despite this applicability, Gyssling was unable to use Article Fifteen against *The Mad Dog of Europe* for the simple reason that the company producing the picture did not do business in Germany. Gyssling was left with only one option: he could inform the Hays Office that if *The Mad Dog of Europe* were made, then his government might place a ban on all American movies in Germany. It is uncertain whether Gyssling actually did this at this particular point in time—the evidence is inconclusive—but he probably did, because very soon Will Hays invited Sam Jaffe and Herman Mankiewicz to his office to discuss their upcoming production.

The meeting was not a friendly one. Hays told Jaffe and Mankiewicz that their activities were endangering the business of the major Hollywood studios. He accused the pair of "selecting a scarehead situation for the picture, which, if made, might return them a tremendous profit while creating heavy losses for the industry." In response, Jaffe simply said that he would go ahead with his production despite any ban that Hays might attempt to impose on it. Mankiewicz agreed and added that he had written the story for the same reason the Hollywood studios had made *Baby Face*, *Melody Cruise*, and *So This Is Africa*—namely, to entertain the public.[111]

Hays needed to adopt a different approach, so he asked his representative in Los Angeles, Joseph Breen, to reach out to important figures in the local Jewish community. He was very particular about whom Breen should approach. He did not want Breen to go to the local branch of the American Jewish Congress, for he had already failed to enlist the support of this group in the suppression of the picture. Instead, he wanted Breen to go to the people who were just then setting up an advisory council for the Anti-Defamation League in Los Angeles.[112]

Breen approached the group and connected with a man named Leon Lewis, a former national secretary of the Anti-Defamation League. He offered Lewis a peculiar argument. He said that if Jaffe and Mankiewicz produced *The Mad Dog of Europe*, there would be a tremendous anti-Semitic backlash in the United States. According to Breen: "Because of the large number of Jews active in the motion picture industry in this country, the charge is certain to be made that the Jews, as a class, are behind an anti-Hitler picture and using the entertainment screen for their own personal propaganda purposes. The entire industry, because of this, is likely to be indicted for the action of a mere handful."[113]

When Lewis first heard this argument, he was extremely suspicious. He noted down that the Hays Office did not want *The Mad Dog of Europe* produced "because (sic) it is afraid it will produce an anti-semitic reaction." His use of "sic" in a sentence that contained no error presumably implied that he did not think the Hays Office actually believed its own argument.[114] A few weeks later, he wrote that he was not convinced by Breen because he had "not noticed a very strong protective influence exerted by the Hays organization in the past."[115] Nevertheless, he used his contacts to obtain a copy of the script of *The Mad Dog of Europe* from Sam

Jaffe, and he promised Jaffe that he would examine it carefully and provide feedback and suggestions.[116]

On August 16, 1933, one of the first meetings of the new advisory council of the Anti-Defamation League in Los Angeles took place. All the local members were present, and several other important figures had come as well, including Rabbi Isadore Isaacson of the Temple Israel in Hollywood. First, Lewis read out the entire script of *The Mad Dog of Europe*. Then a discussion took place. Everyone in the room agreed that the direct references to Hitler and Nazi Germany might be dangerous. Nevertheless, "if modified so as to apparently have reference to a fictitious country, and if the propaganda elements were toned down and made more subtle, it was almost the unanimous opinion that the film would be a most effective means of arousing the general public to the major implications of Hitlerism."[117]

Before the meeting came to an end, a few members expressed one last concern. Even if the script were toned down, they said, the Hays Office would probably object to the film anyway as the major Hollywood studios were still doing business in Germany. Nobody at the meeting knew exactly how much business was being done. Some suspected that Germany was banning films starring Jewish actors; others thought that Germany was banning entire "companies supposed to be controlled by Jews." Nobody had the slightest idea that the Nazis were actually facilitating the distribution of American movies in Germany.[118]

Nevertheless, given this point about business dealings, Lewis decided to put the situation to the test. He asked a well-known screenwriter to prepare an outline of *The Mad Dog of Europe* that contained none of the obvious objections. He then submitted the outline to three different agents, and without any hesitation, they all told him the same thing: "It was no use submitting any story along this line as the major studios had put 'thumbs down' on any films of this kind."[119]

Lewis then reported his findings to the headquarters of the Anti-Defamation League. He wrote to the national director, Richard Gutstadt, passing on everything he had learned and pointing out that two courses of action were possible. The Anti-Defamation League could either attempt to prevent all propaganda pictures on the subject of Nazi Germany—a policy that would obviously please the Nazis and the Hays Office—or it could "sponsor and assist in the distribution of the right kind of propaganda films." If the Anti-Defamation League took the second option, the implication was that it would help shape the content of *The Mad Dog of Europe*.[120]

When Gutstadt read the screenplay, however, he had quite a different reaction from everyone who had attended the meeting in Los Angeles. So did his daughter. ("She happens to be majoring in literature and has pretty keen judgment on literary values," Gutstadt explained.) Their position was as follows: "The film, in its present form at least, can do absolutely no good and may do considerable harm. . . . It is amateurish and such a thing as a high school student would prepare upon instructions to work up a script with the avowed purpose for which this script was written."[121]

Gutstadt's opinion of *The Mad Dog of Europe* was in fact based less on his daughter's expertise than on a policy that the Anti-Defamation League had recently adopted to deal with a change in local conditions. From the moment that Hitler had come to power in Germany, there had been a dramatic rise in anti-Semitism in the United States. Nazi rallies had been held in many American cities, and domestic fascist organizations like the Silver Shirts had come into existence.[122] One of the most common charges of these groups was that the Jews were influencing American public opinion through their control of the mass media, particularly motion pictures. Under these conditions, the Anti-Defamation League had become extremely wary of openly protesting the situation in Germany, fearing that such protests would only fuel American anti-Semitism.[123]

After much deliberation, the Anti-Defamation League had come up with an alternative strategy to deal with the persecution of the Jews in Germany. "We are endeavoring in most of our activities to show gentile sponsorship of anti-Hitler sentiment," Gutstadt said. "It will be expected that Jews will be vociferous in their opposition to everything of an anti-semitic character, whether it be domestic or foreign. It is not anticipated that gentiles will rouse themselves on behalf of the Jews and this is the element that we must utilize to impress non-Jewry." Since *The Mad Dog of Europe* did not fit in with the Anti-Defamation League's new policy, Gutstadt urged Lewis to use his powers to suppress the production.[124]

Lewis did as he was told. Even though his committee had unanimously found that *The Mad Dog of Europe* had the potential to be an effective piece of propaganda, he went around Hollywood, and he informed the relevant parties that the Anti-Defamation League disapproved of the picture. "I have not even discussed this matter at any stage with the Advisory Council," he noted, "but have acted solely on my own initiative and responsibility."[125] The word spread fast. On September 1, he was able to report to Gutstadt that the picture would not be made. The producer, Sam Jaffe, had been trying to raise $75,000 to cover his costs, but "circles where he might look for these funds are now pretty well informed and the chances are that the project is dead."[126] In fact, unbeknownst to Lewis, Jaffe had recouped his costs by selling the production rights to somebody else, and the picture was closer to being made than ever.

The person now in possession of the rights was a highly unusual Hollywood figure named Al Rosen.[127] Rosen was an agent—a "ten-percenter" in those days—and he had a reputation for getting what he wanted. His first major client, the actor Fredric March, described his methods as follows: "He would never go through a front door if there was a side door or a subterranean passage. . . . We never had an appointment. Al was never expected anywhere, but never unexpected anywhere. I would be getting nervous about being arrested for unlawful entry when the door would open and [Louis B.] Mayer or some other great magnate would come in. His face would light up and he would greet Al as an old friend, and they would start arguing as to whether the studio could live without me."[128]

If anyone was going to be able to convince a major Hollywood executive to make *The Mad Dog of Europe*, it was Rosen. He was fearless and ferocious, and in this particular case he was making no excuses for his motivations. "It would be idle to insist I am doing this film as an act of altruism; that I am crusading for the comfort of a race," he said. "My standpoint is that I have reason to believe there is a public demand for a film such as I have in mind."[129]

When the trade papers reported that Rosen was going ahead with *The Mad Dog of Europe*, the usual series of preventive measures took place. Georg Gyssling went to the Hays Office—the evidence is conclusive this time—and the Hays Office urged Rosen to abandon the production. The same excuses were made: a picture like this would jeopardize the major studios' business dealings in Germany and would promote anti-Semitism in the United States. The same threats were issued: if Rosen did not immediately cease and desist, the Hays Office would do everything in its power to see that the film was never produced.[130]

Rosen was a very different figure from Jaffe, however, and upon being threatened in this way, he responded aggressively. First, he enlisted the support of members of the American Jewish Congress who were pushing for a national boycott on German goods.[131] Then he did something unusual: he sued the Hays Office. He went to the Superior Court of Los Angeles, and he accused the Hays Office of malicious interference with contracts and conspiracy. He sought damages totaling $1,022,200: $7,200 for the cost of the script, $15,000 for incurred obligations, and $1,000,000 for punitive damages.[132]

On the same day that Rosen filed suit against the Hays Office, he issued a remarkable statement to the Jewish Telegraphic Agency. His words were blunt and fragmented, but they revealed to the public for the first time what was going on behind the scenes in Hollywood:

> I have it on good authority that the Hays organization was approached by representatives of Dr. Luther and of Dr. Gyssling of Los Angeles to use its influence with the producers in Hollywood to make me stop the production of "The Mad Dog of Europe." But I shall go ahead nevertheless.
>
> The German officials have intimated that the property of the large Hollywood producers in Germany would be confiscated and further American pictures would not be imported into Germany unless they use their influence and pressure upon me to make me withdraw this film. Most of these large producers are Jewish firms, and they call themselves Jews. . . .
>
> They say that if my picture is produced, the Jews in Germany will be harmed. Any normally informed American knows that the Jews in Germany have suffered exile, imprisonment, brutality, denial of the privilege of earning their living, and are not infrequently executed. Could a race thus outraged be inflicted with newer or greater outrages? The press is full of the stories of Nazi brutality. Have these organs created any greater outrage upon the German Jews by printing these stories? Then why should they object when we are going to visualize the actual scenes before the American public?[133]

Over the next seven months—from November 1933 until June 1934—Rosen continued his preparations for *The Mad Dog of Europe*. He obtained ten thousand feet of newsreel footage from Germany to incorporate into the picture.[134] He discovered an actor who looked exactly like Hitler to play the part for the first time on the screen.[135] And he sent a letter to one thousand exhibitors across the United States seeking their reaction to his plans.[136]

Rosen also tried to convince a few of the most powerful executives in Hollywood to pour money into the project. Here he was completely unsuccessful. Louis B. Mayer told him that no picture would be made "because we have interests in Germany; I represent the picture industry here in Hollywood; we have exchanges there; we have terrific income in Germany and, as far as I am concerned, this picture will never be made."[137]

And so *The Mad Dog of Europe* was never turned into a motion picture. Announcements continued to appear in the trade papers that Al Rosen was embarking on the next stage of the process, but nothing ever came to fruition. The only comparable production from the period was a minor anti-Nazi picture called *Hitler's Reign of Terror*, which was not a feature film but an awkward mixture of real and staged newsreel footage that reached a few theaters in May 1934. This independent production received uniformly negative reviews, however, and even the German government recognized that it posed no threat: "The film is rather bad from a technical perspective. It contains a rapid series of mostly incoherent images. . . . The film will not have the effect that our opponents would like it to have. . . . Even our opponents, who probably expected a series of atrocity images, will be disappointed."[138]

The Germans obviously understood that they had nothing to fear from this ineffective production. Georg Gyssling therefore paid little attention to it, but he approached the Hays Office every time he read an announcement about *The Mad Dog of Europe* in the trade papers. Only on one occasion did he encounter a problem. In June 1933, he had infuriated Frederick Herron by banning Warner Brothers from the German market on account of *Captured!* The next time he read a newspaper report about *The Mad Dog of Europe*, therefore, he did not go to the Hays Office. He went instead to the counselor of the German embassy in Washington, DC, who in turn lodged a complaint with the State Department. The State Department then brought up the matter with its contact in the Hays

Office, Frederick Herron. "Herron thereupon characterized the German Consul in Los Angeles, whom he knows personally, in vigorous and entirely unrepeatable terms."

Herron added with some indignation that he intended to wash his hands entirely of the matter, and that he had been willing to play ball with the German authorities as long as they behaved like gentlemen, but that since their action in regard to "Captured," he saw no reason for going out of his way to do them a service. He said that the attempts of the Hays organization to prevent the production of "The Mad Dog of Europe" had involved the organization in lawsuits involving approximately $1,500,000. The German Government had shown no appreciation whatever of his efforts in this matter or of the annoyance to which his organization had been subjected on its account.[139]

Herron seemed to be changing his mind about *The Mad Dog of Europe*—he seemed to be pushing the Hays Office in a different direction—but in reality, this was just another one of his outbursts. Within a few weeks, he would be back to playing ball with the German authorities. And now, thanks to his organization's alliance with the Anti-Defamation League, the Hollywood studios had a perfect justification for not making movies about the Nazis. Privately, the studio heads had admitted that they were not making these movies because they wanted to preserve their business interests in Germany. But they could now cite a more high-minded aim: they were trying to prevent an anti-Semitic reaction in the United States. There is no evidence, at this point or later on, that they were actually afraid of the potential anti-Semitic reaction that an anti-Nazi film might provoke. They were, however, exploiting the position of the Anti-Defamation League to carry out their own policy, which was very simple: they would not make movies about the Nazis; they would do business with the Nazis instead.

The decision not to make *The Mad Dog of Europe* was the most important moment in all of Hollywood's dealings with Nazi Germany. It occurred in the first year of Hitler's rise to power, and it defined the limits of American movies for the remainder of the decade. There was an additional consequence to the decision, however, for only half of *The Mad Dog of Europe* was about Hitler; the other half was about his persecution of a minority group. In agreeing not to make the picture, the studio executives were setting a limit not only to what they could say about Nazis but also to what they could say about Jews.

Up to this point, Jewish characters had appeared with great frequency on the American screen. From 1900 to 1929, there had been around 230 movies about Jews, and audiences across the country had seen Jews in a variety of roles—as pawnshop owners, clothing merchants, sweatshop workers, historical and biblical personalities, and hilarious tricksters.[140] "The Jew was a comic, crazily human figure to be encountered everywhere," one commentator said in an account of this period. "His foibles were part of the American curriculum. His oddities and his accents were known to all."[141]

The arrival of talking pictures had continued this tradition. There had been several movies about Jews in the early sound period, including two landmark productions. In *The Jazz Singer*, the son of a cantor had become a popular performer.[142] And in *Disraeli*, a politician stigmatized as a Jew had shown the foresight necessary to turn England into a great power.[143] The renowned British theater actor George Arliss had won the Oscar for Best Actor for his performance as Benjamin Disraeli, and the film had narrowly lost the Best Picture category to *All Quiet on the Western Front*.[144]

The decision not to make *The Mad Dog of Europe* changed all this. From the moment that the studios chose not to comment on the persecution of the Jews in Germany, they embarked on a completely different path, and in the months that followed, a highly unfortunate series of events took place.

Back in April 1933, the head of production at Warner Brothers—the young and talented Darryl F. Zanuck—had realized that Jack and Harry Warner would never allow him to rise to the top of their studio. He decided to take a chance. He called a press conference, and he said that he was personally raising all studio salaries. Jack Warner was furious and overruled the decision immediately. On April 15, Zanuck announced that since he no longer enjoyed the confidence of his superiors, he was leaving Warner Brothers for good.[145]

Two days later, he was having breakfast with the president of United Artists, Joseph Schenck. Schenck waved a check in front of Zanuck's eyes, signed by Louis B. Mayer and made out for $100,000. "We're in business,"

Schenck said. "We got it." Schenck had convinced Mayer to fund a new production company in which Zanuck could enjoy a much greater degree of control. It was a big moment for Hollywood. Twentieth Century Pictures was born.[146]

Zanuck's first move was to convince some major stars from Warner Brothers to follow him to his new studio. Constance Bennett and Loretta Young joined Twentieth Century when they noticed that their contracts with Warner Brothers had expired.[147] Then George Arliss did the same. "Although I had been very happy with Warner Brothers, I made my next contract with Zanuck," he recalled. "This was an obvious step for me to take since my association had been entirely with him ever since I started in talking pictures."[148]

Arliss told Zanuck that he had an exciting new idea for a Twentieth Century production. Two years earlier, he had come across a play about the Rothschilds, the Jewish banking family of Europe, and he had convinced Warner Brothers to purchase the rights to the script. Given his great success as Benjamin Disraeli, perhaps he was now ready to play the part of Nathan Rothschild. Although Harry and Jack Warner were extremely angry about Arliss' move to Twentieth Century—they had written a concerned letter to Will Hays claiming that Zanuck had lured Arliss away—they somehow agreed to sell the script to Zanuck for the same price that they had paid for it.[149]

Zanuck knew that he was on to a good thing. He needed a picture to draw attention to his new company, and he had hit on a promising subject.[150] At just that time, Herman Mankiewicz and Sam Jaffe were going around Hollywood in an attempt to make *The Mad Dog of Europe*, and Zanuck knew that nothing would ever come of their efforts. He also understood that their abandonment of *The Mad Dog of Europe* would create an opening for a different kind of picture—not a direct attack on Hitler but a general treatment of the subject of anti-Semitism. The Rothschilds' struggles for equal rights in the previous century provided a perfect parallel for what was happening in Germany, and the best part of all was that Georg Gyssling would have no basis for objection. Zanuck could show images of Jewish persecution from the previous century, and he could have his hero, Nathan Rothschild, speak out about it: "Go into the Jewish quarter of any town in Prussia today, and you'll see men lying dead . . . for but one crime—that they were Jews."[151]

Joseph Schenck (left) and Darryl Zanuck (right), founders of Twentieth Century
Pictures, which merged with Fox in 1935 to become Twentieth Century-Fox.
Courtesy of Peter Stackpole; Getty Images.

Zanuck had considerable experience with this kind of material. He had
personally supervised two of Hollywood's most important productions
about Jews, *The Jazz Singer* and *Disraeli*. In another fourteen years, he
would put out his next installment, *Gentleman's Agreement*.[152] Now, he was
about to make his most important contribution of all. But there was something very unusual about Zanuck, and it emerged in a letter he wrote in
late 1933. A censorship official had suggested that he show the script of
his new movie to Georg Gyssling, and Zanuck had declined, stating that
the Nazis disapproved of the Jewish origins of the Hollywood producers.

Then he added, "It just so happens that I am of German-Swiss descent and not a Jew."[153]

Here lay the true significance of Zanuck's move from Warner Brothers to Twentieth Century. In the past, his movies about Jews had been supervised by Jews. Jack Warner spent every afternoon on the studio lot watching the unedited footage from the previous day and cutting whatever he disliked.[154] Harry Warner was even more concerned about Jewish matters than Jack.[155] If Zanuck had tried to make a picture about the Rothschilds at Warner Brothers—especially at the exact moment that the persecution of the Jews was beginning in Germany—he would have had both men making sure that his footage was acceptable.

At Twentieth Century, Zanuck was in quite a different position. The president of the company, Joseph Schenck, actually seemed to think that Zanuck was Jewish. He often put his hand on Zanuck's shoulder and said, "We Jews should stick together."[156] He generally did not involve himself in the production process, and on the one occasion that he did read an early version of the Rothschild script, he brought up the villain's anti-Semitic tirades. When Zanuck told him not to worry—the film would not be interpreted as a plea on behalf of the Jewish people—Schenck just laughed. "Oh no, not like that," he said. "I'm afraid people will cheer."[157] Even if Schenck had been seriously concerned with the script, he hardly would have been able to make changes anyway. He had gone into business with Zanuck as an equal, and the whole point of the arrangement was to allow Zanuck to make movies on his own.

And so the one major American studio that was not run by a Jew turned out to be the one to broach the situation in Germany for the first time. Zanuck had escaped Warner Brothers, and now he was going to cause some real damage.

The original idea for *The House of Rothschild* had come from a Boston newspaperman named George Hembert Westley, who had sent George Arliss a copy of the script knowing that the actor had a reputation for taking on unknown material.[158] Now that Twentieth Century owned the rights, Arliss reread the script—a historical drama in which Nathan Rothschild funded the British army's campaign against Napoleon—and although he was still taken with the idea, he could see why Westley was unknown.[159] He asked his usual writer, Maude Howell, to work on a new script with screenwriter Sam Mintz.[160]

Arliss had a reputation not only for taking on unknown material but also for meddling with the writing process. And the Jewish question was on his mind, for he had recently received letters from his Jewish fans expressing their disappointment that he had traveled on a German ship. "I confess I felt rather guilty about this because the Jews have always been good and faithful adherents of mine both in the theatre and in the cinema," he wrote. "No one has a keener appreciation of what the world of science and art and literature owes to the Jews than I, and no one has greater sympathy with them in their unequal fight against savagery and ignorance."[161]

Once in England, Arliss began conducting research into the history of the Rothschild family. He became fascinated with the most up-to-date work on the subject, Count Egon Caesar Corti's *The Rise of the House of Rothschild*, which had recently been translated from German into English.[162] The count had made his biases clear from the start: he was telling "the story of an unseen but infinitely powerful driving force which permeated the whole of the nineteenth century."[163] The story began with a speculation: an old man named Mayer Amschel Rothschild had supposedly kept one set of accounts for himself and another for the tax collector and had built a well-concealed cellar under his house to hide his money. The old man passed his cleverness on to his son Nathan, who many years later supported the British army with one purpose in mind— the first principle of the House of Rothschild: to "increase the possibility of financial gain, which in turn would serve to increase its power."[164]

Arliss was inspired by all of this—much more inspired than by Howell and Mintz's adaptation of Westley's play. The adaptation contained a few connections to the current situation in Germany, but it needed something more.[165] Just then Arliss had an idea. He would start the film by playing Mayer Amschel in the Frankfurt ghetto, and after a brief sequence indicating the passage of time, he would play Nathan in England. He sat down in the tiny study of his country cottage, and he typed out fourteen pages of suggestions, which he sent immediately to Zanuck.[166] At this point, Sam Mintz disappeared from the project and Maude Howell wrote a new outline based on Arliss' suggestions.[167] Then Zanuck asked Nunnally Johnson to rewrite the script once again.[168] In a matter of weeks, *The House of Rothschild* had become an entirely different film.[169]

Here was how Arliss and Zanuck chose to represent the Jew on the screen just one year after the Nazis came to power in Germany:

It was close to 6:00 PM, the time when the Frankfurt ghetto had to be locked up for the night, and an old man with a long beard and a yarmulke was peering out his window. He seemed very worried. "Mama," he murmured to his wife, "the money hasn't come yet." His wife replied that he should wait until the morning. "Yes," he said, "but if anything should happen—*all that money.*" The old man rubbed his hands together: "*Ten thousand gulden!*" The figure seemed to surprise his wife, so he explained: "Seven thousand in one lump from Prince Louis' crown agent, and then all the small sums—ten thousand at least." "Ah, we should be thankful Mayer," she said with a laugh. "Business is good, eh?"

Mayer Amschel sat down at his desk to count his earnings. He chuckled as he remembered how one of his customers had tried to outsmart him earlier in the day. "There he sat," Mayer recalled, "sly and smiling, planning to rob this poor old Jew Rothschild!" Mayer laughed out loud, but then he noticed something terrible. One of the coins that the customer had given him was a fake. "A whole gulden!" Mayer shouted. His wife chewed on the coin to confirm that he was right. "And I gave him some wine too," Mayer complained, "some of the *good* wine!" Then his temper subsided, and he even started to smile. The customer would return. Mayer would make his gulden back.

Suddenly, there was a knock at the door. It was Mayer's son Nathan, a fifteen-year-old boy, and he was frantic. "Mama," he said, "the tax collector!" His words set off a familiar routine. Mayer packed up the money and the account books. Nathan opened the trapdoor to the cellar and carried the incriminating materials downstairs. His brothers Solomon and Amschel hid everything behind the casks of wine. Meanwhile, Mayer took out a different account book and changed into dirty old clothes. His wife gave her youngest sons a few crusts of bread. She asked them whether they were hungry and they said no. "Then look hungry," she said sternly.

When the tax collector entered the house, Mayer started complaining: "Never have I known such a bad month." But the tax collector was no fool. He looked at the fake books and threw them down. He announced that he was going to assess Mayer 20,000 gulden. Mayer wailed and said that he could barely raise 1,000. The tax collector was not listening, though, for he had just noticed the trapdoor leading to the cellar. He walked down the stairs and looked around, and he was about to discover the real books when Nathan diverted his attention by pouring him a glass of wine. The tax collector fell for the trick, but then said he was going to assess Mayer 20,000 gulden anyway. After some bargaining, he agreed to accept 2,000, along with a personal bribe of 5,000 more, and then he left.

At 6:00 PM exactly, Mayer's messenger arrived with bad news. The 10,000 gulden that Mayer had been expecting had been stolen. The old man's mood suddenly changed. He had been celebrating his good luck with the tax collector and explaining—as someone at the studio put it—"the Jewish psychology and necessity for giving bribes."[170] Now he flew into a rage. He ranted about the mistreatment of Jews everywhere, and just before fainting from exhaustion, he screamed the only solution: "WORK AND STRIVE FOR MONEY! MONEY IS POWER! MONEY IS THE ONLY WEAPON THAT THE JEW HAS TO DEFEND HIMSELF WITH!"

The film up to this point had been more or less consistent with Corti's account in *The Rise of the House of Rothschild*. Corti had tried to characterize Mayer as a stingy old man who sought only to acquire wealth, and, problematic as that account was, it provided the basis for George Arliss' portrayal. The next scene was different.

Mayer was lying on his deathbed, surrounded by his sons. He told them always to obey their mother if they wanted to grow rich. Then he signaled for them to come closer, and he spoke under his breath. "Much money is lost through sending gold by coach from one country to another. . . . You are five brothers. I want you each to start a banking business in a different country. One to go and open a house in Paris, one in Vienna, one in London. Choose the most important centers. So that when money is to be sent from here to London, let us say, you won't have to risk life and gold. Amschel here in Frankfurt will just send a letter to Nathan in London saying 'Pay so-and-so,' and that will be offset by loans from London to Frankfurt.

"In your day, there will be many wars in Europe," Mayer continued, "and nations that have money to transport will come to the Rothschilds, *because it will be safe*." Mayer's wife cautioned him not to get too excited, but he went on: "Remember: unity is strength. All your lives you must stand by one another. No one brother must be allowed to fail while another brother succeeds. Your five banking houses may cover Europe, but you will be one firm—one family—the Rothschilds, who work always together. *That will be your power.* . . .

"And remember this before all: that neither business, nor power, nor all the gold in Europe will bring you happiness, till we—our people—have equality, respect, dignity. To trade with dignity; to live with dignity; *to walk the world with dignity*."

This brief scene of Mayer Amschel Rothschild on his deathbed was a hugely important moment for the representation of Jews in American cinema. Arliss claimed that the scene was based on historical evidence from Corti's book, but Corti had made it clear that only two sons were living in Frankfurt at the time of Mayer's death. Nathan had left for England of his own accord, and James and Solomon were living in France. "These facts," Corti had written, "proved as they are by French police records, and the records of visés issued, are fatal to the well-known legend, according to which [Mayer Amschel] gathered his five sons about his deathbed and divided Europe amongst them."[171] In other words, Mayer could never have imagined, much less engineered, a grand scheme by which his sons would control the finances of Europe.

Furthermore, Mayer's final words in the film—"to walk the world with dignity"—were not quite as straightforward as they seemed. Although Mayer did strive to obtain equal rights for Jews in his lifetime, Arliss and Zanuck did not put these words in his mouth for the purpose of historical accuracy.[172] They were much more interested in making a poignant remark about the fate of the Jews of Europe. They undoubtedly supposed that no one in Hollywood would fault them for such high-mindedness at this particular point in time. But the head of the advisory council of the Anti-Defamation League in Los Angeles, Leon Lewis—who had been so wrongheaded in his treatment of *The Mad Dog of Europe*—instantly recognized that the message at the end of this scene hardly canceled out the sheer lack of dignity that characterized the rest of the picture.

When Lewis first received word that Twentieth Century was working on *The House of Rothschild*, he was deeply dismayed. "Just between us," he wrote to Richard Gutstadt, "the lack of understanding upon selecting this particular story for production at this time is a good illustration of the mental calibre of some of our outstanding movie magnates."[173] Lewis knew that whatever angle the producers adopted, the subject of the film was bound to cause innumerable problems. By late December, the Anti-Defamation League's experts on anti-Semitism had all read the script and found that it contained "chicanery and other despicable incidents and traits."[174] They could barely believe that this script was being used for a major Hollywood production.

The Anti-Defamation League eventually formulated a very clear position about the dangers of *The House of Rothschild* by envisioning the impact of the two main parts of its plot. The opening sequence, they said, portrayed the Jew as an international banker who outsmarted the tax authorities and amassed so much wealth that he possessed even greater power than the government. The rest of the film—in which Nathan Rothschild made bargains with various European nations so that they could defeat Napoleon—characterized the Jew as the secret power behind the throne who regulated the destiny of the world.[175]

The Anti-Defamation League recognized that, on the surface, the film appeared to have a noble message: the Rothschilds were unfairly discriminated against, they wanted to obtain equal rights for their people, and they used money for peace and not war. The League even imagined that some Jewish audiences might respond positively to these moments: they might be so glad that a film spoke out against anti-Semitism that they would overlook the anti-Semitic content of the film itself. But the League was not concerned with the Jewish response to the film; it was only interested in the response of non-Jews. And the organization was absolutely convinced that to the non-Jewish mind, the redemptive elements would either go unnoticed or would not be considered justification for the Rothschilds' behavior. "The impression which will be made," the League noted, "is that the concentration of wealth in the hands of one international Jewish family invested that family with indisputable power to determine the destinies of nations. The very fact that Christian nations must beg of the Jewish Rothschild family for money with which to protect their own existence will in itself create a most undesirable reaction."[176]

After coming up with this analysis, Leon Lewis wrote to Joseph Schenck and said that *The House of Rothschild* threatened to be "one of the most dangerous presentations" of the time. He explained that a wave of anti-Semitic propaganda was just then sweeping across the country and convincing millions of people that the "international Jewish banker" was in control of the world's finances. *The House of Rothschild* by its very subject matter would enforce this myth. In case Schenck had any uncertainty whatsoever, Lewis urged him to communicate "with those among our people . . . who have been devoting all their energies in the past few months to stemming the rising tide of hatred against the Jews."[177]

Schenck read the letter and passed it on to Zanuck. Zanuck replied immediately. He had no intention of abandoning his production of *The House of Rothschild*. "I am not a Jew," he added, "and I have never heard of this 'rising hatred of Jews' that you speak about in your letter, and I am inclined to believe that it is, more or less, imaginary as far as the general public is concerned. We make pictures for the broad general public rather than the minority and I will guarantee you that if there is such a thing as a 'rising hatred for the Jew in America' our film version of ROTHSCHILD will do more to stop it than anything, from the standpoint of entertainment."[178]

The representatives of the Anti-Defamation League ceased all communication with Zanuck at this point and focused their energies on Will Hays.[179] This was a wise move because Twentieth Century was just then trying to obtain membership in the Hays organization. That same day, Hays wrote an urgent letter to Zanuck: "It is important that nothing be done now that might possibly feed the unreasoning prejudice against the Jews which is in some places. A widespread factor in this unfair and prejudiced attack is the false allegation that all Jews acquire money for power, with the inference that such power may be misused. The historical prominence of the house of Rothschild is such that hostile propagandists have tried to make the very name a synonym for sinister, worldwide political power, growing out of accumulated riches. The fact that in the case of the Rothschilds the power of money was rightly used may be overshadowed by the greater impression of the Rothschilds as an example of Jewish power through domination by money."

Hays repeated that he was extremely worried about the situation. He said that there would probably be some difference of opinion within the Jewish community, but that "thinking Jews" might interpret *The House of Rothschild* as anti-Semitic propaganda.[180]

Zanuck found himself in a bit of trouble. He obviously needed to change Hays' mind about the film. He quickly obtained a whole series of positive reactions to *The House of Rothschild* and forwarded them to the Hays Office. He included 175 preview cards that praised the picture and said almost nothing about its "Jewish flavor"; a letter from Joseph Jonah Cummins, the editor of a Jewish newspaper, who said the picture was extremely entertaining and contained no trace of propaganda; and a sermon by Reverend C. F. Aked entitled "George Arliss in *The House of Rothschild*: A Joy and an Inspiration."[181]

The material had a definite impact. Hays soon informed the Anti-Defamation League that most audiences were finding *The House of Rothschild* so entertaining and captivating that they were not picking up on its offensive implications. He also pointed out that the National Council of Jewish Women had recently previewed the picture and officially approved of it. He was now less worried about the film itself and more worried about potential public disagreement between the two Jewish organizations.[182] The Anti-Defamation League understood his concern, and was angry with the National Council of Jewish Women, but was more worried about the film.[183]

The Anti-Defamation League therefore went to its last resort: the heads of the other Hollywood studios. Upon discovering that Louis B. Mayer was the majority owner of Twentieth Century Pictures, the Anti-Defamation League sent him a cable: "OUR SITUATION AT THIS TIME MORE CRITICAL THAN ANY TIME HERETOFORE DEMANDING OF EACH THE GREATEST CAUTION STOP IN NORMAL TIMES NO HARM MIGHT BE ANTICIPATED ACUTE CONDITIONS NOW MUST BE CONSIDERED STOP WILL YOU COOPERATE TO PREVENT PICTURE AT LEAST DURING CRITICAL PERIOD."[184]

Mayer replied straight away. He was unwilling to take action by intervening in the running of Twentieth Century, since his stake in the company was not generally known, but he agreed to examine the picture with Harry Cohn, the head of Columbia Pictures. A few days later, the two executives watched the movie together and cabled back their response. They disagreed with the position of the Anti-Defamation League. There was nothing wrong with *The House of Rothschild*, and in fact both executives had received requests to make such a picture before.[185]

The Anti-Defamation League quickly urged Jewish leaders everywhere to inundate Mayer with letters of protest.[186] At the same time, Richard Gutstadt contacted his secret weapon, Edgar Magnin, who was Mayer's rabbi and close friend. "His influence with Mayer ought to be utilized *now*," Gutstadt wrote.[187] As it turned out, Mayer got to Magnin first. The most powerful man in Hollywood had received many telegrams about the film and was worried and did not know what to do. Magnin responded without sympathy. He "lit into Mayer": "He told him that the conditions in the industry were responsible for a great deal of the prejudice existing and that it is ironical that on top of it they should show so little sense as to promote a film of this type at this time. He said they were digging their own graves and that they would alienate the Jews as well."[188]

At the same time as Magnin was working on Mayer, another member of the Anti-Defamation League was working on Harry Warner. It turned out that Warner did not need much working on. He probably felt responsible for the mess, since he had sold Twentieth Century the script in the first place. He told the Anti-Defamation League that the film threatened to be one of the most dangerous productions of all time. He was so concerned that he even considered offering Twentieth Century $16,000 to have the print destroyed. "IN ALL OF THIS, HE DOES NOT WANT HIS NAME MENTIONED," the Anti-Defamation League noted. The organization suspected that Warner did not want word to get out that he had tried to suppress the production of a rival company.[189]

In the end, though, neither Louis B. Mayer nor Harry Warner used their money or their power to buy out Darryl Zanuck. The primary documents provide no hint as to why the two executives backed down at this critical stage. One possible reason is that they were worried they might have been imitating behavior from the film itself. At one key moment in *The House of Rothschild*, Nathan Rothschild had bought wildly on the stock exchange to bankrupt his gentile competitors, and Mayer and Warner would have been doing something similar to Zanuck.

The more likely scenario, of course, is that Mayer and Warner simply did not want to involve themselves in a film that they had not made. And yet maybe the film involved *them*. After all, it began with a Jewish father named Mayer who schemed with five branches of his family to create a powerful empire. Was Zanuck creating a disguised attack on the studio system as a conspiracy run by Jews, with "Mayer" at the top, and the heads of the other five studios directly beneath him: Jack Warner, Harry Cohn, William Fox, Carl Laemmle, and Adolph Zukor? If this had been Zanuck's intention, nobody pointed it out at the time.

On March 14, 1934, *The House of Rothschild* premiered at the Astor Theater in New York. For the most part, it received excellent reviews. A few critics picked up on the parallels to the situation in Germany; everyone picked up on the jokes. One and a half weeks later, *Time* magazine featured George Arliss "in whiskers and skullcap" on the cover, and praised the film's superb entertainment in the accompanying article: "The House of Rothschild (Twentieth Century) begins with old Mayer Amschel Rothschild . . . as a wheedling Frankfort moneybroker. The loss of a few gulden in a messenger robbery sets him yowling like an alley cat. When the tax-collector comes down Jew Street, stingy old Rothschild whisks his money bags into the cellar, gives each of his children a crust to gnaw, pops the roastbeef into a garbage box, and talks the collector into taking a bribe. As shrewd as he is stingy, Mayer Amschel Rothschild gets a good idea on his death bed. . . ."[190]

A typical review. Of course, later in the film the inhabitants of "Jew Street" experienced persecution, and in these images, Hollywood alluded to the situation in Germany for the first time. But as the review in *Time* magazine proved, this allusion came at a terrible cost: the reinforcement of the stereotype of the international Jewish banker.[191]

Some were prepared to accept that cost. Rabbi Stephen Wise gave a sermon on *The House of Rothschild*, which was "one of the most magnificent tributes ever paid a picture."[192] And a small Jewish group in Hollywood whose motto was "A smile will go a long way" offered Zanuck an honorary fellowship in recognition of his "outstanding achievement benefitting the Jewish people" ("an atrocious thing," in the opinion of the Anti-Defamation League).[193] Zanuck was too busy to attend the ceremony. His film had come close to winning the Oscar for Best Picture and was now propelling him to even greater glory. In May 1935, Twentieth Century merged with Fox, and Zanuck became the head of the third largest studio in Hollywood, Twentieth Century-Fox.[194]

But the Anti-Defamation League remained convinced that *The House of Rothschild* had been a travesty and wanted to make sure that nothing like it would ever happen again. "It is just too bad that it was made at this time," one representative wrote, "for it corroborates the basic Nazi propaganda, and this corroboration is furnished by Jews."[195] The irony was almost unbearable. The Anti-Defamation League had gone through all the established channels and had not been able to prevent the release of the picture. Clearly, the organization needed to adopt a different approach.

Will Hays agreed. Up to this point, he had helped the Anti-Defamation League achieve a few small successes, but *The House of Rothschild* proved that something else needed to be done. "The objectionable films," one of Hays' employees pointed out, "are made so often in studios controlled by Jews . . . that [the Hays Office] cannot be expected to carry on a program of education without some direct approach . . . by a Jewish group to these producers themselves."[196] The Anti-Defamation League, in other words, needed to meet more regularly with the producers and provide more systematic guidance for the representation of Jews on the screen.

So, at precisely the moment that *The House of Rothschild* was hitting theaters across the United States, the Anti-Defamation League was taking preventative measures for the future. In March 1934, a new organization came into existence in Hollywood, the Los Angeles Jewish Community Committee.[197] Leon Lewis, the founder of the organization, quickly created a separate motion picture committee and was joined by representatives from each of the major studios including Irving Thalberg, Harry Cohn, Joseph Schenck, and Jack Warner. This distinguished group met once per month for the sole purpose of discussing Jewish matters.[198] "For the first time," Lewis wrote, "we have established a real basis for cooperation with the Motion Picture Industry and I hope for splendid results hereafter."[199]

When Will Hays announced a major campaign to clean up American movies four months later and named Joseph Breen as the enforcer of the Production Code, the Los Angeles Jewish Community Committee seized on the moment to solidify its own new arrangement with the motion picture companies. On the afternoon of July 11, 1934, all the major film executives met with Hays about the new censorship plan.[200] Immediately afterward, the Jews among them adjourned to Harry Cohn's office at Columbia Pictures to meet with Richard Gutstadt. The usual members of the motion picture committee were present along with Louis B. Mayer, David Selznick, Harry Warner, and Carl Laemmle Jr. Gutstadt pleaded with the group to avoid the carelessness that had characterized their productions of the previous year. The various executives then discussed ways of preventing offensive depictions of Jews in the future. The meeting was a great success, and the Anti-Defamation League was convinced that from then on there would be "a much quicker and much more hearty cooperation" between the two groups.[201]

The following year, most references to Jews were cut out of Hollywood productions. Adolph Zukor, the head of Paramount, promised that Cecil B. DeMille's *The Crusades* would "not refer to the Jews in any manner or form."[202] RKO agreed to turn a ruthless Jewish businessman in

*Success at Any Price* into a non-Jew.[203] Twentieth Century cut Jewish characters out of its picture *Born to Be Bad*.[204] And Louis B. Mayer canceled *The Merchant of Venice* as well as a picture about the crucifixion of Christ called *Two Thieves*. "We need have no fear as to the outcome," Lewis wrote, "in view of the splendid cooperation that we have always had from M.G.M."[205]

Still, Gutstadt was not entirely satisfied. After the traumatic experience of *The House of Rothschild*, he wanted to get rid of all possible references to Jews. "It is just as essential to avoid obviously pro-Jewish propaganda in films as it is to obviate the drawbacks of anti-Semitic films," he wrote.[206] Over the course of the decade, his letters became more extreme. He wrote to Lewis about foreign films, shorts, and cartoons, and then he started writing about films that had nothing to do with Jews whatsoever because—as he put it—"you can't tell what might come out of Hollywood."[207]

Soon the Anti-Defamation League's efforts started to have a broader impact. On the stage and over the radio, Jewish dialect comedians were being heard less frequently. In Hollywood, Jewish character actors were finding it virtually impossible to obtain work at all.[208]

And so the Jew, once so prominent in American culture, was suddenly nowhere to be found. One commentator wrote: "The greatest single Jewish phenomenon in our country in the last twenty years has been the almost complete disappearance of the Jew from American fiction, stage, radio, and movies."[209] More than any other single factor, *The House of Rothschild* was responsible for this disappearance. Even after bringing about such a monumental change, however, the film still had one last piece of damage to inflict.

The Nazis had been fascinated by *The House of Rothschild* ever since the picture first appeared in theaters worldwide. Back in May 1934, when the screenings were in full swing, the German ambassador in London and the German consul in Seattle had watched it with interest. Both had picked up on the film's double-edged portrayal of Jews. The ambassador in London had noted that the film provided unfortunate parallels to the situation in Germany at the same time as it showed the Jews' "sleazy greed for money." He continued: "The film emphasizes that they use their financial power for liberation, but it is not convincing."[210] The consul in Seattle had made a similar observation before concluding that the film would never be shown in Germany. He was not exactly right.[211]

On November 28, 1940, the notorious propaganda picture *The Eternal Jew* (*Der ewige Jude*) premiered at theaters throughout Germany. This documentary about "the problem of world Jewry," which was released to coincide with some of the first deportations of Jews to Eastern Europe, began by contrasting the Aryan's inclination to work with the Jew's inherent tendency to live off the work of others. Outwardly, Jews often looked like everyone else. But, according to the film, their inner nature compelled them to loan, barter, and trade, and during the reign of Alexander the Great, they spread like rats throughout Europe. They gravitated toward the wealthiest places, growing richer and richer, and in the early nineteenth century, a few Jews acquired international power.[212]

At this point—twenty minutes into the picture—the narrator of *The Eternal Jew* made an announcement. "Here we show a scene from a film about the Rothschild family. It was made by American Jews, obviously as a tribute to one of the greatest names in Jewish history. They honor their hero in a typically Jewish manner, delighting in the way old Mayer Amschel Rothschild cheats his host state by feigning poverty to avoid paying taxes."

And there it was: the original scene from *The House of Rothschild* with accurate German subtitles. The Nazis had made their own feature film about the Rothschild family just a few months earlier, but they did not use it here.[213] They found the American version far more effective and entertaining. No embellishment was necessary. They simply allowed the drama to unfold before the viewers' eyes. When the scene shifted to Mayer on his deathbed, the narrator interjected just once: "Transfer of money by check was not a Jewish invention nor was it cultivated by Jews for the good of mankind. It served them as a means of obtaining international influence over their host peoples."

The rest of the scene was self-explanatory. Old Mayer Amschel made his sons promise to support each other, and he told them about the power they would soon acquire. The film cut just in time to leave out the line about Jewish dignity at the end.

For years, *The Eternal Jew* has been denounced as one of the most atrocious examples of Nazi propaganda. But the picture was unthinkable without *The House of Rothschild.* The images of Mayer Amschel provided structure to what would otherwise have been a jumble of the regime's usual anti-Semitism. The first twenty minutes of the documentary established the Jew's natural cleverness with money. Then the images of Mayer Amschel pointed to the real threat: the wealthiest Jews were taking

The cover of *Time* from March 26, 1934. George Arliss "in whiskers and skullcap" as Mayer Amschel Rothschild in *The House of Rothschild* (1934). Courtesy of *Time Magazine.*

**A promotional poster for the Nazis' anti-Semitic film** *The Eternal Jew* **(1940).**
**Courtesy of the Holocaust Museum.**

over the world. The narrator explained this so-called connection. "The House of Rothschild is just one example of the use of this tactic by the Jews to spread their net of financial influence over the working man. . . . By the beginning of the twentieth century, the Jews are sitting at all the junctions of the world's money market. They are an international power.

Though they make up only 1 percent of the population of the earth, their capital enables them to terrorize world exchanges, world opinion, and world politics."

There was just one possible course of action. The film turned to the supreme authority on the Jewish problem, Adolf Hitler, in his speech to the Reichstag on January 30, 1939. "Should the international finance Jews inside and outside Europe push people into another world war," he said, "the result will not be a victory of Jewry but the annihilation of the Jewish race in Europe."

On December 5, 1930, the day that the Nazis rioted against *All Quiet on the Western Front* in Berlin, one of the most unusual diplomatic agreements of the twentieth century was born. As a result of the riots, the German government told the Hollywood studios that they could only do business in Germany if they did not harm German prestige in any of their films. At first, this meant that the studios could not make pictures that distorted the German experience of the World War. Then, when Hitler came to power, it meant that they could not make pictures that attacked the core principles of Nazism.

The first crucial moment in the studio's dealings with the Nazis was one of pure collaboration: the studios collectively boycotted the anti-Nazi film *The Mad Dog of Europe* to preserve their business interests in Germany. The next step in the process, however, was more complicated. The only Hollywood film that addressed the persecution of the Jews in this period, *The House of Rothschild*, contained ideas so compatible with Nazi ideology that it was incorporated into the most extreme Nazi propaganda film of all time. The Anti-Defamation League, which had shown such poor judgment in the suppression of *The Mad Dog of Europe* a few months earlier, was more clear-sighted in its opposition to this new picture. And yet despite these ambiguities, the outcome was unambiguously injurious: not only was *The House of Rothschild* incorporated into Nazi propaganda, but it also led to the erasure of Jews from the American screen.

In the years that followed, Hollywood movies were marked by two distinct absences: that of the Nazis and that of the Jews. Only when Hollywood stopped doing business with Germany did the Nazis make their dramatic appearance on the American screen. The Jews, on the other hand, did not return quite so easily.

In the meantime, the business dealings between Hollywood and the Nazis continued. The Nazis examined more than four hundred American movies from 1933 to 1940, and they had to put these movies into categories. They eventually adopted the very same categories that Hitler had established from the start: "good," "bad," and "switched off."

# THREE

# "GOOD"

Here's one picture Germans spot as OK[1]

The Reichstag meeting of March 23, 1933 started out calmly enough. At around 2:00 PM, the representatives of the German people—the Nazis, the German Nationalists, the Social Democrats, and the Center Party deputies—filed into the Kroll Opera House, the temporary quarters since the burning down of the official building. The Communists, who had been blamed for the Reichstag fire, had either been taken into custody or fled the scene in time. Outside the building, units of SS men were standing guard in their first official public duty; inside stood long rows of SA men in brown shirts. A huge swastika flag hung behind the stage.[2]

After a brief introduction by Reichstag President Hermann Göring, Hitler rose to give his first parliamentary address. He began in his usual manner, describing the misery and despair into which Germany had fallen. Under his administration, he said, there would be a "far-reaching moral renewal" supported by education, the media, and the arts. The unemployment problem would be solved through work-creation schemes, and the size of the army would remain unchanged, as long as the rest of the world agreed to a radical disarmament. But it would be against the spirit of the national uprising for the Reichstag to involve itself in any of these efforts. In a crisis like this, there needed to be a clear decision in every case. Hitler therefore proposed an Enabling Act, which transferred all power to his administration. The measure would be a temporary one, and the existence of the Reichstag would not be threatened. As he left the stage to wild cheering, most of the deputies rose to sing "Deutschland über Alles," and a three-hour recess was called.[3]

Although the Nazis and their coalition partners had won the elections of March 5, they needed a two-thirds majority for the Enabling Act to pass. With the Communists absent, they could obtain the numbers by winning the support of the Center Party. Hitler had made various assurances to the party leader, Prälat Ludwig Kaas, and in a closed meeting, Kaas now argued that Germany was in the greatest danger. There had been talk of civil war if the measure did not go through. Meanwhile, the guards outside were chanting, "We want the Enabling Act—or there'll be hell to pay." Eventually, all the Center Party deputies agreed to support Kaas' position.[4]

At the end of the recess, the Reichstag reconvened and Otto Wels, the chairman of the Social Democrats, took the floor. For a moment the room was silent, and only the distant voices of the SS men could be heard. Then Wels, who was carrying a cyanide capsule to swallow in the event of his arrest, explained why his party would not be supporting the Enabling Act. He said that the Nazis and their nationalist allies had won the elections, and that they therefore had an opportunity to govern constitutionally. In fact, they had more than an opportunity—they had an obligation. For the German Reich to remain healthy, criticism must remain in place, and it must not be persecuted.[5] He ended with a moving appeal to future generations: "In this historic hour, we German Social Democrats solemnly profess our allegiance to the basic principles of humanity and justice, freedom and socialism. No Enabling Law gives you the right to annihilate ideas that are eternal and indestructible.... We greet the persecuted and the hard-pressed. Their steadfastness and loyalty deserve admiration. The courage of their convictions, their unbroken confidence, vouch for a brighter future."[6]

The Nazis in the chamber responded with laughter.[7] Meanwhile, Hitler raced to the platform, pointed at Wels, and yelled, "You come late, but still you come! The pretty theories you have just proclaimed here, Mr. Deputy, are being communicated to world history just a bit too late." Then, working himself into an even greater rage, he continued:

You talk about persecutions. I think there are only a few of us here who did not have to suffer persecutions from your side in prison. . . .

You seem to have forgotten completely that for years our shirts were ripped off our backs because you did not like the color. . . . We have outgrown your persecutions!

You say furthermore that criticism is salutary. Certainly, those who love Germany may criticize us; but those who worship an International cannot criticize us. Here, too, insight comes to you very late indeed, Mr. Deputy. You should have recognized the salutary nature of criticism during the time we were in the opposition. . . . In those days our press was forbidden and forbidden and again forbidden, our meetings were forbidden, and we were forbidden to speak and I was forbidden to speak, for years on end. And now you say: criticism is salutary![8]

The Social Democrats were shouting in protest at this point, so Göring rang the bell and said, "Stop talking nonsense now and listen to this." Hitler picked up from where he had left off:

You say: "Now they want to shunt aside the Reichstag in order to continue the revolution." Gentlemen, if that had been our purpose we would not have needed . . . to have this bill presented. By God, we would have had the courage to deal with you differently!

You also say that not even we can abolish Social Democracy because it was the first to open these seats here to the common people, to the working men and women, and not just to barons and counts. In all that, Mr. Deputy, you have come too late. . . .

From now on we National Socialists will make it possible for the German worker to attain what he is able to demand and insist on. We National Socialists will be his intercessors. You, gentlemen, are no longer needed![9]

Hitler concluded by saying that the meeting taking place was nothing more than a formality: "We appeal in this hour to the German Reichstag to grant us that which we could have taken anyway."[10] He looked over at the Social Democrats one last time and told them he did not even want them to vote for the bill. "Germany shall be free," he yelled, "but not through you!"[11]

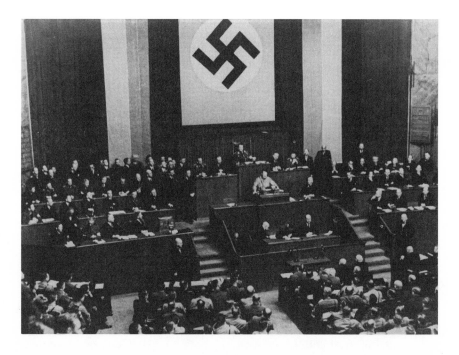

**Hitler dissolves the Reichstag on March 23, 1933. Courtesy of Keystone-France; Getty Images.**

After that, there were no more disruptions. The remaining party leaders rose to declare their support for Hitler's proposal, and a vote was taken. The result—441 to 94—led to the passage of the "Act for the Removal of Distress from People and Reich."[12] For all practical purposes, the Reichstag ceased to exist.

The events made front-page headlines around the world the following day. "Hitler cabinet gets power to rule as a dictatorship; Reichstag quits *sine die*," the *New York Times* announced.[13] Another report continued: "Never was there such a brute exaltation of mere strength. . . . In the very proclamation of the absolutely independent and ruthless Germany that is to be . . . the new German Government found itself confronted with the moral condemnation of almost all the rest of the world."[14]

Buried in these sentences was the implication that such a thing could never happen in America. One week later, however, on March 31, 1933, a remarkably similar series of events unfolded before a large number of American citizens. They saw a president of their country give almost exactly the same speech to a joint session of Congress, and when it was over, they all laughed and went home. It was a fateful moment for American democracy; it was the premiere of the Hollywood movie *Gabriel over the White House*.[15]

The joint session in the film began as follows: one courageous senator, a certain Mr. Langham, called for the impeachment of the newly elected president, who he said had been acting inappropriately, and the room erupted with a mixture of protest and applause. Then the president walked through the door, and the room turned silent. He stood in front of a gigantic American flag, and everyone waited for him to speak.

Like Hitler, he began gloomily. He said that he had arrived as a representative of the American people in their hour of darkest despair. For years, Congress had been throwing away money on schemes that did not benefit ordinary Americans. Countless hours had been wasted on futile discussion. Now it was time to take action. The president asked the representatives to declare a state of national emergency and to adjourn Congress until normal conditions were restored. For this temporary period,

Hitler's oratorical skills on display. Copyright © KPA/ZUMA/Corbis.

The fictional president dissolves Congress in *Gabriel over the White House* (1933).

he would assume full responsibility for the government of the United States.

There was a murmur in the crowd, but only Senator Langham dared to respond. "Mr. President, this is dictatorship!" he yelled. "The United States of America is a democracy! We are not yet ready to give up the government of our fathers!"

The president hardly flinched. "You *have* given it up," he said. "You've turned your backs. You've closed your ears to the appeals of the people. You've been traitors to the concepts of democracy upon which this government was founded.

"I believe in democracy," he continued, "as Washington, Jefferson, and Lincoln believed in democracy. AND IF WHAT I PLAN TO DO IN THE NAME OF THE PEOPLE MAKES ME A DICTATOR, THEN IT IS A DICTATORSHIP BASED ON JEFFERSON'S DEFINITION OF DEMOCRACY: A GOVERNMENT FOR THE GREATEST GOOD OF THE GREATEST NUMBER!"

The majority of congressmen responded with overwhelming applause, but Senator Langham did not give up. "This Congress refuses to adjourn," he called out, not quite as confidently as before.

"I think, gentlemen, you forget that I am still the president of these United States," was the reply. "AND AS COMMANDER-IN-CHIEF OF THE ARMY

The president's threat worked. A vote was taken and the result was announced: 390 to 16, in favor of the Emergency Act.[16] "Congress accedes to president's request, adjourns by overwhelming vote," the *Washington Herald* reported. Like Hitler, the president had won through legal means what he said he could have taken anyway.

This episode was as dramatic as the one in Germany; it involved people who were as high up in the nation's political and cultural elite, and it took place at the same point in time. From January to March 1933, some of the most important men in the United States conducted a serious discussion about how to portray the most pressing issues of the day on the screen—and this was the result.

Everything about the new president was unusual, not least his origins. In the summer of 1932, Thomas F. Tweed, political advisor and chief of staff to the former British prime minister David Lloyd George, took a holiday aboard a cargo vessel in the Mediterranean. Just before his departure, Tweed had read an interesting item in the news: apparently, a well-known department store owner named Harry Gordon Selfridge had declared that democracy in America was coming to an end. The nation would soon be managed by an "inspiring, unselfish spirit," and the people would be able to tend to their own affairs.[17] Tweed was deeply impressed by this idea, and he found himself discussing it with the other passengers on board. Was Selfridge right that a benevolent dictator should adjourn Congress, abolish prohibition, and impose a sales tax? Eventually he lost interest in their replies and found that his confinement to the freighter provided the boredom necessary to come up with an answer of his own.[18] This Englishman who had never before written a book nor set foot on American soil started working on what would become *Gabriel over the White House.*

Soon the legend of Jud Hammond was born. Originally a cynical politician who had risen to the presidency as a result of his good humor and charm, Hammond suffered a terrible car accident early in his administration, and when he awoke, he was possessed by an unshakeable will to solve all of America's problems. After dissolving Congress, he single-handedly managed to end unemployment, put a stop to racketeering, and bring about world peace.[19] In a country suffering its worst-ever economic depression, these were very appealing prospects.

In early January 1933, just before *Gabriel over the White House* was published in the United States, a copy of the novel somehow ended up in the hands of William Randolph Hearst, the head of one of the biggest media empires in the country.[20] Hearst not only ran dozens of newspapers but also a film company called Cosmopolitan Pictures, and he jumped at the idea of turning *Gabriel over the White House* into a movie. For years, he had compensated for his failed political ambitions by writing forceful editorials on the front pages of his newspapers. Now was his chance to create a president in his own image. Working with screenwriter Carey Wilson, he fashioned a story that dramatized his plans for the economic rehabilitation of the country. He wrote large portions of Hammond's speeches on his own. *Gabriel over the White House* became his pet project.[21]

But whereas Hearst could say whatever he wanted in his editorials, he was not entirely in charge of this film. Cosmopolitan Pictures depended on MGM for distribution and exhibition, and consequently, the film had to meet with the approval of the most powerful man in Hollywood, Louis B. Mayer. This was a problem, because although Hearst and Mayer were close friends, they had opposing political allegiances. In the previous year, Hearst had used all his influence to support Franklin D. Roosevelt in the lead-up to the elections.[22] Mayer, on the other hand, supported Herbert Hoover, and now, upon viewing the rough cut of *Gabriel over the White House*, he was outraged. "Put that picture in its can, take it back to the studio, and lock it up!" he is reported to have yelled after the screening.[23] Apparently, he had interpreted the earlier, cynical Hammond as a parody of President Hoover and the later, effective Hammond as powerful validation for Roosevelt.

The following month, MGM spent an enormous amount of time editing and reshooting *Gabriel over the White House*. Mayer went to great lengths to ensure that the film did not reflect on any national administration.[24] He revised Hammond's speeches, and he cut out an address to Congress about unemployment relief. As a result, the film did not promote Hearst's agenda as literally as it had before.[25]

Finally, Mayer consulted the least likely person of all during the editing process: Franklin D. Roosevelt himself. The incoming president watched the first cut of the film and expressed concern that it was at times promoting the wrong political agenda. As one report explained, "We run the risk of [Roosevelt's] belief that we are shaping public opinion contrary to what he may have to do."[26] To reduce this risk, Roosevelt proposed some changes, all of which were adopted, and he seemed very pleased with the final result. His secretary sent a thank-you letter to MGM, and he wrote to Hearst himself: "I want to send you this line to tell you how pleased I am with the changes which you made in GABRIEL OVER THE WHITE HOUSE. I think it is an intensely interesting picture and should do much to help. Several people have seen it with us at the White House and to every one of them it was tremendously interesting. Some of these people said they never went to movies or cared for them but they think this a most unusual picture."[27]

Despite this praise from the president, Hearst was unhappy. On March 25, he wrote to Mayer to express frustration and disappointment that his vision had been compromised. He reluctantly accepted Roosevelt's suggestions, pointing out that they detracted from the drama of the film. "Still," he continued, "there were a lot of alterations in the picture which were not requested by the government and which in my humble opinion were in no way necessary. . . . I think you have impaired the effectiveness of the President's speech to the Congress, because you have been afraid to say the things which I wrote and which I say daily in my newspapers and which you commend me for saying, but still do not sufficiently approve to put in your film. . . . I believe the picture will still be considered a good picture and perhaps an unusually good picture. Nevertheless, I think it was a better picture."[28]

The end result of all this was that several men were responsible for the creation of Jud Hammond. Hearst had wanted the ideal president to be all his own, but he had been forced to accept the changes of the real president, Franklin D. Roosevelt, and the studio executive, Louis B. Mayer.

There was one final person who suggested changes to *Gabriel over the White House*: Will Hays. Upon viewing the rough cut in March, Hays found himself in substantial agreement with the changes proposed by Mayer and Roosevelt. He also came up with a critique of his own. Given the tremendous strain of the times, he said, it seemed dangerous to suggest that the answer to the economic crisis lay somewhere other than in the accepted form of government. "The fact is hundreds of thousands of people have one eye on [Roosevelt] and one eye on God and it is a temper and state of mind that in my opinion will resent seriously a reflection on the institutions and the factors in government that have to find the solution," he wrote. "The people, in my opinion, will not sense in this picture the fact that it points to the people themselves behind their elected representatives as the source of all government power but will regard it as a direct indictment of the puerility and fallibility of today's government machinery and personnel and that only by a blow in the head of the president and the consequent acts of a deranged man is enough righteousness and wisdom put into the executive branch of the government to lead."[29]

Hays may not have been the most articulate writer, but he was calling attention to a problem that no one else seemed to have noticed. It was all very well for Hearst and Mayer and Roosevelt to argue about what kinds of changes their ideal president should bring about. If anything, Hays agreed with the compromise they eventually reached. But this fictional president dissolved Congress. He threw the entire concept of democracy out the window. He proposed dictatorship as the solution to America's problems.

In Hays' opinion, the film urgently needed to be changed. His first suggestion was to rework the opening scenes so that viewers would not be as disenchanted with the current form of government. The screenwriters at MGM obviously did not listen to his advice, for they came up with the following:

*Hammond:* Goodnight, Mr. Vice President. Hope you sleep well.
*Vice President:* When did the vice president ever do anything else?

*Hammond:* When I think of all the promises I made the people to get elected. . . .
*Brooks:* You had to make some promises. By the time they realize you're not going to keep them, your term will be over!

*Hammond:* Oh, thanks for those unexpected votes from Alabama.
*Congressman:* Wait till you get the bill for them.

So much for Hays' first suggestion. But he had another. When a man is nominated as a candidate or elected as a president, he wrote, a distinctively American phenomenon occurs. The man undergoes a spiritual transformation that leads him to do everything possible to achieve his objective, even if he kills himself in the process. With a few changes, the same thing could happen to Hammond. If this president had even a hint of responsibility upon being elected, then his later actions could be seen as the result of inspiration stemming from the democratic process.[30]

Here was how Hammond's transformation was eventually depicted: Not long after his inauguration, he was driving recklessly down a road. He said it was the first time he had been ahead of the newspaper men since he had been elected. He asked how fast he was going, and one passenger responded ninety-eight miles per hour. After the ensuing crash, Hammond lay in bed unconscious for several weeks, and when he awoke, he looked the same but seemed completely different. In the novel, the first character to see him was his favorite nephew, who sobbed, "That isn't my Uncle Jud!"[31] In the film, the president's physician recognized the transformation. "What does he say?" someone asked. "He says nothing," the physician replied. "He sits there silently, reading or thinking, like a gaunt gray ghost with burning eyes that seem to see right down into you."

Hammond had suddenly acquired mysterious powers. His famous smile had disappeared. He did not make jokes anymore. And when he did speak, his authority was absolute. He met with his cabinet and fired the secretary of state for questioning his orders. Then he told the press what had happened without any embellishment. Soon Hammond was no longer regarded as a cheap politician but as the supreme leader whose orders always had to be obeyed. As his secretary, Miss Malloy, explained in the book, "There's something about him, something new and terribly strange which deprives you of volition—of any capacity to think and act for yourself. It is easier to give way than to continue fighting for your ego. You become content to serve—to serve—and wait his pleasure."[32]

It was on the eve of the joint sitting of Congress that the source of Hammond's power was revealed. Miss Malloy entered his study late that night to give him the final draft of his speech, and although he had written it himself, he did not know what it was. He looked up, stared into space for a few seconds, and in that moment, Malloy became aware of the presence of a third being. She had known for some time that there were two Jud Hammonds. Now she understood that God had sent the angel Gabriel to inhabit Hammond's body and turn him into a messenger of revelations for the United States. The president took the speech and said he recognized it; in dissolving Congress, he would be doing the will of God.

So it was that the first major fascist motion picture appeared neither in Italy nor in Germany, but in the United States. The idea of "American fascism" has often been associated with Huey Long and Charles Coughlin, men whose beliefs and actions were reminiscent of fascist leaders in Europe.[33] Before Long and Coughlin became household names in America, however, this film argued that what the country needed was a dictator president. The men who made it came not from the fringes of American politics and culture but from the center. The one person who questioned its premise was not Roosevelt, the great democrat, but Will Hays, the puritanical motion picture reformer. For three years, Hollywood had avoided making movies that drew attention to the economic depression and the horrendous conditions under which people were living. Finally, one was released that cited all the major issues of the day—mass unemployment, racketeering, Prohibition, war debts, the proliferation of armaments—and the solution it proposed was fascism.

MGM was completely aware of this. Five months after *Gabriel over the White House* premiered in the United States, MGM marketed it in Germany. The local manager, Frits Strengholt, gave a promotional interview in which he declared, "We have demonstrated a strong trust in Germany and in the German market. . . . We believe that the efforts of your government in the struggle against unemployment, culminating in the generous work procurement program whose effects are already starting to be apparent, will also have pleasing consequences for theater attendance." Strengholt then said that his company was distributing a few pictures in the coming season that were of particular interest to the German public. These pictures used American examples to show that the principles of the New Germany were valid for the entire world. The most important by far was *Gabriel over the White House*. "This film has met with extraordinary praise in the press of the countries where the original version has already been screened," Strengholt said. "We are sure that in Germany, where these issues lie closer to reality, the film will have an even more favorable reception."[34]

"We believe in a satisfying collaboration [*Zusammenarbeit*] of all parties," he added, "just as we have . . . been able to work together smoothly with all German governmental authorities up to now."[35]

*Gabriel over the White House* premiered in Berlin in February 1934, and it played for fifteen consecutive days in its first run.[36] Not surprisingly, Hollywood's all-star productions from the same year outperformed it: *Queen Christina*, starring Greta Garbo, played for forty-four days; *Cleopatra*, starring Claudette Colbert, played for thirty-four days; and *The Scarlet Empress*, starring Marlene Dietrich, played for twenty-five days.[37] But *Gabriel over the White House* was more than mere entertainment. The Prussian minister of justice, the president of the German Film Chamber, and several high-ranking members of the Foreign Office attended a special screening of the picture, and the reviews were uniformly excellent. The main Nazi newspaper, *Völkischer Beobachter*, picked up on the parallels to the situation in Germany.[38] And the film reviewer for Goebbels' newspaper, *Der Angriff*, gave a truly insightful account of what these parallels meant.

The reviewer, a man named H. Brant, said that at first he had simply assumed that the producers of *Gabriel over the White House* had taken inspiration from recent events in Europe. But then he had discovered something fascinating: the idea for the film actually predated Hitler's rise to power in Germany. If ever one needed proof that the National Socialist principle had penetrated the thoughts and feelings of the citizens of all modern nations, this was it. Even in democratic America, the principle was so deeply embedded in the collective unconscious that it had led to the creation of this remarkable film.[39]

Brant then marveled at the distinctive personality of Jud Hammond. The contrast between Hammond's earlier self, inhibited by the old political system, and his new, better self, enabled by the breakthrough of the car accident, was masterly. "At first the smiling, somewhat complacent . . . parliamentary politician," Brant wrote, "then the completely transformed figure of a man possessed by a holy fanaticism, one who sees himself as above all party authority, as Leader, and as patron of the interests of his entire people and of all humanity."[40] In Brant's view, it was this sudden understanding of the leader principle that enabled Hammond to solve the problems first of the nation and then of the world.

When *Gabriel over the White House* was released in the United States, film critics tended not to label it outright fascism. Some excused the film by calling it a satire; others agreed with its agenda.[41] In Germany, however, its meaning was more straightforward. Yes, the film was a satire, but it was a *fascist* satire: it made fun of democracy and the inefficiency of the parliamentary system. And yes, President Hammond brought about positive changes, but these were no different from the ones the actual leader was busy delivering. As the Nazis and MGM agreed, each of the film's main reforms—ending unemployment, solving the gangster problem, and bringing about world peace—ultimately served to validate the supremacy of Adolf Hitler.

The first reform in *Gabriel over the White House* fit most closely with actual events in Germany. Immediately upon taking office, Hitler declared in a radio broadcast that his priority was the "salvation of the German worker in an enormous and all-embracing attack on unemployment." In 1933, he invested five billion Reichsmarks in work-creation schemes, and by 1934, the unemployment rate had dropped to less than half that of the previous two years. Even though these figures were not entirely accurate, and even though the work-creation schemes were actually an initiative of the previous government, there was widespread belief that Hitler had brought about an "economic miracle."[42]

*Gabriel over the White House* reinforced this belief, for Hammond—or as Brant called him, the leader—achieved the same outcome. He met with a group of unemployed men in Baltimore, and he said what Hearst had been saying since the Depression had begun: the government needed to create a large number of jobs in order to restore prosperity.[43] With no Congress to interfere, he was able to keep his promise. He invested $4 billion in work-creation schemes, and soon the problem of unemployment was solved.

The film critic, H. Brant, was impressed, but he could not help noting an important difference between Germany and the United States. "All the things that have already been overcome in Germany, namely parliamentarianism, political parties, and the liberal business principle," he wrote, "the American film can only bring about as a visionary wish in a dream sequence."[44]

Brant was right, but, to be fair, the American film also wished for things that had not yet come to fruition in Germany. The leader, after all, needed to do more than just solve the unemployment problem; he also needed to destroy an evil menace that threatened the very existence of the nation. Of course, the menace in the United States was not the same as the one in Germany. But the style of response was the same. *Gabriel over the White House* stigmatized one group as the source of all the nation's problems, and this was something to which German audiences could easily relate. In *Gabriel over the White House*, the villain was known as the gangster.

Hollywood had already put out many gangster films. Just the previous month, Cecil B. DeMille's *This Day and Age* had been a hit in Germany.[45] It told the story of a group of schoolboys who united, kidnapped the head gangster of their town, and lowered him into a pit full of rats. The film was banned in Holland because censors there felt that it contained "strong Fascist tendencies."[46] In Germany, however, Paramount renamed it *Revolution of Youth* and promoted it with a poster of a leader hailing a group of boys. The film played for twenty days in its first run in Berlin.[47]

*This Day and Age* was an unusually cruel picture, but even it did not propose a concrete solution to the gangster problem. *Gabriel over the White House*, on the other hand, did. Back in October 1932, Hearst had commissioned Benito Mussolini to write an article on the subject, and Mussolini's argument formed the basis for this part of the film. Mussolini had said there was only one answer to organized crime: "complete annihilation." When he had come to power in Italy, he had selected only those men who had the will, determination, and firmness to act without hesitation. "The real lofty democracy," he said, "is one which helps the people advance, protects and educates the masses, and punishes whenever necessary both wickedness and the wicked."[48]

That was exactly the position of *Gabriel over the White House*. In a speech over the radio, the leader, Jud Hammond, first outlined his plans for the protection of the American worker, and then raged against the enemy, "a malignant cancerous growth eating at the spiritual health of the American people." There was just one way of dealing with the problem: "These evil forces must be, shall be, eliminated, so that our citizen pursuing his peaceful way will be no longer forced to conduct his business in the shadow of extortion and debt."

But the leader was a generous man. A few days after speaking over the radio, he invited the head gangster, Nick Diamond, to the White House, and he gave him the chance to return to his home country. Then two government officials entered the room, and the gangster became frightened. "I thought I was guaranteed there'd be no frame-up," he said. The leader looked up at a painting of George Washington on the wall, and smiled. "Diamond," he said, "I don't think you're quite ready for framing."

The next night, Diamond organized a drive-by shooting outside the White House. No one was killed, but the repercussions were extreme. The leader put his personal assistant, Harley Beekman, in charge of eliminating all gangsters, and Beekman acted swiftly and mercilessly. He summoned Diamond and his men to a court martial, and he sentenced them all to death. "You're the last of the racketeers," he announced, "and why—because we have in the White House a man who has enabled us to cut the red tape of legal procedures and get back to first principles. An eye for an eye, Nick Diamond, a tooth for a tooth, a life for a life."

The course was clear. Beekman set up a concentration camp on Ellis Island in New York Harbor, where he personally supervised the shooting of the enemy. "I want to exterminate them like rats," one of his associates said in the book. And later, Beekman himself said, "I had no regrets, no compunctions about the fate of the beasts of prey we had destroyed."[49]

With the unemployment problem solved and the enemy completely annihilated, the leader had one last thing to do. He organized a meeting with the most important political figures of the world, and he bullied them with a display of American military power. "Is the president of the United States going to plunge the world into another war?" one statesman asked. "No, the United States must have the greatest navy in the world because we want peace," the leader replied. Another statesman pressed for further conferences, but the leader said that the Americans were always viciously exploited at such events. There was a much better solution. He forced every nation to sign a disarmament treaty that he himself had written, and with his work complete, he suffered a heart attack and died.

The leader of Germany, Adolf Hitler, also understood the benefits of talking in terms of world peace. In an address to the Reichstag on May 17, 1933, he said that Germany was prepared to renounce weapons of aggression if other countries would do the same. Two years later, he created the new German army, saying he wanted nothing more than "the power, for the Reich and thereby also for the whole of Europe, to be able to uphold peace." In response to condemnation for his actions from the League of Nations, he gave yet another "peace speech" to the Reichstag. "What else could I wish for other than calm and peace?" he proclaimed. "Germany needs peace, and wants peace."[50]

Of course, the one thing missing from Hitler's proclamations was the eventual reality—not total employment but millions off to war, not the weeding out of evil but genocide, not world peace but destruction on an unprecedented scale. These developments would emerge later. For the time being, Hitler promised the German people that he would solve their problems, and *Gabriel over the White House* reinforced everything he said. The film made the same promises as Hitler at the same point in time, and in this way, it performed a very specific function: it served as propaganda for the new Nazi regime.

It was not just any kind of propaganda. As H. Brant explained at the end of his review, it set the standard for all future production. "The danger of this film is that it risks turning into a boring set of debates," he wrote. "Through rapid cutting, the varied lighting of individual actors, and inserted short scenes, [the director] has instead turned the film into an exemplary propagandistic artwork. From beginning to end it leaves the spectator completely breathless."[51]

*Gabriel over the White House* was, in this critic's eyes, the perfect propaganda film. It showed the exact process by which Hitler became leader. It explained the actual reforms he would soon bring about. And it was absolutely captivating and entertaining. In a regime that was making propaganda central to its existence, Hollywood had supplied the first model picture. More were coming soon.[52]

From the day Hitler became chancellor of Germany to the day he invaded Poland, American movies were massively popular in the Third Reich. Between twenty and sixty new titles hit the screens every year, and they performed much better than the German productions of the time. They were admired by everyone from ordinary German citizens to the highest officials, they were discussed extensively in the press, and they were awarded a whole series of national prizes. Even in 1940, when only six American feature films were screened, at least two went on to become major hits.[53]

There were several reasons why American movies were so popular in Nazi Germany. One reason was that they were technically superior. Another was that they contained so many stars. Still another was that the Germans loved musicals, and the most dazzling musicals came from Hollywood. Of all the movies (both foreign and domestic) that were screened in the Third Reich in the 1930s, the second most popular was *Broadway Melody of 1936* (which played for 129 consecutive days in its first run in Berlin), and the third most popular was *Broadway Melody of 1938* (which played for seventy-four days).[54]

But there was a more important reason why American movies were so popular in Germany in this period. As a large number of critics pointed out, these movies possessed a unique quality: a "light comedy touch."[55] To cite a few examples from the press:

*After the Thin Man:* Just the right mixture of seriousness and fun, lightness and suspense, charm and brutality, to make the public erupt with laughter.[56]

*Forsaking All Others:* We are unable to make films like this, in which silliness is everything and nothing, both the focus and the entwining accoutrements, and all with such understandable, lively, natural and unnatural, easy-going jabber.[57]

*Desire:* A new victory in American humor . . . that is enabled by the Americans' open, uninhibited mentality.[58]

Very quickly, the various German production companies started emulating this distinctive quality of American movies. "Virtually every week," one newspaper reported, "several German production managers ask the American companies to borrow copies of a film so that they can learn from it."[59]

The head of the newly formed Propaganda Ministry, Joseph Goebbels, was troubled by the Americans' obvious superiority in the realm of film. Like Hitler, he watched movies every night, and he was frequently left with the impression that something needed to be done. After watching Frank Capra's Oscar-winning comedy *It Happened One Night*, for example, he noted his reaction in his diary: "A funny, lively American film from which we can learn a lot. The Americans are so natural. Far superior to us. The terrible German film *Leichte Kavallerie* proves that. Deadly boring."[60] He had a similar reaction to the second most popular movie in Germany in 1937: "*San Francisco* with Clark Gable and Jeanette MacDonald. Wonderfully acted, directed, and produced. *Stärker als Paragraphen*, a German botch containing a National Socialist message. Absolutely atrocious."[61]

Goebbels admired American movies, just like Hitler, but he found himself questioning Hitler's judgment in one respect. In Hitler's opinion, a propaganda film should never attempt to be entertaining: "I want to exploit the film fully as an instrument of propaganda, but in such a way that every viewer knows that today he's going to see a political film. Just as in the Sportpalast he doesn't expect to hear politics mixed with art. It makes me sick when I see political propaganda hiding under the guise of art. Let it be either art or politics."[62] This understanding led to the creation of *Triumph of the Will*, which, for all its power, contained very little humor or lightness.

Goebbels came up with a more imaginative approach. If a propaganda film were to be successful, he thought, it also needed to be entertaining: "Even entertainment can be politically of special value, because the moment a person is conscious of propaganda, propaganda becomes ineffective. However, as soon as propaganda as a tendency, as a characteristic, as an attitude, remains in the background and becomes apparent through human beings, then propaganda becomes effective in every respect."[63] Goebbels was reiterating what H. Brant had said about *Gabriel over the White House*: the film worked by using human drama to sustain the audience's attention at every moment. Far from getting in the way of propaganda, this was just what made it succeed.

At the end of 1935, a good year for the American companies, Goebbels gave a speech to a group of German filmmakers in which he took his observation even further. He began by criticizing German film actors for delivering their lines as if they were reading from a script or performing on a stage. The secret of film, Goebbels said, was that it was like real life, and consequently, film actors needed to speak more naturally. Only the Americans, who were unburdened by a long theatrical tradition, had understood this.[64] The acting in films like *It Happened One Night* and *The Lives of a Bengal Lancer* was unforced and completely convincing. Then, as Goebbels came to the end of his speech, he made a fascinating remark. In the two films he had mentioned, "a hero does not always speak heroically, but he acts heroically."[65]

Goebbels' remark applied interestingly to *It Happened One Night*, the most successful film in Germany in 1935.[66] The film told the story of a millionaire's spoiled daughter, played by Claudette Colbert, who ran away from home and met an out-of-work reporter, played by Clark Gable. The

**Joseph Goebbels, head of the Propaganda Ministry. Copyright ©
Bettmann/Corbis.**

pair fought throughout their travels but ended up falling in love, and just
when Gable was about to propose, a misunderstanding occurred. Colbert
returned home angry and heartbroken, and several weeks later, her father
confronted Clark Gable.

"Do you mind if I ask you a question, frankly?" the father said. "Do you
love my daughter?"

"Any guy that'd fall in love with your daughter ought to have his head
examined," Gable answered.

"Now that's an evasion," the father said.

"What she needs is a guy that'd take a sock at her once a day whether
it's coming to her or not," Gable yelled. "If you had half the brain you're
supposed to have, you'd have done it yourself long ago."

"Do you love her?"

"A normal human being couldn't live under the same roof with her without going nutty! She's my idea of nothing!"

"I asked you a simple question," the father yelled back. "Do you love her?"

"Yes. But don't hold that against me, I'm a little screwy myself!"

And so the couple fell into each other's arms, but hardly in the normal way. Gable never declared his undying love for Colbert. Instead he yelled it at her father. "A hero," in other words, "does not always speak heroically, but he acts heroically."

*It Happened One Night* was a romantic comedy with no obvious political message, so the stakes in this case were not very high. *The Lives of a Bengal Lancer*, starring Gary Cooper, was different.[67] It too was extremely successful—the third most popular film in Germany in 1935, playing for forty-three days in its first run in Berlin.[68] Unlike *It Happened One Night*, however, it was regarded as a *Tendenzfilm*, that is, a film exhibiting "strong National Socialist tendencies." And this particular combination—a *Tendenzfilm* that was a huge hit at the box office—was the first of its kind.

A few statistics are instructive at this point. The most popular Nazi propaganda film of the 1930s was *Triumph of the Will*, which premiered a few weeks after *The Lives of a Bengal Lancer* and played for twenty-nine days in its first run in Berlin.[69] But *Triumph of the Will* did not come close to making the top-ten most popular films of 1935 in Germany. In fact, there were nine American films alone that year that outperformed it. In a sense, the most successful Nazi propaganda film of the 1930s was not *Triumph of the Will*, commissioned by Hitler, but *The Lives of a Bengal Lancer*, produced by Paramount.

The significance of the film was immediately recognized by the German authorities. Just after its premiere, *The Lives of a Bengal Lancer* was deemed not only "artistically valuable" (an honor that exempted it from a variety of taxes) but also "useful for national education" (which meant it could be used to indoctrinate the young).[70] The leaders of the Hitler Youth were always on the lookout for such pictures, and when the group began organizing film screenings for its members, *The Lives of a Bengal*

*Lancer* was one of the first to be shown. "The practical importance of these performances," an American trade commissioner explained, "lies in the fact that in Berlin alone 20 to 30,000 young people see these films and, if the younger children are included, as many as 60,000 persons."[71] The Hitler Youth had found the perfect educational tool in *The Lives of a Bengal Lancer*. Here was how it went:

Lieutenant Alan McGregor (played by Gary Cooper) was dissatisfied. He had joined the Forty-First Regiment of the Bengal Lancers to fight rebels in colonial India, but the head of his regiment, Colonel Stone, always insisted on withholding fire. When this policy led to the death of two fellow lancers, a curious situation arose. One of the replacements was Lieutenant Forsythe, an accomplished soldier from another regiment. The other was Donald Stone, the colonel's own son. And here was the intolerable thing: the colonel treated his son just like any other soldier. At a certain point McGregor could not stand it anymore. He took the boy aside and told him that the colonel had no human feelings. "What's a son to him compared to his blasted regiment," he yelled, but just as quickly, he apologized for the outburst and told him to forget it.

Then one day Stone Jr. was kidnapped by Mohammed Khan, the colonel's archenemy. It was obviously the boy's fault, for he had left the campsite against orders. Even so, McGregor was horrified to learn that the colonel had no intention of sending out a search party for his son. "I'd just begun to think I was wrong about you, but I wasn't," McGregor yelled. "You haven't a human bone in your body, there's not a drop of blood in your veins!" When McGregor had finished yelling, the colonel arrested him for insubordination and placed him under the charge of the other new recruit, Lieutenant Forsythe.

It was time for the film's first lesson. Major Hamilton, the colonel's loyal assistant and the most inexpressive man in the regiment, came storming in to McGregor's quarters. He was furious. How could McGregor possibly think that the colonel did not care about his son? Of course he cared. His son meant everything in the world to him.

"I suppose if it were your son you'd sit here too like a dummy," McGregor said. "You would not."

"No, I should probably have ordered the regiment out," the major replied. "But that's because I'm not the man the colonel is. Nor the soldier."

"Well, if that's what you call being a man or a soldier, I don't want any part of it," McGregor yelled.

"Man, you are blind!" the major yelled back. "Have you never thought how for generation after generation here, a handful of men have ordered the lives of 300 million people?" (Or, as the German version put it, how "a handful of white men protect 300 million Indians from chaos?")[72] "It's because he's here, and a few more like him. Men of his breed have made British India. Men who put their jobs above everything. He wouldn't let death move him from it, and he won't let love move him from it. When his breed of man dies out, that's the end. And it's a better breed of man than any of us will ever make."

The film was preaching an idea that was in common circulation in Germany: according to common doctrine, Hitler too had given everything up for his people. He was the loneliest man in the country because he carried its entire weight on his shoulders. As Goebbels once said, "He stands alone facing his and our fate in order to battle out to a victorious conclusion the titanic struggle imposed on us for the life of our nation."[73]

But that was just the regular propaganda. There was something about this film, in Goebbels' opinion, that made it more effective than any of his own proclamations. It was that Colonel Stone did not need to use words like "titanic struggle" or "victorious conclusion"—he did not need to speak heroically in order to be heroic. When he tried talking to his son, his words were awkward. When his son was kidnapped, he said nothing at all. For over an hour, the audience—in this case the Hitler Youth—wondered why Colonel Stone was acting so coldly, and then, because he would never say it himself, his loyal friend provided the answer. The colonel was making an immense personal sacrifice for the good of the nation.[74]

There was another side to Goebbels' remark, however, and it was no less important in explaining the effectiveness of the film. The young soldiers in the Forty-First Regiment, particularly Forsythe and McGregor, never spoke heroically because they were constantly joking around. The reviewer for one of the daily newspapers, the *Berliner Tageblatt*, found this aspect of the film fascinating, and he described a scene in which Forsythe deliberately annoyed McGregor by playing a bagpipe: "The cheeky Forsythe is brought to reason in a masterly way. He is driving his superior mad by playing a creaky bagpipe. A cobra misinterprets the noise, thinking that the Scottish atonalities are actually the call of a local snake charmer. Now the cobra dances in front of Forsythe's nose, and Forsythe must continue playing in a nervous sweat until his superior rescues him, barely concealing the ironic smirk on his face as he does so."

In this reviewer's opinion, the cobra scene revealed the secret behind the entire picture. Even though the boys were constantly in danger, he said, they were still able to keep their sense of humor: "We are stirred and moved to see that bravery can exist at the same time as fear, but at every moment, even in the utmost crisis, humanity is there as well."[75]

That was especially the case after Major Hamilton gave his climactic speech about Colonel Stone. As soon as he left, Forsythe could not resist commenting on the highly unusual outburst.

"There's a great deal of speaking of minds going on here tonight," he said. "I didn't think the old boy had it in him—*but he's right*."

Forsythe was trying to make a joke, but it came out serious, and the cheekiness of the impulse only added to the gravity of the conclusion. Even McGregor was starting to see the error of his ways. Still, this stubborn soldier was determined to go out against orders and search for the colonel's son. Once again, Forsythe displayed both wit and courage in his response: since McGregor was his prisoner, he could hardly let him out of his sight, so he would have to go too.

The expedition was very precarious. The two men were dressed in ridiculous disguises, and Forsythe was singing obnoxiously until McGregor threw a piece of fruit at him. Somehow they were admitted into Mohammed Khan's stronghold, but they were identified in no time. The next thing they knew, they were sitting down to a civilized dinner with Khan himself, and Forsythe was complimenting Khan on the mutton. Khan then asked where their regiment intended to pick up its next munitions supply. "Well," Forsythe quipped, "when the furry little animal jumped out of the bag, he really jumped, didn't he?" Then, after telling Khan what he really thought of the mutton (it was rotten), the comedic part of the experience ended, and the serious part began.

Khan had an original way of making his victims speak: he placed tiny bamboo slivers under their fingernails and lit them. Neither McGregor nor Forsythe gave in under torture, but the colonel's son did, and the next day, Khan had enough ammunition to wipe out the entire Forty-First Regiment. As the reviewer for the *Berliner Tageblatt* noted, even at this point the soldiers did not lose their sense of humor: "Forsythe movingly sings a song about England in his moment of greatest depression, only to regret the lack of violin accompaniment."[76] It was then that McGregor and Forsythe came up with a plan. One would sacrifice his life by blowing up the entire munitions supply, and the other would provide cover. They bet on who would do the main job, and Forsythe "won." At the last moment, however, McGregor punched Forsythe in the face and did the deed himself. In his final words, he said that Stone Jr. should repay him by never telling Colonel Stone what had really happened. McGregor was sacrificing himself for the leader he had once doubted and protecting the leader from the knowledge of his son's betrayal.

Here lay the second lesson of *The Lives of a Bengal Lancer*: young people should be prepared to sacrifice their lives for their leader, who had already given up so much for them. As *Der Angriff* pointed out, they should do it without asking questions: "These men say nothing about the issues of the nation that have brought them here. For them that [silence] goes without saying. Perhaps it would offend them if someone started to talk about it."[77] Yet despite the seriousness of this message, humor was used at every point to support it, and the humor only made the message more convincing. The emotion of the final scene—in which Stone Jr. held back tears as McGregor was posthumously awarded the Victoria Cross—was all the more profound because of the jokes that had come before. It was no coincidence that *The Lives of a Bengal Lancer* was screened to tens of thousands of members of the Hitler Youth for educational purposes. The film put them in the position of boys slightly older than themselves, who joked around just like they did, and then led them through the appropriate learning process.

In the months that followed, several other high-ranking Nazis issued statements about the significance of *The Lives of a Bengal Lancer*. Gerd Eckert, a leader in the Hitler Youth, complained that there were nowhere near enough German propaganda films and that the few in existence were unconvincing and full of clichés. "It is shameful," he wrote, "that our filmmakers lack the courage to make a movie like *The Lives of a Bengal Lancer*."[78] And Leonhard Fürst, a leader in the German Film Chamber, described the terrible state of the local industry and asked, "Where is a script like *The Lives of a Bengal Lancer*?"[79] Even Hitler, who officially disapproved of the combination of entertainment and propaganda, said that *The Lives of a Bengal Lancer* was one of his favorite movies.[80]

The picture was a sensation, and thanks to its success, Gary Cooper soon became a celebrity in Germany. In late November 1938, just two weeks after the brutal pogroms against the Jews on *Kristallnacht*, Cooper paid tribute to his German audiences by making a publicity trip to Berlin. If they were expecting another lesson about leadership, though, they were disappointed. He just muttered a few banalities to the press—"Life is too precious to drive quickly"; "Fly German lines"; "The Bremen is the best ship"—and then he left.[81]

At the time of the actual release of *The Lives of a Bengal Lancer*, however, Gary Cooper was the most important exponent of the leader principle on the screen. By the end of 1935, it was clear that the Hollywood studios had supplied Germany with not one but two pictures that enforced this central aspect of Nazi ideology. And yet neither picture had been entirely perfect. *Gabriel over the White House* had borne an uncanny resemblance to the political situation of the time, but it had only been moderately popular. *The Lives of a Bengal Lancer* had drawn in massive crowds, but it had not emphasized the present need for fascism—it had harkened back to an earlier era. The next Hollywood movie that delivered a National Socialist message would be both popular and contemporary, and as a result, it would set a new standard for future German production.

The film was called *Our Daily Bread*, and it was made by the Hollywood director King Vidor outside the studio system. Vidor later explained why he had made the film this way: when the United States was in the midst of the Great Depression, Hollywood only wanted to show riches and glamour. "But," he said, "I also felt I didn't want to be a complete prostitute as far as making money in the studios was concerned. I didn't feel just like being the good company boy."[82] Upon discovering that unemployed workers were returning to the land to form cooperative farms, he was inspired to write a screenplay about their plight. Then, when the major studios turned his screenplay down, he "returned to the land" himself. He borrowed money on his house, his car, and everything that looked valuable in his safe-deposit box, and he made the picture independently. *Our Daily Bread* did well at the box office, and it won a prize in Moscow and a League of Nations award "for its contribution to humanity."[83]

Vidor left a few things out of his account, however. He did not mention that he actually started making the film at RKO and that his contract was terminated when the studio realized that he would have earned too great a share of the profits. He forgot to say that he later obtained distribution through United Artists, which all but guaranteed that he would make his money back.[84] And finally, he did not point out that *Our Daily Bread* was deemed "artistically valuable" in Nazi Germany, where it played for fifty-four days in its first run in Berlin.[85]

There was a reason for the film's disproportionate success in Germany. Viewers there understood Vidor's sensibility better than anyone else because it so closely resembled their own. "Laudable is the attitude of the author and director, who propagates the leader principle," the *Völkischer Beobachter* said.[86] The *Berliner Tageblatt* agreed and added that "the Americans have the advantage over us of being able to depict such things with humor (as in *The Lives of a Bengal Lancer!*)."[87]

An earlier film that did not exactly "depict such things with humor" was *Triumph of the Will*. One-third of the way through that film, during the official review of the Reich Labor Service, a group of men told Hitler about their daily routines. Some planted trees, others built roads, still others provided farmers with soil. In reply, Hitler gave a speech on how much he valued their efforts. The film was making an important ideological point: it was portraying the Führer as the figure around whom the concept of work was organized.[88]

*Our Daily Bread* enacted a more amusing version of the same scene. An unemployed man named John Simms had inherited a run-down farm, and he had put up some signs advertising for help. The next day, dozens of people arrived. "Wow!" Simms said; he barely knew the difference between carrots and weeds, and now he was going to lead a gigantic venture in farming. "Line up men!" he yelled as authoritatively as he could, and they did exactly as he said. There was a plumber, a carpenter, and a stone-mason (all very helpful) and then there was a concert violinist. Simms tried to stay positive—he believed that the man's strong wrists would come in handy—but another man was an undertaker, and he did not known how to be optimistic about that.[89]

Later that night, he gave a speech. He started out with a few jokes about Indians to warm up the crowd, and then, barely able to conceal his excitement, he told them, "You don't have to stay—you can go whenever you want to—but if you do stay, make up your minds to *work*!" Simms was making the same point as Hitler, with one slight difference. As *Der*

*Angriff* observed, "The call of community here is no empty phrase; it enters the picture lushly and with humor, with the boldly cast lights of real life."[90]

When Simms got to the end of his speech, an odd-looking man in the crowd asked an important question. "Mr. Chairman and friends," he said, trying to sound as official as possible, "What form of government are we going to have?"

Simms obviously had not thought this far ahead. "Well," he said, "whatever most of the crowd wants."

"Then I suggest, my friends, that we bind ourselves together in sacred covenant, *and establish an immortal democracy!*"

The crowd responded with a loud murmur of disapproval. "It was that kind of talk that got us here in the first place," one man said, and everyone laughed in agreement.

Then someone else made a suggestion. "We must have a socialistic form of government. The government must control everything, including the profits."

A few people seemed interested in this idea at first, but then a dispossessed Swedish farmer named Chris Larsen stood up. "Vait a minute," he yelled. "Let me talk! I don't even know what those words mean them fellers been talkin'! All I know is, we got a big yob here, and we need a big boss! And Yohn Simms is feller for boss!"

Everyone went wild in approval. Even the man who had originally proposed a democracy was excited. "Simms for boss!" he announced, and as he called for three cheers, Simms looked very pleased with himself.

The reviewer for *Der Angriff* was deeply impressed by what he had just seen. "There wasn't much discussion because discussion was the cause of all their misery," he wrote in his review. "The first man who was there should give orders and lead. And that's that!"[91]

What this reviewer did not say was that a subtle change had been taking place over the course of these films. From Jud Hammond in *Gabriel over the White House* to Colonel Stone in *The Lives of a Bengal Lancer* to John Simms in *Our Daily Bread*, the leader was becoming more and more human. And in this latest installment, a new kind of drama was about to unfold, one that had been unthinkable in the earlier films. *Our Daily Bread* was about to call the abilities of the leader into question.

A beautiful blonde had joined the farm under suspicious circumstances, and as the days went by, Simms seemed to be spending an increasing amount of time with her. The farm was experiencing a terrible drought, and everyone was blaming him for it, but the blonde had a way of making him feel better about himself. One day he tried complaining to his wife, but what she told him was not as comforting.

"They look up to you, John," she said. "They want to believe in you—they picked you as their leader."

"Well, who asked them to pick me?" he said. "I can make mistakes too, can't I? I'm only human. Can I help it if it don't rain?"

"No one expects you to. But keep your perspective. Be the boss again. Let them think you're not worried. Let them think you know more than they do."

Her advice did not help. The blonde had convinced him that he was destined for better things, and one night they ran off together. As they were driving away, Simms was plagued by doubts. He was thinking about one of his former workers, a wanted criminal who had turned himself in to the police to obtain the reward for the farm. He pulled over to the side of the road and tried to think, and it was then that he heard the sound of a nearby stream. What if the men dug a massive ditch from the stream to the crops, he wondered? Wouldn't that solve all their problems? The blonde held his neck tightly and told him not to go, but he pushed her away and ran back to the farm.

It was time to give the speech of his life. The men all hated him by now, and he needed to convince them to work harder than ever. As Hitler had once said, the point of the spoken word was "to lift . . . people out of a previous conviction, blow by blow to shatter the foundation of their previous opinions," and that was just what Simms did.[92] He yelled with all the emotion he could muster, and when he was done he turned to a member of the crowd, his old friend Chris Larsen, and asked him what he was going to do. "I go get my shovel Yohn," Chris replied. "If you go," someone else said, "I'm going too." Soon everyone had agreed to do the job, and after hours of grueling work, the men had built the ditch. The film ended with images of water gushing from the hilltop down to the parched corn fields.

The Nazis responded to *Our Daily Bread* with unqualified praise. From their perspective, by turning the leader into an ordinary man, the film validated the leader principle in an even more effective way than before. In reality, Hitler himself was not so different from John Simms: he would agonize for days before making decisions, and then he would act with great firmness, as if to suggest that the course of action were inevitable.[93] He never imagined that it might be fruitful to expose his human fallibility to the public. *Gabriel over the White House* perpetuated the mystery by claiming that President Hammond was doing the will of God, and *The Lives of a Bengal Lancer* only briefly hinted at the difficulties that Colonel Stone was experiencing. *Our Daily Bread* finally introduced a leader with whom audiences could identify, someone who they could feel was just like them. The Nazis had been praising Hollywood movies for a while, but this latest development prompted the production chief at Ufa, Ernst Hugo Correll, to write a report on what the Americans had achieved.

*Our Daily Bread*, Correll said, was so striking that it seemed to have been made under the direct instructions of the Propaganda Ministry. Indeed, if the film had been made in Germany, it probably would have won the state prize. And here was the truly shameful thing: there was a whole series of American films just like it. Columbia Pictures had recently released *Mr. Deeds Goes to Town*, in which an honest man (played by Gary Cooper) inherited a massive fortune and then gave it away to decent, respectable farmers whom the state had left in poverty. "In this film as well," Correll wrote, "a National Socialist idea is inserted—incidentally in a very amusing way."[94] A few years later, the Nazis would describe the sequel, *Mr. Smith Goes to Washington*, as yet another example of "excellent propaganda that ridicules corruption and parliamentarianism in Washington."[95]

"Unfortunately," Correll continued, "I cannot spare our German writers from this reproach: they have seldom expressed . . . National Socialist ideas in the relaxed, lively way that we see in the examples I have just given. Our German writers have been able to find the form to depict nationalist and, to some degree, National Socialist ideas in film. . . . But they have not yet mustered up the freedom to shape their work in the way I have described. Naturally, we will continue making films about our own history. . . . But something entirely new, something like *Our Daily Bread*, would considerably expand our propagandistic abilities."[96]

Correll had correctly identified the problem—he had pointed out that the Hollywood studios were providing the most effective, seductive propaganda films—but his dream never came true. In the remaining years of the Third Reich, German filmmakers did not release a single picture that addressed the leader principle in an innovative way. Every picture on the subject harkened back to an important figure in German history: Schiller in *Friedrich Schiller*, Frederick the Great in *The Great King*, and Bismarck in *Bismarck* and *The Dismissal*.[97] Some of these films performed quite well at the box office, but none of them were as entertaining as *Gabriel over the White House*, *The Lives of a Bengal Lancer*, or *Our Daily Bread*.[98]

The Americans, on the other hand, continued to release even more inventive treatments of the leader principle. Around the time that Correll criticized German film propaganda, MGM released its all-star production *Mutiny on the Bounty*, which, like *Mr. Deeds Goes to Town*, showed how an ordinary man could rise up against the tyranny of a corrupt power. It played for forty-two days in its first run in Berlin, and the reviewer for *Der Angriff* was ecstatic. "We take this film to be the harshest American production in recent years," he wrote, "and would like to say that even *The Lives of a Bengal Lancer* pales in comparison."[99] The *Berliner Tageblatt* added, "Don't forget the laughs, which occur at the most serious moments (and which make the film lighter, more enjoyable, yet no less serious)."[100] Hitler himself was intrigued, and one of his adjutants ordered a copy of the print for his retreat at the Obersalzberg.[101]

Over the years, the Hollywood studios provided Germany with many other similar pictures. *Looking Forward* (released in Germany in 1934) was, in MGM's words, "a film in which the healthy, life-affirming, masculine optimism—the optimism of the New Germany—finds expression." *Night Flight* (1934) showed one man's determination to fly airplanes in darkness and was deemed "useful for national education." *Queen Christina* (1934) dramatized a woman's struggle between love and duty and was deemed "artistically valuable." *West Point of the Air* (1935) unveiled the heroism of a young aviator and was deemed "artistically valuable." *Souls at Sea* (1938) showed an individual's struggle against tyranny and was deemed "artistically valuable." *Captains Courageous* (1938) told the story of a spoiled boy who learned the value of sacrifice and was deemed "artistically valuable."[102]

The list went on. This was the high point in Hollywood's relationship with Nazi Germany. The various studios had found a special market for their films about leadership, and this, along with the success of their politically innocuous movies, justified further business dealings. But the experience of the American studios in Germany was by no means entirely positive. Some American movies were deeply unpopular in Germany; others were rejected by the censors and never even reached the screen. It is time to turn to these less fortunate productions.

# " B A D "

"*Tarzan*: Bad"[1]
Adolf Hitler

In the early days of Hitler's rise to power in Germany, the American studios were cautiously optimistic. They had reason to believe that their sales would improve under the new Nazi regime, and the first round of statistics seemed to prove them right: the studios sold sixty-five movies in Germany in 1933, up from fifty-four in 1932.[2] After hearing for over a year that the Nazis were "absolutely in favor of international exchange and collaboration," the studios were starting to think that it might actually be true.[3]

Then, on March 2, 1934, a major Hollywood motion picture came up for appeal at the highest censorship board in the country. An obscure minister from the region of Württemberg had lodged a complaint against the film, and the censorship board needed to determine whether or not the complaint was valid.[4] It was an unusual case, for the film had premiered more than a year earlier and by this stage was playing only at minor theaters and bringing in negligible proceeds. Anyone who had any interest in seeing the film had already seen it. It was called *Tarzan the Ape Man*.[5]

Under normal circumstances, the production company, MGM, would not have been overly concerned about the case. The chief censor, Dr. Ernst Seeger, had recently approved a series of similar pictures, including

*King Kong*, and in one of his decisions, he had even made the following pronouncement: "The Americans . . . have now treated so many versions of the *Tarzan* problem in film that an immoral effect upon adults and normal viewers can no longer be expected from these improbable events."[6]

MGM was worried in this particular case, however, and the reason was simple: two weeks earlier, a new film law had come into effect in Germany. In the past, films could only be banned if they "endangered public order, harmed religious feelings, provoked a threatening or immoral effect, or endangered the German image or Germany's relations with other nations."[7] Now films could also be banned if they "endangered the vital interests of the state" or if they "harmed National Socialist . . . ethical, or artistic sensibilities." There was one other notable change: a sentence of the old law—"Permission must not be denied for reasons that lie outside the content of the film"—had been cut.[8]

The meeting that was about to take place was therefore of great importance. One year after coming to power, the Nazis had introduced a new film law in Germany, and *Tarzan* was going to be the new law's first test case.

A small group assembled in the screening room of the supreme censorship board, and the picture was shown from start to finish. Then Dr. Seeger read out a summary of the plot: "Jane Parker is the daughter of an ivory merchant in Africa. She accompanies him and his partner on an expedition to an elephant cemetery, where they hope to find vast quantities of ivory. On the way there they discover Tarzan, the ape man, who has been raised by apes and has never seen a human being. Tarzan kidnaps Jane but soon he is her best friend; she tries to communicate with him in her language. Tarzan then rescues Jane's father, his partner, and Jane from imprisonment by a group of pygmies, but when the small expedition finds the elephant cemetery, Jane's father dies. Jane remains with Tarzan in the jungle."[9]

After reading out this summary, Seeger turned to the Württemberg minister and asked him to explain why he had brought the film up for appeal. Here is what the minister said: "This film is one of those Africa pictures that would aim to awaken the thrill of sadistic instincts in the spectator by deliberately and subtly emphasizing the atrocities in the struggle between humans and animals, as well as that between animals of different kinds. Its immoral and bestializing effect is illuminated in the fact that the audience laughs at the mortal danger of a nice little monkey who lets out atrocious death screams while clumsily running from a roaring panther, and furthermore titters with pleasure when a herd of elephants stampedes through a Negro village . . . and when an elephant hurls a pygmy through the air onto the ground where the unfortunate soul perishes, writhing in pitiable death convulsions and shrieks.

"The cruelty to animals that occurred in the making of this picture is a cultural disgrace, which has been barred from taking place in the New Germany because of the animal protection law that we have instituted. The film law should spare no means in preventing foreign pictures of this type from reaching the screen in Germany, for the producers of these pictures are breaking the fundamental precepts of humanity in their pure obsession with profit."[10]

When the Württemberg minister had finished talking, Dr. Seeger did a strange thing. Usually, his next move would have been to ask the MGM representative to respond to these charges, but instead, he said that he had found it necessary to obtain a second opinion on the case. He had wanted to ascertain whether the film harmed German racial feelings, and thereby "endangered the vital interests of the state," so he had requested a written evaluation from the Propaganda Ministry. He now proceeded to read out the Ministry's response.[11]

"Because the people's consciousness has been heightened by a month-long intensive propaganda campaign on all questions of genetic biology," he read, "this film must be considered dangerous. The Nazi state has been tirelessly trying to awaken in public opinion the highest sense of responsibility in the selection of a husband. It has also put a great deal of effort into freeing the ideas of marriage, womanhood, and motherhood from the superficial distortion of the past epoch, which was completely aimed at sexuality, and making them honorable again. A film that puts pure libido in the foreground, that tends to imply that a jungle man, virtually an ape, is capable of the noblest impulses of the soul and is a worthy marriage partner, certainly runs against the tendencies of National Socialism with regard to population politics.

"The film must be rejected," the letter concluded, "for it contradicts the fundamental ideas of National Socialism and the official propaganda, even if the impartial spectator does not immediately and clearly recognize it."[12]

That was enough for Seeger. He said that the national government had put a great deal of effort into keeping alive the healthy racial feelings of the German people, and that it contradicted these efforts to show a civilized woman court, love, and protect a jungle man. Seeger banned *Tarzan* for this reason and said that there was no need to consider the position of the Württemberg minister.[13]

In the months that followed, censorship grew stricter in Germany. Seeger had previously been a relatively lenient judge of American movies: he had banned only two titles in 1931 and only three titles in 1932.[14] Now he took it upon himself to protect the German nation from American immorality. When a Marlene Dietrich film called *Blonde Venus* reached his censorship board, he criticized the way the central female character left her husband to look after her child on her own. "Such a lax depiction of marriage and morality," he said, "contradicts the nation's current emphasis on the importance of the family."[15] Eight months later, he turned down another American film starring Marlene Dietrich, *The Song of Songs*, on the grounds that this German actress was once again revealing her preference for "prostitute roles."[16]

Seeger also seized on his new moralizing tendencies to ban entire film genres. When the gangster film *Scarface* reached his censorship board, he said that the film glorified criminal life and made crime seem like a legitimate profession. The main character walked around town in a tuxedo, he went to fashionable nightclubs and drank champagne cocktails, and he constantly surrounded himself with beautiful women. At this point in the meeting, the film company made a clever argument: since the Nazis had all but wiped out crime in Germany, audiences would automatically disapprove of the action in the picture. But Seeger did not agree. *Scarface*, like all other gangster pictures, threatened to undermine the government's efforts and reintroduce crime in Germany.[17]

Next, Seeger outlawed all horror movies on the grounds that they had an immoral, threatening effect. He explained that the images contained in these movies whipped up the nerves of normal spectators and targeted their lowest instincts.[18] Back in 1932, Seeger had permitted *Frankenstein*; now, he banned *The Invisible Man* and *Dr. Jekyll and Mr. Hyde*.[19]

Finally, Seeger rejected a few pictures for more unusual reasons. When a medical drama entitled *Men in White* reached his censorship board, he said that the disturbing images of an American hospital had no place in the Third Reich. It would be frightening and alarming for German spectators to see patients stamped with a number, wrestling with death in an enormous building, while people in the adjoining rooms did not seem to care.[20]

As strange as some of these decisions may have seemed, none were unique in the history of international film censorship. Many countries disapproved of gangster pictures and horror movies in the 1930s, and all countries developed their own set of criteria for evaluating Hollywood productions. Mexico and Britain, for example, prohibited religious scenes; China prohibited westerns; and Japan excluded all pictures that reflected badly upon royalty, were derogatory to the military, or contained kissing scenes. Even Seeger's analysis of *Tarzan* was not that unusual: at around the same time, a Fox film called *Caravan* was banned in France because it depicted a romance between a high political figure and a gypsy girl. The local manager explained, "The picture is as offensive to Central Europe as would be a film in the United States showing the Secretary of State consorting with a wanton of another race and color."[21]

The tightening of film censorship in the Third Reich therefore did not come as much of a surprise to the American studios, nor was it a major cause for concern. Every country in the world had worked out reasons for rejecting Hollywood movies in this period, and Germany was simply developing some reasons of its own.[22] The studios sold only forty-one films to Germany in 1934—down from sixty-five in 1933—but as soon as the preferences of the Nazi authorities were known and understood, the studios would be able to adjust their offerings accordingly.[23]

At least that would have been the case were it not for one final development. A couple of weeks after the *Tarzan* hearing, another top-grossing American picture reached the supreme censorship board. There was something that distinguished this case from all others around the world— namely that the problem had nothing to do with the film itself.

In late April 1933, the former world heavyweight boxing champion, Max Schmeling, was getting ready to leave Germany for a fight in the United States. One evening, he was dining at a restaurant in Berlin when an SA officer came over to his table and made a surprising announcement: "Herr Schmeling, the Führer requests that you join him for dinner at the Reich Chancellory." Schmeling, who was not a Nazi, replied that he would gladly go, and soon he was having a conversation with Hitler. At the end of the night, Hitler wished Schmeling good luck in his upcoming fight.

"I've heard that you're going to America," he said. "If anyone over there asks how it's going in Germany, you can reassure the doomsayers that everything is moving along quite peacefully."[24]

Schmeling's opponent in the United States was a rising young boxer named Max Baer. And Baer, whose grandfather was a Jew from Alsace-Lorraine, decided to turn the fight into a great symbolic event. He sewed a gigantic Star of David onto the left side of his trunks, and he announced to the press, "Every punch in the eye I give Schmeling is one for Adolf Hitler."[25]

The fight took place at Yankee Stadium in New York City on June 8. It did not begin well for Baer. By the ninth round, his trainer told him that he was losing, and suddenly, without any warning, Baer came back. He began the tenth round by delivering a devastating punch to Schmeling's jaw, knocking the German down, and when Schmeling somehow got up, Baer hit him again. "That one's for Hitler," he said, and at that point—one minute and fifty-one seconds into the round—the referee stopped the fight.[26]

Max Baer (center) immediately after defeating Max Schmeling (second from right) on June 8, 1933. The Star of David is sewn onto Baer's trunks. Copyright © Bettmann/Corbis.

Baer's victory turned him into a hero, and soon afterward, he received an exciting proposition from Louis B. Mayer of MGM. Mayer offered him $30,000 to star in a major motion picture about a heavyweight boxing champion, entitled *The Prizefighter and the Lady*.[27] In September and October, the film was shot, and on November 10, it premiered in the United States. The film showed Baer winning boxing matches and having affairs with beautiful women, and it was a big hit.[28]

MGM naturally intended to distribute *The Prizefighter and the Lady* all around the world, and in January 1934, the head of MGM in Germany, Frits Strengholt, submitted a subtitled version of the film to the German censors. It was approved instantly. Since the film promised to do very well at the box office, Strengholt then spent $25,000 to have it dubbed into German, and he submitted the new version to the censors as well.[29] (This was common practice: the studios generally released their pictures first with subtitles, and then dubbed the more lucrative ones into German.)[30] While Strengholt was awaiting the result of the second censorship meeting, a series of unrelated events caused him to worry a great deal. The events almost seemed to be a repeat of the controversy around *All Quiet on the Western Front* three years earlier.

On the evening of March 8, a British picture called *The Rise of Catherine the Great* premiered at the Capitol Theater in Berlin, and it starred Elisabeth Bergner, a Jew who until recently had been one of Germany's leading actors. When the guests arrived at the theater, a mob that included Nazis in uniform pelted them with eggs and rotten oranges. "We don't want Jewish pictures," the mob yelled. Then a prominent Nazi leader gave a speech, the uniforms disappeared, and the police were able to restore calm.[31]

The following morning, the president of the Film Chamber announced that *The Rise of Catherine the Great* was being taken out of circulation in Germany because it endangered public order. The representatives of the American studios in Berlin were skeptical. "It is clear that such danger can be supplied readily at any time and at a moment's notice," wrote one American trade commissioner.[32] "It is not clear . . . whether it was deliberately arranged in order to make it appear as if public opinion were responsible," wrote another.[33] And Frits Strengholt, whose subtitled version of *The Prizefighter and the Lady* was scheduled to open at the same theater eight days later, decided to take preemptive action. On March 15, he wrote to the German Foreign Office to explain the severe consequences that would result from the banning of *The Prizefighter and the Lady* in Germany.[34]

First, MGM would give up its Berlin office, for it was not in the habit of conducting business in this way. As a result, around 160 employees would lose their jobs, and the German company that manufactured MGM's film prints would lose its biggest customer.[35]

Second, MGM was 100 percent owned by Loew's Incorporated, and a very considerable portion of Loew's was owned by William Randolph Hearst. Up to this point, the Hearst press had regularly attacked France and had treated the new regime in Germany with objectivity and good favor.[36]

Third, if *The Prizefighter and the Lady* were banned, there would automatically be massive reprisals against German films and German sportsmen in America. This would be a great shame, for up to this point MGM had "always been anxious to maintain good relations between Germany and America." The studio had secured distribution deals for German pictures in the United States and had produced *Gabriel over the White House*, which the German government had recognized as "politically valuable." If the premiere of the Max Baer film did not go ahead as planned, Germany would stand to lose a lot more than MGM.[37]

Frits Strengholt had one more trick up his sleeve. One of his employees happened to be the nephew of the German foreign minister Konstantin von Neurath.[38] He must have made use of the contact, for at eleven-thirty the next morning, the foreign minister was on the phone with Joseph Goebbels.[39] Here is an account of their conversation from the perspective of the foreign minister's assistant, Alexander Führ: "Baron von Neurath stressed that the English version was approved without objection in January, and that a sudden belated ban would have such bad consequences, and would be such an insult to the organizers and the foreign press, that the matter would be known throughout the entire world within two hours. In reply to this statement, Reichsminister Goebbels said something which I didn't hear. From the further words of the Foreign Minister, however, it became clear that Reichsminister Goebbels had agreed to go ahead with the premiere, and that he would provide protection against any potential disturbance."[40]

When the phone call was over, the foreign minister called Alexander Führ over to his desk and asked him to carry out a couple of important assignments. First, he wanted him to meet with the chief censor, Dr. Seeger, under whose authority *The Prizefighter and the Lady* had initially been permitted. Then he wanted him to report the results of the conversation to Frits Strengholt of MGM.

That afternoon, Führ visited Dr. Seeger, who had no qualms with *The Prizefighter and the Lady*, but who felt that Goebbels' guarantee of no violence could not be upheld. Führ replied that he would contact the police himself and instruct them to take the necessary precautions.[41]

Führ then called Frits Strengholt to inform him of the results of his efforts. He said that he had spoken to the police and to the local Nazi Party leader, and that the evening's events would run smoothly. Nevertheless, the Film Chamber would undoubtedly issue a ban the next day, and the wisest move for MGM (and one involving no loss of prestige) would be to withdraw the picture from circulation the following morning. Führ said that the most he could obtain for the company was this brief respite.[42]

Strengholt had just one question for the assistant to the foreign minister: Why, he asked, was Goebbels objecting to the film in the first place? Führ said that he believed it had something to do with an insulting remark that Baer had made about Hitler. Strengholt was prepared for just this response, and he directed Führ's attention to an article in the most recent edition of *Der Angriff*: "Max Schmeling speaks with respect about his former opponent. He emphasizes that up until his return to Europe, they were the best of friends. Why, then, this stupid claim that Baer said he would crush 'the representative of Hitler'? Schmeling never heard anything like this when he was in America."[43] If Goebbels' own newspaper was categorically denying the rumor about Baer, Strengholt said, then what was the problem? Führ replied that MGM could always provide any documentation to the authorities at a later date, but that, for the moment, the only course of action was to withdraw the film from circulation.[44]

The premiere of *The Prizefighter and the Lady* went ahead that night without any interruptions. At the end of the screening, the crowd responded with tumultuous applause, and the critics were deeply impressed. The reviewer for *Der Angriff*, H. Brant (the same man who had written the perceptive review of *Gabriel over the White House* two and a half weeks earlier) had only kind words for Max Baer. Baer, he said, gave a marvelous performance as a boxer who rapidly rose to stardom, even if he did have a few adulterous affairs on the side. This man was always a winner—whether as a boxer or as an actor, whether he put his efforts into chasing women or simply allowing himself to be surrounded by them.[45]

One of the only complaints about the film, in fact, was that it had not yet been dubbed into German. "Why," the reviewer for *Völkischer Beobachter* asked, "instead of dubbing the picture, must the company resort to this careless procedure of printing German titles on the screen with the English sound, which is spoken at such a rapid tempo that the spectators' eyes miss half of the acting? In the future, please use either the German language or nothing at all!"[46]

Strengholt was encouraged by the reviews, and the following morning, he did not pull *The Prizefighter and the Lady* out of circulation. To his surprise, the German authorities did not take any action either. The film was in its thirteenth consecutive day of sold-out showings at the Capitol Theater and seemed likely to become one of the biggest hits of the year in Germany when the dubbed version finally came up for review.[47] Strengholt was not too worried at this point, for even if the picture were rejected, he could always appeal the decision to Seeger's supreme censorship board—and even if Seeger then rejected it, the subtitled version would still bring in excellent returns.

The meeting opened with the first-ever screening of *The Prizefighter and the Lady* in German. Then Arnold Bacmeister, the head of the regular censorship board, turned to the only invited guest, a representative from the Propaganda Ministry. "Do you object to the showing of this picture because it is not in the spirit of the New Germany," he asked, "because the main actor is the Jewish boxer Max Baer?"

"Yes," the representative replied.[48]

In the discussion that followed, Bacmeister said that the events in the film revolved around Max Baer, and that Max Baer had all the internal and external features of a Jew. The German public would inevitably recognize Baer as a typical representative of his race.[49]

It was bad enough, Bacmeister said, that the main character of the film was a Jew. The decisive point, though, was that despite his inherent moral defects, he was portrayed as a sports hero and moral victor. His victory took place not only inside the ring but also outside it—with non-Jewish women. He grabbed them indiscriminately and slept with them, and his non-Jewish wife was so addicted to him that she forgave him every time. Such a portrayal could not be tolerated in the New Germany. Bacmeister therefore turned down MGM's application for the dubbed version of *The Prizefighter and the Lady*, and he ordered that the subtitled version currently playing at the Capitol Theater be taken out of circulation immediately.[50]

Strengholt was outraged. He called a press conference and announced to fifty journalists that *The Prizefighter and the Lady* had been banned because the main actor was a Jew. His company stood to lose 350,000 Reichsmarks as a result. If the Nazis intended to ban all pictures containing Jews, then not only MGM but all the American studios would be forced to leave the country. In that case, around five thousand local employees would lose their jobs. MGM had already lodged an appeal with the highest censorship board in the country, and the other studios would be paying close attention to the outcome.[51]

In the days that followed, several high-ranking Nazi officials spoke out against the banning of *The Prizefighter and the Lady*.[52] The Reich Ministry of Economics became heavily involved, and Foreign Minister Konstantin von Neurath wrote a concerned letter to Goebbels. Von Neurath reminded Goebbels of their earlier telephone conversation, and then stated his position in no uncertain terms: "In view of the extraordinary influence that the American film industry exerts on our economy, we will have to deal with the most detrimental reactions . . . from Washington if the lower censorship board's decision is upheld. The Americans think of film not as a cultural asset but as a commodity, and the former ambassador Schurman emphasized a few years ago that it is one of their most significant exports. From this perspective, the uncertainty in this sector generated by the censors' decision will cast serious doubts on our reliability as a partner in a new trade agreement." After reiterating the basis of MGM's claim, the foreign minister urgently requested that Goebbels intervene in the upcoming meeting of Dr. Seeger's supreme censorship board.[53]

Three weeks later, the meeting took place. The proceedings began with a screening of the picture, followed by a summary of the plot. Then the lawyer for MGM gave several reasons for contesting the earlier decision. He first argued that *The Prizefighter and the Lady* neither glorified Max Baer nor made him seem superior to other people. Furthermore, even if German spectators did emerge from the film idealizing Baer, they would never think of him as a "typical representative of his race." They would consider him merely an exception.[54]

Seeger refuted both of these claims. "The entire film is a singular apotheosis for Max Baer, whose life and times serve as its principal content, and whose fight at the end has all the sympathy of the public on his side. . . . This committee believes that Baer is furthermore a particularly Negroid type [of Jew]. When the claimant questions the determination of the committee . . . that the German public will not consider Baer to be a 'typical representative of his race,' he remains alone in this view."[55]

The MGM lawyer moved on. He turned to Baer's sexual relations with non-Jewish women, and he said that German feelings were only hurt when relations between Jews and non-Jews took place in *Germany*. Since the film was set in America, it was not offensive in any way.[56]

"Such relations [between Jews and non-Jews] are offensive to German feelings regardless of where they are set," Seeger replied. "The German people have collectively adopted a hostile attitude toward Jews, and as numerous recent incidents prove, are provoked whenever a film is screened in which a Jew plays a leading role. In this matter it makes no difference whether the Jew is of German or foreign origin, or whether the film is set in Germany or abroad."[57]

The MGM lawyer had one last objection. Even if the authorities insisted on banning the dubbed version of the film, they had no basis for pulling the original version out of circulation as well.

"The inclusion of the original approved English version in the ban is not to be criticized," Seeger said. "It is to be explained by the fact that in the time between the certification of the original version . . . and its resubmission in dubbed German . . . the new film law became effective . . . which forbids pictures that harm National Socialist sensibility." After responding to this final objection, Seeger announced that no further appeals were possible, and he brought the meeting to a close.[58]

The upholding of the ban on *The Prizefighter and the Lady* changed the nature of film censorship in the Third Reich. In the past, films had only ever been banned in Germany on account of objectionable content—a policy consistent with the policies of other nations. Now, films could also be banned because of the racial origins of the members of the cast. The Nazis were applying their anti-Semitic views to the film selection process, a practice without precedent anywhere in the world.

All this might have signaled the end of the Nazis' relationship with the American studios. The Nazis had targeted one prominent Jew in Hollywood, and more cases would inevitably follow. Soon business dealings between the two groups would be unthinkable. The collaboration would come to an end.

In fact, things turned out quite differently. Years later, Arnold Bacmeister wrote a memoir in which he explained the true meaning of *The Prizefighter and the Lady* decision. "Of particular significance," he wrote, "was the question of whether and to what extent *the participation of Jewish artists* in a film would necessitate a ban on account of 'harming National Socialist sensibility.' . . . When the American film *The Prizefighter and the Lady* was submitted to the board, with the Jewish boxer Max Baer in the leading role, I took the principal position that the mere participation of a Jewish artist did not justify a ban. A film should only be rejected if the artist were playing a leading role and, in addition, were well known to the German public. This restrictive interpretation seemed necessary to me out of practical considerations. If the interpretation of the ban had been any broader, barely a single foreign film could have been shown in Germany."[59]

The banning of *The Prizefighter and the Lady*, in other words, was a pragmatic decision that balanced Nazi ideology with economic reality. The censors had merely intervened in an extreme case—a film that starred a well-known, threatening Jew who had publicly criticized Hitler. There was no way that they could have rejected Hollywood's entire output, for that would have been disastrous for theater attendance in Germany. The Nazis were therefore not ending their relationship with the American studios; they were announcing the only way that the relationship could continue.

But there was one more side to the Nazis' decision, one final reason why they could not possibly have stopped doing business with the studios at this particular point in time. If the Nazis had banned all American movies in Germany, then their representative in Los Angeles, the German consul Georg Gyssling, would have lost all his bargaining power. He would have had no further basis for objecting to the production of anti-Nazi films in Hollywood. The Nazis needed to maintain friendly relations with at least a few of the studios, or else they almost certainly would have become the villains in the most popular form of entertainment that the world had ever known.

Hitler himself had been very clear about his priorities here. In a society fighting for its existence, he had said in *Mein Kampf*, propaganda acquires supreme importance, and all other considerations become secondary.[60] In accordance with this precept, he was willing to sacrifice virtually anything to obtain the advantage in the field of propaganda. His film workers followed his example. They were prepared to permit most American movies starring Jewish actors in Germany if it meant that Georg Gyssling could continue to exert his influence over the really important cases.

So, in the end, the banning of *The Prizefighter and the Lady* was not the most significant moment in the Nazis' dealings with Hollywood. The Nazis simply did not consider the appearance of Jewish artists on the German screen to be anywhere near as pressing as the preservation of German prestige in movies to be screened all around the world. On several occasions, the Propaganda Ministry explained this policy to the German press and issued clear instructions on what to say about the showing of "Jewish pictures" in Germany: "Jewish writers, directors, and composers in foreign pictures must not be emphasized. At present, it is impossible to prevent the screening of all foreign pictures in which Jews have participated due to the existing agreements."[61]

That, at least, was the Nazis' position. But there were two sides to the relationship, and the Hollywood studios had some bargaining power too. After all, Frits Strengholt had threatened to quit the German market if *The Prizefighter and the Lady* were banned, and his superiors could easily have transferred him out of the country as soon as the decision was announced. Instead they told him to remain, so he returned to work, defeated and demoralized, and it was around this time that the balance of power shifted discernibly to the German side.

In November 1934, the German government raised the price of import permits for foreign movies from 5,000 to 20,000 Reichsmarks per title.[62] The representatives of the American studios quickly paid a visit to Dr. Seeger's subordinate in the Propaganda Ministry and said that a compromise needed to be reached. They showed him a series of statistics to prove that both parties would benefit from a lower fee, and the following month the fee was adjusted to 10,000 Reichsmarks.[63]

In 1935, the studios encountered more difficulties. Fifty of their movies were permitted in Germany—a decent number—but once again an MGM movie was banned for unknown reasons.[64] The movie in question was a musical that had promised to do very well in Germany, entitled *The Merry Widow*. Frits Strengholt sent his employee, the nephew of the German foreign minister, to meet with Dr. Seeger about the case, and Seeger explained that the film had been banned on account of its director, Ernst Lubitsch. The MGM representative asked whether the problem was that Lubitsch was a Jew, and Seeger refused to say.[65]

In 1936, the American studios' business dealings in Germany reached a critical level. The censors rejected dozens of films, sometimes giving vague reasons (the cast was unsatisfactory, the story was silly), sometimes giving no reasons at all. The smaller companies— Warner Brothers, RKO, Disney, Universal Pictures, and Columbia Pictures—had all left Germany by this point, and only the three largest companies—MGM, Paramount, and Twentieth Century-Fox—remained. By the middle of the year, these three companies had managed to have a combined total of only eight pictures accepted by the censors, when they really needed ten or twelve each just to break even.[66] The new American trade commissioner in Berlin, Douglas Miller, sent an urgent report to his superiors in Washington, DC, in which he explained the reality of the situation:

> It would . . . be unfortunate for German-American relations if our motion picture companies no longer feel that they have any possibility of selling films in Germany or any further interest in considering the German point of view. American film companies are always working under the temptation of portraying foreign countries in an unfavorable light. They must have villains but through the desire of selling pictures in foreign countries are barred from any unfavorable treatment in their pictures of nationals of such countries. . . . If all our film ties with Germany are severed, American film companies will jump at the chance of using stories which will portray Germany and the Germans in an unfavorable light, not because they desire to

injure Germany but because they are hungry for villains and desire a relief from the monotony of always using Americans or unnamed foreigners in this connection.[67]

As the above explanation made clear, the American studios were faced with a difficult decision: they could continue doing business in Germany under unfavorable conditions or they could leave Germany and turn the Nazis into the greatest villains of all time. On July 22, MGM seemed ready to take the plunge. The company announced that it would bow out of Germany if the other two remaining companies, Paramount and Twentieth Century-Fox, did the same.[68] But Paramount and Fox said no. Even though they were not making any money in Germany (Paramount announced a net loss of $580 at the end of 1936), they still considered the German market to be a valuable investment.[69] They had been there for years. They gave direct employment to 400 German citizens, and they employed thousands more for manufacturing purposes. Despite the difficult business conditions, their movies were still extremely popular. If they remained in Germany a while longer, their investment might once again yield excellent profits. If they left, on the other hand, they might never be permitted to return.[70]

A few days later, the studios discovered another reason for remaining in Germany: the head of the local branch of Twentieth Century-Fox, P. N. Brinck, was invited to become a permanent member of the Import and Export Committee of the German Film Chamber. This was quite an honor. The Nazis on the committee assured Brinck "that they [had] no desire to see the American companies leave Germany . . . that they [hoped] to make relations more friendly and [would] try to assist American companies in their difficulties with the censor and the Propaganda Ministry."[71]

The Film Chamber also arranged a meeting between Brinck and Dr. Seeger, and at the meeting Seeger announced, somewhat surprisingly, that the American companies could not bring in pictures employing Jews in any capacity. Brinck asked Seeger on what law he was basing this statement, and Seeger replied that he had been given definite instructions even though there was no official statute in the books. Seeger then said "that the German Government could not very well prepare a list of persons who are considered undesirable, as this would give rise to undesirable publicity, but a working agreement with American motion picture companies might be achieved so that they could get an approximate understanding of what the German Government's attitude was."[72]

The American studios took Seeger's advice to heart. Over the next few years, they put great effort into establishing a new working agreement with the Nazi authorities. Instead of criticizing the anti-Semitic approach to film censorship, as they had done several times in the past, they actively cultivated personal contacts with prominent Nazis. In 1937, Paramount chose a new manager for its German branch: Paul Thiefes, a member of the Nazi Party.[73] And Frits Strengholt adopted a more deferential attitude than he had before: at the request of the Nazi authorities, he divorced his Jewish wife, and she ended up in a concentration camp.[74]

The American studios also became more conciliatory in their regular business activities. Whenever films were rejected by the censors, the studios sent polite letters to their contacts in the administration to propose mutually acceptable solutions. A typical example was Paramount's reaction to the banning of three films, *Give Us This Night*, *The General Died at Dawn*, and *The Texas Rangers*. Upon hearing about the bans, Paramount wrote to the German Film Chamber and speculated on what was objectionable in each case. *Give Us This Night*, the company imagined, had been turned down because the Jewish composer Erich Korngold had written the score, so the company offered to dub in music by a German composer instead. *The General Died at Dawn* had been directed by Lewis Milestone, who had also directed *All Quiet on the Western Front*, so the company offered to slash Milestone's name from the credits. Finally, *The Texas Rangers* contained battle scenes that were too brutal, so the company put together a much milder version.[75] The Film Chamber considered Paramount's request and ended up approving *The Texas Rangers*, which turned out to be a big hit the following year in Germany.[76]

The three remaining American studios carried out a variety of these kinds of schemes in the late 1930s, and at a certain point, one of the studios attempted something particularly ambitious. In January 1938, the Berlin branch of Twentieth Century-Fox sent a letter directly to Hitler's office: "We would be very grateful if you could provide us with a note from the Führer in which he expresses his opinion of the value and effect of American films in Germany. We ask you for your kind support in this matter, and we would be grateful if you could just send us a brief notification of whether our request will be granted by the Führer. Heil Hitler!"[77] Four days later, Twentieth Century-Fox received a reply: "The Führer has heretofore refused in principle to provide these kinds of judgments."[78]

Despite this setback, the studios gradually managed to obtain an understanding of the Nazis' new censorship methods. They figured out which Hollywood actors the Nazis considered undesirable, and they made sure not to submit any films in which these actors played a role. They also found that they could still submit pictures employing Jews as long as they made appropriate adjustments to the credits.[79] As a consequence of their efforts, the studios actually managed to improve their sales figures in this period. In 1937, the studios sold thirty-eight movies in Germany, and in 1938, they sold forty-one, almost as many as in the year before Hitler had come to power.[80] The new working agreement between the Hollywood studios and the Nazis was yielding some good results.

Then came *Kristallnacht*: the savage destruction of thousands of Jewish homes and businesses on November 9 and 10, 1938, followed by a wave of increased anti-Semitic measures around the country. The new spirit pervaded everything in the ensuing weeks, including the film business. On November 22, *Der Angriff* made an announcement that could not have appeared in earlier years: "One-third of Hollywood stars are Jews." The paper proceeded to give sixty-four names of the most prominent Jewish producers, directors, and actors, and added, "There are seven producers named Cohn."[81]

The next day the Propaganda Ministry released an extraordinary document: a "black list" containing the names of around sixty Hollywood personalities (see note).[82] The Ministry explained that if anyone on the list played an important part in an American film, the censors would "not permit [the film's] entry into Germany." Some of the people on the list were well known as Jews, such as Al Jolson and Paul Muni. Others were German émigrés, such as Fritz Lang and Ernst Lubitsch. Still others were prominent anti-Nazis, including Herman J. Mankiewicz and Sam Jaffe, who had attempted to make the first anti-Nazi film *The Mad Dog of Europe*, and even Ernest Hemingway, who had worked on an anti-Nazi documentary. The list went on: it included Jean Arthur, James Cagney, Joan Crawford, Bing Crosby, Theodore Dreiser, Fredric March, Lewis Milestone, Norma Shearer, and Sylvia Sidney. The Nazis had been carefully monitoring events in Hollywood for almost a decade, and the blacklist was the result of their efforts.[83]

From that moment onward, the studios did not need to guess which of their films would be banned in Germany. They could simply go through their holdings and submit the films that did not involve the participation of anyone on the blacklist. Even so, their exports fell dramatically. Only twenty Hollywood movies were screened in Germany in 1939.[84]

But still the studios did not give up. Even when the Second World War broke out in Europe, the studios kept selling their movies in Germany. And while business continued as usual for Paramount and Twentieth Century-Fox, the advent of war brought one final unexpected benefit for MGM.

All the way back in June 1933, the Nazis had passed a law preventing foreign companies from taking their money out of the country. According to the law, foreign companies were required to keep their money in blocked German bank accounts, and they could only spend their money in Germany.[85] The American studios were among the last companies to be subject to the law, but by the end of 1934, they were rapidly accumulating German mark balances in their accounts, and they were trying to decide what to do with their assets.[86]

For Paramount and Twentieth Century-Fox, the solution was simple. Both of these studios were major producers of newsreels in Germany, and they could invest their money locally in cameramen and film stock. They could then capture footage of the latest Nazi events, and they could incorporate this footage into newsreels that they sold all around the world.[87] Here are some of the stories that Twentieth Century-Fox covered in this period:

*Rally of Allegiance to the Führer*: Adolf Hitler greets the national police force from the window of the Chancellery as the Berlin population erupts with thunderous shouts of "Heil!"[88]

*The First Monument of the National Socialist Movement*: In Bayreuth, the head of the German Labor Front Dr. Robert Ley solemnly unveiled a cenotaph in honor of National Socialism.[89]

*Celebration of the Workers of the German Nation*: The Führer speaks at the construction zone of the Autobahn in Unterhaching (from Munich to the border) to open the great labor battle for the year 1934.[90]

*National Holiday of the German People:* The Chancellor gives his salute to the entire Berlin school community in the Berlin Lustgarten. Reichsminister Dr. Goebbels speaks during the festival session of the German Culture Chamber in the Berlin Opera House. On the national labor holiday, the biggest rally that the world has ever seen took place on the Tempelhof field, where the Führer spoke in front of two million comrades.[91]

The law governing the withdrawal of money out of Germany therefore did not adversely affect the business activities of Paramount or Twentieth Century-Fox. These two companies could reinvest their money in local newsreels, and they could then use the German footage all around the world, bringing in excellent profits. But MGM did not make German newsreels, and for years, the company had been trying to work out how to get its money out of the country.[92] Only one method up to this point had been successful: MGM had managed to sell its blocked Reichsmarks to a German bank in exchange for American currency. In the conversion process, however, MGM had incurred massive losses.[93]

In December 1938, one month after *Kristallnacht*, MGM discovered a way to export its profits more effectively. An American trade commissioner explained the process: MGM first loaned the money to certain German firms where credit was "badly needed." MGM then received bonds in exchange for the loan and finally sold these bonds abroad at a loss of around 40 percent—which was a substantial improvement over previous losses. There was just one catch, and it had to do with the firms that were receiving MGM's money in the first place. "The firms in question," the American trade commissioner said, "are connected with the armament industry especially in the Sudeten territory or Austria."[94]

In other words—the largest American motion picture company helped to finance the German war machine.

The collaboration of American movie studios with Nazi Germany was complex and multifaceted, and as the decade progressed, it evolved in a clearly discernible way. More and more, the Nazis dictated the terms of every encounter, and the studios, instead of leaving the German market, did everything they could to remain. As the years passed, fewer American movies were shown in Germany, but as long as the studios pandered to the whims of the Nazi regime, the collaboration remained as strong as ever.

Only at one point late in the decade did anyone mount a serious challenge to the prevailing state of affairs. A powerful organization questioned the very morality of the relationship between Hollywood and Germany and even suggested that the relationship should not be permitted to continue. The organization was not one of the American studios, however, nor was it a pressure group based in the United States. It was the SS.

In order to understand the significance of the challenge, it is necessary to turn back slightly, to the first half of the 1930s. In that period, film critics in Germany had been more than eager to say what they thought about Hollywood movies. The vast majority treated the movies with a sense of awe and astonishment. They praised the Americans' technical superiority, they delighted in the "light comedy touch," and they complimented the deep understanding of the leader principle. Time after time they announced: "Our directors could learn a lot from this American film."[95]

Occasionally, some reviewers gave less favorable opinions. In May 1934, for example, the critic for *Völkischer Beobachter* went to see what was perhaps the worst American movie that ever reached Nazi Germany, *Miss Fane's Baby Is Stolen*. This critic found it painful to watch the main star's dreadful overacting, and the next day his review appeared. "Fine," he said, "we adore and love children too . . . but it would have been better not to show us this film if one intended to invoke the American mentality now as an excuse."[96]

This was a common complaint: a significant number of German film critics felt that the movies they were watching were too American. They therefore dismissed Hollywood productions as kitsch, they attacked the excessive sentimentality of the story lines, and they made fun of the happy endings. Taken as a whole, German film criticism of Hollywood in this early period consisted of a curious mixture of unbridled enthusiasm and predictable anti-Americanism.

Then, in late 1936, Joseph Goebbels abolished film criticism in Germany and ordered journalists to provide "film description" instead.[97] His employees in the Propaganda Ministry began issuing instructions on how to write about specific American movies that were being shown around the country. Here are a couple of examples of what they said: "The American film *Honolulu* (Metro) is full of humorous ideas, refreshingly fast-paced, and contains dance sequences, catchy music, and gags about mistaken identity—a very pleasant entertainment. It is gratifying that it is able to bring harmless amusement to these serious times"; "*Rose-Marie* belongs to that genre of films that wins over an audience seeking entertainment with endearing melodies and beautiful open-air shots. Reviewers can point out that the film is four years old, and that there is a noticeable difference in American film technology between then and now."[98] The vast majority of reviewers adhered to these directives, and as a result, German film writing in the latter half of the 1930s became increasingly bland. The reviews simply gave brief plot summaries along with a few trivial observations about the films in question. True criticism all but disappeared.

Every now and then, however, an article appeared in the German press that was not only thoughtful but also questioned the whole validity of showing American movies in Germany in the first place. In April 1938, a critic named Wilhelm Frels published one such article about the latest technological innovation in Hollywood: the arrival of Technicolor. Frels examined two of the earliest Technicolor movies, *Ramona* and *Wings of the Morning*, both of which had recently been shown in Germany, but unlike everyone else he was not interested in how these films had been improved by the new technology.[99] He was more concerned with how these films had fooled the unsuspecting German public. As he explained: "Colored films love to use colored people because of their more effective skin tone."[100]

He was absolutely right. Both *Ramona* and *Wings of the Morning* had told stories about nonwhites, and both films had lingered on their characters' bodies as objects of attraction and fascination. It is unlikely that any other reviewer had picked up on this connection before.

The first Technicolor picture to be screened in Germany, Frels said, was nothing more than a dirty trick. In its provocative opening scene, an Indian chief named Alessandro stumbled upon a beautiful white woman who was stuck in a tree. He helped her down, and later that evening, he learned that her name was Ramona and that dozens of men had ridden more than forty miles to meet her.[101]

It was one thing for an Indian to be attracted to a white woman, but it was quite another when she was attracted to him. In the days that followed, Ramona and Alessandro spent an increasing amount of time together, and at the peak of their courtship, the Technicolor film captured something absolutely shocking: a white woman in the arms of a man dressed in colorful Indian garb.

That was when the trick was revealed. Ramona's stepmother walked in on the scene and sent the Indian away. Then she took Ramona aside. "You've been brought up in my house . . . as my own daughter," she said. "All the time I've lived in fear that sooner or later the blood of your mother would come out."

"How can you speak that way of my mother?" Ramona protested. "Why, she was your own sister."

"She was not!" the stepmother yelled. "She was an Indian squaw." The stepmother proceeded to explain that Ramona's father, "a man of good family," had made a tragic mistake with a native woman.

Later that night, Ramona left the ranch on which she had been brought up and ran back into Alessandro's arms. As the couple kissed, the image on the screen tried to atone for the earlier, shocking one. Maybe it was the darkness of the night, or maybe it was that of the revelation—whatever the case, the contrast between the two lovers did not seem anywhere near as sharp as before.

Wilhelm Frels was unimpressed by this erasure of racial difference. He thought that it was in bad taste to play games with the issue of mixed marriage, especially after the Nazis had put so much effort into eradicating the problem in Germany. If *Ramona* was bad, however, the next film was even worse. "This subject, which is a bluff in *Ramona*," Frels said, "in *Wings of the Morning* turns out to be a completely unambiguous statement."[102]

Frels was probably not that surprised that *Ramona* had been passed by the censors. He had almost certainly read the Karl May stories that were extremely popular in Germany and that gave a romantic account of the dying Indians. A film like *Ramona* was more or less acceptable in Germany, and it could even be described in Goebbels' newspaper as "the conflict between the brave Indian and the evil white men."[103] *Wings of the Morning* was something else entirely. This film dealt with one of the groups that the Nazis had explicitly selected for persecution. Its title in Germany was *The Gypsy Princess*.

Here, once again, was a Technicolor film that took the side of "colored people." The film showed a white man falling in love with a colorfully dressed gypsy woman and even apologizing to her for the prejudice of his friends: "These people, they've got no imagination, no understanding."[104]

Only this time, it was not a trick. The man did not turn out to be a gypsy in the end. The film was making a completely unambiguous statement in favor of mixed marriage. Frels was disgusted. The first two Technicolor movies that had been screened in Germany, he said, used Technicolor to glorify colored people. He was not sure whether the Americans were doing this out of principle or out of foolishness, but he, for one, was not going to watch the next Technicolor movie to find out.[105]

It was certainly very strange that *Wings of the Morning*—a movie that glorified gypsies—had been permitted in Germany at this particular point in time. Only nine months earlier, Dr. Seeger had banned a Laurel and Hardy picture called *The Bohemian Girl* because it portrayed gypsies in a sympathetic light. "This film essentially gives a false image of the objectionable life of gypsies in a kitschy form," Seeger had explained, "and it has no place in our nation."[106] How, then, could the censors have permitted *Wings of the Morning*, a much more serious picture that explicitly spoke out on behalf of this persecuted people?

Here is the likely answer: Ever since the censors had started checking up on the racial origins of a film's cast and crew, they had been paying less attention to the film itself. They had spent so much of their time researching the background of Hollywood personalities that they had sometimes forgotten to take into account a film's actual content. Consequently, a few titles had slipped through their fingers.

For the remainder of the decade, this phenomenon continued to occur. In the middle of 1938, for example, Paramount submitted a movie called *Shanghai* to the German censors. The movie was about a successful businessman whose father was white and whose mother was a Manchurian princess. (For some reason, whenever a man had relations with a woman of a different race, she always turned out to be a princess.)[107] The entire film was a plea for tolerance and understanding, and it ended with the following lines: "Someday prejudice may die, convention go stale. Men will be judged not for their creed or color but for their merits. We may not live to see that day—I pray God we will."[108]

Because *Shanghai* dealt with the race problem—a subject that was just then very popular in Germany—Paramount submitted it to the censors and promoted it to the Propaganda Ministry. After a long discussion, *Shanghai* was approved, "after much hemming and hawing because [Paramount] didn't have anything better, but not because it dealt with the race problem."[109] The film premiered in Germany in September 1938, and although Hitler found it boring and could not watch it to the end, the German press reviewed it very favorably: "Whenever an earth-shattering problem can be included, like the race problem, the American production companies gladly include it. . . . The fact that the Asian-American intermarriage problem is acted out and solved by two such striking actors as Charles Boyer, the unforgettable lead in *La Bataille*, and Loretta Young will ensure that this film will receive particular attention [in Germany]."[110]

And so *Shanghai*, like *Ramona* and *Wings of the Morning*, was blindly accepted by most German film critics. Only Wilhelm Frels and a few others had noticed (or had dared to notice) that these movies contradicted the official ideology of the Third Reich. But while a small group of isolated film critics could not possibly make a difference, a larger, more powerful organization might.

At the beginning of 1940, a Shirley Temple movie entitled *Susannah of the Mounties* was screened in Germany. The German public adored Shirley Temple—Goebbels called her "a wonderful child"—but this film, like *Ramona*, was about the relationship between whites and Indians in the United States.[111] Given the sensitivity of this subject matter, the Propaganda Ministry carefully told the press how to review it: "In *Susannah of the Mounties* (Fox), the little Shirley Temple reveals her incredible gift with great poignancy. The Wild West plot she has been placed in provides a good setting for this entertainment, too."[112]

The newspapers all followed these instructions and reviewed *Susannah of the Mounties* as an example of harmless entertainment. But the SS—Hitler's major paramilitary organization—appeared to have picked up on something truly disturbing about the picture. Just a few minutes before the end, Shirley Temple pricked her finger and exchanged her blood with the blood of a young Indian boy.[113] The SS soon expressed anger "that films with Shirley Temple are currently being screened in Munich," and added: "We are lodging particular complaints against the press articles that cast *Susannah of the Mounties* in a most positive light."[114]

A few months later, the SS reacted to a different film that was still being screened at theaters throughout Germany: *Ramona*. "The main criticism of the plot was that an Indian, whom the whites had originally hated, was suddenly considered their equal at the moment he converted to Catholicism," the SS said. "It was felt to be incomprehensible that a film whose content so grossly contradicts National Socialist ideology could still be shown."[115]

The SS had picked up on a glaring contradiction, but even this powerful organization could not bring an end to the relationship with the Hollywood studios. The relationship continued, and more American movies that contradicted National Socialist ideology were shown in Germany. The SS was unable to understand how such a thing was possible, but there were two simple reasons: the censors were approving films with little or no regard to content, and the Propaganda Ministry was issuing instructions on how these films needed to be reviewed in the newspapers.

There was one final reason for this strange phenomenon, and it had to do with the people in the audience. The majority of film viewers in Germany were neither as radical as the SS nor as perceptive as Wilhelm Frels. When they went to the movies, they almost certainly did not connect a film's overall message to the purported aims of the Nazi regime. They simply did what everyone else around the world did: they identified with the good guys and against the bad guys. And if the racial policies of the Nazi regime fit more in line with the ideology of the bad guys, it is unlikely that the people in the audience stopped to think about it.

The reception of one last film provides a useful illustration of this point. The film was a musical called *Let Freedom Ring*, and it premiered in Berlin at the end of February 1940. It was written by one of the most prolific screenwriters in Hollywood, Ben Hecht, and Hecht used to play a little game with himself. He would have his hero utter a "few semi-intelligent remarks," and he would try his best to prevent these remarks from being cut out by the producer. In this case, he managed to get them past the Nazi censors.[116]

The setup was conventional enough: A railroad owner named Jim Knox was using dirty business methods against the honest inhabitants of a small town. He offered to buy their land at a low price, and if they refused to sell, he had his men burn their houses down. One evening, he paid a visit to a landowner named Thomas Logan, who was being particularly stubborn. Logan said that his son Steve, a Harvard-educated lawyer, would soon be back to stand up for everyone's rights. At just that moment, Steve walked through the door. He chided his father for getting in the way of the railroads, and he expressed his willingness to cooperate with Jim Knox.[117]

Of course he was lying. He was on the side of his family and friends, but he could not say so openly. His plan was to save the town by seizing on an inalienable right: the freedom of the press. He printed a large number of inflammatory pamphlets, and he secretly distributed them to Knox's foreign workers, urging them to unite and stand up against their tyrannical leader. When this failed, he sang them a song in which he tried to tell them that, as Americans, they were all free. But still he was having difficulties. All the characters in the film, even the bad guys, were simply enjoying the song. Audiences in Germany probably would have enjoyed the song too if it had not been cut from the German version.[118]

One scene in the film, however, was definitely not cut. At the climax, Steve had a debate with Jim Knox in front of the foreign workers, and the dialogue remained. Steve was telling them to stand up for their rights, and Knox was telling them to return to their quarters.

"Will you listen to me once more?" Steve said. "The cattle boats brought you over here but I say you're men."

"Get back to your bunkhouses, all of you!"

"I say you came here looking for . . . liberty and freedom, and you'll not lie down in the mud at Jim Knox's feet."

"Don't listen to him; I'm boss here."

"Your boss calls you the pick of the swill barrels and the riffraff from everywhere. I call you something else. I call you Americans."

"Come on, come on, I'm giving orders"

"THERE'S NO TYRANT TO GIVE ORDERS IN THIS COUNTRY! THERE'S NO MAN BIGGER OR STRONGER THAN YOU ARE IF YOU'LL RAISE YOUR HEADS!"

"Come on sheriff, get him out of here."

And that was when something extraordinary happened. The camera cut to a close-up of Steve, who looked the Third Reich in the face and said: "You Germans and Italians, you Jews and Russians and Irish, *all you who are oppressed*—" And just as Steve was about to give up all hope, his girlfriend Maggie started singing "Let Freedom Ring," and the workers overthrew their tyrannical leader.

It is impossible to know for certain whether the line about Jews was ultimately included in the German version of the film. According to the American records, only three deletions were made for the German version: Steve Logan's song praising the United States as the land of liberty, a reference to a character as an "Irish windmill," and a violent fistfight.[119]

And according to the German censorship report: "Steve speaks to the people who still do not dare to rebel against Knox. When Knox thinks that Steve has lost, Maggie starts to sing the national anthem. Everyone joins in, and the defeated Knox runs away."[120]

Regardless of whether the line about Jews was included, however, the bulk of the speech undoubtedly remained. At this very late point in time, a Hollywood movie was shown in Germany that argued against prejudice and oppression and that urged its audiences to rebel against a tyrannical ruler. The movie was quite successful, playing in Berlin for twenty-one days in its first run, and according to all the reviews, it was generally well liked.[121] But was it really subversive in Nazi Germany? There is no evidence to suggest that anyone thought the film was criticizing Hitler, and one of the reviewers actually came out with the opposite interpretation. After giving a summary of the plot—Steve Logan had stood up to the railroad owner Jim Knox—the reviewer attacked Knox as a "dirty Jewish exploiter."[122] In other words, the reviewer thought that the villain of the film was meant to be a Jew.

More than anything else, this interpretation highlighted the powerlessness of Hollywood movies in this period. Even the movies that contained veiled references to fascism were useless: audiences in Germany could watch them and still come out with interpretations that suited their own purposes. They could identify with the same good guys and against the same bad guys as audiences all around the world and still emerge from the screenings thinking that their system of government was superior to all others.

There was just one type of movie for which this could never be the case: the anti-Nazi movie. Audiences in Germany could not possibly interpret Hollywood feature films favorably if *they* were the bad guys. And consequently, these were the only movies that the German government treated with genuine concern. In turning to these movies, it is necessary to shift back slightly, to the time before the collaboration between Hollywood and the Nazis began.

# "SWITCHED OFF"

"I wrote 'It Can't Happen Here,' but I begin to think it certainly can."[1]
Sinclair Lewis

Hitler was late. He had appointments with two foreign journalists at the Kaiserhof Hotel in Berlin, and he was making them wait.[2] He despised such encounters with strangers. These people expected to meet a great orator, the future dictator of Germany, but for some reason they often emerged disappointed.[3]

He walked through the hotel lobby with his bodyguard and up the stairs to his salon. He said he would see the Italian journalist first. For half an hour, he spoke to this man, and then it was time to meet Dorothy Thompson, an American journalist and wife of the novelist Sinclair Lewis.[4]

As usual, he had requested the questions in advance so he was not surprised by her words. "When you come to power, as I take it you will," she said, "what will you do for the working masses of Germany?"[5]

He found it hard to respond: "Not yet is the whole working class with us . . . we need a new spirit . . . Marxism has undermined the masses . . . rebirth in a new ideology . . . not workers, not employers, not socialists, not Catholics . . . but Germans!" Throughout the tirade, he looked off to a far corner of the room and banged his fist on the table, desperately working himself into a frenzy, all for nothing.[6]

Thompson proceeded to her next question. "When you come to power will you abolish the constitution of the German Republic?"[7]

This time his response was clearer, although his eyes were still searching for the crowd that was not there. "I will get into power legally," he said. "I will abolish this parliament and the Weimar constitution afterward. I will found an authority-state, from the lowest cell to the highest instance; everywhere there will be responsibility and authority above, discipline and obedience below."[8]

Thompson moved on to her final question. "What will you do for international disarmament, and how will you handle France?"[9]

On previous occasions, Hitler had told his people of the need to rearm and then destroy France. But he was being more cautious with foreign correspondents these days. "When the German people are at last really unified, and secure in their own honor," he said, "I believe even France will respect us."[10]

The interview was over. Thompson stood up, chatted briefly with one of the adjutants, and then she was gone.[11] Hitler went on with his regular activities.

A few months later, in March 1932, the interview appeared in William Randolph Hearst's *Cosmopolitan* magazine. It began as follows: "When I walked into Adolf Hitler's salon, I was convinced that I was meeting the future dictator of Germany. In less than fifty seconds I was sure I was not. It took just that time to measure the startling insignificance of this man who has set the world agog."[12]

Previous interviewers had provided transcripts of Hitler's responses, and some had even reflected on his strange manner. But none had thought as deeply about the contrast between his inner and outer selves, and none had ridiculed him to quite this extent: "He is formless, almost faceless, a man whose countenance is a caricature, a man whose framework seems cartilaginous, without bones. He is inconsequent and voluble, ill-poised, insecure. He is the very prototype of the Little Man. A lock of lank hair falls over an insignificant and slightly retreating forehead. The back head is shallow. The face is broad in the cheek-bones. The nose is large, but badly shaped and without character. His movements are awkward, almost undignified and most un-martial. There is in his face no trace of any inner conflict or self-discipline. . . . There is something irritatingly refined about him. I bet he crooks his little finger when he drinks a cup of tea."[13]

Such a man, Thompson said, was not destined to become dictator of Germany. He simply would not get the votes. He might serve briefly as chancellor if he formed a coalition with the Center Party, but ultimately he would be pushed aside. "Oh, Adolf! Adolf!" Thompson wrote, "You will be out of luck!"[14]

Her prediction would later be called a "blunder," a "comico-terrible gaffe"[15]—but Hitler did not see it that way. For a full year following the article's publication, he refused all interviews with American journalists.[16] Upon coming to power, he set up a "Dorothy Thompson Emergency Squad" to translate every word she wrote. He planned to make an example of her as soon as he had the chance.[17]

In August 1934, more than two years after the article first appeared, Thompson was on her way to Germany to cover the political situation. She had made five such trips since the Nazis had come to power, but this time was different: Hitler had just wiped out the dissident elements of his Party by murdering Ernst Röhm and other SA leaders on the Night of the Long Knives.[18] Sinclair Lewis became hysterical for his wife's safety, and it required an entire evening to calm him.[19] But Thompson had no intention of abandoning her trip. She began by investigating conditions in Austria. She then crossed the border into Germany and drove past a youth camp whose motto—"WE WERE BORN TO DIE FOR GERMANY"—sent chills down her spine. She pressed down hard on the accelerator and eventually arrived in Berlin.[20]

Ten days passed without any notable incident occurring. Thompson spent the time interviewing witnesses to the Röhm purge and learning how indiscriminate the murders were. "Men didn't know why they were shot," one storm trooper told her under condition of anonymity. "[Hitler] never forgets anything or forgives it."[21] Shortly afterward, she received a phone call in her hotel room from the porter downstairs. A member of the secret police was waiting to see her, and he presented her with a letter: "It has come to the attention of the authorities that you have recently again arrived in Germany. In view of your numerous anti-German publications in the American press, the German authorities, for reasons of national self-respect, are unable to extend to you a further right of hospitality. To avoid formal expulsion you are therefore requested to interrupt your sojourn in Germany as quickly as possible and leave the domain of the Reich immediately."[22]

Thompson quickly called the U.S. ambassador, William E. Dodd, who told her that she was being expelled primarily for the Hitler interview and also for some articles she had written on the Jewish question. If she did not leave within twenty-four hours, she would be officially escorted to the border. She could not appeal the decision because it came from "the highest authority in the Reich."[23]

Thompson's account of her treatment by the German authorities later appeared in the *New York Times*. "My offense was to think that Hitler is just an ordinary man, after all," she wrote. "That is a crime against the reigning cult in Germany, which says Mr. Hitler is a Messiah sent by God to save the German people—an old Jewish idea. To question this mystic mission is so heinous that, if you are a German, you can be sent to jail. I, fortunately, am an American, so I merely was sent to Paris. Worse things can happen to one."[24]

Thompson was already a well-known critic of Hitler. Now she became a national celebrity. For the remainder of the 1930s, she was the leading American agitator against the Nazis. Her regular column "On the Record" appeared in hundreds of newspapers and reached millions of people. One study estimated that three-fifths of the 250,000 words she wrote in a two-year period were devoted to attacking the Hitler regime.[25]

Her rise to prominence had troubling effects on her marriage, however. Various socialites visited her household to hear about her experiences in Germany, and Sinclair Lewis resented the intrusion. He often walked into the room and saw them all huddled around her, and he said, "Is she talking about *It*?" Then he walked out again. "You with your important little lectures, you with your brilliant people," he later complained. "*You* want to talk about foreign politics, which *I* am too ignorant to understand." More than once he was heard to remark, "If I ever divorce Dorothy I'll name Adolf Hitler as co-respondent."[26]

But he was more interested in the political gatherings than he was letting on. And one topic of conversation particularly fascinated him. Back when Thompson had written up the Hitler interview, she had included one very memorable sentence: "If you want to gauge the strength of the Hitler movement, imagine that in America, an orator with the tongue of the late Mr. Bryan and the histrionic powers of Aimee MacPherson, combined with the publicity gifts of Edward Bernays and Ivy Lee should manage to unite all the farmers, with all the white collar unemployed, all the people with salaries under $3000 a year who have lost their savings in bank collapses and the stock market and are being pressed for payments on the icebox and the radio, the louder evangelical preachers, the American

Legion, the D.A.R., the Ku Klux Klan, the W.C.T.U., Matthew Woll, Senator Borah, and Henry Ford—imagine that, and you will have some idea of what the Hitler movement in Germany means."[27]

Now, Sinclair Lewis was not particularly interested in "what the Hitler movement in Germany means." He was, however, looking for a subject for his next book. Throughout the previous decade—in which he had written numerous best sellers including *Main Street* (1920), *Babbit* (1922), *Arrowsmith* (1925), *Elmer Gantry* (1927), and *Dodsworth* (1929)—critics had often pointed out that he had an uncanny ability to seize on a popular mood and give it definition. "If *Main Street* lives," one critic had shrewdly observed, "it will probably be not as a novel but as an incident in American life." Since winning the Nobel Prize for Literature in 1930, Lewis had struggled to find an idea with as much potency as the ones that had animated him in the past. This one was suddenly starting to seem quite promising.[28]

By 1935, Thompson's sentence had acquired new meaning in American life. There were speculations that the democratic system of government was failing, and certain politicians had arisen whose actions were being interpreted as examples of domestic fascism. If the implication of Thompson's long list of names was that there were already fascist tendencies in the United States, now some people were saying that the United States could actually turn fascist.[29]

By far the most frequently cited example of a fascist American leader was Huey Long, the governor of Louisiana from 1928 to 1932. Long's record of achievements was actually quite impressive: he provided free textbooks to Louisiana students, he vastly improved the state's highway system, and he revised the tax codes to increase the burden on the wealthy gas and oil interests. But Long's methods were questionable. He took jobs away from anyone who opposed him. He treated the passing of legislation as a mere formality. Even some of his supporters considered him a virtual dictator.[30] In Long's own words, "First you must come into power— Power—and then you can do things."[31]

In 1932, Long became a U.S. senator, and in 1934, he announced his Share Our Wealth Plan. He proposed to give every needy family $5,000 per year and to limit the fortunes of the wealthiest citizens to a few million dollars.[32] To achieve this goal, he founded the Share Our Wealth society, and by 1935, the society had 27,000 local branches and more than seven and a half million members. Long had by this stage shaken off his allegiance to Franklin D. Roosevelt and was seriously considering running for president in the 1936 election on a third-party ticket.[33]

It was clear, however, that if Long became president of the United States, and if he were indeed a fascist, he would not be an exact replica of the dictators of Europe. One commentator writing in early 1935 claimed that the difference lay in his casual and even humorous ruling style: "Huey in his green pajamas, holding court in his bedroom, is the natural man . . . Hitler looks through a solitary listener and goes into a near-trance, forgetting everything except the flow of ideas which pours from him. Huey does not ignore his listener; he stands over him shouting, prods him with a gesticulating finger, thumps him with an articulate fist." In other words, this commentator was saying, Huey Long was a fascist of the American variety.[34]

No author was better qualified to handle such material than Sinclair Lewis. He combined firsthand knowledge of the situation in Germany with his unique insights into American life. In the summer of 1935, he followed his wife's instructions from years earlier and imagined what an American dictatorship would look like. His old work routine returned with a vengeance. When some friends asked to come over for a quick visit, Thompson replied that her husband was "working nine hours a day on a novel which he is writing all in one flood with great enthusiasm and to the exclusion of everything else." By mid-July, he had completed the first draft, and in early August, he sent the final product to the printers.[35]

The book, which he called *It Can't Happen Here*, was the most important anti-fascist work to appear in the United States in the 1930s. Lewis envisioned fascism overtaking not only the government but also the mindset of the country. "For the first time in America, except during the Civil War and the World War," he wrote, "people were afraid to say whatever came to their tongues. On the streets, on trains, at theaters, men looked about to see who might be listening before they dared so much as say there was a drought in the West, for someone might suppose they were blaming the drought on the Chief! . . . Every moment everyone felt fear, nameless and omnipresent. They were as jumpy as men in a plague district. Any sudden sound, any unexplained footstep, any unfamiliar script on an envelope, made them startle; and for months they never felt

WHAT WILL HAPPEN WHEN
AMERICA HAS A DICTATOR?

IT CAN'T
HAPPEN
HERE

A Novel by

SINCLAIR LEWIS

The cover of the original edition of Sinclair Lewis' *It Can't Happen Here* (Doubleday, 1935).

secure enough to let themselves go, in complete sleep. And with the coming of fear went out their pride." Lewis probed deeply into this world without ever losing his sense of humor to arrive at sentences that were chillingly convincing. "Under a tyranny," he wrote, "most friends are a liability."[36]

His novel recounted the rise of Berzelius (or "Buzz") Windrip, a Democratic senator who stole the 1936 presidential nomination from Roosevelt and became the first American dictator. Windrip adopted many of Hitler's methods—he recruited uniformed troops to terrorize opponents, he took control of the press, he created an official salute, and he became known as "the Chief"—but he persistently denied that he was a fascist, and he did so with such good humor that everyone believed him. Even the hero of the book, a sixty-year-old newspaperman named Doremus Jessup, briefly succumbed to Windrip's charms before risking his life in an effort to destroy the dictatorship.

The plot of *It Can't Happen Here* was therefore relatively straightforward. The politics were not. Up to this point, the loudest warnings against an imminent fascism in America, and the harshest attacks on Huey Long, had come from the left. In early 1935, *The Nation* had run numerous articles on homegrown fascism, and later in the year, the public intellectual Carey McWilliams had published a pamphlet on anti-Semitic organizing in Los Angeles.[37] But Sinclair Lewis had no intention whatsoever of uniting with the left out of a common anti-fascist sympathy. Indeed, Lewis' whole motivation for writing *It Can't Happen Here* was uncertain. He may have genuinely believed that Long was the American version of Hitler, or he may have despised Long for the same reason that intellectual elites often despise populist leaders—out of a need to assert superiority. Whatever the case, he lampooned everyone in the book—Huey Long, the Communists, and liberals for thinking "It can't happen here" in the first place—only to return to a passionate defense of traditional American values at the end. "More and more, as I think about history," his hero concluded, "I am convinced that everything that is worth while in the world has been accomplished by the free, inquiring, critical spirit, and that the preservation of this spirit is more important than any social system whatsoever. But the men of ritual and the men of barbarism are capable of shutting up the men of science and of silencing them forever."[38]

Soon after the publication of *It Can't Happen Here*, a group of writers affiliated with the Communist Party tried to win Sinclair Lewis over to their cause. They invited him to a dinner where half a dozen members praised his book profusely. Lewis stood up to respond. "Boys, I love you all," he said, "and a writer loves to have his latest book praised. But let me tell you, it isn't a very good book—I've done better books—and furthermore I don't believe any of you have *read* the book; if you had, you would have seen I was telling you all to go to hell. Now, boys, join arms; let all of us stand up and sing, 'Stand Up, Stand Up, for Jesus.'" And as a couple of the guests rushed out of the room, the others did exactly as Lewis said.[39]

Lewis knew why the Communists were trying to get him on their side: his book had been a big success. The trade sales in the United States amounted to more than 94,000 copies and the total sales to more than 320,000.[40] Lewis would never attain such figures again. And yet there was a definite limit to his achievement. His book had sold very well, but it was hardly popular on a mass scale. If *It Can't Happen Here* were to have any real impact, it would need to reach a much wider audience.

And here was where Dorothy Thompson's perceptions became especially relevant. Unlike other critics, she had actually learned from Hitler. She had been profoundly influenced by his whole approach toward propaganda. She quoted him as follows: "One must judge a public speech not by the sense it makes to scientists who read it next day, but by the effect which it has on the masses." She agreed. In her famous interview, she announced that she had no intention of writing about Hitler in the manner of a meticulous historian. The times were moving too fast to allow for such a luxury. Rather, she said, "Ours is the age of the reporter."[41]

In a slightly expanded, book-length version of the Hitler interview that Thompson released a few months later, she said something even more revealing. She included dozens of documentary photographs that had not appeared in the original article, and, once again, she quoted Hitler to justify her decision: "Many would rather look at the presentation of a case in pictures, than to read a long text. The Picture clarifies everything immediately and often does all that long and boresome reading can accomplish."[42] Thompson was very consciously turning Hitler's own methods against him: first using unpretentious writing to make fun of him, then using photos to enforce her claims. There was just one further step she could take. In a sentence that had appeared on the same page of *Mein Kampf* as the above passage, and that Thompson had left out of her book, Hitler had mentioned the most powerful weapon of all. "The picture *in all its forms up to the film*," he had said, "has greater possibilities."[43]

Thompson undoubtedly brought these statements to her husband's attention, for the fictional dictator in *It Can't Happen Here*, Buzz Windrip, said many of the same things. "You can win over folks to your point of view much better in the evening, when they are tired out from work and not so likely to resist you," Windrip once proclaimed.[44] Hitler had said exactly this in *Mein Kampf*, but unlike the fictional dictator, he had gone on to draw out the implications for his favorite form of entertainment:

"The same applies even to a movie. This is important because in the theater it might be said that perhaps the actor does not take as much pains in the afternoon as at night. But a film is no different in the afternoon than at nine in the evening. No, the *time* itself exerts a definite effect."[45]

Now, none of this might have amounted to much under ordinary circumstances. Thompson might simply have been alerting her husband to these passages to round out his portrayal of an American dictator. Her references to the power of the picture in her own work might have been another joke at Hitler's expense. But a single fact casts her contribution in a different light. By the time Sinclair Lewis' novel was published in October 1935, MGM had already purchased the screen rights.[46] From the beginning, it seems, *It Can't Happen Here* had been envisioned as a movie.

And not just any movie: MGM planned to assemble some of its greatest talent to make one of the most controversial productions of the decade. With its business in Germany dwindling, the studio was actually thinking of turning Hitler's own methods against him. *It Can't Happen Here* was going to be the first piece of anti-fascist propaganda to reach a mass audience.

No expense was spared. MGM asked one of the highest-paid screenwriters in Hollywood, Sidney Howard, to do the script. Howard was the obvious choice. He had been nominated for the Academy Award for Best Adapted Screenplay for his version of Sinclair Lewis' *Arrowsmith*, and his stage version of *Dodsworth* was still playing at theaters around the country.[47] MGM gave him an advance copy of the novel and offered him $22,500 plus $3,000 per week to write the script.[48] This was a colossal sum, and Howard badly needed to pay off the mortgage on his farm.[49] It did not take him long to accept.

Still, the job was not going to be an easy one. Howard was a tireless worker and a perfectionist, and Lewis' book, which frighteningly recast the nation under the Chief, was not without its problems. Above all—and this was a criticism of Lewis' work in general—his characters had no real depth. "I loathe this stinking, synthetic, phoney piece of tripe that Lewis has written," Howard told his wife early in the process.[50] "It isn't easy to write about marionettes and there isn't room, with all this synthetic material, to make people of Lewis' marionettes. . . . As I said yesterday to my director [J. Walter Ruben]: anybody can put two marionettes into bed together but when they get there nothing happens and you have to make the little marionettes yourself."[51] Howard was considered an expert at adapting material for the screen, and his method—which he termed "dramatizing by equivalent"—often led him to invent rather than replicate scenes to achieve the novelist's intended effect.[52] The problem in this case was that he did not know what Lewis' intended effect was, despite the fact that Lewis was available for consultation.

Nevertheless, Howard believed in the project. "Almost for the first time," he told one executive, MGM was going "to carry the American screen into the field of living controversy."[53] The sheer magnitude of the project inspired him. He reread *It Can't Happen Here*, and he started to have some ideas. The novel, he thought, was a chronicle of protest against an imaginary political situation. Its hero, Doremus Jessup, courageously defended American institutions from the tyranny of fascism.[54] This part he found plausible enough. But he was unsure how to convince American audiences that they would ever have surrendered their rights to a demagogue in the first place. He could not accept Lewis' idea "that a charlatan who is nothing but charlatan could get to be president of this country." The characterization simply seemed wrong. Finally, after much deliberation, he came up with a solution. The fictional president, Buzz Windrip, could be a convincing figure if he actually believed what he was saying. His sincerity might win the confidence of the people.[55]

The film was starting to take shape in Howard's mind. He envisioned a vehicle for two stars, both of whom were key players at MGM. Lionel Barrymore—an instantly recognizable, middle-aged actor with a warbly voice full of conviction—was well suited to play Doremus Jessup. And Wallace Beery—a huge, likeable villain who was so honest and ordinary that he probably could have been an American dictator—would play Buzz Windrip. The film would shift between the experiences of these two men through a sustained technical device: the scenes involving Jessup would be shot normally, while the scenes involving Windrip would be shot like newsreels. The result would be a distinctive picture combining human drama with a believable account of the new political conditions.[56]

That was the idea, anyway. But as Howard sat down to write, he found that he was having trouble getting started. The material was more challenging than anything he had done before, and it did not help that his office at MGM was noisy and unpleasant.[57] "I was an idiot ever to take this assignment," he told his wife.[58] "The crux is to get 'It Can't Happen Here' into production and that cannot happen here or anywhere until I have completed . . . the script."[59] He was getting frustrated. He snapped at his wife whenever she forgot to call him.[60] Then, one day in late November, something clicked. He had been planning to begin the picture with the largest possible close-up of Buzz Windrip's face ("how fine," he thought, "if it is also Wallace Beery's face") and to follow this with a long, drawn-out political campaign.[61] But he changed his mind. He threw out everything he had and started again.

The setting was Fort Beulah, a small town in Vermont. A family was out on picnic on a sunny afternoon. It was a pleasant occasion, and the view was spectacular, and at just the right moment, the father, Doremus Jessup, crept back into his car and switched on the radio. The presidential candidate for one of the major parties was screaming over the airwaves: "I, Buzz Windrip, am the only true, genuine and permanent remedy! And they can throw all the legal and political switches they've got on the line! I'm one locomotive they can't derail or sidetrack!" The crowd responded with an ovation, but Doremus just shook his head.[62]

The scene shifted to Washington. The men behind the Windrip campaign, Lee Sarason and Dewey Haik, were obvious bad guys—ruthless schemers who preached the wonders of fascism whenever they were alone. But Windrip himself was "not at all a bad fellow," and to prove it, he told everyone with complete sincerity that he was on their side. He was a friend of business and he was a friend of labor, he loved immigrants and he loved hundred percent Americans, he was in favor of disarmament and he was in favor of rearmament. And one fateful night, when the country was drunk on his promises, he was elected president of the United States. All around the country, people were celebrating. Nobody seemed to be wondering what the Minute Men—Windrip's paramilitary organization—would do now that he was in power. Even in the small editorial office of the *Daily Informer* in Fort Beulah, Doremus was not overly worried. "There's no harm in 'em, though," he told himself. "Not way up here in Vermont . . ."[63]

A few days later, Windrip moved into the White House. He entered the Oval Office, removed his shoes, and wiggled his toes. "Bet this was the first thing Lincoln did when he got here," he said. Meanwhile, Sarason and Haik were taking care of more important matters. They armed the Minute Men, they abolished the Supreme Court, and they suspended Congress. A mob surrounded the White House in protest, and Sarason and Haik convinced Windrip to give a terrible order to his Minute Men. "Get that mob, boys!" Windrip yelled. "Help me to help you save America!" Journalists condemned the gunning down of innocent civilians, but once again Sarason and Haik knew what to do. They took control of the press, they announced that the mob had been composed of dangerous radicals, and they adopted a series of measures to fight the "Communist plot." Jobs were taken away from foreigners. Concentration camps were created for anyone who opposed the new regime.[64] ("The brutality of the concentration camp," Howard noted in his treatment, "is so much a part of today's world history that it requires full development in this picture.")[65]

Then the setting changed again, this time to a movie theater somewhere in America. A title flickered on the screen—"Official Government Newsreel No. 1"—and Windrip appeared. "Well, folks," he said, "we've been turning our minds to making your government more efficient and we're blest if we see any use keeping all these separate states." He pointed to a map that revealed that the country was now divided into seven new provinces, and Lee Sarason walked onto the screen. "Subject to your approval, Mr. President, I've taken the liberty of revising the national flag. You will see that the now antiquated stars have given way to a steering wheel symbolizing your guidance of the ship of state." Windrip looked on in approval, and the announcer said: "And those of you who've been wondering about that five thousand a year you were promised. . . ."[66]

The scene shifted back to Doremus Jessup, and the music turned somber. As he wandered the streets of his hometown on a sad autumn afternoon, he saw nothing less than the end of America. Women were waiting in illegal breadlines, Minute Men were spying on their friends and on each other, immigrants had all been taken away. A book burning was in progress, and a little girl was crying because she had lost her copy of *Alice in Wonderland*. Doremus made sure not to console her because he knew that such actions would be reported to the authorities. He just turned around and headed for home. As he walked through his front door, his eight-year-old grandson gave him the Windrip salute. His daughter mumbled something about the horror of bringing children into this world.[67]

And then came the turning point. The unsuccessful presidential candidate from the previous election, Walt Trowbridge, escaped to Canada and began a movement to restore democracy in America. Trowbridge had not appeared much in the picture up to this point ("Old Americanism is dismally undramatic," Howard had noted), but now Trowbridge was back, and he asked Doremus to be his man in Vermont.[68] The sixty-year-old newspaper editor saw the error of his ways. "All us lazy-minded Doremuses are responsible," he declared. "I used to think that wars and depressions were brought on by diplomats and bankers. They were brought on by us liberals . . . because we did nothing to stop 'em."[69]

Doremus was awake now. He spent all his time writing and editing an underground newspaper that exposed the horrors of the Windrip regime. He worked tirelessly, and one night, his family asked him to read something aloud. As he began to speak, the crimes of the Minute Men came to life on the screen. One horrific image dissolved into another. And as more and more people around the country became aware of what was really going on—and as they recognized that the official newsreels were full of lies—the opposition to the Windrip government steadily grew.[70]

Meanwhile, Sarason and Haik were getting worried. They turned all their attention to figuring out who was responsible for publishing the damaging newspaper. It did not take long. One afternoon a truck pulled up in front of Doremus Jessup's house, and Minute Men hauled him off to a concentration camp. The scenes that followed were the bleakest of the entire picture. The camp was a converted old boys' school; barbed wire sealed off the area; "Hurrah for the Chief!" was written on the walls. Doremus passed through two gates and was placed in a cell where he experienced terrible pain.[71] ("A little torture goes a long way on the screen," Howard noted.)[72]

After several months, Doremus was close to death. The guards called him "a living corpse. Like the American spirit." Only when he had almost given up hope did the country's fortunes start to change. Doremus escaped from the camp. His daughter Mary, a trained pilot, flew head-on into Lee Sarason's plane. Dewey Haik assassinated Windrip and became the new American dictator. An organized resistance to the fascist tyranny emerged, and the United States became embroiled in a civil war.[73] ("Lewis has written our picture for us here, almost shot for shot, and at greater length than we can use.")[74]

And then, one hot day, an old truck inscribed "Dr. Dobb's Famous Remedies" was pulled over at the side of the road, and thirty Minute Men on motorcycles were passing by. When they were out of sight, Dr. Dobbs—or, as it turned out, Doremus Jessup—got back in his truck and drove to a local farmyard. He gave machine guns and ammunition to a group of farmers, and they gave him shelter for the night. The next thing he knew, he was dreaming about the family picnic from the beginning of the movie, and his wife was calling out to him. But the noise turned out to be one of the farmers telling him that it was 5 AM, so Doremus lit a cigarette and got ready to leave. Another farmer started whistling the verse of a well-known Union song ("John Brown's body lies a-mouldering in the grave"), and as Doremus drove away he sang, "But his soul goes marching on!" The music rose to full volume, and the film ended with America still up for grabs.[75]

Howard stopped writing. He looked over the script. He felt almost elated.[76] It was, in his words, "the toughest job I have ever done in my life."[77] He sent a copy to Sinclair Lewis with the usual modesty ("I don't know why you should want to read this script. I don't know how anyone can ever read a motion picture script. . . . If you do look through it and feel like making any notes requesting either cuts or additions, you may be sure that your observations will receive all possible attention.")[78] One week later Lewis replied: "I have read it word for word. I have the greatest admiration for it and had a great deal of excitement out of reading it." Lewis offered just a few suggestions for the ending of the picture, which Howard discarded immediately.[79]

Meanwhile, following normal practice, MGM sent a preliminary copy of the script to the Hays Office for inspection. Ever since July 1934, when Will Hays had put Joseph Breen in charge of the enforcement of the Production Code, the Office's censorship recommendations had become more stringent. Breen tended to give detailed recommendations to the studios, and most of the time, although certainly not always, the studios followed his advice.

In the case of *It Can't Happen Here*, Breen had a different reaction. The Production Code dealt mostly with issues of morality, and his main problem with the script was political. He therefore admitted that *It Can't Happen Here* was more or less acceptable under the provisions of the code, and he took the unusual step of referring the matter back to Will Hays. He explained to Hays that he had two major concerns with the proposed picture. First, he said, "it is hardly more than a story portraying the Hitlerization of the United States of America. It is an attempt to bring home to American citizens, that which is transpiring in Germany today." He wondered whether as a matter of policy the American film industry should be willing to sponsor a picture of this kind. Second, he worried that *It Can't Happen Here* would have a damaging impact on Hollywood's foreign markets.[80]

He then wrote to Louis B. Mayer to inform him that Hays was now reviewing the case.[81] Several weeks passed, and Mayer heard nothing from Hays—so Mayer did nothing himself. *It Can't Happen Here* went straight into preproduction. Basil Rathbone and Jimmy Stewart took on small parts.[82] Lionel Barrymore grew a beard and was looking more like Doremus Jessup every day.[83] Sidney Howard cut all of Barrymore's romantic scenes from the picture, explaining to Sinclair Lewis that "Old actors who can play love scenes without being revolting on the screen are extremely hard to find. Turn to your novel scenes of Doremus and Lorinda in bed together and then try on your mind's eye a photograph of any old actor you can think of and you will see that the picture is both ludicrous and unpleasant."[84]

After making these and other revisions, Howard decided to remain in Los Angeles on MGM's payroll. He had grown so attached to the project that he could not bear the thought of someone else making changes to his script.[85] He was especially worried that Louis B. Mayer would attempt to turn *It Can't Happen Here* into an anti-Roosevelt picture in anticipation of the upcoming election.[86] He ended up accepting an offer from Samuel Goldwyn to adapt Sinclair Lewis' *Dodsworth* for the screen partly so that he could watch *It Can't Happen Here* go into production.[87]

This turned out to be a good decision, for a couple of weeks before shooting was scheduled to begin, Louis B. Mayer received a seven-page letter from Breen in which he was urged not to make the picture at all. "This story is of so inflammatory a nature, and so filled with dangerous material that *only the greatest possible care* will save it from being rejected on all sides," Breen wrote. Breen requested sixty sets of cuts—an outrageous number—and then said that even if these cuts were made, *It Can't Happen Here* would be subjected to "the most minute criticism on all sides," and that "this criticism may result in enormous difficulty to your studio."[88]

Yet despite the harshness of Breen's words, the warning was ultimately a hollow one. Six weeks earlier, Breen had turned the entire matter over to Hays, asking whether industry policy should permit such a picture to be made—and Hays had not said no. Breen's only remaining course of action was to cause difficulties for the studio by recommending a massive number of cuts. Even as he did this, he was forced to add the disclaimer: "The Production Code Administration has no responsibility from the policy angle. . . . The judgment ventured herein is *not* to be construed as having any bearing whatsoever on this policy angle."[89]

Upon receiving Breen's letter, MGM sought out legal advice. Alvin M. Asher of the firm Loeb, Walker and Loeb read Howard's script and found thirteen instances that could potentially give rise to litigation or were simply in bad taste. "In most of the cases," Asher wrote, "I think the possible grounds for objection can be removed with slight changes."[90] Sam Eckman, the head of MGM in England, was more pessimistic. "Have read Can't Happen script," he cabled, "and if treatment reflects on dictatorship prevalent European countries will have extreme difficulty getting picture passed censors." He went on to cite six problematic aspects of the script.[91]

Louis B. Mayer was told about all these objections, and he decided to push ahead with *It Can't Happen Here* anyway. "[The squawks] have been loud and agonized," Sidney Howard wrote to a friend, "and I find myself amazed at the stubbornness with which Metro-Goldwyn persists in its determination to make the picture. The only instructions I have received from Mr. Louis B. Mayer were not to pull my punches. Explain his interest if you can. I can't explain it."[92] Howard spent nearly two weeks going through all sixty of Breen's recommendations and making the necessary changes, and on February 12, 1936, he noted in his diary, "Finally got the script in—and pray God it may not be longer than ever!"[93] Little did he know that just as he was putting the final touches on his script, someone else was taking much more effective action against the film.

The trouble began with a real estate agent in Philadelphia named Albert H. Lieberman. When Lieberman heard that Louis B. Mayer was turning *It Can't Happen Here* into a motion picture, he panicked and wrote to his local rabbi: "It seems inconceivable to me that men of their intelligence do not understand that the making of a few more dollars for their Company out of a piece of business of this kind will result in repercussions that will make even them uncomfortable."[94]

Under ordinary circumstances, Lieberman's letter would have had absolutely no impact on MGM's plans to make the picture. But Lieberman's rabbi happened to be William H. Fineshriber, the chair of the film committee of the Central Conference of American Rabbis, and in the preceding years, this organization had been fighting the prevalent charge that Jews were responsible for bringing immorality to the screen. In 1934, Fineshriber had joined with Protestant and Catholic leaders in a crusade to eradicate such immorality, and in early 1935, he had spent three weeks in Hollywood with some of the most powerful men in the business. By the end of his stay, he had cultivated excellent relations with Louis B. Mayer and Will Hays, both of whom he had praised publicly for their efforts to reform motion pictures.[95]

On February 7, 1936, Fineshriber wrote to Mayer about *It Can't Happen Here*: "I have considered the problem at great length, and I am of the opinion that a film version of that story, howsoever interpreted and directed, will have anything but a beneficial effect upon the Jewish Problem. More and more, I am convinced that during these highly critical days for the Jewish people, here and elsewhere, we ought not to thrust the Jew and his problems too much into the limelight. I am quite sure that any interpretation of the story made by your firm will be forceful and certainly not seemingly detrimental to the Jewish cause, but there are times when to say nothing is better than to say something favorable."[96] Then Fineshriber wrote to Will Hays: "The only wise method to pursue in these days of virulent anti-Semitism is to have no picture in which the Jewish Problem is ventilated."[97] Finally Fineshriber wrote to another powerful executive at MGM, Nicholas Schenck: "I know full well that the picture, if produced by you, will be a splendid pro-Jewish and anti-Fascist interpretation, but I believe that now is the time for us to keep silent. If the story could be told without allowing the Jewish problem to be presented, it might not be so bad, but I can't, for the life of me, see how you can divorce the two."[98]

As it happened, MGM had gone to great lengths to divorce the two. In April 1934, the problematic picture *The House of Rothschild* had played at theaters throughout the United States, and ever since then, the Anti-Defamation League had urged the studios not to refer to Jews in any of their productions. In the case of *It Can't Happen Here*, Sidney Howard had originally included numerous instances of anti-Semitism and persecution, but MGM had ordered significant revisions.[99] In the new version, the Windrip government continued to persecute Jewish-looking characters and even hauled many of them off to concentration camps, but these characters were never officially classified as Jews. Instead they were simply called "foreigners."[100]

Fineshriber did not know that MGM had taken these steps, and he probably did not even know about the Anti-Defamation League's efforts to remove Jewish characters from American movies. But his letter provided the Hays Office with exactly the ammunition it needed. Will Hays discussed the matter privately with Louis B. Mayer, and a few days later, on February 13, 1936, MGM canceled *It Can't Happen Here*.[101] Hays wrote to Fineshriber the next day to say that he was pleased and to tell him that Louis B. Mayer would call later that day.[102]

The actual combination of factors that led Mayer to cancel *It Can't Happen Here* will probably never be known. The decision was shrouded in mystery from the day it was announced.[103] Even Sidney Howard was never given any satisfactory explanation. On February 14, just before leaving Hollywood to seek solace with his family, the screenwriter expressed his confusion to MGM: "The only feeling that comes clear to me is that I have somehow cracked Metro-Goldwyn's safe and made off with a lot of money to which I am not entitled." Then he edged closer to his true feelings: "One of the heart-aches about writing for pictures is that writers are not often allowed to maintain any continuous enthusiasm for them."[104] His diary entry for the same day revealed an even more troubled state of mind: "Too upset by the fate of 'It CAN'T HAPPEN HERE' to make any sense at all. To Berkeley by the night train and an awful time catching it. Rain in sheets and streets in rivers."[105]

Sinclair Lewis had a different reaction. He knew all about the Hays Office's criticism of the screenplay, and he naturally assumed that Will Hays had banned the picture himself. On February 15, he publicly lashed out at the so-called "movie czar": "The world is full today of Fascist propaganda. The Germans are making one pro-Fascist film after another, designed to show that Fascism is superior to liberal democracy. . . . But

Mr. Hays actually says that a film cannot be made showing the horrors of fascism and extolling the advantages of liberal democracy because Hitler and Mussolini might ban other Hollywood films from their countries if we were so rash. Democracy is certainly on the defensive when two European dictators, without opening their mouths or knowing anything about the issue, can shut down an American film causing a loss of $200,000 to the producer. I wrote 'It Can't Happen Here,' but I begin to think it certainly can."[106]

Will Hays immediately denied all of Lewis' charges. He said that he was not in a position to ban the film and that MGM had acted alone.[107] Louis B. Mayer agreed. "The picture was abandoned because it would cost too much," he said in an official statement. "If all this talk continues perhaps we will find it profitable to make it at once."[108] Samuel Goldwyn also rushed to Hays' defense: "It is well known that the Hays organization does not ban films, but cooperates with the producer while the picture is being made." Goldwyn added that the picture was withdrawn from production "probably" because of "casting difficulties"—the standard excuse that was given whenever movies were canceled.[109]

Officially, of course, Sinclair Lewis had made a mistake. The Hays Office did not ban *It Can't Happen Here*, nor did it have the power to do so. In every other respect, however, Lewis' statement was accurate. The Hays Office had discouraged MGM from making *It Can't Happen Here* even though the German and Italian governments had apparently not said a word against the picture. Indeed, if anything, Lewis should have gone further in his attack, for ever since MGM's *Gabriel over the White House*, the Hollywood studios had themselves released "one pro-Fascist film after another"—films that expressed dissatisfaction with the slowness and inefficiency of the democratic form of government.

But as Lewis pointed out, the opposite—a film advocating liberal democracy over fascism—could not have been made in the United States at this time. If fascist tendencies existed in America, Lewis was saying, the events around the film revealed them more forcefully than he ever could have in a novel. After all, he was not at all certain that the United States was headed for dictatorship when he wrote *It Can't Happen Here*. Even Dorothy Thompson had told him, "I really think you should consider making it an uproarious satire. I don't believe we *could* make fascism."[110] On top of everything else, there was a very simple reason why the United

States could not have adopted a fascist system of government in this period: on September 8, 1935, Huey Long was shot as he walked from the chamber of the State Capitol in Baton Rouge, and thirty hours later, he was dead. Sinclair Lewis had just sent his manuscript to the publishers at the time, and he had been forced to make a few last-minute changes as a result.[111] But he understood as well as anybody that the event had profound implications for his book. With Huey Long out of the picture, there was no longer any obvious figure threatening to bring fascism to the United States. *It Can't Happen Here* had turned from an urgent warning to a cautionary tale overnight.

And yet five months later, with Long all but forgotten, with Lewis' book sales in the hundreds of thousands, and with Howard's screenplay finally completed, the most powerful men in Hollywood had decided in a closed meeting that they could not film a purely imaginary portrayal of fascism in America. The final sentence of Sinclair Lewis' statement to the press was more than just a quip. Lewis was saying that while his book was hypothetical at best, the decision to cancel the movie had actually happened. The authorities had chosen not to screen a warning about the fragility of the democratic system of government to the American people. And it was no coincidence that the day after Lewis issued his statement, representatives of the German and Italian governments came forward to lend MGM their support. The representatives announced that they were pleased that *It Can't Happen Here* was not being turned into a movie, and the German spokesman said that the United States had avoided an official protest from Berlin by arriving at the decision. He added that Sinclair Lewis was a "full-blooded Communist."[112]

The very same day, like any full-blooded Communist, Lewis seized on all the publicity to promote his book. "Read it and see for yourself!" proclaimed a massive advertisement in the major newspapers. "Hollywood can censor every motion picture theatre in the country, *but it cannot yet censor your bookseller.*"[113] Six months later, Lewis profited even further from the decision by accepting a commission from the Federal Theater of the Works Progress Administration. His stage version of *It Can't Happen Here* opened simultaneously in eighteen cities across the United States on October 27, 1936, and it enjoyed an enormously successful run. Only the critics were disappointed, and with good reason: the play was an unconvincing, diluted piece of work compared to Sidney Howard's magnificent screenplay.[114]

Over the next two years, many people tried to get their hands on that screenplay, but MGM owned the rights, and Howard did not want to give it to anybody anyway. He seemed to want to forget the whole experience.[115] He wrote a few more scripts for the studios, including the first draft of *Gone with the Wind*, and then, on August 23, 1939, the day that the German-Soviet Nonaggression Pact was signed, he was crushed to death by a tractor on his farm in the Berkshires.[116] His abandoned screenplay lay untouched in the MGM vault.[117]

*It Can't Happen Here* could have been Hollywood's first great anti-fascist picture. It could have been the moment at which the studios abandoned their policy of collaboration and attacked Hitler's chosen form of government. It could have been a triumph for democracy and American culture. Instead, it was canceled at the last moment, and Hollywood remained at peace with Germany. In the long series of events leading to the cancellation of the picture, however, one voice was curiously absent: that of the German consul in Los Angeles, Georg Gyssling.

Gyssling had been born in 1893 in the village of Walzen, which at the time was a part of Germany. He had joined the German Foreign Office shortly after the World War, and he had served as a consul in a few cities, including a six-year stint in New York. In 1931, he had become a member of the Nazi Party, and in March 1933, he had been sent to Los Angeles, where he had quickly forged close ties to the Friends of the New Germany (later the German American Bund).[118] His efforts to spread Nazi propaganda throughout California had greatly worried local Jewish organizations, and on one occasion in 1935, a Jewish representative had tried to meet with Gyssling at the German consulate.[119]

"Have you any relatives or friends in Germany?" Gyssling's subordinate had asked as he looked at the visitor's card.

"No," the Jewish representative replied. "Do you think for a moment I would give you my card if I had any relatives in Germany?"

The subordinate laughed. "You really believe that I wanted your card so I could have your relatives killed in Germany?"

The Jewish representative laughed too. "There have been rumors to that effect," he said, and then he left.[120]

Georg Gyssling's propaganda activities in the 1930s were well known, but he had another, even more sinister job: to collaborate with the American studios. Within a few months of his arrival in Los Angeles, he worked out exactly how to do this. He told the studios to make changes to their pictures about Germany, and he threatened to expel them from the German market, in accordance with Article Fifteen of the German film regulations, if they did not cooperate. Very quickly, he kicked Warner Brothers out of Germany for not making changes to *Captured!*, a film set in a German prison camp during the World War. Then, in early 1934, he convinced the studios to boycott *The Mad Dog of Europe*, a film about his government's persecution of the Jews.

In all of the remaining archival materials, there is no evidence to suggest that Gyssling issued any complaint about *It Can't Happen Here*. But Gyssling was by no means inactive in this period. In late 1935, when *It Can't Happen Here* was being adapted for the screen, he took action against a different MGM picture called *Rendezvous*. This picture was concerned with German espionage agents operating in the United States during the World War, and while it was still being previewed, Gyssling wrote a letter to the Hays Office: "Though I have not seen this picture myself, I beg to draw your attention to it, as its showing might result in the unfortunate difficulties so well known to us."[121]

The Hays Office responded to Gyssling by suggesting that he watch the film and note down his objections to it. At this point, the official correspondence ended: Gyssling did not send any reply. Nevertheless, within a short time MGM made several physical changes to *Rendezvous*. The studio cut around ten minutes of footage from the print, including one crucial word from the climax. In the original version, the U.S. assistant secretary of war had announced to the hero, "You've helped us trap the head of the German spy ring." In the final version—and it is still noticeable in the remaining copies of the print—the word "German" was muted from the assistant secretary of war's speech.[122]

The official correspondence on *Rendezvous*, along with the physical evidence of the film itself, provides indisputable proof that Gyssling was in contact with MGM during this period. He first complained to the Hays Office about the film, and then, without any assistance from the Hays

Office, the film was changed. If he had made a complaint about *It Can't Happen Here* a few months later, he would not have bothered going to the Hays Office; he would have gone straight to the studio. And in such a scenario, no evidence of his complaint would remain, for there is no archive of MGM production correspondence for this period.

Whether Gyssling was involved in the cancellation of *It Can't Happen Here* will probably never be known. But even if Gyssling were not directly involved, his presence in Los Angeles undoubtedly affected MGM's decision. Ever since 1933, he had been putting his energies into "educating and training" the Hollywood studios about German national feeling.[123] He had created the system of collaboration that made his position on any potential anti-fascist film obvious. Consequently, to paraphrase Sinclair Lewis, Gyssling did not need to open his mouth to have *It Can't Happen Here* abandoned. The producers at MGM already knew what he would have said.

Finally, regardless of whether Gyssling took any action against *It Can't Happen Here*, he certainly benefited from the outcome. The following year, he did a couple of things that he had never attempted before.

In early February 1937, Gyssling called up Warner Brothers, the studio that he had personally expelled from the German market several years earlier. He had heard that the studio was making a film about the French government's wrongful conviction of Alfred Dreyfus, a Jewish officer, for the transmission of military secrets to the German government in 1894. The film was obviously going to condemn one of the most notorious instances of anti-Semitism in the recent past, and Gyssling was determined to take action.

The associate producer, who was of course under no obligation to speak to Gyssling, picked up the phone: "I naturally received several calls from Dr. Gyssling, the German Consul, and could not avoid talking with him—which I did. He was well aware, I don't know through whom, that we are making a Dreyfus picture and he was very much worried in what respect Germany would figure in this. He wanted to make a date with me immediately, and wanted further information in regard to this—I presume in order that he might notify Washington or his government. I succeeded in telling him that the Dreyfus case plays a very small part in our picture. . . . This seems to have satisfied him very much and I hope that we won't hear from him any further."[124]

A few days after this phone call took place, Jack Warner dictated some important changes to the Dreyfus picture (which would eventually be titled *The Life of Emile Zola*):

Scene 80: Start the speech of the CHIEF OF STAFF with "He's a man! . . ." losing the line—"And a Jew!"

Scene 190: Do not use the word "Jew" in the speech by the COMMANDER OF PARIS. Use DREYFUS' name instead.

Scene 235: Use DREYFUS' name here again instead of—". . . that Jew."[125]

After all of Warner's changes had been implemented, the word "Jew" was not spoken a single time in *The Life of Emile Zola*. The only reference that remained was a shot of a piece of paper on which Dreyfus' religion was written. And before the film was released, there was a request for this to be cut out too: "Take out the last part of the insert where the finger runs across under the line, 'Religion—Jew.'"[126] But for some reason the request was not carried out, and hard as it may be to believe, this one-second shot turned out to be one of the few explicit references to a Jew in American cinema for the remainder of the 1930s.[127]

This unfortunate episode revealed what an aggressive figure Georg Gyssling had become. He had dared to exert his influence over a studio that he had expelled from the German market. He was obviously prepared to adopt harsher measures against the studios still doing business in Germany, and one year after the cancellation of *It Can't Happen Here*, he went further than anyone had expected.

Back in 1931, the foundation for the agreement between the Hollywood studios and the German government had been laid when the head of Universal Pictures, Carl Laemmle, had edited *All Quiet on the Western Front* in accordance with the wishes of the German Foreign Office. In 1932, Laemmle had continued along the same path by postponing the sequel to *All Quiet on the Western Front*, entitled *The Road Back*. "Naturally," the German Foreign Office had observed at the time, "Universal's interest in collaboration is not platonic but arises from the company's interest in its Berlin branch and in the German market."[128]

In April 1936, Carl Laemmle had lost control of Universal Pictures, and the American financier and sportsman John Cheever Cowdin had become the new chairman of the company. Cowdin found the old script of *The Road Back* and, given Universal Pictures' vastly reduced business in Germany, he put the film back into production. "When this story originally came in 4 or 5 years ago," a Universal Pictures employee explained to the Hays Office, "we were loathe to produce same then, solely due to the jeopardy in which its production would have placed our German business at the time. However since then the situation with regard to the American Film Industry has completely changed and we are now ready and anxious to produce this story."[129]

In fact, despite this proclamation, Universal Pictures had not lost interest in the German market. In February 1937, soon after reviving *The Road Back*, Cowdin made a business trip to Berlin, and according to the U.S. ambassador, he made an "unusual offer" to the Nazi authorities: "The company in question was previously controlled by Jewish interests but after recent reorganization it is understood that it is now non-Jewish. The representative mentioned had certain discussions with government officials and film interests with a view to explaining this particular point. He has reported success in convincing them in the matter, and thereafter a plan was considered whereby, probably in collaboration with German interests, his company might re-enter the German market."[130]

In a very sly way, Cowdin was attempting to make Universal Pictures the preeminent American studio in Germany. He had non-Jewish origins on his side, and now he had *The Road Back* as a bargaining chip. If his company were allowed to re-enter the German market, he would agree to make the picture palatable from the German standpoint. He held numerous meetings with Propaganda Ministry officials, and he repeatedly assured them "that everything would be done to make the film apolitical and that he was very interested in cultivating good relations with Germany."[131]

Cowdin remained true to his word. In the book on which the film was based, a group of German soldiers had returned from the World War and had clashed with their former officers on the streets in the aftermath of the Revolution.[132] Since this contradicted the Nazis' interpretation of the postwar period, Cowdin instructed his screenwriters to make major changes. In the new script, there were jokes at the expense of the revolutionaries, the officers were portrayed sympathetically, and the conflicts between the two groups were, as Cowdin had promised, apolitical.[133]

Georg Gyssling did not know about these changes, however, so when he heard that Universal Pictures was going ahead with *The Road Back*, he sent a letter of protest to Joseph Breen in the Hays Office.[134] Breen then met with the director, James Whale, and he asked Whale about the scene in which the revolutionaries clashed with the army officers. Whale "insisted . . . that the scene would be shot in such a way as to remove any possible danger. . . . He further stated . . . that he had so changed the story from the book, that the finished picture was not likely to give serious offense to anybody and more especially to the Germans." As if to prove his point, Whale agreed to meet with Gyssling and to iron out any problems directly with him.[135]

The meeting took place one month later at Whale's home near Santa Monica. An account of the conversation between the film director and the Nazi consul has survived, and it is worth quoting at length because it conveys Gyssling's increased sense of entitlement since the cancellation of *It Can't Happen Here*:

> Consul Gyssling was, characteristically, never openly threatening in his attitude. . . . He simply insinuated "he'd be very sorry to have to take counter measures." The script for "The Road Back" was shown to him, but he would give no reply as to whether it satisfied the requirements of the Nazi regime. It was pointed out that nothing in the story in any way represented Nazi Germany, since it deals with a period immediately after the end of the World War. Not a word is said at any point about Hitler or Nazism. In fact, the story makes fun of inadequacies of the leading Social Democratic politicians of the time for their failure to take decisive steps in fulfillment of their program. Dr. Gyssling had the monumental cheek to suggest that the author, Erich Remarque, famed German novelist, should not be given screen credit in the completed picture. This, of course, the studio representatives were unable to grant.
>
> Consul Gyssling again insinuated that he would be very sorry to have to be forced to report to his government that the picture was unsatisfactory.[136]

A few weeks later, Gyssling had a second meeting about *The Road Back*. He visited the Universal studio lot, and he watched an early version of the picture. Once again, however, he refused to commit himself in any way.[137]

Then, on April 1, 1937, Gyssling made his boldest move yet. He had already threatened to invoke Article Fifteen of the German film regulations against several major Hollywood studios. Now he threatened to invoke it against individuals. He sent letters to around sixty people involved in *The Road Back*—the director, the entire cast, even the wardrobe man—and he warned them that any films in which they participated in the future might be banned in Germany.[138]

This was a shocking move, and it created an uproar. Georg Gyssling had directly threatened American film workers for their activities on home soil. He had used the U.S. Postal Service to frighten and intimidate individuals who were just going about their regular business. Universal Pictures told everyone to keep the matter a secret, but the news quickly leaked out.[139] Several actors sought out legal advice, complaints were lodged with the State Department, and one member of the Hays Office hoped that Gyssling would finally be expelled "on account of his viciousness."[140]

In the days that followed, the matter was considered at the highest level. A representative of the secretary of state met with the counselor of the German embassy in Washington, DC, and asked whether Gyssling had been acting under the direct instructions of his superiors. The counselor replied that he had. The American representative pointed out that such actions did not fall within the proper functions of a consular officer and then emphasized that he did not want to lodge an official complaint. He simply asked the counselor to bring the matter up with the German government and insisted "that we would consider the whole matter to have been discussed only through this informal approach . . . that we are looking into the matter and that my conversation with him was not considered to be a protest."[141]

In the meantime, Universal Pictures made twenty-one cuts to *The Road Back* and sent the new print off to the German ambassador, Hans-Heinrich Dieckhoff.[142] By this stage, there was hardly anything in the film to which the ambassador could object. So many scenes had been cut out that the plot

Georg Gyssling, German consul, welcomes Leni Riefenstahl to Los
Angeles in 1938. Copyright © Bettmann/Corbis.

barely made any sense. The ending, which had criticized the rise of militarism in Germany, now criticized the rise of militarism all around the world. The film was a muddled piece of work, and there was little risk that it would offend anyone.[143] Nevertheless, the German government was through with Universal Pictures. The company was not permitted to resume operations in Berlin.

For Gyssling, on the other hand, the news was less bleak. The German Foreign Office sent a brief, unapologetic letter to the State Department to explain that the consul in Los Angeles had been instructed not to issue future warnings to American citizens.[144] As a result, the State Department considered the matter closed.[145] Not only was Gyssling permitted to remain in his position, but within a few days, he was defending his actions to the press: "I have been authorized by His Excellency the German Ambassador in Washington D. C., to deny emphatically reports that I have been rebuked by the German government for having issued on instruction warnings to some Hollywood actors in connection with the making of a certain film. All reports to the contrary are just fiction and fabrications not based on any facts."[146]

Gyssling had acted boldly and successfully. Fourteen months after MGM's abandonment of *It Can't Happen Here*, he had managed to terrorize an entire community. Very soon, with his name cleared, he was back to his usual methods. He read in the trade papers that another film about the World War was being made, so he wrote to the Hays Office: "I feel a little alarmed, as I hear that the film THE LANCER SPY, which is under production at Westwood (Fox) will contain several scenes apparently objectionable from the German standpoint. Will you therefore be kind enough to give this matter your attention, the more, as from what I hear, many Fox films are being shown in Germany at this time." He followed this with a second letter that contained the same obvious threat: "The production of a film of such a character will arouse very bad feeling in Germany against the producing company and may lead to serious difficulties which should be avoided in mutual interests."[147]

The Hays Office forwarded these letters to Twentieth Century-Fox, and soon afterward, Gyssling was invited to preview *Lancer Spy*. He did not like what he saw. In his opinion, none of the German officials in the film were portrayed sympathetically. He also felt that the film was even more dangerous than *The Road Back* because it was so "thrilling and entertaining." At the end of the screening, he made some suggestions, and three months later, he was invited to the studio lot to watch the new version of *Lancer Spy*. He still did not like it—he thought that ideally half of it should be reshot—but he agreed that several changes had been made. Consequently, Twentieth Century-Fox was permitted to continue doing business in Germany.[148]

In all of these dealings with the Hollywood studios, Gyssling was doing something very strategic. He was objecting to a series of films about the World War—*Captured!*, *Rendezvous*, *The Road Back*, *Lancer Spy*—when his real target lay elsewhere. Ever since he had heard about *The Mad Dog of Europe*, he had understood that Hollywood was capable of producing a much more damaging type of film from his perspective: a film that attacked Nazi Germany.[149] His reaction to *The Road Back* was therefore carefully calculated. He was focusing his energies on the films set in the past in an attempt to prevent the studios from moving into the present. He was acting shocked and outraged by a few titles that had all but lost their relevance so that the studios would not dare to embark on something truly dangerous. He had managed to bring about significant changes to a series of movies about the war, but for him, the real benefits were still to come.

In May 1937, one month after Gyssling issued his warnings to the actors, the very film that he had objected to years earlier—*The Mad Dog of Europe*—was put back into production. The agent Al Rosen, who still owned the film rights, had conducted a survey of tens of thousands of people and had determined that 82 percent of Americans now supported the picture. Rosen cast several well-known actors in leading roles, and he announced that he was not releasing their names to the press in light of Gyssling's recent actions. Soon rumors started circulating that John Wray (the down-and-out farmer in *Mr. Deeds Goes to Town*) had been cast as Hitler and that Sam Jaffe (the high priest in *Lost Horizon*) had been cast as the persecuted Jewish professor.[150]

Gyssling quickly swung into action. He informed the Propaganda Ministry that *The Mad Dog of Europe* would be extremely detrimental to Germany, and he recommended that a warning be issued to the Hays Office. He continued: "Although the Hays Office, which is not affiliated with New Era Productions [Al Rosen's company], will declare that it will have nothing to do with this, it would nevertheless convey the warning to its member companies [the major Hollywood studios]. These companies would then at the very least warn the prominent actors against participating in the film, because their employability in future films would be restricted."[151] Not surprisingly, the production plans for the new version of *The Mad Dog of Europe* never went ahead.

As Gyssling knew well, though, the real danger at this point was not that a minor production company would embark on an anti-Nazi film—it was that a major Hollywood studio would do so. And the final volume of Erich Maria Remarque's trilogy, *Three Comrades*, which was prime Hollywood material, had just been published in the United States. Whereas *All Quiet on the Western Front* had been about the World War and *The Road Back* had been about its aftermath, *Three Comrades* was set in the late 1920s, when the Nazis were emerging as a significant political force. The novel told the story of three war veterans—Gottfried Lenz, Robert Lohkamp, and Otto Köster—who were struggling to survive in a broken Germany. As they worked hard to keep their auto repair shop open, Lenz discovered politics, Lohkamp discovered love, and Köster tried to keep the comrades together. In the end, though, defeat was inevitable. Lenz was shot on the street by a storm trooper, Lohkamp's wife died of tuberculosis, and *Three Comrades* ended without hope and without meaning.[152]

Unlike *All Quiet on the Western Front* and *The Road Back*, which had both been produced by Universal Pictures, the film rights to *Three Comrades* were in the possession of MGM. The company considered canceling the picture when Gyssling threatened the actors but eventually decided to push ahead with it, and the screenwriter of *The Road Back* came up with something politically innocuous.[153] In May 1937, MGM sent the script to Joseph Breen in the Hays Office for inspection. Breen could not have been particularly surprised to receive it, for he had already read three typical letters from Georg Gyssling on the subject ("I beg to say that I still feel a little concerned about Metro-Goldwyn-Mayer's alleged plan to film the Remarque story titled 'Three Comrades,'" etc.).[154] Still, as sensitive as Breen was to the concerns of the Nazi consul, he could not find anything wrong with the script. He wrote to MGM to say that it met the requirements of the Production Code, and he offered just a few suggestions regarding coarse language and drinking.[155]

In the meantime, the producer assigned to *Three Comrades*, Joseph L. Mankiewicz (whose brother Herman had come up with the idea for *The Mad Dog of Europe* four years earlier) had a change of heart about the picture. Many commentators, including Remarque himself, had complained bitterly about Universal Pictures' production of *The Road Back*, and the script for *Three Comrades* looked just as bad.[156] Mankiewicz therefore asked none other than F. Scott Fitzgerald to come up with something better.[157]

Fitzgerald plunged into the adaptation of *Three Comrades* with great seriousness. He read the novel and found it comparable to Ernest Hemingway's

*The Sun Also Rises* and *A Farewell to Arms*. He tried to summarize it in his head. "A story of a generation growing up in a poor and defeated country," he thought. "A life without hope amid sordid surroundings. . . . Relations with women cynical and unromantic. Then a girl drops into it. The struggle goes on, assuming for a while a sort of hope and glory; even the grief of the girl sinking gives it color. Then the girl is dead and presumably the world is empty and hollow again."[158]

Fitzgerald tried to work out how to translate the spirit of the book onto the screen. "No story . . . must be lifted from its context and written as if it did or could happen in America out of time or space," he thought. Upon reading the original screenplay, he became only more convinced of this. The screenplay omitted the emptiness of the surroundings, the particularity of the German landscape. "It is a lovely story only if we show from what desolation and waste it was snatched, with what difficulties, in how short a time, with such luck," he wrote. "These are things I want to accentuate even more than in the book if possible."[159]

In Fitzgerald's opinion, *Three Comrades* needed to reflect the exterior surroundings—the German political situation—more clearly. Consequently, he started to write Hollywood's second explicitly anti-Nazi screenplay. He worked under the supervision of the man whose brother had written the first. His first full draft, dated September 1, 1937, mounted a powerful attack on the rise of Nazism in Germany.[160]

What came next was one of Hollywood's notorious run-ins with a great American author. Joseph Mankiewicz read Fitzgerald's script and found that it badly needed revisions. He hired a rewrite man at MGM to do the fixes, and he wrote some of the new dialogue himself. Fitzgerald was furious, but Mankiewicz was adamant that the changes were necessary. "I personally have been attacked as if I had spat on the flag because it happened once that I rewrote some dialogue by F. Scott Fitzgerald," he recalled. "But it needed it! The actors, among them Margaret Sullavan, absolutely could not read the lines. It was very literary dialogue, novelistic dialogue that lacked all the qualities required for screen dialogue. The latter must be 'spoken.' Scott Fitzgerald really wrote very bad spoken dialogue."[161]

After four months of revisions, the script of *Three Comrades* contained a mixture of material by Fitzgerald, Mankiewicz, and a few MGM staff writers. It bore little resemblance to what Fitzgerald had originally intended. Nevertheless, the jabs at the Nazis remained, and if anything they were even more intense than they had been before, so when Joseph Breen read the new script, he panicked. He had just received a fourth warning from Gyssling about *Three Comrades*, and he knew exactly what the German consul was capable of. He therefore wrote to Louis B. Mayer in the strongest possible terms: "This screen adaptation suggests to us enormous difficulty from the standpoint of your company's distribution business in Germany. . . . I raise the question . . . as to whether or not the production by your company of this picture may not result in considerable difficulty in Europe for other American producing organizations."[162]

Mayer read the letter from Breen and understood the problem immediately. According to Budd Schulberg, here was what happened next: "When they tried to make some, I think there was *Three Comrades*, there were some films that Louis B. Mayer of MGM would actually run those films with the Nazi German consul and was willing to take out the things that the consul, that the Nazis, objected to. . . . I heard about the way that Louis Mayer would kowtow, we were amazed when we heard it, but he was definitely doing it. I think the consul even came to the studio and looked at his pictures and said yes, that's all right, no take that out, it was unbelievable."[163]

Shortly after alerting Mayer to the dangers of *Three Comrades*, Joseph Breen was in possession of a list of changes that needed to be made to the film. He organized a meeting with Joseph Mankiewicz and four other MGM executives, and he discussed the contents of the list with them.[164] It is very unlikely that Breen came up with the list himself, for he had his own separate set of suggestions (relating to sex, foul language, etc.).[165] In all likelihood this secret document, which contained ten unusual changes, was the list that Mayer compiled with Gyssling at the end of their screening of *Three Comrades*.

Breen went through the items on the list one by one. According to the first item, the film now needed to be set several years earlier, in the two-year period immediately following the end of the World War. "Thus," Breen told the MGM executives, "we will get away from any possible suggestion that we are dealing with Nazi violence or terrorism."[166] He read out the scenes that needed to be cut, and he pointed out that these cuts

**Louis B. Mayer, president of MGM. Courtesy of General Photographic Agency; Getty Images.**

could be made without interfering with the romantic plot at the center of the picture. The MGM executives agreed. They said they would date the story back to 1920 and remove all references to the Nazis and all images of swastikas and book burning.

As if this were not enough, the second item on the list demanded that all implied attacks on the Nazis be removed as well. Early in the film, Lenz, the most political of the three comrades, had expressed his preference for a different ideology. "There's more to fight for—better than food—better than peace," he had shouted. "Democracy—freedom—a new Germany! Isn't *that* worth fighting for?"[167] The instructions regarding such sentiments were clear: "Delete references to 'democracy' in scenes 3, 31, and 75." Once again, the MGM executives agreed.[168]

The studio now had on its hands a picture that was almost ready to be distributed on the world market. There was just one more change necessary. Back in F. Scott Fitzgerald's original script, the three comrades had purchased a taxi very cheaply from a poor, desperate couple, and Lenz had expressed sympathy for their plight.

"I know," Lenz had told them as he had given them their money. "It all goes for debts. But that's what Germany *is* today—A rotten, moldy corpse of a country!"

"Oh, don't say that," the owner had replied. "I love my country. Mamma and I gave our two sons to Germany—one killed in Poland—one at sea. That's all right. I don't complain. And now if Germany is too poor to feed me and mamma *after* the war—that's all right too. . . . And I'll tell you why. Because Germany is still my fatherland. She still protects me and my people. You see—*I* am a Jew."[169]

Upon reading this dialogue by F. Scott Fitzgerald, Joseph Mankiewicz had been forced to give the eminent author a history lesson. "Forget that you're writing about a Jew," Mankiewicz had said. "It should be a man who does not call his wife 'mama.' He has not got a beard—nor should he talk as if he has one. He is not full of self-pity."[170] Mankiewicz had then dictated a new version of the speech, and here was how it eventually read: "Please don't talk that way. It was very sad to lose our sons, of course, but it was for the Fatherland—it was for our country. . . . And I'll tell you why. Because Germany has given us something worth anything we can give in return. A home. Peace—and security. You see, we're Jews."[171]

Not surprisingly, this scene was cited in the list of changes. "The speech about 'We are Jews' . . . will be rewritten," Breen announced.[172] The executives agreed, and the screenwriters eventually came up with the following: "Please don't talk that way. It was very sad to lose our sons, of course, but it was for the Fatherland—it was for our country. . . . And I'll tell you why. Because Germany has given us something worth anything we can give in return. A home—and security. A country to be proud of—always."[173] The new version of the speech no longer had the same impact, however, and in the end, it was simply cut from the film.

After all these changes had been made, *Three Comrades* neither attacked the Nazis nor mentioned the Jews. The picture had been completely sanitized, and the German government could not possibly have been offended by it. There was just one more suggestion on the list that Breen read out to the MGM executives at the end of his meeting with them: "It might be well to make the communists the 'heavies.' If this is done, then it seems to us that several of Lenz's speeches . . . could stand as they are."[174]

At this point in the meeting, Joseph Mankiewicz erupted. He slammed his script on the table and stormed out of the room, "threatening to tear up his contract if any such thing were done."[175] He preferred to cut out Lenz's speeches entirely than to have them fit the exact position of the Nazi Party. And on this issue, he managed to get his way. "The next day," he remembered, "I went into the commissary, and Scott was there. He ran up, threw his arms around me, and kissed me."[176]

And so, after a tense meeting, Joseph Breen had managed to implement nearly all of the changes on the list. He made a quick note of what he had accomplished. He put a check mark next to seven of the ten items, he put a question mark next to two very minor items, and next to the suggestion about communists, he wrote "NO." Finally, he told Louis B. Mayer that virtually all of the changes had been made.[177]

Over the next four months, the director Frank Borzage shot the new version of *Three Comrades*. In May 1938, Georg Gyssling was invited to preview it again, and this time he found that he had only a few trivial requests: he wanted a shot of drums in a parade to be eliminated, and he wanted a scene containing a fistfight to be shortened. MGM did as he said, and then, finally, the picture was released.[178]

From Gyssling's perspective, the removal of all the offensive elements of *Three Comrades* was the true benefit of his behavior from the previous year. He had reacted so dramatically to the second film in the trilogy that he had now managed to get his way on the third. And this was no small feat, for *Three Comrades* would have been the first explicitly anti-Nazi film by an American studio. At this critical moment, when a major Hollywood production could have alerted the world to what was going on in Germany, the director did not have the final cut; the Nazis did.

A few weeks after the edited version of *Three Comrades* reached theaters in the United States, another situation arose. For the second time in 1938, an anti-Nazi script arrived at the Hays Office.[179] The script was written by John Howard Lawson, a talented Jewish screenwriter, and it was loosely based on Vincent Sheean's memoir *Personal History*, an award-winning account of an American reporter's experiences abroad.[180] The film was scheduled to go into production in nine days under the supervision of Walter Wanger of United Artists, and Henry Fonda had been cast in the leading role.[181]

As Joseph Breen read the script of *Personal History*, his latest encounter with Gyssling was fresh in his mind. Before he had even reached the halfway point, he was very concerned. The story—the final one that needs to be recorded in all of its details—was unlike almost any other he had read before. Here was how it went:

An American college student named Joe Sheridan was questioning the value of his education in a world on the brink of war. He dropped out of college and obtained a job in a newsreel company, and just as he was about to leave on his first assignment in Spain, he fell in love with a beautiful woman named Miriam. A few months later, Miriam learned that something had happened to her mother, and soon the two of them were in Berlin with her father, Dr. Bergemann, a world-famous physician.[182]

"Your mother killed herself," Dr. Bergemann said. "Because I'm a Jew! My wife was not! You don't know how complete the social boycott has been." Dr. Bergemann explained that his wife had chosen to die rather than comply with the Nazis. He turned to his daughter, who was sobbing. "There's no shame in that, Miriam. I want you to be proud—my faith has always been proud of its heritage."

Miriam looked up slowly. "I am proud, father," she said.[183]

The next day, another crisis emerged. An Aryan woman named Viktoria von Rhein visited Dr. Bergemann and told him that she was worried about her health. Dr. Bergemann examined her and discovered that she was dangerously ill. Unless he operated on her soon, she would die. It was strictly forbidden for a Jew to operate on an Aryan, he said, but he had known her for years, and he was willing to take the risk. That night, Joe went to Viktoria's house and pleaded with her not to expose the doctor to any trouble. She understood his concern and agreed not to go ahead with the operation.

After several weeks in Berlin, Joe had become fiercely anti-Nazi. He filmed images of the persecution of the Jews and he smuggled the footage out of the country. He also devised a way to get Jewish children out of Germany. The description of their departure was haunting: "PLATFORM OF BERLIN RAILROAD STATION—NIGHT. . . . Refugees grouped with families and baggage on the platform beside a train. . . . Someone in the crowd begins to sing a Jewish song—others pick it up. . . . Parents who are staying behind are feverishly saying good-bye to their children. The singing grows in volume. There are cries of ['Shalom,'] etc. from the crowd. . . . The mournful singing, expressing the courageous tragic feeling of the race, mingles with the increasing clatter of the wheels as they gain momentum."[184]

After rescuing the Jewish children, Joe had one last thing to do: he wanted to take Miriam back to the United States. He proposed to her, and she said yes. Then, just as they were about to get married in the American consulate, Miriam was arrested by the secret police. The reason given for her arrest was typical: she was a Jew, and she had been spending too much time with Joe, who was considered an Aryan. Joe appealed to the one man he knew with any power, Herr von Rhein, the husband of the woman who badly needed an operation.

"I'm asking you to help your own friends," Joe said.

"Jews are not my friends," Herr von Rhein replied. "We now consider that Jews are not part of the German people."

"That's crazy," Joe said.

"That's a matter of opinion—I think it's crazy for you to come to me with a request to help a Jewish prisoner. I'll have nothing to do with it."[185]

Eventually, Miriam was released. She crossed the border to Austria, and she married Joe in Vienna. In the middle of the celebration, Dr. Bergemann received an urgent telegram: Viktoria von Rhein was extremely sick, and she was coming to Vienna to be operated on immediately. She arrived on March 12, 1938, the day that German troops marched into Austria in the lead-up to the *Anschluss*. Her operation went well, but she still needed a blood transfusion, and the only person with her blood type was Miriam. Dr. Bergemann carried out the transfusion, and just then German troops burst through the door.

"This woman is very ill," Dr. Bergemann told them. "You'll be responsible for her life."

"One of you Jews?" an officer asked.

"If she's not, you know the punishment," another officer said.

"Yes," Dr. Bergemann replied. "I can assure you that Jewish blood flows in her veins."[186]

In the aftermath of the operation, Herr von Rhein saw the error of his ways. "We've tried to make hate into a religion!" he said. "This is supposed to be the greatest moment in the history of my country—but I know better. I've known for some time, but I've been afraid to speak!"

Herr von Rhein had an urgent piece of advice for Joe. "Go back to your country," he said, "and warn them."[187]

Joseph Breen put down the script. He was extremely concerned. He had come across only one other screenplay that mounted such a direct attack on Hitler's persecution of the Jews: *The Mad Dog of Europe*. Georg Gyssling had managed to have that picture suppressed, and he had been taking dramatic measures against far less threatening pictures ever since. There was no telling what he would do if he heard about this one. Not only was it as radical as *The Mad Dog of Europe*, but it was far better written. It was both gripping and original, Breen thought, and it would have "the inevitable result of arousing audience feeling against the present German regime, in the matter of its treatment of the Jews."[188]

Breen invited the producer, Walter Wanger, to the Hays Office. He told him that although *Personal History* met the requirements of the Production Code, he was not sure whether industry policy should permit the picture to be made. He said that he would consult Will Hays about the matter, and in the meantime, he suggested a large number of changes that would help to portray the Germans more favorably.[189]

Breen then wrote to Hays about the case. "The theme of the story," he wrote, "is to be the conversion of a half-baked young radical college boy, away from his exaggerated ideas, to an enthusiastic belief in American democratic ideals. The hero quits college . . . goes to Europe, gets a position as a newsreel cameraman, is involved, first, with the Spanish War, and more importantly, in Nazi Germany, where he assists in the rescue of the Jews, who are being persecuted, and falls in love with a half-Jew girl, whom he eventually marries."[190]

As Breen and Wanger awaited a decision from Hays, they both grew impatient. Breen wrote to Hays again on June 21, and he cabled him on June 22: "WANGER AWAITING WORD . . . PERSONAL HISTORY . . . PICTURE SCHEDULED START MONDAY."[191]

Wanger in the meantime continued his preparations for the film. He hired Budd Schulberg to implement all of Breen's changes, and he asked William Dieterle (who had worked on *The Life of Emile Zola*) to direct. Then, on June 29, 1938, Wanger announced that *Personal History* had been indefinitely postponed. He cited "casting difficulty" as the reason, and he said that he would resume work on the picture at some point in the future.[192]

He kept his word. Nearly two years later, in March 1940, he hired Alfred Hitchcock to direct a new version of *Personal History*. He sent the provisional script to Breen, who in turn sent a reassuring letter to Will Hays: "It occurs to me that you may want to know that the story in hand has not the even remotest semblance to the story we were concerned about two years back. It is a new, and complete, and entirely different story."[193]

This was true. *Personal History* was now called *Foreign Correspondent*; it was a typical adventure film set in London; and it contained no mention of Hitler's persecution of the Jews. There was one vague similarity, however. At the end of the film, the main character spoke into a microphone in a dark room, and he told the American people about the war: "I've been watching a part of the world being blown to pieces. . . . It's death coming to London. Yes, they're coming here now. You can hear the bombs falling on the streets and the homes. . . . It's too late to do anything here now except stand in the dark and let them come."[194]

This scene was the one remnant from the original script of *Personal History*. At the end of that script, the main character (Joe) had also stood in a dark room and told the American people about the German aggression. Only what he had said had been quite different: "Oh, it didn't take long. In five hours it was all over but the shouting. The freedom of Austria was wiped out in five hours. Many were not so fortunate as to get away— doctors—lawyers—professors—committed suicide—killed—gone to concentration camps."[195] And as he spoke, shocking newsreel footage of these things had appeared on the screen. Joe had managed to smuggle the footage out of the country during his escape, and it had become a part of *Personal History*. Another character looked at the footage and smiled. "Lucky they didn't get this film," he said.[196]

But he was wrong. They did.[197]

Nineteen thirty-nine is often remembered as the greatest year in American film history, the peak of Hollywood's golden age. It was the year that the studios put out some of the most celebrated movies of all time. In the opinion of the film critic André Bazin, it was also the year that American cinema approached the level of a classical art.[198] For all the achievements and for all the glory, however, nobody remembers how 1939 began.

In early January, perhaps even during the New Year's celebrations, a producer at MGM named Lucien Hubbard found a copy of the old script of *It Can't Happen Here*, and reading through it, he realized how timely it had been. Hubbard had been slated as the original producer, and he thought, Why not try to make it again? Hitler had recently annexed Czechoslovakia at the notorious conference in Munich and afterward had launched the attacks on German Jews during *Kristallnacht*. A film version of *It Can't Happen Here* seemed more urgent than ever before.

Hubbard had some experience as a writer, and as he went through the earlier versions of the story, he found that he had just one reservation. "Both the Sinclair Lewis novel and the Sidney Howard script were written too soon to enlighten us," he thought. "We have had three years and more to find out. In the novel and the scenario, a lot of witless sadists were running at large, committing senseless acts of cruelty. They were bogeymen out of nightmares. Instead, we must have a clear picture of the calculated horror of Fascism today."[199]

Hubbard proposed a simple way of bringing *It Can't Happen Here* up to date. Whereas Sidney Howard had deliberately restricted his screenplay to America, Hubbard wanted to include recent developments in Germany. He introduced a new character, a former American diplomat in Berlin, who suggested all sorts of ways that the United States could emulate the Nazis. He also changed the climax so that the American dictator suggested an alliance with Germany, Italy, and Japan—"a four-way split of the world"—as appropriate foreign policy.[200]

Finally, Hubbard had never been satisfied with the original ending of *It Can't Happen Here*. The image of Doremus Jessup struggling to restore democracy in America was too pessimistic for his taste. Instead, he felt, Doremus should win in the end. "The picture must say there is something in the soil of America nourished by the blood of those who gave their lives for liberty that will not allow tyranny to flourish," he decided. "And that is the thought which should make this picture the most talked-about one of the year . . . IT CAN'T HAPPEN HERE can be America telling the world."[201]

For over four months, Hubbard reworked Sidney Howard's old script. He rewrote the first seventy pages entirely, and he added the decisive victory at the end. By the time he was done, he had almost completely butchered the original work. Howard's screenplay had been universally appealing: he had managed to write a kind of parable about the fragility of the democratic system of government. Hubbard's screenplay, on the other hand, was simplistic and crude, and his writing was mediocre. Nevertheless, he still spoke out against fascism, and unlike Howard, he attacked the Nazis specifically. If the new version of *It Can't Happen Here* was nowhere near as good as the old one, it was also capable of causing the German government greater offense.[202]

On June 7, 1939, Georg Gyssling spoke to his contact at MGM—whoever that was—and expressed concern over several of the studio's upcoming productions. One was *Thunder Afloat*, a picture about German submarines in the World War; another was *It Can't Happen Here*. The MGM representative assured Gyssling that nothing in *Thunder Afloat* would cause offense to the German government. In the case of *It Can't Happen Here*, the MGM representative made no promises.[203]

By this point in time, Gyssling had all but lost his credibility in Hollywood. The Hays Office had ceased all communication with him, and the director of the Federal Bureau of Investigation, J. Edgar Hoover, considered him a dangerous threat. "The present Consul at Los Angeles . . . is an ardent Nazi and a member of the Nazi Party in good graces with the Hitler Government," Hoover had reported. "He willingly carries out the instructions from Berlin."[204] In this changing political climate, a film version of *It Can't Happen Here* would hardly have been a subversive undertaking; if anything, it would have supported the position of the U.S. government. The Hays Office had read various drafts of the script and had found it to be free of any difficulties under the Production Code.[205]

Nevertheless, two days after Gyssling made his phone call, MGM made a surprising announcement: once again it was abandoning *It Can't Happen Here*.[206] There was little controversy this time around. The decision received almost no attention in the press, and Sinclair Lewis issued no statement. A spokesman for MGM simply explained that the times were "not propitious" for the making of the picture.[207]

Then, two weeks later, a scandalous rumor began to circulate throughout Hollywood. Apparently the editors of ten prominent Nazi newspapers, including the editor of *Völkischer Beobachter*, Carl Cranz, had been treated to a "good will tour" of one of the major studios.[208] Similar tours had been organized in the recent past: in September 1937, Vittorio Mussolini (son of Benito) had been shown around by producer Hal Roach, and in December 1938, Leni Riefenstahl had been publicly snubbed by all the major studios except Disney.[209] Ever since that last episode, nobody had imagined that a studio would open its doors to a prominent Nazi again.

Upon hearing the rumor about the newspaper editors, an organization called the Hollywood Anti-Nazi League became deeply concerned. The group was composed of actors, screenwriters, and prominent Hollywood personalities, and it was one of the most active anti-Nazi organizations in the country. Ever since it had come into existence in 1936, the Hollywood Anti-Nazi League had launched protests against fascist activities in Germany and the United States. The organization could not make movies, however, and up to this point, it had avoided all criticism of the Hollywood executives' dealings with Georg Gyssling. The news about the Nazi editors led to a change in policy.

The Hollywood Anti-Nazi League called up the various studios and asked whether the rumors were true. Every studio but one denied the charge: the League was unable to get through to Robert Vogel, the head of the international department of MGM. A secretary explained that Mr. Vogel was "busy because there have been many visitors." Finally, after three days, Vogel returned the call and said that the ten Nazi editors had indeed visited his studio. He explained that an MGM director, Richard Rosson, had been arrested in Germany while shooting a film. The tour of the studio was arranged "at the request of the German Consul, Dr. George Gyssling, who was very helpful to us in the Rossen case."[210]

"This was the regular line of business," Vogel said. "We handle newspapermen from 48 countries and we think we should handle these the same as anyone else."[211]

Not everyone agreed. Harry Warner wrote to several people he knew at MGM: "I just can't bring myself to believe that your people would entertain those whom the world regards as the murderers of their own families. . . . I am not writing L.B. Mayer because I've written him several times on matters of charity which he has not even answered. Therefore, I consider it a waste of time to write him."[212] An American sociologist named Henry Pratt Fairchild adopted a different approach. He wrote to Mayer directly about the two recent events, and the Hollywood Anti-Nazi League reprinted the letter in its weekly newspaper: "Quite honestly, we do not understand your position in this matter. . . . Your abandonment of 'It Can't Happen Here' in the middle of production was doubly surprising as you are not only a leading personality in our country, but also a Jew. It is sufficiently proven by now we believe, that people of your race are the first to feel the wrath of fascism, whether it be delayed six months or a year, depending on the income bracket, it strikes nevertheless." After making this point, which contained just a trace of anti-Semitism, Fairchild continued: "We are honest in saying that the complete abandonment of this picture would be a severe blow to the rising forces of democracy, and when the announcement appeared in the press, we were inclined to believe it was possibly confusion on the part of your company, but since that date, we learned that you were the only studio to entertain nine Nazi editors. This, we believe, is a shocking indication of your possible attitude toward this production. One is almost forced to believe the comments in the industry that you are more interested in appeasing Nazism than protecting the welfare of your own country."[213]

Louis B. Mayer refused to take the bait. His studio made no comment, and it seemed that nothing more would be said on the subject. When a series of similar letters from other organizations started to appear, however, an anonymous MGM spokesman agreed to a single interview about the recent events.

"Why did you drop 'It Can't Happen Here?'" the interviewer asked.

"We dropped 'It Can't Happen Here' because we think it is not politically propitious," the MGM representative said.

"Politically propitious? They are two words. What do they mean?"

"That's all I can say. The studio has decided 'It Can't Happen Here' is not politically propitious."

"Who decided it wasn't politically propitious?"

"Mr. Mayer, Mr. Schenck, Mr. Katz and six or seven other executives."

"The publishers thought 'It Can't Happen Here' politically propitious and published it as a novel. The U.S. government thought it was politically propitious and made it a play. Both times the public thought 'It Can't Happen Here' was politically propitious, making it a best selling novel and a hit play. How can six or seven men in Culver City ignore all this public opinion?"

"Don't quote me on this but my private opinion is that certain groups protested."

"What groups?"

"I don't know."

"You had $200,000 invested in 'It Can't Happen Here,' didn't you?"

# SWITCHED ON

**With all hope of profit gone, we can, at last, become properly indignant and raise our voices in shocked protest without any pecuniary regrets.[1]**

At the beginning of 1939, Hitler was stationed at his private retreat near Berchtesgaden. He was only months away from his fiftieth birthday. On January 5, he had a disappointing meeting with the Polish foreign minister, Joseph Beck.[2] Later that day, he met with Joseph Goebbels. The two men spoke for hours and unwound by watching an American film and exchanging memories. The next day, they discussed the possibility of war. Was there a way out? Only the future could tell. They watched another movie together, and afterward Hitler left to carry out important business in Munich and Berlin.[3]

On January 8, Goebbels discussed some "film matters" with one of his assistants, and on January 9, a Propaganda Ministry official named Ernst von Leichtenstern made a surprising announcement to the editors of all the major newspapers: "In the near future, the screening of American films in Germany will be stopped by order of the Führer. . . . The film dealings between Germany and the United States will probably come to an end completely."[4] Von Leichtenstern emphasized that the announcement was strictly confidential and that the press was only being informed because there had been too much fanfare around Hollywood in recent times. From this point on, he said, there should be no mention of banned American movies in the newspapers and no publicity around American movie stars.

"Yes, we paid Sinclair Lewis $75,000 for the book. . . ."

"But you didn't ignore the protests of this group? Is it such an important group?"

"Listen, we want to make the picture and it's my private opinion we will make it."

"Who knows why it was really withdrawn?"

The MGM representative was getting sick of all the questioning. He looked up at the interviewer and just before terminating the meeting, he gave his answer. "Mr. Mayer knows."[214]

"Please don't praise American films to the skies anymore," he said. "Instead just describe them factually." The editors needed to prepare the public in a gentle way for the removal of American movies from screens in Germany.[5]

After making this announcement, von Leichtenstern rambled on about all the problems that the Germans had encountered with the American movie studios. He spoke about money (the Americans had a lot of it and could afford to invest millions of dollars in individual productions) and about distribution (the Americans exported their pictures all around the world whereas the Germans could hardly sell their pictures in America). He said that American movies starring Jewish actors would never be shown in Germany, nor would movies starring actors who had participated in hate pictures. "The American companies know all this, and Fox has already complied with most of our wishes," he said. "But it's no use. We now want to suppress American films."[6]

Just a few days earlier, von Leichtenstern had informed the same group of newspaper editors of another development: the Propaganda Ministry had been receiving regular reports about the production of two new anti-Nazi films in Hollywood.[7] The first film was an "impudent satire" of dictatorship by Charlie Chaplin with a very offensive plot: "The joke of this film is that Chaplin, the 'little big Jew,' is mistaken (!) for the Führer (!) by the guards and thereby ends up in the position of Adolf Hitler (!)."[8] The second was a "Nazi spy" film by Warner Brothers, which had led Georg Gyssling to ask the Hays Office "whether this firm has really the intention to make a picture like that."[9]

Of course, various people in Hollywood had been attempting to make anti-Nazi pictures since 1933, and Gyssling had been more involved in the suppression of such pictures than anyone else. But, as Ernst von Leichtenstern explained, there was a big difference in these two cases. In his words: "Up to now I have initiated measures against the production of American hate films only when we have stood a real chance of success and wouldn't make fools of ourselves in the process. We stand a chance of success only when the film is being produced by an American studio that is still doing business in Germany, namely Fox, Metro-Goldwyn-Mayer, and Paramount. In these cases I can threaten countermeasures in Germany; to threaten countermeasures against the other American firms would be absurd because they would have no effect, especially since the purely Jewish studios—Universal, Warner Brothers—would certainly be happy if their competition were to suffer setbacks in Germany."[10] Von Leichtenstern was obviously referring to Article Fifteen of the German film regulations, which stipulated that if a studio made an anti-German picture, then all of its productions would be banned from the German market. He was saying that by this point in time, Article Fifteen could only be applied to a limited number of American studios.

Neither United Artists, the company that distributed Chaplin's pictures, nor Warner Brothers, the company that was contemplating the Nazi spy movie, had any investment in the German market. United Artists had been banned from Germany in 1933 and Warner Brothers in 1934. These two companies had nothing to lose by making anti-Nazi pictures, and they may even have had something to gain, so von Leichtenstern ordered the newspaper editors to proceed with great caution: "It would be pointless to attack such film plans in the press because then we would be dignifying things that are based mostly on rumor. I consider it appropriate to remain silent until one of these films is actually completed."[11]

The reason for suppressing American movies in Germany was therefore clear: after years of relatively peaceful negotiations, the system of collaboration set up in 1933 was finally breaking apart. Two studios with no financial investment in Germany had begun to make anti-Nazi pictures. In response to this new development, von Leichtenstern recommended a policy of absolute silence. Hitler, however, adopted a different approach.

On January 30, 1939, the sixth anniversary of the Nazis' rise to power in Germany, Hitler gave a speech to the Reichstag in which he made a terrible prophecy: "If international finance Jewry inside and outside Europe should succeed in plunging the nations once more into a world war, the result will be not the bolshevization of the earth and thereby the victory of Jewry, but the annihilation of the Jewish race in Europe!"[12] This speech has frequently been cited as the first mark of Hitler's emerging genocidal mentality, but it was also something else. A few minutes after making the above pronouncement, Hitler extended his threat even further: "And the announcement of American film companies of their intention to produce anti-Nazi—i.e. anti-German—films, will only lead to our German producers creating anti-Semitic films in the future."[13]

For six years, Hitler had avoided making official pronouncements about Hollywood. He had allowed the American studios to distribute their product in Germany, and he had barely said a word about the movies that he watched so avidly in his daily life. In his speech of January 30, 1939, all that changed. Instead of ignoring the latest rumors about Hollywood, he indicated that he took them as seriously as the possibility of physical aggression against Germany. He threatened the American studios in the same way and in almost the same breath as he threatened the Jewish people.

His words were not lost on the German press. Various commentators noticed that Hitler had singled out Hollywood in his speech, and a few film critics meditated on what he had said. The most astute article was entitled "Film Hatred in the USA: Will the Führer's Warning Be Heeded?" The author of this article pointed out that unlike the written word and even photography, the cinema possessed a powerful reality effect that the Americans had harnessed against Germany since the World War. They had made disgraceful, believable pictures including *The Kaiser, the Beast of Berlin*, and when the hostilities had ended, they had released a series of German spy pictures and, of course, *All Quiet on the Western Front*. Ever since 1933, this critic admitted, the Hollywood studios had behaved themselves relatively well in their treatment of Germany. Nevertheless, there had been a steady increase in demands for anti-Nazi pictures, and two projects in particular—a Nazi spy film by Warner Brothers and a caricature of dictatorship by Charlie Chaplin—were very worrying. Hitler's warning had been loud and clear, but it was uncertain whether the Hollywood studios would listen: "Only time will tell how far the United States can and will take this film hatred against Germany. . . . The preparations and first reports lead us to suspect the worst."[14]

On the other side of the globe, relations between the various American studios were growing increasingly tense. Warner Brothers had begun work on its anti-Nazi film and did not appear overly concerned about any difficulties that its competitors might suffer in Germany as a result. Charlie Chaplin, on the other hand, was having second thoughts. According to various newspaper reports, he had decided to shelve his parody of Hitler. Presumably, he felt that the treatment of the Jews in Germany was so horrendous that the subject of dictatorship could no longer be treated humorously.[15]

The announcement of Chaplin's decision was received in Hollywood with a mixture of relief and dismay. For the studios still doing business in

Germany, it was a moment of opportunity. The foreign manager of Paramount—the one studio that had never even contemplated making an anti-Nazi picture, and therefore had never gotten into trouble with Georg Gyssling in the 1930s—took the unusual step of writing to the Hays Office to express concern about Warner Brothers' latest undertaking: "I think the big mistake that Warners are making in this matter is that they have not heeded the action taken by Charlie Chaplin in dropping his plan to make a burlesque on Hitler. . . . I feel sure that if [their] picture is made and is in any way uncomplimentary to Germany, as it must be if it is to be sincerely produced, then Warners will have on their hands the blood of a great many Jews in Germany."[16]

While Paramount was making these kinds of proclamations (and doing business with Germany), Jack Warner was campaigning in the opposite direction. He met with Franklin D. Roosevelt who, somewhat surprisingly, brought up Chaplin's abandonment of the Hitler picture. Roosevelt said that he hoped the picture might still come to fruition. Warner was of course delighted to hear Roosevelt's opinion on this matter, and he wrote to Chaplin immediately: "I . . . assured the President you had not planned to drop the making of it. . . . I remember your telling me . . . you were going ahead with it, and I hope you do, Charlie, for if the President of our country is interested in your making the picture it certainly has merit."[17]

Upon receiving this letter, Chaplin issued an official statement in which he denied that he had ever considered canceling the project. He was going ahead with it, and he was "not worried about intimidation, censorship or anything else."[18] The only problem was that he was a perfectionist, and he would need more than a year and a half to complete the film. Warner Brothers was not alone in its efforts, but its schedule was a lot tighter than Chaplin's, and it would eventually be credited as the first major studio to break the peace with Hitler.

The idea for its spy picture came from one of the most sensational stories to hit American newspapers in the previous year. From May 1936 to February 1938, a U.S. Army deserter named Günther Rumrich had carried out research for the Abwehr (the German military intelligence agency) from his home in New York City. He had managed to purchase the Z-Code—the signal used by the U.S. Army for transmitting messages ship to shore—and he had then been caught in an attempt to obtain fifty blank passports and the army mobilization plans for the eastern seaboard. His subsequent interrogation by a special agent in the Federal Bureau of Investigation, Leon G. Turrou, had led to the arrest of a Nazi spy network operating in the United States.[19]

On June 20, 1938, the day that eighteen individuals were indicted by a New York Grand Jury for espionage, Turrou resigned from the Federal Bureau of Investigation and three days later, he sold the film rights to his story to Warner Brothers.[20] The studio began working on a script, and when the trial concluded at the end of the year, a copy was sent to the Hays Office for inspection. Not surprisingly, Joseph Breen was very concerned. He had read the letter of protest from Paramount, and he understood that a controversial picture by Warner Brothers might endanger the business of other studios still selling movies in Germany. Nevertheless, after going through the script, he was forced to admit that the picture was technically within the provisions of the Production Code: it represented Germany "honestly" and "fairly" because it told a story of espionage that had not only been verified in a court of law but was also common knowledge throughout the United States.[21] Furthermore, Warner Brothers had been promised "indirect, if not direct, aid, assistance, and cooperation" from certain important government officials.[22] With relatively little fuss, Breen issued a certificate of approval for the project now entitled *Confessions of a Nazi Spy*.[23]

The actual production of the picture, which began on February 1, 1939, did not proceed quite as smoothly. Warner Brothers was forced to print only a limited number of scripts because Georg Gyssling and the German American Bund were desperately trying to get their hands on it. The regular studio workers received threatening phone calls, and several actors and producers received death threats. When the filming began, security guards were hired to prevent unauthorized people from entering the sound stage. The studio at least benefited by sending photographs of the security measures to the press for publicity purposes.[24]

After only six weeks of production, Warner Brothers had completed the first major anti-Nazi film. The names of the characters had been changed, but in every other respect, *Confessions of a Nazi Spy* turned out to be a remarkably faithful account of the events that had taken place in New York.

The film also pulled no punches, depicting all Nazis—whether spies or members of the German American Bund—as radical fanatics who took their orders directly from Berlin. American citizens were urged to be extremely vigilant and to stand up against this evil menace that threatened the democratic form of government.[25]

*Confessions of a Nazi Spy* was released on May 6, 1939, and the Nazis and their sympathizers reacted dramatically. Theaters were vandalized, critics in the Midwest were urged to write negative reviews, and Hollywood was denounced as a Jewish conspiracy. The German American Bund sought an injunction against the film and sued Warner Brothers for slander.[26] Hans Thomsen, acting chief of the German embassy in Washington, DC, submitted an official complaint to the State Department, and the German Foreign Office managed to have the picture banned in over twenty countries around the world.[27]

Despite all the drama and secrecy, however, *Confessions of a Nazi Spy* was by no means a great film. Warner Brothers claimed to have spent over $1.5 million on it, but the actual figure was closer to $656,000.[28] *Confessions of a Nazi Spy* was an obvious B-picture with exaggerated German characters, a cheesy narrator, and a simpleminded script. Unlike the abandoned productions of the past, it did not broach important subjects such as the persecution of the Jews (*The Mad Dog of Europe*, *Personal History*) or the fascist tendencies in American life (*It Can't Happen Here*). It was just a formulaic spy story with the Nazis playing the role of the villains. Many reviewers picked up on the cheapness of the production and wished that Warner Brothers had pitched its battle on a higher plane. "Hitler won't like it; neither will Goebbels," the *New York Times* commented. "Frankly, we were not too favorably impressed either."[29]

The *New York Times* was wrong about one detail. A copy of the film eventually ended up in the hands of the Propaganda Ministry, and one night, Goebbels actually watched it. Thirty-five minutes into the film, he saw a fictional version of himself appear on the screen. The character was giving instructions to the head of the German-American Bund on how to spread Nazi propaganda in the United States: "There is to be a slight change in our methods. From now on National Socialism in the United States must dress itself in the American flag. It must appear to be a defense of Americanism. But at the same time, our aim must always be to discredit conditions there in the United States and in this way make life in Germany admired and wished for. . . . In the ensuing chaos, we will be able to take control."

Goebbels was overwhelmed to see himself in a Hollywood movie. His fictional counterpart had made just a two-minute appearance, but Goebbels could not help exaggerating the part in his diary. "I myself play a main role and not even a particularly unpleasant one," he wrote. "But I do not consider the film dangerous otherwise. It arouses fear in our enemies rather than anger and hate."[30]

Even Goebbels had recognized that *Confessions of a Nazi Spy* was nothing to get worked up about. The unfortunate truth for Warner Brothers was that the production had not lived up to the controversy that surrounded it.[31] The reviews were of course dramatic. "Hollywood declares war on the Nazis," was a typical headline. "This film starts the war."[32] But the world remained at peace after Warner Brothers released *Confessions of a Nazi Spy*, and the other American studios did not even notice any great change in business conditions in Germany. If anything, their situation slightly improved. German exhibitors indicated that American pictures were still needed, and Goebbels himself was having second thoughts about Hitler's new policy. "Should we really suppress American films?" he asked himself. "I myself am not at all certain."[33]

Under these circumstances, the three remaining studios managed to continue with their regular business activities. They kept selling their movies in Germany, and they did not engage in any attacks on the Nazis. An executive at Twentieth Century-Fox, Walter J. Hutchinson, was asked whether the companies were pulling out, and he replied, "I never heard of such a thing. We'll stick in Germany as long as we can do business there." An executive at Paramount agreed: "It is only logical for us to do business wherever profitable as an obligation to our stockholders." The official attitude at the biggest studio of all was the same too: "M-G-M will make pictures without regard to politics and with only boxoffice and entertainment in mind."[34]

And so in the summer of 1939, Hollywood movies were still playing to packed theaters throughout Germany. In July and August alone, five new American features premiered in Berlin.[35] Then, on September 1, something happened that was much more significant than the release of a picture like *Confessions of a Nazi Spy*. German troops marched unannounced into Poland, and the Second World War began.

Within a few weeks, Britain, France, and the Soviet Union were all embroiled in the conflict. The United States remained neutral, however, and the Propaganda Ministry was determined that American movies should play unhindered in Germany as long as this was the case.[36] Will Hays did his part by issuing a statement on behalf of the American film industry: "There will be no cycle of 'hate' pictures. The primary purpose of . . . motion pictures is entertainment."[37] The system of collaboration therefore remained in place. The American studios continued to pander to the whims of the Nazi regime in a variety of ways. MGM, which was already financing the production of German armaments, now donated eleven of its most popular films, including *After the Thin Man* and *Viva Villa*, to the German government to help with the war relief effort.[38]

For the most part, American movies were well received in Germany in this period. Three MGM musicals were hugely successful: *Rose-Marie* played for forty-two days in Berlin, *Broadway Serenade* for fifty-six days, and *Honolulu* for sixty-nine days.[39] And in October 1939, just when the first newsreels of the successful campaign against Poland were hitting the screens in Germany, a Clark Gable film called *Too Hot to Handle*—which spoofed the newsreel business in America—was at the beginning of a thirty-five-day run. Audiences first applauded the German army during the actual newsreel footage and then watched what they perceived to be "the sequel": "a great plot involving a newsreel reporter—a kind of swindler with a big heart—in the South American wilderness. . . . And such irresistibly crazy things happen that by the end, the audience in the Marmorhaus could not stop laughing."[40]

As the war continued, however, serious doubts started entering the minds of the studio executives in Hollywood. Although a few of their films were still being shown in Germany, the hostilities were drastically reducing their much more significant business in England and France. This was a devastating development. Twentieth Century-Fox estimated its average weekly income for European countries before the war as follows: England, $200,000; France, $50,000; Germany, between $28,000 and $30,000. With the loss of most of this income, the studio executives were forced to take desperate measures. At Twentieth Century-Fox, MGM, Paramount, and Warner Brothers, hundreds of employees were dismissed; at Columbia Pictures, Harry and Jack Cohn took voluntary pay cuts of 33 percent; and various producers and advisory staff across the board took cuts ranging from 10 to 50 percent.[41]

Soon the heads of the studios were reconsidering their options. They started to think in terms similar to those laid out by William C. DeMille (the brother of the director) one year earlier: "By killing the sale of American films in most of Europe, Mr. Hitler, aided by the leaders of various other totalitarian states, has finally removed that chance of commercial gain which lies so close to the heart of international politeness. With all hope of profit gone, we can, at last, become properly indignant and raise our voices in shocked protest without any pecuniary regrets."[42] DeMille had made this statement prematurely, back when Warner Brothers was working on *Confessions of a Nazi Spy*. His words were much more relevant now. Hitler had cut Hollywood's foreign revenue by around half—not by prohibiting American movies but by initiating a war that was impacting European distribution—and the heads of the studios were having a change of heart. As the war raged in Europe, a commercially viable idea was starting to take shape in their minds.

Of course, there was nothing they could do about the situation in Europe. They were forced to accept that their markets had been severely damaged. But the Second World War was at least promising in one respect: it provided a terrific subject for future productions. And while the studio heads had avoided criticizing the Nazis in peacetime out of concern for the German market, they now had on their hands a topic so promising that the German market was starting to seem insignificant by comparison. They still had no intention of leaving Germany. They simply changed their priorities. In the words of one reporter, ideas were "creeping their way into the production agenda despite the cries of reactionary critics whose contention has been that the sole content of the motion picture should be 'escapist' entertainment."[43]

The change took place gradually. In early 1940, two of the studios still doing business in Germany—Twentieth Century-Fox and MGM—embarked on their first anti-Nazi films. The studio heads, who were breaking a policy that had been in place for nearly a decade, made sure to supervise every aspect of the production process. When Darryl Zanuck read an early draft of Twentieth Century-Fox's first anti-Nazi film, *Four Sons*, for example, he assembled his writers and announced his reaction:

"Generally speaking, Mr. Zanuck likes very much the way Mr. Lawson has handled the story. However there is one major mistake we must rectify, and that is: our personal story has been submerged to give prominence to the march of Events. It must be the other way around. . . . Mr. Zanuck mentioned NAZI SPY as a case in point, where the story concerned itself with a *problem*, and therefore the entertainment values suffered and the picture was not a success."[44]

Zanuck continued, "Hitler's name should be mentioned only once—in the early part of the story. When someone asks what it's all about, or whatever it is, he is told: 'Oh, there's some fellow by the name of Hitler who's doing so-and-so—' And from then on, Hitler's name should be kept out of it, although we do everything in connection with the Nazi activities just as you do it now."[45]

*Four Sons* was a relatively minor film set in Czechoslovakia that ignored the specific dangers of Nazism.[46] It greatly annoyed Georg Gyssling, who began "raising the roof" with the studio, but it made very little impact on anyone else.[47] In the meantime, however, a much more important film was underway at MGM. A few executives at that studio were finally being forced to confront a subject that they had been avoiding ever since Hitler had come to power in Germany.

The idea for the film was first suggested by an obscure MGM employee who had read Phyllis Bottome's best-selling novel *The Mortal Storm*, which had been published in the United States in 1938.[48] This employee had been deeply moved by the story and had sent a persuasive memorandum to the studio's production department: "This is not a book of propaganda, but a fair picture of the situation in Nazi-Germany. . . . If a picture is made on this controversial subject this book is recommended for aside from the politics involved it is a great story."[49]

MGM quickly purchased the film rights to *The Mortal Storm*, and four writers—Anderson Ellis, George Froeschel, John Goulder, and Claudine West—set about adapting it for the screen. They worked hard to convey the novel's central conception of a German family torn apart by the rise of Nazism. Here was the structure that they came up with:

On January 30, 1933, in a small university town in Germany, a happy family was sitting down to dinner. The family consisted of Professor Roth, a famous Jewish scientist; Emilia Roth, his non-Jewish wife; Freya and Rudi, their children; and two sons from Emilia's previous marriage named Otto and Erich von Rohn. As they were enjoying their meal, one of the servants burst into the room and announced that Adolf Hitler had been named chancellor of Germany.

Then everything disintegrated. Otto and Erich became ardent Nazis and joined the SA. Professor Roth was taken to a concentration camp, where he died under mysterious circumstances. His wife escaped to Austria with Rudi, and his daughter was killed in an attempt to escape at the end.[50]

This dramatic storyline represented a radical departure from Hollywood's previous policy toward Nazi Germany. Ever since 1933, the various studios had vowed neither to attack the Nazis nor to defend the Jews in their films. With the sudden loss of revenue in Europe, the studios had just started to rethink the first side of their policy; now they were being forced to rethink the second. The script for *The Mortal Storm* brought a Jewish character back into American cinema in dramatic fashion, and in one particular scene—taken straight from the book—it did even more.

The scene began this way: One afternoon, Rudi came home from school and told his mother and sister that he had been having problems with his friends. One boy had refused to sit next to him in the classroom, and a few others had thrown stones at him. At the end of the day, the headmaster had given him a form for his father to fill out. The form was headed "PROOF OF ARYAN DESCENT," and it ended with the question: "PERCENTAGE OF JEWISH BLOOD."[51]

His sister quickly understood what was going on. Just a few days earlier, she had used a strange term to describe her father—"Non-Aryan"—and now she was starting to see that the term applied to her and Rudi too. She said nothing, however, so Rudi decided to bring up the matter with his father.[52]

"I'm not a Jew, am I, Father?" Rudi asked. "Mother isn't—nor Otto and Erich—"

"You're right—they're not," Professor Roth answered. "But, Rudi, I am—"

"I know that, Father," Rudi said impatiently. "But it doesn't make any difference to me, does it?"

"It does, Rudi. . . . Since the new Government came into power, it's no longer a question of faith—it's a racial question—"

"What does that mean?"

"It means that no matter what your religion may be—if you have a certain percentage of Jewish blood, the Government considers you of Jewish race."

"You mean—I *am* Jewish?"

"From their standpoint, yes—"[53]

A look of dread appeared on Rudi's face. Professor Roth understood what Rudi was going through and decided to tell his son about his heritage. "I'm proud to be a Jew," he said. "I'm proud to belong to the race that gave Europe its religion and its moral law—much of its science, too—much of its genius, in art, literature and music. Mendelssohn was a Jew, and Rubenstein—the great English statesman, Disraeli, was a Jew, and so was our poet Heine, who wrote the 'Lorelei.'"[54]

But Rudi was not convinced, and he begged: "Father, do we *have* to put it on the form?"[55]

Professor Roth looked at his son sympathetically. "Things are not going to be easy for you, son," he replied, "but to know you're right is half the battle. Our race has . . . outlived persecution. God willing, we shall survive the injustice and cruelty of these bewildering days. When you're caught in a storm you must bow to it, but you mustn't be ashamed or afraid."

There was a brief silence. Then Rudi lifted his head and said, "I'm not afraid—now."

"I know I can rely on you and be proud of you," Professor Roth said. "You have gifts and qualities of *my* people—be true to them . . . Now, first the name—Rudolph Ulrich Roth—" Then, according to the script, "He starts to write—the camera goes to a close shot of Rudi—he looks out into the bleak future, first with bewilderment—then with tightening lips and defiant eyes as we FADE OUT."[56]

In early February 1940, just before *The Mortal Storm* went into production, a version of the script was sent to Phyllis Bottome, who had written the novel. Bottome was extremely impressed with what she read, but she had a few concerns, so she wrote to the producer, Sidney Franklin.

"I would not put in Freya's mouth the word: 'Non-Aryan' instead of Jew," she wrote. "In the early days of the Hitler regime, when the story takes place, the word 'Jew' was always used by proud and self-respecting

Jews of themselves. . . . Freya would have flung up her head and said with pride . . . 'My father is a Jew!' "

Next, Bottome turned to the father-son scene. "Rudi is a German boy," she said, "and it is a pity not to show him from the first, as far more proud of his father and loyal to him than anxious to escape his Jewish heritage. He would never have *begged* not to be a Jew." Bottome emphasized that this question of Jewish pride was "the crux of the book and the crux of the world today."[57]

Meanwhile, following normal practice, MGM sent every new copy of the script to the Hays Office for inspection. Joseph Breen read a total of sixteen scripts over eight months, including thirteen scripts while the film was in production. In this period, Breen did not hear a word of protest from the German consul, nor did he write to the studio with any objections of his own. He simply approved a picture in which the main character had expressed pride in being a Jew.[58]

The shooting took place over the next two months, and there was just one interruption. According to Sidney Franklin, "Every time I went on the set, it was like a private Germany of our own. I loathed the very sight of the swastika and all it stood for, and as production proceeded, I became increasingly disturbed. We were about half way through, when I went down on the set; stormtroopers were singing the Horst Wessel song, and some of them jumped a Jewish character and beat him into insensibility. It made me ill. The scene on the stage was like seeing the real thing that I'd been reading about in the newspapers."[59] Franklin approached the senior management of MGM and asked to be relieved of his duties, and in mid-March he was replaced by the British producer Victor Saville, who was of Jewish descent.

The production continued under Saville, and the father-son scene was shot. The scene lasted just a few minutes, and by all accounts it was deeply moving. The director Frank Borzage managed to get fine performances out of his actors, including Frank Morgan, who played the part of Professor Roth.[60] (Morgan had played the Wizard in *The Wizard of Oz* just the previous year.)[61]

Then, in late March or early April, a surprising announcement was made to the cast. One of the actors, Gene Reynolds, who played the part of Rudi, remembered it this way:

"There was a scene in which Rudi comes home and says to his father, 'I have been mistreated at school; they're threatening me . . . because I'm a Jew, and I don't understand.' And his father in this scene explains to him what it is to be a Jew, about the heritage, and so forth.

"The producer, I recall, coming down to the set, and he says, 'We cut that scene, and you'll notice that in the whole film nobody ever says "Jew." It's "Non-Aryan" but nobody ever says that "I am a Jew," "He's Jewish," and so forth.' And he said that with a certain amount of pride."[62]

Gene Reynolds, who had one Jewish parent himself, remembered more. "The scene ran several pages, and it was carefully written and intelligently written. . . . The boy said, 'They say at school that I'm a Jew, and I don't understand because we haven't emphasized being Jewish in the house. What is it to be a Jew?' And Frank Morgan, who was a beautiful actor and who later in the film went to a concentration camp . . . explained to me the long history of Jews, the great value of the religion, and the great accomplishment of Jews."[63]

When asked whether Victor Saville was personally responsible for cutting the scene, Reynolds said: "I do recall him smiling and pointing out how kind of clever he was. He sounded very much in charge of the opera-

Rudi (Gene Reynolds) brings a letter home to his father (Frank Morgan) in a scene from *The Mortal Storm* (1940). The scene, which broached the question of anti-Semitism in Germany, was cut from the film.

tion. But I don't think for a moment that this was done without counsel with L. B. Mayer and Mannix and whatever heavyweight producers there were that I'm sure were consulted. I'm sure they were all very into this.

"Certainly Saville could not have done it on his own. He'd have to have it approved. So it went to L. B. But I don't know who advised him, or whether it was just him alone."[64]

In the days that followed, all references to Jews were removed from the film. The father-son scene was completely eliminated, and many other lines of dialogue were changed as well. Some lines were simply deleted; other lines were reworked so that they lost their impact, such as the following: "Is it your opinion that there is no difference between the blood of an Aryan and the blood of a Non-Aryan?"

When *The Mortal Storm* was released on June 14, 1940, it was without any doubt the first truly significant anti-Nazi film. It starred Jimmy Stewart and Margaret Sullavan, it was actually set in Germany, and it attacked the Nazis for their persecution of a minority group. But in refusing to identify who that group was, the film ultimately made very little impact. According to a survey of three hundred people conducted two weeks before the film's release, "Outstanding impressions left by the picture were ACTING, 62 per cent . . . CHANGE DUE TO HITLER, 65 per cent . . . PROPAGANDA, 46 per cent . . . SCENIC BEAUTY, 45 per cent. JEWISH PERSECUTION impressed only 7 per cent."[65]

MGM conducted one final survey before releasing the new version of the film. A screening was organized for Edgar Magnin, the rabbi and close friend of Louis B. Mayer, and after the screening, Magnin was asked what he thought. "I think you've told a wonderful story," he replied. "There was a doubt in my mind whether that passage ("Father-Son" scene) should be in or out. When I spoke to Ida [the sister of Louis B. Mayer], she said they had the feeling there was no use overdoing it; whereas, others I spoke to wanted to present the Jewish side. I tried to take this into consideration as I looked at the picture and I think it is right just as it is—without it. . . ."

Magnin then edged closer to his real thoughts. "One thing in favor of our side now is that people may be sympathetic, (but not much), when they fear," he said, "and now they are afraid. They hate the thing they fear— that is the answer. They can still hate Jews and still fear Germany!"[66]

These comments, which were sent directly to Louis B. Mayer, captured the essence of the problem in Hollywood—namely that the studio heads had no desire to defend their Jewish heritage. They preferred (in Rabbi Magnin's words) to let the people hate Jews. This was extremely ironic in light of the dialogue that they had cut from the film. In the father-son scene, Professor Roth had declared pride in being a Jew. He had said that he was neither ashamed nor afraid of his heritage. He had faced his reality with great dignity. When his son had asked whether it was really necessary to declare one's Jewish identity—"Father, do we *have* to put it on the form?"—he had said yes. In cutting these lines, MGM was saying no.

Behind MGM's decision lay a powerful timidity—a sense that even in the United States, it was better to hide one's Jewish heritage. Several reasons have generally been given for this timidity: the studio heads, who mostly originated from Eastern Europe, wanted to see themselves as Americans rather than as Jews; they feared the likely reaction of anti-Semitic groups who were targeting their control of motion pictures; and they were constantly nervous about rocking the boat.[67]

But the most important reason lay in MGM's own past. Back in 1933, in an effort to hold onto the German market, Louis B. Mayer had agreed not to make *The Mad Dog of Europe*, a film that was remarkably similar to this one.[68] From that moment onward, the various studio heads, in compliance with the wishes of Georg Gyssling, made sure neither to attack the Nazis nor to defend the Jews in their films. And as a result of this new policy, the studio heads naturally became a lot warier of projecting their own Jewish identity into the world. In the past, they had made hundreds of movies about Jews. Now they acted as if Jews did not exist at all. Their timidity, in other words, was not inherent; it derived from their years of collaboration with Nazi Germany. In this context, it was perfectly logical that when they finally released a picture about the horrors of Nazism, *The Mortal Storm*, they would consciously erase all references to Jews at the end.

The problem with all of this was that the heads of MGM were setting a dangerous precedent. They were proposing the idea that Hollywood should attack the Nazis without engaging in any special pleading on behalf of the Jews. They were abandoning the first half of their agreement with Nazi Germany while leaving the second half intact.

In the months that followed, both MGM and Twentieth Century-Fox began work on new anti-Nazi pictures. MGM filmed a story about the imprisonment of a non-Jewish character in a German concentration camp (*Escape*).[69] And Twentieth Century-Fox carefully eliminated most Jewish references from a story about an American woman whose husband became an ardent Nazi (*I Married a Nazi*, later renamed *The Man I Married*). According to the studio records, "Mr. Zanuck was in complete agreement with the suggestion that we keep the Jewish element in the background as much as possible, except at the end when the husband learns that he is himself of Jewish blood."[70]

Even Charlie Chaplin toned down his picture, which was now nearing completion. Back on November 10, 1938, when the first reports of *Kristallnacht* were hitting American newspapers, Chaplin had rushed the first version of his story to the U.S. Copyright Office. The story had gone as follows: Hinkle, the dictator of Ptomania, had devised a scientific test to separate Jews from Aryans. All Jews were sent to concentration camps, and one named Charlie, who bore an uncanny resemblance to Hinkle, broke out. He was mistaken for the dictator, and he gave a speech that convinced the country to abandon fascism. Suddenly music filled the streets. Everyone started dancing. Prisoners were released from the camps. Storm troopers were dancing with Jews.

The script ended with an epilogue: "Through the music comes the playing of a bugle call. The scene shifts back to the concentration camp. Charlie wakes up with a smile as a storm-trooper enters. Charlie smiles at him. The storm trooper starts to smile back, then ashamed at his softness he bellows: 'Get up, Jew! Where the hell do you think you are?' "[71]

Chaplin took this chilling idea and turned it into a hilarious but less effective film. He shifted the location of the persecution of the Jews from a concentration camp to a ghetto. He gave a long, rambling speech at the climax that had virtually nothing to do with the Jewish question. And he replaced the twist at the end—in which his speech turned out to be the dream of a concentration camp prisoner—with his audience responding with cheers and applause.[72]

Obviously Georg Gyssling did not appreciate any of these efforts. From his perspective, *Escape*, *The Man I Married*, and *The Great Dictator* were virulent anti-Nazi films, and he informed the German ambassador in Washington, DC, about the two similar films already in distribution, *The*

*Mortal Storm* and *Four Sons.* The German ambassador then registered an official complaint with the State Department: "Both pictures are in all their details deliberate attempts to arouse public sentiment and hate in this country against the German people and their government. . . . Pictures like those mentioned above may . . . lead to a complete lack of interest to show any films of those two companies in Germany."[73] The State Department forwarded the letter to the Hays Office as a courtesy to the German government.[74]

The letter ended up in the hands not of Will Hays but of his foreign manager, Frederick Herron. Herron had always disapproved of the Germans' business methods, and he was not about to apologize for the fact that the studios had finally turned anti-Nazi. "We beg to disagree with the opinion of the German Consulate regarding the two pictures they mention," he told the State Department. "These two pictures are dramatic portrayals of stories laid in Germany and were produced solely for the purpose of supplying the theatres and their public throughout the world with amusement. . . . The motion picture business differs in no way from any other form of business and it would be ridiculous to suppose that a producer would deliberately place any material in a picture that would tend to drive people away from the box office."[75]

It was the final straw. The German government had issued an official warning in accordance with Article Fifteen of the film regulations. Now the government could act. On July 5, 1940, the Propaganda Ministry informed Twentieth Century-Fox that it could no longer distribute motion pictures or newsreels in Germany, Norway, Bohemia, or Moravia.[76] The management of Twentieth Century-Fox was astounded to hear that the ban extended beyond the traditional German border and asked the State Department to intervene: "If our local companies are prohibited from the continued distribution of our films in the countries enumerated, this corporation will suffer huge losses in income due to the interruption and stoppage of our business."[77] The head of the film department of the Propaganda Ministry stood firm, however, and announced that the decision would be upheld and that the other American motion picture producers should "take the measure as a warning."[78]

MGM paid no attention and kept its anti-Nazi film in circulation. Then, on August 15, the studio was expelled from Germany and all German-occupied territories.[79] The reason for the expulsion was the production and distribution of the anti-Nazi film *The Mortal Storm*.[80] MGM responded to the news by announcing that it was being forced to dismiss 660 employees in Germany, France, Belgium, Czechoslovakia, Holland, Denmark, and Norway. The German government was directly responsible for these job losses throughout Europe.[81]

That left Paramount as the one American studio still doing business in Germany, and on September 12, it was officially expelled as well.[82] "Although Fox and Metro-Goldwyn-Mayer were accused of making anti-German pictures," the official report stated, "no such accusation is made of regular Paramount films." The reason for the expulsion order was flimsy by comparison: apparently the captions of a few Paramount newsreels had been unfriendly toward Germany.[83] There was some cause for hope, though. "When the war ends," the Paramount manager was told, "American film producers will be allowed to engage in business on a restricted scale providing they guarantee corresponding showings of German films in the United States."[84]

The enforcement of Article Fifteen had turned out to be much more damaging than the studios had imagined. Instead of losing the relatively small German market, they had lost all German-occupied territory, which by this point covered a lot of ground. The studios were forced to take solace in the offhand comment about future dealings. "Later," one trade paper reported, "a more co-operative attitude may be adopted by the Nazis, especially if German product fails to satisfy."[85] The implication of this sentence, of course, was that Hitler would win the war.

For the present, however, the greater German market had been lost. The Nazis had finally enforced a section of the film regulations that they had reserved as a threat for almost eight years. When the enforcement was complete, the Foreign Office informed all German consulates and embassies of the reason behind the government's decision: "Because the American film companies MGM, Twentieth Century-Fox, and Paramount have continued to distribute hate films of the worst sort (*The Mortal Storm*, *Four Sons*, etc.) all around the world—despite repeated requests from the Propaganda Ministry to their representatives in Berlin to cease production of anti-German hate films or to withdraw from circulation those already made—it has been ordered that from now on *none of their films* may be screened in the greater German Reich."[86]

As a result of this development, the Hollywood studios were free to make as many anti-Nazi films as they liked. They no longer needed to pay attention to the German authorities. In the year that followed, however, the studios released only a handful of such films, none of which contained any reference to the persecution of the Jews. Twentieth Century-Fox made *Man Hunt*, Warner Brothers made *Underground*, Columbia Pictures made *They Dare Not Love*, and United Artists released *Foreign Correspondent*.[87]

Hollywood was still apprehensive about making anti-Nazi pictures, but the reason for its apprehension had changed. While most Americans at this point supported President Roosevelt's provision of aid to Britain and the other allied nations, a significant isolationist movement had emerged in the United States.[88] The isolationists were accusing Hollywood of producing insidious propaganda designed to draw the country into the European conflict, and in September 1941, their efforts came to a climax when they spearheaded an investigation into propaganda in motion pictures before a subcommittee of the Committee on Interstate Commerce of the U.S. Senate. Most of the senators on the subcommittee were isolationists, including Gerald P. Nye of North Dakota. The only senator in favor of Roosevelt's policies was Ernest McFarland of Arizona.[89]

The first person to testify was Gerald P. Nye, who pointed out that he was not an anti-Semite ("I have splendid Jewish friends in and out of the moving-picture business"). Nye then said that the Hollywood studios had by this stage produced fifteen or twenty propaganda pictures whose purpose was to draw the United States into the European war.[90]

Senator McFarland eventually asked an important question. "You stated that you had seen some of these war pictures?"

"That is right," Senator Nye said.

"Which of those pictures was the most objectionable that you saw, from your point of view?"

Senator Nye stumbled through his response. "Senator, you have propounded to me a question that is most difficult of answer," he said. "It is a terrible weakness of mine to go to a picture tonight and not be able to state the title of it tomorrow morning. . . . I could not tell you what I would consider the worst of them all. Somehow or other I have a rather lasting impression of what I recall as having been a picture under the title 'I Married a Nazi.'"

"All right. We will take that picture. What was there in that picture that was particularly objectionable from your point of view?"

"Why, primarily it was the injection of scenes that could only have the effect of making us hate not only a fictional individual but an entire race of people."

"What was portrayed that created that feeling?"

"Senator, I have not reviewed a picture in a long, long time."

"What is another picture that you think of that you saw, that was objectionable to you?"

"Oh, Senator, I have seen three or four or five of them."

"Can you name one other?"

"I am afraid I cannot."

"Let me see if I can help you a little bit. Did you see Escape?"

"Perhaps if you can tell me a part of the story I could tell you better whether I had seen Escape or not."

McFarland confessed that he had not seen the picture himself, and then moved on. "Flight Command?"

"I do not believe I did, Senator."

"That Hamilton Woman?"

"I did not see that."

"Man Hunt?"

"I think not."

"Sergeant York?"

"I think not."

"You mean, you have not seen it?"

"I have not seen it."

"Did you see The Great Dictator?"

"I have."

"What in that picture was particularly objectionable to you?"

"Why, it was a portrayal by a great artist, not a citizen of our country, though he has resided here a long, long while, that could not do other than build within the mind and heart of those who watched it something of hatred, detestation of conditions and of leadership that existed abroad."

There was a brief interjection in which the defense pointed out that *The Great Dictator* had been made outside the studio system. Senator McFarland then mentioned one last title. "The Confessions of a Nazi Spy, did you see that picture?"

"I do not know whether I have been talking about The Confessions of a Nazi Spy or I Married a Nazi. For the life of me I could not tell you which was which."[91]

The hearings continued for several days, during which time a variety of other witnesses spoke unconvincingly about Hollywood's warmongering tendencies. Then the executives of the major studios were given a chance to respond. Nicholas Schenck appeared for MGM, Harry Warner for Warner Brothers, and Darryl Zanuck for Twentieth Century-Fox.[92] The executives all spoke with great passion, but Zanuck's speech was the most rousing of all. He denied that Hollywood had ever produced anything resembling propaganda, and then he declared his pride in the motion picture industry: "I look back and recall picture after picture, pictures so strong and powerful that they sold the American way of life, not only to America but to the entire world. They sold it so strongly that when dictators took over Italy and Germany, what did Hitler and his flunky, Mussolini, do? The first thing they did was to ban our pictures, throw us out. They wanted no part of the American way of life."[93] At the end of Zanuck's speech, there was great applause, and one of the isolationist senators even found himself admitting that the speech was very convincing. No one pointed out that Zanuck's own studio had been doing business in Germany just the previous year.

The Hollywood executives had one last trick up their sleeve. They had appointed Wendell Willkie, the Republican presidential candidate who had lost to Roosevelt in 1940, as their representative. And Willkie made sure to attack one of the isolationists' most persistent claims, namely that the studios were motivated only by profit. Willkie began by summarizing the isolationists' position: "Senator Nye adds . . . that the men who hold the trusteeship of the motion-picture industry oppose nazi-ism and support the British for mercenary reasons. . . . This, obviously, we do not admit." Then Willkie made a powerful move:

But, taking Senator Nye's assumption as correct and following his line of reasoning, then the motion-picture industry, for its own financial advantage, should at once become the great appeasers of nazi-ism. As is well known, the advocates of doing business with Hitler and of a negotiated peace, maintain that if the policies they advocate were adopted, peace would reign in the world and Nazi

Germany and the United States could [continue] extensive trade relations. Under such assumed conditions, the motion-picture industry would not alone retain its business in Great Britain, but would regain the very large volume of business which it lost in Germany and in Central Europe even before the outbreak of the war as well as since then. The motion-picture industry would be against appeasing Hitler even if such a result for it would follow.[94]

Willkie's claim in front of this committee of the U.S. Senate was remarkable. He was not merely agreeing with Zanuck's rewriting of history. He was also giving a designation to the Hollywood studios in the hypothetical (and presumably absurd) situation that they did do business with Hitler. In this situation, he said, the studios would become "the great appeasers of nazi-ism."

On September 26, 1941, after two and a half weeks of hearings, the investigation into the motion picture industry came to an end. The Hollywood studios had managed not only to clear their reputation but also to erase their record of business dealings with Nazi Germany. The isolationists, on the other hand, had made fools of themselves. But they could never have achieved anything anyway. On December 7, the Japanese bombed Pearl Harbor, and the United States entered the greatest armed conflict the world had ever known.

In the period that followed, from 1942 to 1945, Hollywood went to war. The various studios together produced a staggering number of films to support the nation in the struggle against fascism. According to one study, more than 800 of the 1,500 feature films that reached theaters in this period were concerned in some way with the Second World War. Of these films, 242 referred explicitly to the Nazis and 190 to Hitler.[95]

The sudden transformation of the motion picture industry was due in part to the efforts of the U.S. government. On June 13, 1942, Franklin D. Roosevelt created the Office of War Information (OWI), a propaganda agency with a separate motion picture division, and within a short time, the OWI began examining the scripts of Hollywood films. For every title, the OWI asked the relevant studio a series of questions, beginning with the most important: "Will this picture help win the war?"[96]

The OWI, like the Propaganda Ministry in Germany, adopted a flexible approach toward the concept of propaganda. In Joseph Goebbels' opinion, "Even entertainment can be politically of special value, because the moment a person is conscious of propaganda, propaganda becomes ineffective. However, as soon as propaganda as a tendency, as a characteristic, as an attitude, remains in the background and becomes apparent through human beings, then propaganda becomes effective in every respect."[97] The head of the OWI, Elmer Davis, agreed: "The easiest way to inject a propaganda idea into most people's minds is to let it go in through the medium of an entertainment picture when they do not realize that they are being propagandized."[98]

The similarities between the two agencies ended here, however, for whereas the Germans made only a few propaganda films that were popular on a mass scale, the Americans made many. This was the period in which Hollywood released some of its most celebrated productions, including *Casablanca* (1942), in which the ideological message was powerfully embedded in the drama between the two main characters. The OWI was impressed with the way these characters, played by Ingrid Bergman and Humphrey Bogart, subordinated their feelings for each other to the central task of defeating fascism. In the OWI's words, "The heroine and the man she loves sacrifice their personal happiness in order that each may carry on the fight in the most effective manner. They realize that they cannot steal happiness with the rest of the world enslaved."[99]

Even more successful than *Casablanca* was the top-grossing film of 1942, *Mrs. Miniver.* The OWI classified this account of the struggles of a British family in the early days of the Second World War as "a very thoughtful, a very moving, and a very handsomely mounted picture."[100] The British prime minister Winston Churchill went even further, announcing that the effect of the film "on public sentiment in the USA was worth a whole regiment" during the war.[101] The most enthusiastic viewer of all, however, was Joseph Goebbels, who managed to obtain a copy of the film one year after its release: "This evening I'm going to have the much-discussed American-English film *Mrs. Miniver* screened. It shows the destiny of a family during the current war, and its refined, powerful propagandistic tendency has up to now only been dreamed of. Here you can see the achievement of everything that I have been demanding from German filmmakers for months, indeed for years now. The Americans have a masterful way of turning marginal details into artistic flourishes. The life of an English family is described, and you are forced to find them likeable. There is not a single angry word spoken against Germany; nevertheless, the anti-German tendency is perfectly accomplished. I will show this film to German producers to explain how it must be done."[102]

The above testimonies demonstrate that from 1942 onward, the Hollywood studios mounted an effective, coordinated attack on Nazi Germany. All the studios except Paramount submitted their scripts to the OWI, and they generally complied with the OWI's suggestions and recommendations. But how did the studios depict the persecution of the Jews? That was quite a different question.

The OWI's position, at least, was straightforward. The organization praised a minor aspect of a film called *The Pied Piper* in 1942: "An interesting insight . . . is provided by the character of the Gestapo official whose little niece is half Jewish. . . . He is beginning to question the morality . . . of a system that persecutes innocent children."[103] The organization also praised *Margin for Error*, a film about a Jewish policeman providing protection for the German consul in New York: "Although this Jew dislikes the assignment to protect a man who represents Jewish persecution, he agrees with his Irish police captain that . . . it might be a good idea to show the Nazi the meaning of our way of life."[104]

The OWI was especially enthusiastic about a third film called *Once Upon a Honeymoon* (RKO), which starred Cary Grant and Ginger Rogers. This was a comedy about an American woman named Katie O'Hara (Ginger Rogers) who was living in Vienna and pretending to be an aristocrat so that she could marry a wealthy Austrian, Baron von Luber. When a foreign correspondent named Pat O'Toole (Cary Grant) told Katie that Baron von Luber was a member of Hitler's inner circle, she at first refused to believe him, but she eventually realized that he was right. She then traveled with him throughout war-torn Europe, where they witnessed all sorts of atrocities, and finally they returned home to the United States.[105]

In the official report, the OWI reviewers explained just what made *Once Upon a Honeymoon* so distinctive. Like other anti-Nazi movies, they said, this film showed terrible German aggression and the defeat of one country after another. But the film also showed something else: "the Nazis' special oppression of the Jewish people." According to the report, *"An attempt is made to show the cruelty and unreasonableness of minority discrimination. The*

Jewish problem is brought out with extreme frankness, and in two important instances the full terror and pathos of the plight of these tragic people is depicted."[106]

The OWI reviewers went on to describe these two instances. In the first, Katie O'Hara was in her hotel room in Warsaw during the German occupation of Poland. Her chambermaid entered the room with two children and announced that the Germans were going to take them away. "We are Jewish," the chambermaid explained. Katie reacted quickly. She put a photo of the chambermaid in her own passport and she noted down the names of the two children. She then exchanged passports with the chambermaid, and she escorted the family to a truck that was about to leave the country. "Go somewhere where it's safe," she said as the truck pulled away. "Where?" the chambermaid replied.

A few days later, Katie and Pat (the American reporter) were wandering the streets of Warsaw. They were stopped by two Gestapo officers, and after a brief search, the passport of the Jewish chambermaid was found. As a result, they were thrown in a concentration camp. They sat with a group of Polish Jews behind a barbed-wire fence, and a cantor sang a prayer in the background. "We're really in a mess, aren't we?" Katie said. Pat replied, "What about these people?" Then, for about a minute, the characters sat in silence, and in the words of the OWI, "they—and we—get the full impact of the suffering and terror experienced by thousands of these unfortunate people throughout Europe."[107]

The concentration camp scene in *Once Upon a Honeymoon* was unprecedented in American cinema, and the OWI reviewers strongly approved of it. "The above portions of the film are immensely effective," they wrote, "and the film deserves great commendation for its treatment of this important problem."[108] But their report did not end there. The film, they said, also contained a couple of scenes that threatened to undo all this good work. They proceeded to explain what they meant.

They began with the first scene, which occurred immediately before Katie and Pat were interned in the concentration camp. The two Gestapo officers had just discovered the passport of the Jewish chambermaid, and one of them read out the name—"Anna Sarah Beckstein. Juden." The officer then turned to Pat. "Und sie sind der Jude Beckstein?" he asked ("And you are the Jew, Beckstein?"). Pat of course said no. That was when the German officer came up with an idea. He noticed a derby hat hanging on the wall behind him, and he remembered the popular stereotype of the Jewish performer who wore a derby hat crammed down over his ears and who waved his arms about in an exaggerated manner. The German officer decided to put the stereotype to the test. According to the stage directions: "trooper jams derby down on Pat's head—pushes his ears down—hits hat down . . . [Katie] puts hand to mouth—starts to laugh—[Pat] stares down at her . . . waving his hands—trying to explain—Katie going into hysterics . . . doubles up laughing." This routine went on for some time until Katie, who had been laughing so hard that she had been unable to speak, finally looked up at Pat and said, "Why don't you . . . just give yourself up?"[109]

*Once Upon a Honeymoon* contained another scene that was no less offensive. Toward the end of the film, Pat gave a radio broadcast in which he told a few stories about the chief villain, Baron von Luber. He ended by pointing out that von Luber had married a Jew. He then called Katie over to the microphone and she started to speak:

> KATIE (in Jewish accent): Hallo! . . . Hah do yah do . . . (moves on to a rather Semetic-looking German woman) By any chance is your name, Kaplan? . . . (moves on among people) . . . Are you all getting enough to eat? If the Baron had only told me . . . the schlemiehl—I could have made blinzes. . . . Of cuss, I don't make them like my mamma—my sweet softic mamma . . . "Ketzelleh", she'd say . . . she always called me "Ketzelleh" . . . "Ketzelleh, dolling, sit donn bime table and in two seconts I'll fix fa you some knishes, believe me you'll positively gung to lick by you the fingess!" And her potato lotkess . . . my sweet mama would say "is mine pahtateh lotkess simply gudjuss udder not?"[110]

The OWI reviewers were concerned about the above two scenes, and they wrote to the studio in question, RKO. They accepted RKO's assurances that the director of the film, Leo McCarey, had always gone to great lengths to avoid anything in bad taste.[111] They also accepted that the scenes had occasioned much laughter among preview audiences. Nevertheless, they said, "if there is any chance that the scenes may be misinterpreted or cause bitterness among our Jewish population, they would better be omitted."[112] Their recommendation was taken seriously.

In the final cut of the film, there was no trace of either of the offensive scenes.

The OWI's record with respect to the Jewish question, therefore, was impressive. The organization encouraged the studios to expose the persecution of the Jews and discouraged offensive or demeaning stereotypes. The record of the studios themselves, however, was quite another matter. In the period stemming from America's entry into the war in December 1941 to Franklin D. Roosevelt's creation of a War Refugee Board in January 1944, the studios released only one other picture that mentioned the Jews in Germany (*Hitler's Children*) and one other that mentioned Jews at all (*Bataan*).[113] There were hundreds of anti-Nazi films, of course—films that gave audiences the impression that Hollywood was a bastion of democracy—but with respect to the persecution of the Jews, there were a few brief references in *The Pied Piper* and *Margin for Error*, and the two-minute concentration camp scene in *Once Upon a Honeymoon*.

The reason for this reticence was clear. After a decade of training themselves to avoid any mention of Jews in their films, the studio heads were simply not ready to engage in what they understood as special pleading. Their years of collaboration with Nazi Germany had marked them too deeply. The German market was closed now, and the United States had entered the war, but the heads of the Hollywood studios—most of whom were Jews themselves—were unwilling to say anything about the plight of the Jews of Europe.

And yet despite their best efforts, they could never have prevented what came next. Out of their own empire there suddenly emerged a new kind of voice, one that could only have emerged in this particular time and place. The voice, which provided a corrective to their silence and which questioned their whole attitude toward their Jewishness, belonged to one of their most valued employees: the prolific screenwriter Ben Hecht.

Hecht had been born in New York City in 1894 to Jewish immigrant parents, and by the age of seventeen, he had already become an established reporter for the *Chicago Daily News*. In 1924, he had moved back to New York to write books and short stories, and soon afterward, he had found himself in financial difficulties. Then—at least according to his version of the story—one spring day in 1925, a telegram had arrived from his friend Herman Mankiewicz: "Will you accept three hundred per week to work for Paramount Pictures. All expenses paid. The three hundred is peanuts. Millions are to be grabbed out here and your only competition is idiots. Don't let this get around."[114]

Hecht accepted the offer, and he quickly became one of the highest-paid writers in Hollywood. He received the first-ever Academy Award for Best Story for his gangster picture *Underworld* (1927), and he went on to write such classics as *Scarface* (1932), *Design for Living* (1933), *Viva Villa* (1934), *Nothing Sacred* (1937), and *His Girl Friday* (1940). In total he wrote nearly 100 screenplays, many of which he churned out in a matter of days. One of his favorite boasts was that he had written the final script of *Gone with the Wind* in a week without actually having read the book.[115]

Ben Hecht, screenwriter and Jewish activist. Courtesy of Keystone; Getty Images.

Despite this stunning record, Hecht had little respect for the movies, mainly because he felt his own work was constantly being butchered at the last moment. He frequently lost his temper about this, and on several occasions he complained to the producer in question. One of his letters to Samuel Goldwyn in 1938 was particularly brutal: "The wanton and amateur rewriting of the last half of the material I gave you, the idiot sabotage played with my lines, scenes and plot points; the totally psychopathic mania for change . . . all these items make it impossible for me ever to write anything more for your use or discarding. . . . I am sorry to start rabbit punching, Sam, because outside of your lack of respect for my work and your curious urge to change, lessen and debauch it, I found you charming and pleasing to be with and work for. Allow me to walk out with nothing more offensive than a pout, a sigh and a friendly 'never again.' Good luck . . ."[116]

Although Hecht rarely kept such promises (he was back working for Goldwyn the following year), the above letter made one thing clear. He had guts. He could stand up to anyone, even the person who paid his salary. And in November 1938, after hearing about the brutal pogroms against the Jews on *Kristallnacht*, he found himself standing up for a political cause for the first time in his life. The news from Germany transformed him. Until he heard it, he later explained, he had never really considered himself a Jew. Now he looked upon the world with Jewish eyes, and he spoke out against what the Germans were doing. "No such urgent decision," he said, "had ever commanded me before."[117]

His first contribution to the Jewish cause was astounding. In June 1939, a collection of his short stories was published, and in the second story, "The Little Candle," he revealed how well he understood the situation in Germany:

On that dreadful July morning when we Jews opened our morning newspapers to see what kind of face the world had made overnight we expected to read the usual accounts of other people's troubles, and a few of our own. . . . We learned that overnight some five hundred thousand Jews had been murdered in Germany, Italy, Rumania, and Poland. . . . The need to purge these lands of the contaminating Jew—finally and forever—had become so urgent that to have delayed any longer would have been to endanger the racial welfare of all

Germans, Rumanians, Italians, and Poles. So the mad face with the comedian's mustache, called the Fuehrer, informed us.[118]

Hecht wrote these words two months before the outbreak of the Second World War and two years before the commencement of the extermination program. He seemed to have little doubt about where Hitler's anti-Semitic policies were leading. But he was not only interested in the situation in Germany. He quickly moved on to his main subject: the reaction of a small Jewish community in New York to the news. In his story, the members of the community all raced to their local synagogue to ask their rabbi, a man they absolutely trusted, what to do. The rabbi simply told them to go home. Then, when the rabbi was alone, he started to argue with God. He did not blame God for the massacre—he blamed the Germans—but he was nevertheless angry. "It is this that I have thought," he told God, "that in order to have Your Name written in a book, You have driven a handful of Your children mad. . . . O Mighty God, recall Your error. Withdraw Your mistake from the earth. Unbind the mummy of Israel. Make him into a man, O Lord of Hosts. You need us no more."[119]

The prayers ran for several hours. Then, late in the night, the "Shabbes-goy"—the gentile whose job it was to light the candles on the Sabbath—entered the synagogue and found the body of the rabbi hanging from a beam. He cut the body down, he performed his cleaning duties, and for some reason he lit a small candle before he left.

When the congregation visited the synagogue the next morning, they learned of the passing of their rabbi. They started to pray, and suddenly they noticed that a single candle was still alight even though the others had burned down. "A miracle—a miracle!" they cried, and all was forgiven. "For such is the trusting heart of the Jew that the little candle dispelled the darkness of the great massacre," Hecht wrote. "The Jew was such a light, feeble and powerless, but never to be extinguished. God had placed him in a world of cruelty and darkness and had bidden him to keep His image glowing."[120]

In this remarkable fable, Hecht was revealing his thoughts and feelings about his newly discovered Jewish identity for the first time. All the traits of his future activism—his anger at the Nazis, his shame and bitterness at the Jewish response—were there. At the same time, he knew very well that only a small group of people would read "The Little Candle." If his voice were to be heard, he would need to venture beyond the realm of literature. And so, at the beginning of 1941, he accepted a position as a columnist for *PM*, a left-wing daily newspaper based in New York that featured cartoons by Dr. Seuss and Crockett Johnson. The slogan of the paper was "We are against people who push other people around."[121]

Hecht was exhilarated by his new role. He was given free rein by the editor, Ralph Ingersoll, to write about whatever he wanted, and he used the opportunity to explore his new ideas about the plight of the Jews. His first article on the subject was addressed to the heads of the Hollywood studios. He pointed out that they had recently received a visit from Joseph P. Kennedy, the former U.S. ambassador to Great Britain, and that Kennedy had urged them not to use their movies as a propaganda weapon against the Nazis. Hecht told the studio heads not to buy into Kennedy's argument that such pictures would lead to an increase in anti-Semitism in the United States. He said that such thinking had been designed merely to play on their fears.[122]

Then, in late March, he wrote an article that angered a large number of his readers. In it, he made fun of a group of Jews in the United States who were desperately trying to escape their Jewish identity. These people, he said, most of whom were wealthy and sophisticated, were clutching at the idea that they were Americans rather than Jews. They believed that if they proved that there were no Jews in the world—that no such race existed—then there would be no problem. Hecht called the article "Run, Sheep—Run!" and he received a large number of angry letters soon after it was published.[123]

He responded with an even harder-hitting article—a manifesto that he titled "My Tribe Is Called Israel." "I write of Jews today," he proclaimed, "I who never knew himself as one before, because that part of me which is Jewish is under a violent and apelike attack. My way of defending myself is to answer as a Jew." He then addressed his critics who were trying to hide their Jewish origins: "It is not I who am bringing this Jew-consciousness back into the world. It is back on all the radios of Europe and on an alarming proportion of them in the U. S. A. . . . I suggest . . . that you stop wasting your angers on me. I am not attacking you. I am only asking you to fight. And I have tried in my small way to bring into the long battered soul of the Jew the pride and mental stamina many Jews like myself feel under attack." Hecht ended his article by announcing his plan of action

for the remainder of the war. "Since we are Jews in the eyes of our enemies," he said, "since they have with great cunning and malice reinvented
us—all I suggest is that we turn into Frankensteins."[124]

Hecht continued writing for *PM* throughout 1941, and in late August,
one of his articles caught the attention of a Palestinian Jew named Peter
Bergson. Bergson had moved to the United States to raise money for the
Irgun, an armed underground that was pushing for the immediate estab-
lishment of a Jewish state in Palestine, but in 1940, with the war raging in
Europe, Bergson had changed his priorities. He had decided to focus his
energies instead on the creation of a Jewish army to fight Hitler. He now
read the latest article by Hecht in *PM*, and he decided to write to the eminent Hollywood screenwriter. "Thanks for giving in Sundays PM magnificent expression to the pride and spiritual heroism which for centuries
accumulated in the soul of the genuine and conscious Jew. By the creation
of a Jewish army we intend to transform this heroic spirit into heroic
deeds."[125]

Hecht was intrigued. A second letter from Bergson soon arrived, and
eventually Hecht agreed to meet the Committee for a Jewish Army at the
Twenty One Club in New York. He listened carefully as the representatives outlined their plans, and he felt some uncertainty. On the one hand,
he did not share their hope for the creation of a Jewish state in Palestine.
On the other, he was impressed with their courage and tenacity. In the
end, he decided to join the group under two conditions. First, the Jewish
Army should not include American Jews (who were eligible to serve in the
U.S. Army). Second, all Palestinian politics should be put aside.[126]

In the year that followed, Hecht spread the committee's message to
everyone he knew. He told his friends and colleagues that the idea of a
group of Jews fighting Germans under their own flag would "thrill all the
Jews of the world." He said it would finally "bring respect back to the
name of Jew."[127] Then, on November 25, 1942, the situation suddenly
changed. Something happened that stopped Hecht in his tracks.

He read in the newspaper that some two million Jews in Poland, Germany, Austria, and the Netherlands had been murdered by the Nazis.
According to a report that had been confirmed by the State Department, these murders represented the "first step toward complete liqui-
dation." A whole brutal scheme had been established: first, the old and
disabled Jews were taken to a cemetery and shot. Then the rest were

packed into freight cars that had been covered with a thick layer of lime or chlorine. Many of the passengers died from inhaling the fumes, and the ones who survived were sent to extermination camps at Treblinka, Belzec, and Sobibor. "Thus under the guise of resettlement in the east," the newspaper announced, "the mass murder of the Jewish population is taking place."[128]

This brief article, which appeared on page ten of the *New York Times*, did not come as a surprise to the American authorities. Back in August, the American legation in Bern had cabled Washington about "a plan to exterminate all Jews from Germany and German controlled areas in Europe." The State Department had then suppressed the news and urged the head of the World Jewish Congress, Dr. Stephen Wise, to say nothing on the subject. At the time of the original report, one and a half million Jews had been killed by the Nazis; in the three-month delay leading to the announcement, one million more.[129]

Then, two weeks after the announcement, the leaders of the major Jewish organizations in America joined together to meet with President Roosevelt. The meeting—the only one that Roosevelt granted to Jewish leaders on the subject of the genocide—lasted half an hour. Roosevelt began with a humorous anecdote about his plans for a postwar Germany. Then he got to the point. "The government of the United States is very well acquainted with most of the facts you are now bringing to our attention," he said. "Unfortunately we have received confirmation from many sources." He quickly agreed to the Jewish leaders' one demand, namely for a warning to be issued to the Nazis about war crimes, and he asked for further suggestions. The Jewish leaders had none.[130]

The leaders then went their separate ways, and in the months that followed, the major Jewish organizations did not radically change their agendas. The American Jewish Congress developed several concrete proposals for rescue but implemented very few. The other organizations, including the American Jewish Committee and the B'nai B'rith, focused on the question of rescue even less.[131]

The members of the Committee for a Jewish Army were stunned by these developments. Their militant Zionism had alienated them from the mainstream Jewish organizations in the past, and as a result, they had not been invited to the meeting with Roosevelt. But after hearing about the genocide they changed their course. Just as they had put aside their Zionism after their meeting with Ben Hecht, they now more or less shelved the Jewish army idea. They put their energies into a single goal: the immediate rescue of the Jews of Europe.[132]

Their first action was to take out a full-page advertisement in the *New York Times* on December 5 addressed "To the Conscience Of America." In it they declared: "Let an American Commission of military and governmental experts not only prepare an indictment against those guilty. . . . Let it find a way to stop this wholesale murder!"[133] Throughout the following year, the Committee for a Jewish Army put out dozens of advertisements in the major newspapers, always pushing for the same thing: "It is . . . our primordial demand that an inter-governmental commission of military experts be appointed with the task of elaborating ways and means to stop the wholesale slaughter of the Jews in Europe. This must be done now—before the greatest homicidal maniac extends his policy of extermination to other peoples; before he dares introducing poison gas and bacteriological warfare."[134]

Ben Hecht wrote many of these advertisements himself, and on several occasions he even took responsibility for them. In early February 1943, for example, he heard that the Rumanian government had offered to transport 70,000 Jews to safety at a rate of 20,000 lei per person. He thought through the implications of the offer, and he came up with a shocking headline:

For Sale to Humanity
70,000 Jews
Guaranteed Human Beings at $50 a Piece

Underneath he wrote: "Roumania is tired of killing Jews. It has killed one hundred thousand of them in two years. Roumania will now give Jews away practically for nothing. Seventy thousand Jews are waiting death in Roumanian concentration camps. . . . It is an unprecedented offer! Seventy thousand souls at $50 a piece! The Doors of Roumania Are Open! Act Now!" In the middle of the advertisement he signed his name: Ben Hecht.[135]

The representatives of the State Department, who had already decided that they would not participate in the Rumanian proposal, ignored the advertisement.[136] The leaders of the major Jewish organizations, on the other hand, were outraged. They accused the Committee for a Jewish Army of implying that every $50 contribution would save a Jewish life, and they continued to distance themselves from the group.[137]

As the weeks passed, that distance grew. When the leaders of the American Jewish Congress heard that Ben Hecht was planning a rally at Madison Square Garden on March 9, they quickly scheduled a rally at the same location on March 1. Twenty thousand people came to hear speeches that night by American Federation of Labor president William Green, New York mayor Fiorello La Guardia, the head of the World Jewish Congress Stephen Wise, and the Zionist leader Chaim Weizmann. After neglecting the rescue question for several months, the American Jewish Congress was suddenly putting it back on the agenda.[138]

Then the Committee for a Jewish Army's event took place, and it surpassed all expectations. The event—a spectacular pageant called *We Will Never Die*—attracted a record forty thousand people. Ben Hecht conceived of the idea for the pageant, and he enlisted the help of many famous friends: Billy Rose was put in charge of production; Moss Hart directed; Kurt Weill composed the score; and Paul Muni, Edward G. Robinson, Frank Sinatra, and the then unknown Marlon Brando all played parts.[139]

There was just one problem: the work was not Hecht's best. The pageant began with one of Hecht's usual images, a rabbi talking to God about the murder of the Jews of Europe. Unlike the character in the short story "The Little Candle," however, this rabbi was not arguing with God. He was simply mourning the deaths. "We are here to honor them and to proclaim the victory of their dying," he said, and he proceeded to give a long list of Jewish achievements. There was no shame or anger on this night; there was only sadness and sentimentality.[140]

Nevertheless, *We Will Never Die* helped to bring the genocide to national attention. In the weeks that followed, the Committee for a Jewish Army organized performances in Washington, Philadelphia, Chicago, Boston, and Hollywood.[141] After that, performances in other cities were blocked by the American Jewish Congress, and the tour came to a sudden halt.[142] By early April 1943, it was clear that two groups were competing to present the case for rescue to the American public: the Committee for a Jewish Army on the one hand, and the mainstream Jewish organizations on the other.

Then, from April 19 to 30, an international conference on the subject of the refugee problem was held in Bermuda. The British and U.S. governments each sent three delegates and several technical experts to the proceedings, and in the pleasant setting of an oceanside resort, these men ruled out all proposals for large-scale rescue. One British delegate warned "that if Hitler accepted a proposal to release perhaps millions of unwanted persons, we might find ourselves in a very difficult position." An American delegate responded "that there was no doubt whatever that the Department of State would oppose any negotiations with Germany." The diplomats then spent the rest of the time discussing the fate of five thousand Jewish refugees in Spain and ignored the huge number of victims in Eastern Europe.[143]

The major Jewish organizations were shattered by the results of the Bermuda Conference. They were so demoralized that from this point onward, they all but abandoned their rescue campaign and focused their energies instead on the postwar creation of a Jewish state. As a result, the Zionist movement grew significantly in the United States in this period.[144]

The Committee for a Jewish Army had a different reaction. Within a few days, a massive advertisement appeared in the *New York Times*: "To 5,000,000 Jews in the Nazi Death-Trap Bermuda Was a 'Cruel Mockery.'"[145] In the weeks that followed, the Committee for a Jewish Army organized a conference of its own to work out what could be done to halt the massacre. The event—a kind of anti-Bermuda—involved the participation of an impressive array of people including Herbert Hoover, William Randolph Hearst, Dorothy Parker, Fiorello La Guardia, Harold Ickes, and Senators Guy M. Gillette, Edwin C. Johnson, William Langer, and Elbert D. Thomas.[146]

After two years of campaigning, the Committee for a Jewish Army had managed to transform itself from a tiny underground movement into the major American organization pushing for rescue. It adopted a new name to reflect the change—the Emergency Committee to Save the Jewish People of Europe—and it stepped up its presence in the major newspapers. In addition to receiving considerable editorial support from Hearst, the committee put out a new series of dramatic advertisements. The headlines spoke for themselves: "Time Races Death"; "They Are Driven To Death Daily, But They Can Be Saved"; "We All Stand Before the Bar of Humanity, History and God"; "How Well Are You Sleeping?"[147]

As usual, Ben Hecht, who seemed to have regained his anger and bitterness in the aftermath of the Bermuda Conference, wrote the most powerful advertisements. One of his best efforts was a chilling poem called "Ballad of the Doomed Jews of Europe," which went as follows:

> Four million Jews waiting for death.
> Oh hang and burn but—quiet, Jews!
> Don't be bothersome; save your breath—
> The world is busy with other news.
>
> . . .
>
> Oh World be patient—it will take
> Some time before the murder crews
> Are done. By Christmas you can make
> Your Peace on Earth without the Jews.[148]

Even more notorious was an advertisement attacking President Roosevelt, who had done little to help the Jews of Europe. In August, Roosevelt had ignored the findings and recommendations of the Emergency Committee to Save the Jewish People ("I do not think this needs any answer at this time. F.D.R."). In October, he had avoided meeting four hundred Orthodox rabbis who had made a pilgrimage to the White House to push for rescue. And in November, he had admitted that he did not know whether any action had been taken to aid the Jews at the Moscow Conference of Russian, British, and American foreign ministers. (None had been taken.)[149]

In response to all this, Hecht penned an advertisement under the title "My Uncle Abraham Reports . . ." The advertisement began: "I have an Uncle who is a Ghost. . . . He was elected last April by the Two Million Jews who have been murdered by the Germans to be their World Delegate. Wherever there are Conferences on how to make the World a Better Place, maybe, my Uncle Abraham appears and sits on the window sill and takes notes."[150]

Very recently, the advertisement continued, this elected Ghost had been in Moscow. He had sat on the window sill of the Kremlin, and he had listened carefully to the fine speeches by the ministers from Russia, Britain, and the United States. Then he had gone back to the two million dead Jews to give his report. He had told them that the ministers had promised to punish the Germans for murdering all the different peoples

# Ballad of the Doomed Jews of Europe

### by Ben Hecht

FOUR MILLION JEWS waiting for death.
Oh hang and burn but—quiet, Jews!
Don't be bothersome; save your breath—
The world is busy with other news.

Four million murders are quite a smear
Even our State Department views
The slaughter with much disfavor here
But then—it's busy with other news.

You'll hang like a forest of broken trees
You'll burn in a thousand Nazi stews
And tell your God to forgive us please
For we were busy with other news.

Tell Him we hadn't quite the time
To stop the killing of all the Jews;
Tell Him we looked askance at the crime—
But we were busy with other news.

Oh World be patient—it will take
Some time before the murder crews
Are done. By Christmas you can make
Your Peace on Earth without the Jews.

•

## You can prevent their doom

**DEMAND OPEN DOORS TO PALESTINE**

Do you remember all the high, brave words of the United Nations' statesmen—saying that the Jews of Europe, the Four Million Unmurdered Ones, must be saved and would be saved?

What has been done?

*Nothing!*

This isn't quite true.

One thing was done. The statesmen met, conferred, debated, and cut off all hope of escape for the surviving Jews of Europe.

*Palestine had been the only land eager and ready to receive the Four Million Jews still surviving the great German murder campaign.*

The doors of Palestine have been closed in the face of the Jews.

Rather than offend the *amour propre* of some unreliable Arab politicians, the United Nations have condemned all the surviving Jews of Europe to death—by closing the only avenue of escape, Palestine.

The murder of the Jews is in full progress.

They are being exterminated at the rate of thousands a day.

*If you are not too busy, and there are not too many things on your mind, if you believe there is something a little amiss with allowing Four Million human beings to be murdered in German lime kilns and gas chambers—Four Million who might be saved* —write to a Statesman, a Congressman, a Senator, an Alderman, a Judge, a Mayor, a President.

**Ask them why the door has been closed.**

Ask them whether the world profits more from catering to the political whims of a few Arabs than from saving the lives of millions of men, women and children who are dying because the doors are shut.

**Help us to carry out the campaign we are launching to "save the Jews of Europe by opening the doors of Palestine."**

## COMMITTEE FOR A JEWISH ARMY OF STATELESS AND PALESTINIAN JEWS

National Headquarters, 535 Fifth Ave., New York 17, N. Y. Murray Hill 2-7237

This Committee, under the Chairmanship of Senator Edwin C. Johnson, is dedicated to the task of saving the lives and dignity of the Hebrew people of Europe and Palestine. It has gained the moral support of leaders from all walks of American life.

Seventy military authorities, 40 Senators, 210 Congressmen, 22 Governors, 115 government officials, 82 jurists and justices, 80 mayors, 314 clergymen and rabbis, 54 labor leaders, 290 educators, 422 authors, newspapermen, columnists, 254 artists, 112 lawyers and attorneys, 98 doctors, and many hundreds more have endorsed the principles and objectives of this movement by signing the "Proclamation on the Moral Rights of the Stateless and Palestinian Jews."

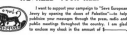

**----------WE NEED YOUR HELP----------**

I want to support your campaign to "Save European Jewry by opening the doors of Palestine"—to help publicize your messages through the press, radio and public meetings throughout the country. I am glad to enclose my check in the amount of $..........

Name ......................................................

Address ...................................................

PLEASE MAKE YOUR CHECK PAYABLE TO ALEX WILF, TREASURER, COMMITTEE FOR A JEWISH ARMY OF STATELESS AND PALESTINIAN JEWS, 535 FIFTH AVENUE, NEW YORK 17, N. Y.

[ By a ruling of the Treasury Department, contributions to this Committee are tax exempt. ]

One of Ben Hecht's attempts to bring the genocide of the Jews to the attention of the American public. This advertisement of the Committee for a Jewish Army appeared in the *New York Times* on September 14, 1943.

of Europe—Czechs, Greeks, Serbs, Russians, Poles—but that the Jews had not been mentioned.[151]

Suddenly a female ghost spoke up. "If they didn't mention the two million murdered Jews in the Conference, isn't that bad for four million who are still alive? The Germans will think that when they kill Jews, Stalin, Roosevelt and Churchill pretend nothing is happening."[152]

The other ghosts let out a great cry, and then their World Delegate raised his hand. "Little Children," he said, "Be patient. We will be dead a long time. Yesterday when we were killed we were changed from Nobodies to Nobodies. Today, on our Jewish tomb, there is not the Star of David, there is an Asterisk. But, who knows, maybe Tomorrow—!"[153]

The advertisement ended: "My Uncle Abraham has gone to the White House in Washington. He is sitting on the windowsill two feet away from Mr. Roosevelt. But he has left his notebook behind."[154]

Roosevelt read many of these advertisements, and according to his wife and his chief speech writer, he was not at all happy about them. He complained in particular about "My Uncle Abraham Reports. . . ." He eventually learned that the Emergency Committee was putting pressure on him not only in the newspapers but also in Washington. On November 9, 1943, a group of senators and congressmen affiliated with the Emergency Committee introduced a resolution urging him to create "a commission of diplomatic, economic, and military experts" to save the Jews who were still alive. The resolution received strong backing in the Senate, but the most prominent Jewish leaders and six out of seven Jewish congressmen refused to support it.[155] Rabbi Stephen Wise explained that the resolution was inadequate because it did not recommend opening Palestine to unrestricted Jewish immigration.[156]

Nevertheless, Roosevelt was being forced into a position in which he had little choice but to act. On January 16, 1944, he received a visit from the secretary of the treasury, Henry Morgenthau Jr. Morgenthau presented him with a damning document entitled "Report . . . on the Acquiescence of This Government in the Murder of the Jews" as well as a proposed executive order to create a rescue commission. Roosevelt suggested a slight change and agreed to go ahead with the plan.[157]

There was one final factor that contributed to Roosevelt's decision to issue his executive order on January 22. At around the same time as he was visited by Morgenthau, he was approached by the influential Jewish businessman Bernard Baruch—and Baruch had been recruited by none other than Ben Hecht. Hecht heard the results of the meeting from a friend: "Our tall white haired charmer [Baruch] has evidently gotten part of his job done with the boss [Roosevelt]. He called me from Washington at the crack of dawn a couple of days before the announcement appeared about the boss's appointment of a Refugee Commission. I have since discussed it with him and the story of how this came about I wouldn't care to entrust to a letter. . . . He's very insistent that his name never be mentioned in connection with any work he may have done for this cause. . . . I am not under-rating the great contribution made by Peter's organization [Emergency Committee to Save the Jewish People of Europe]. I think it helped plenty but I wouldn't be a bit surprised that our friendship with the old boy helped bring this to a head."[158]

Hecht also received a letter from a key member of the Emergency Committee, Samuel Merlin: "I am sending you some clippings about the appointment by the President of the War Refugee Board. . . . I am pretty sure that this tremendous achievement is, at least in part, a result of your, and your friend's, personal endeavors with the White House. I don't think that either my intuition or my sense of judging developments mislead me in this point. Anyhow, I am congratulating you for your endeavors."[159]

And so, finally, the American government took action. More than one year after the announcement of the systematic extermination of the Jews, Franklin D. Roosevelt did what the Committee for a Jewish Army (later the Emergency Committee) had been demanding all this time: he created a governmental agency to rescue the victims. Unfortunately, he acted only at the last moment, when he was pressed to do so by many sides, and he failed to provide the agency with adequate funding or sufficient governmental support. Nevertheless, his executive order had a momentous impact. By the end of the Second World War, the War Refugee Board had helped to save around 200,000 Jewish lives.[160]

After the creation of the board, the Emergency Committee lost steam. The chairman, Peter Bergson, thanked President Roosevelt: "By your action you have become to us a living symbol of Democracy."[161] Only Ben Hecht remained bitter. He took no credit for his role in the creation of the War Refugee Board. He simply thought of the lives that could have been saved. One day, late in the war, he wrote to his wife: "While Hitler played butcher shop with the Jews, Roosevelt and the U.S.A. Govt sat by—not powerless—but indifferent—refusing to save, solace, threaten or even refer to the mass crime. The Roosevelt-Churchill attitude toward Jews will go down in history as part of [the Nazis'] extermination plan."[162]

Hecht's verdict on the Roosevelt administration was harsh, and it never changed. His verdict on the Emergency Committee, which he only arrived at years later, was more sympathetic. He admitted that he and the other members of the committee had failed at their primary objective, namely to save the Jews of Europe. But in another respect, he said, they had made some headway. In a sentence that differed strikingly from Peter Bergson's proclamation to President Roosevelt, he described what he saw as the true achievement of the Emergency Committee: "We were creating a new school of Jews in the U.S.—one which refused to believe blindly in the virtues of their enemies in Democracy's clothing."[163]

While this sentence may have been too strongly worded, it captured Ben Hecht's great contribution to the Jewish cause. At a time when most American Jews were afraid to rock the boat, when a sizeable number of them were too nervous even to identify themselves as Jews, he chose a different path. He did not run away from his Jewish heritage in a desperate attempt to identify himself, whatever the cost, as an American. He understood, rather, that in America he could also be a Jew. He could use his gifts and his talents to expose the failure of the Roosevelt administration to do anything about the extermination of his people. In this critical period, Ben Hecht's voice was the loudest, most courageous Jewish voice in America. His words changed what it meant to be an American Jew.[164]

And here was the truly remarkable thing: Ben Hecht came from a place that for nearly eight years had collaborated with Nazi Germany. He did not know about the collaboration, of course. He did not know that his own movies had been a source of great enjoyment to German audiences throughout the 1930s. He certainly did not know that his employers had reinvested the profits from his movies in Nazi newsreels and German armaments, and that they had gone to all sorts of other extreme lengths to protect their investment in Germany. He only knew that they would not allow him to write a screenplay about what the Nazis were doing to the Jews.

Hecht naturally assumed that his employers, like many other members of the Jewish community, were acting out of fear. He did not guess that they were drawing on this fear for their own benefit. He had no idea that when they said that they were trying not to rock the boat, they were really trying not to lose their business in Germany.

But after participating in this system for so many years, Ben Hecht suddenly went in the opposite direction. He shouted more loudly and more forcefully than anyone else about what the Nazis were doing to the Jews. And in early 1944, around the time of the creation of the War Refugee Board, he wrote a book on the subject. He called it *A Guide for the Bedeviled*, and although he originally envisioned it as a straightforward discussion of anti-Semitism, he gradually changed course. He found himself thinking about something quite different.

"Hollywood," he announced, "is a town, an industry, an empire of toy-making, invented by Jews, dominated by Jews, and made to flourish like unto the land of Solomon—by Jews, and a few embattled Irishmen. Such is its truth, and if you wish to look for its deep meanings, it is into this truth you must look."[165]

Hecht knew that in making this announcement, he would delight anti-Semites all around the world. He also knew that he would infuriate the studio heads. But he did not care. He was proud of the fact that Hollywood had been invented by Jews. He saw Hollywood as one of the great Jewish achievements. The only problem, in his view, was that the studio heads did not share his pride. In fact, they had removed all images of Jews from the screen. "The greatest single Jewish phenomenon in our country in the last twenty years," he said—this was his second announcement— "has been the almost complete disappearance of the Jew from American fiction, stage, radio, and movies. . . . And for this false oblivion and for this dangerous exile, the movies are the most to blame."[166]

Hecht did not know the details behind the disappearance. He had no idea that the German consul in Los Angeles had mounted a fierce campaign against Herman Mankiewicz's *The Mad Dog of Europe*, and that as a result, the studio heads had decided not to make any pictures about Hitler's persecution of the Jews. He had no idea that these events had led to the making of another film, *The House of Rothschild*, which had been so horrendous that the studio heads had decided not to make any pictures about Jews at all. He only knew that when he was young, there had been dozens of movies about Jews, and now there were none.

Hecht had questioned his employers many times about this. Why, he had asked them, did they not "stand up as the great of Hollywood and proclaim in their films against the German murder of their kind"? The answer, they had said, was obvious: "Though they own them, the movies are not theirs to use willy-nilly for special Jewish pleading. . . . For the American people trust them to be Americans and not Jews. It is a pact understood between the movie fans and the movie makers that there is nothing Jewish about the whole thing."[167]

Hecht did not know about the collaboration from the previous decade, so he took these statements at face value. He was at first confused, because his employers had pleaded on behalf of many other oppressed groups in their films. Then he recalled a statement by Romain Rolland: "There are people who have the courage to die for the cause of another who have not the temerity even to speak up for their own."[168]

This was Hecht's way of explaining his employers' actions to himself, and perhaps, to a certain extent, he was right. Perhaps his employers were able to defend others and not themselves. But their past—their actual behavior—was more significant than any speculations about their character. And for nearly eight years, in compliance with the wishes of the German government, they had trained themselves not to say anything about the persecution of the Jews.

This training continued to influence them when they stopped doing business with Germany, and it even continued to influence them in the final year of the war. While the War Refugee Board was saving Jewish lives, the studio heads made only the most sparing references to Jews in their pictures. MGM's contribution, *The Seventh Cross*, showed the escape of seven prisoners from a concentration camp, one of whom, a man named Beutler, was a Jew. According to a production memo, "Reason for identifying Beutler as a Jew: the general notion in this country is that all concentration camp prisoners are Jews. Therefore, make *one* a Jew, implying that the others are not."[169]

In all the years of the war, there was only one minor picture that revealed what the Nazis were doing to the Jews. This was *None Shall Escape* (Columbia Pictures, 1944), a courtroom drama set in the future in which Nazi leaders were brought to justice for their crimes. In a flashback that occurred late in the picture, a group of Jews were being loaded onto a train, presumably to be taken to a concentration camp. As they were boarding the train, their rabbi called out to them. He told them that their peaceful ways had failed and that it was time to stand up to their oppressors. They responded by attacking the Nazis around them, and they were all shot dead. Then the rabbi turned to the chief Nazi, and before he was shot he said, "We will never die."[170]

From Hecht's perspective, this was too little too late. A five-minute scene in a movie about a future war-crimes trial did not satisfy him. After years of standing up as a Jew, he had come up with too many other ideas. And toward the end of *A Guide for the Bedevilled*, he outlined one of them—a movie set in an entirely different time and place, in which human indifference caused a huge number of needless deaths. Then, in an unusual move, he imagined himself pitching the idea to some great executive in Hollywood.

"It is in the world of these indifferent ones that anti-Semitism flourishes," he told the executive. "Anti-Semitism and everything foul. It is these Nice People who make all horror and wretchedness possible—by their unfunctioning Niceness. By their fierce pride in the little they know. By their abominable laziness. . . . If I am looking for the villain responsible for the murder of three million Jews, I must, as an honest man, not single out a few anti-Semites. I must attack a world from pole to pole."[171]

The imaginary executive listened to Hecht and smiled. "You have come to the wrong place for such activity," he said. "Hollywood is not Armageddon. Here we do not seek to make truth triumph by the dubious business of killing off all its enemies. Whom would we sell pictures to, in such a case? To corpses? If you want to fight the world you must not be naive enough to ask the world to line up on your side. You've got to go it alone. And here's your movie. Take it with you. I don't think we can waste any more time on it."[172]

At this point, Hecht's daydream ended. He did not particularly like it. He allowed his mind to wander, and he stumbled upon another. He imagined a world in which Jews contributed so much, so openly, and so enthusiastically that their contributions no longer needed to be called "Jewish." A world in which their talents were embraced without any mark of "alienism." A world in which they could be themselves. "This is a look far off but it is the only land of promise on the horizon," he said. And this land of promise—he knew that it had something to do with Hollywood.[173] He had done more than anyone else to lead his people to this land. But he would never live to see it.

# EPILOGUE

On June 16, 1945, one month and nine days after the German surrender, a dozen motion picture executives gathered at the Pentagon in Washington. They were about to embark on a three-week tour of Europe at the invitation of the supreme headquarters of the commander of Allied forces. The group included Jack Warner of Warner Brothers, Darryl Zanuck of Twentieth Century-Fox, Harry Cohn of Columbia Pictures, Clifford Work of Universal Pictures, Barney Balaban of Paramount, and Eddie Mannix of MGM (Louis B. Mayer's right-hand man). Also present was Francis Harmon, a Hays Office employee who had helped to organize the trip.[1]

After a pleasant lunch with several high-ranking officials, General of the Army George Marshall told the executives why they were going to Europe. He said that he wanted them to acquire a firsthand understanding of the war and of postwar conditions.[2] He handed out a detailed itinerary, which included visits to various European landmarks and a tour of a German concentration camp.[3] Presumably he hoped that these cultural ambassadors would witness the devastation and the atrocities and incorporate them into their motion pictures.

The executives listened carefully to what General Marshall was saying. Naturally, they had their own motivations for going to Europe. Above all, they were eager to re-establish a market for their films in Germany. Back in early 1944, Darryl Zanuck had told one of President Roosevelt's closest advisors that he wanted to abolish the German film industry after the war and replace it with subsidiary units of the American companies.[4] A year after that, Harry Warner had sent a very similar proposal to the president.[5] At the time, these ideas had met with strong resistance from senior government officials, such as the assistant secretary of war, John J. McCloy: "The logical outcome of this almost amounts to continuous Allied control of all [German] industry and culture and I think that approaches nonsense."[6] The executives sitting in the Pentagon in Washington were optimistic, however. Zanuck had just met with the new president, Harry S. Truman, and the meeting had gone very well.[7]

The executives were all wearing official army uniforms as they boarded their plane the next day. In the first two weeks of the trip, they went to a variety of cocktail parties, luncheons, dinners, and conferences in London and Paris. Then they went to Germany. On July 1, they visited Hamburg and inspected the incredible damage to the city. "Beneath our plane," they noted, "the whole vast panorama of urban destruction unfolded."[8] On July 2, they planned to travel to Buchenwald concentration camp to see the "crematories where thousands of bodies were burned" and the "piles of human bones and ashes."[9] They were grounded by the weather, however, so they remained in Hamburg for an extra day and met with local officials, one of whom told them "that a starvation diet does not go well in an unheated house nor does a dancing film with Jive music go well in such an environment."[10]

On July 3, the executives flew to Munich. They were meant to begin the day with a visit to Berchtesgaden: "Those who wish to see Hitler's fabulous Nazi retreat may make [the climb]. 'Nest' is in good shape with furnishings, etc still intact. Others may remain at base. View is lovely."[11] There was not enough time for this, however, so the executives contented themselves with a tour of the Brown House (the Nazi Party headquarters) and the beer hall where Hitler had carried out his putsch. Jack Warner took a photograph of the hall and marked the entrance with his pen.[12]

The executives also made a motor trip to Dachau that day, but they did not leave behind an extensive record of their reaction. "Less than 5,000 of the camp's 38,000 inmates remained at the time of our visit," one member of the group noted. "These were recovering from disease and starvation."[13] Jack Warner took a couple of snapshots, and then the executives left.[14] They drove back to Munich, and they had "a festive dinner and celebration."[15]

In the final days of their tour of Germany, from July 4 to July 6, the executives went to Frankfurt, where they met with General Robert A. McClure, director of the Psychological Warfare Division. McClure asked them: "What can you gentlemen do to help us in our main job of winning the peace?" The executives replied that their visit "marked the first opportunity for any responsible representatives of the American industry to talk with anybody inside Germany"; that they "had a twelve year supply of feature pictures and short subjects which had not been exhibited in Germany"; and that there were "1,400 motion picture theatres for use in winning the battle for Germany."[16]

More conferences followed, and on July 6, the executives enjoyed "a fitting climax" to their visit to Germany. For six hours, they cruised up the Rhine River in Hitler's personal yacht. They saw many beautiful landmarks, including the Lorelei, the Castle of Katz, and the city of Coblenz, and they were served lunch and refreshments on board. A photographer of the U.S. Army Signal Corps was present to capture the occasion. In one low-angle shot, two executives—Jack Warner and Harry Cohn—watched the splendor of the German landscape unfold before their eyes.[17]

A few days later, the trip came to an end, and the motion picture executives returned to the United States. Francis Harmon drafted a report to the War Department, which he sent to the executives for approval. He first expressed gratitude for the once-in-a-lifetime opportunity to see Europe immediately after the war. He then noted that the German film industry would soon be reinstated, and he wrote: "We were advised . . . that when the theatres in Germany are reopened, the films would be shown to paying audiences, hence the terms on which they are to be delivered and played will need to be established. Representatives of the industry are prepared to undertake the necessary discussions at any time."[18]

Very quickly, Harmon received a series of urgent telegrams from Jack Warner. "We should not undertake to advise that the German motion picture industry be reinstated," Warner said. "Am sure we can produce in this country all pictures necessary for Germany. I would not wish to suggest that the German motion picture industry be reestablished or foster in any way the redevelopment of motion picture production in Germany." Warner then added that the production of film stock should also be prohibited in Germany: "Since film is an adjunct to production of TNT it is absolutely inadvisable in my opinion."[19]

Harmon replied to Warner by pointing out that the policy of the U.S. government was "to make the Germans feed themselves clothe themselves and provide themselves with other items needed." Nevertheless, he agreed to delete the section on film stock, and he inserted a carefully worded sentence on domestic film production: "It should be feasible to produce films in Germany exclusively for the German market using German actors and German technicians under the most careful American supervision."[20]

Even after all these changes had been made, Jack Warner was still concerned. He insisted that Harmon attach the following message to the end of the report: "If it is true . . . that 'He who controls the cinema, controls

"Signal Corps Photo: Group of American motion picture executives touring the continent take a trip up the Rhine on Hitler's personal yacht, given to him by the city of Cologne." Eddie Mannix (second from right), Jack Warner (third from right).

"Signal Corps Photo: (L–R) Mr Jack Warner, Exec Prod and Vice Pres. of Warner Bros., and Mr Harry Cohn, Pres. of Columbia, members of group of American motion picture executives on tour of the continent, look over rail while making a trip up the Rhine on Hitler's personal yacht."

Germany' . . . and if the Allies will not permit Germans to rebuild the munitions industry, they should not be permitted for any reason, even if temporary, to rebuild a motion picture industry."[21]

The report was sent, and nothing more was said about the European trip. In the years that followed, however, the results were clearly discernible. The executives had witnessed the devastation wreaked by the war, and they had toured one of the most notorious concentration camps in

Europe. They had seen firsthand one of the sites where the murder of the Jews had taken place. But they did not put it on the screen.[22] Decades would pass before any reference to the crime appeared in American feature films.[23]

In Germany, on the other hand, the domestic film industry took years to recover, and audiences were able to watch all the Hollywood movies that they had missed out on during the war.

# NOTES

PROLOGUE

1. *King Kong*, directed by Merian C. Cooper and Ernest B. Schoedsack (RKO, 1933).
2. Oberprüfstelle report 6910, "King Kong," September 15, 1933, Deutsches Filminstitut, Frankfurt (henceforth Deutsches Filminstitut). All translations are my own unless otherwise noted. In the first half of this introduction, I have turned the record of the discussion at the censorship meeting into direct speech. I have preserved the original meaning throughout.
3. My emphasis.
4. Oberprüfstelle report 6910, "King Kong," September 15, 1933.
5. Ibid. My emphasis.
6. Ibid. My emphasis.
7. Oberprüfstelle report 6910, "King Kong," October 5, 1933, Deutsches Filminstitut. My emphasis.
8. Ibid.
9. Ibid.
10. Thomas Jefferson, *Notes on the State of Virginia* [1785] (New York: Penguin, 1999), 145.
11. Oberprüfstelle report 6910, "King Kong," October 5, 1933.
12. Ibid.
13. George Canty, "Economic and Trade Notes 158," January 25, 1934, Commercial Attachés in Germany 1931–1940, RG 151, National Archives and Records Administration, College Park, Maryland (henceforth National Archives); advertisements for *King Kong*, *Der Angriff*, November 30, 1933, 15, and December 1, 1933, 7.

14. "Filmtechnik besiegt die Urwelt: 'Die Fabel von King-Kong,'" *Völkischer Beobachter*, December 3–4, 1933, 5–6.

15. "Die Fabel von King Kong," *Der Angriff*, December 2, 1933, 6.

16. Ernst Hanfstaengl, *Zwischen Weissem und Braunem Haus: Memoiren eines politischen Aussenseiters* (Munich: R. Piper & Co. Verlag, 1970), 314.

17. André Bazin, *What Is Cinema?* vol. 1 (Berkeley: University of California Press, 1967), 29. For accounts of the studio system in the golden age, see David Bordwell et al., *The Classical Hollywood Cinema: Film Style & Mode of Production to 1960* (New York: Columbia University Press, 1985); Thomas Schatz, *The Genius of the System: Hollywood Filmmaking in the Studio Era* (New York: Pantheon Books, 1988).

18. The records of the Bureau of Foreign and Domestic Commerce at the National Archives (RG 151) contain twenty-two boxes of reports of American commercial attachés stationed in Berlin in the 1930s. These reports include statistics on how long American movies remained in theaters in their first runs. The classic studies of German cinema and German censorship do not discuss the popularity of Hollywood movies in the Third Reich. See Gerd Albrecht, *Nationalsozialistische Filmpolitik: Eine soziologische Untersuchung über die Spielfilm des Dritten Reichs* (Stuttgart: Ferdinand Enke Verlag, 1969); Wolfgang Becker, *Film und Herrschaft: Organisationsprinzipien und Organisationsstrukturen der nationalsozialistischen Filmpropaganda* (Berlin: Verlag Volker Spiess, 1973); Jürgen Spiker, *Film und Kapital: Der Weg der deutschen Filmwirtschaft zum nationalsozialistischen Einheitskonzern* (Berlin: Verlag Volker Spiess, 1975); Kraft Wetzel and Peter A. Hagemann, *Zensur—Verbotene deutsche Filme 1933–1945* (Berlin: Verlag Volker Spiess, 1978); Klaus-Jürgen Maiwald, *Filmzensur im NS-Staat* (Dortmund: Nowotny, 1983); David Welch, *Propaganda and the German Cinema, 1933–1945* [1983] (New York: I.B. Tauris, 2001). There is a chapter on the impact of Hollywood movies on Nazi cinema in Eric Rentschler, *The Ministry of Illusion: Nazi Cinema and Its Afterlife* (Cambridge, MA: Harvard University Press, 1996), 99–122.

19. Prior books on this subject have not uncovered the collaboration between the American studios and the Nazi regime. One book provides a rich exploration of archival materials: Markus Spieker, *Hollywood unterm Hakenkreuz: Der amerikanische Spielfilm im Dritten Reich* (Trier: Wissenschaftlicher Verlag Trier, 1999). A more recent book provides a lively account, but one that is limited to reports that appeared in American trade papers: Thomas Doherty, *Hollywood and Hitler, 1933–1939* (New York: Columbia University Press, 2013). More general studies of Hollywood's portrayal of foreign dictators include Benjamin L. Alpers, *Dictators, Democracy, and American Public Culture: Envisioning the Totalitarian Enemy, 1920s–1950s* (Chapel Hill: University of North Carolina Press, 2003); David Welky, *The Moguls and the Dictators: Hollywood and the Coming of World War II* (Baltimore, MD: Johns Hopkins University Press, 2008). Also see Anthony Slide, "Hollywood's Fascist Follies," *Film Comment* (July–August 1991): 62–67.

20. *The Tramp and the Dictator*, directed by Kevin Brownlow and Michael Kloft (Photoplay Productions, 2002). Budd Schulberg is best known for his con-

troversial novel about Hollywood, *What Makes Sammy Run?* According to Schulberg, when his novel was released, Louis B. Mayer told his father, B. P. Schulberg (a former executive at Paramount), "You know what we should do with him? We should deport him!" Budd Schulberg, "What Makes Sammy Keep Running?" *Newsday*, August 2, 1987, 9. Also see Schulberg, *Moving Pictures: Memories of a Hollywood Prince* (New York: Stein and Day, 1981).

21. For accounts of Hollywood's anti-fascism, see Colin Schindler, *Hollywood Goes to War: Films and American Society, 1939–1952* (Boson: Routledge, 1979); Edward F. Dolan Jr., *Hollywood Goes to War* (Twickenham: Hamlyn, 1985); Clayton R. Koppes, *Hollywood Goes to War: How Politics, Profits, and Propaganda Shaped World War II Movies* (Berkeley: University of California Press, 1987); Allen L. Woll, *The Hollywood Musical Goes to War* (Chicago: Nelson-Hall, 1983); Michael S. Shull and David E. Wilt, *Doing Their Bit: Wartime American Animated Short Films, 1939–1945* (Jefferson, NC: McFarland & Company, 1987); Bernard F. Dick, *The Star-Spangled Film: The American World War II Film* (Lexington: University Press of Kentucky, 1985); Thomas Doherty, *Projections of War: Hollywood, American Culture, and World War II* (New York: Columbia University Press, 1993); Michael S. Shull and David E. Wilt, *Hollywood War Films, 1937–1945: An Exhaustive Filmography of American Feature-Length Motion Pictures Relating to World War II* (Jefferson, NC: McFarland & Company, 1996); Michael E. Birdwell, *Celluloid Soldiers: The Warner Bros. Campaign against Nazism* (New York: New York University Press, 1999).

22. Deutsche Fox-Film to Wilhelm Brückner, January 10, 1938, NS 10, vol. 125, Bundesarchiv, Berlin (henceforth Bundesarchiv).

23. For studies of the business that other American companies did with the Nazis, see Edwin Black, *IBM and the Holocaust: The Strategic Alliance between Nazi Germany and America's Most Powerful Corporation* (New York: Crown Publishers, 2001); Edwin Black, *Nazi Nexus: America's Corporate Connections to Hitler's Holocaust* (Washington, DC: Dialog Press, 2009); Henry Ashby Turner Jr., *General Motors and the Nazis: The Struggle for Control of Opel, Europe's Biggest Carmaker* (New Haven: Yale University Press, 2005); Charles Higham, *Trading with the Enemy: An Exposé of the Nazi-American Money Plot 1933–1949* (New York: Delacorte Press, 1983); Reinhold Billstein et al., *Working for the Enemy: Ford, General Motors, and Forced Labor in Germany during the Second World War* (New York: Bergham Books, 2000).

24. See, for example, George Canty, "German Film Developments," December 27, 1934, Commercial Attachés in Germany 1931–1940, RG 151; Douglas Miller to American Embassy, May 14, 1936, File Class 281: Germany 1930–1945, RG 151, National Archives.

25. For the Jewish origins of the Hollywood executives, see Neal Gabler, *An Empire of Their Own: How the Jews Invented Hollywood* (New York: Crown Publishers, 1988).

26. There are some well-researched studies of Hollywood's export markets in this period, which include sections on how Hollywood changed foreign versions of American movies. One of the central contentions of this book, however, is

that the dealings with Nazi Germany were radically different from the dealings with other nations. First, Hollywood generally changed its movies only for specific markets, not (as the Nazis insisted) for the entire world. Second, regular business dealings with other democracies or constitutional monarchies cannot be compared to a business arrangement with a totalitarian regime. For Hollywood's dealings with foreign countries, see Kristin Thompson, *Exporting Entertainment: America in the World Film Market, 1907–34* (London: BFI Publishing, 1985); Ian Jarvie, *Hollywood's Overseas Campaign: The North Atlantic Movie Trade, 1920–1950* (Cambridge: Cambridge University Press, 1992); Ruth Vasey, *The World According to Hollywood, 1918–1939* (Madison: University of Wisconsin Press, 1997); John Trumpbour, *Selling Hollywood to the World: U.S. and European Struggles for Mastery of the Global Film Industry, 1920–1950* (Cambridge: Cambridge University Press, 2002). For a study from the period, see John Eugene Harley, *World-Wide Influences of the Cinema: A Study of Official Censorship and the International Cultural Aspects of Motion Pictures* (Los Angeles: University of Southern California Press, 1940).

## 1. HITLER'S OBSESSION WITH FILM

1. Nicolaus von Below, *Als Hitlers Adjutant 1937–45* (Mainz: Von Hase & Koehler, 1980), 33, 152, 282–283; Fritz Wiedemann, *Der Mann, der Feldherr werden wollte: Erlebnisse und Erfahrungen des Vorgesetzten Hitlers im 1. Weltkrieg und seines späteren Persönlichen Adjutanten* (Velbert: Bild + Bild Verlag für politische Bildung, 1964), 68–78. Also see Ian Kershaw, *Hitler 1889–1936: Hubris* (London: Penguin, 1998), 534–535; Kershaw, *Hitler 1936–1945: Nemesis* (London: Penguin, 2000), 33.

2. For examples of Hitler's monologues, see Kershaw, *Hitler 1936–1945*, 32–33, 198–199, 500. For examples of Hitler's dictation, see Hitler's agendas for Tuesday, June 28, 1938, Wednesday, June 29, 1938, Thursday, June 30, 1938, and Thursday, July 7, 1938, NS 10, vol. 125, Bundesarchiv, Berlin (henceforth Bundesarchiv).

3. SS-Obersturmführer E. Bahls to Propaganda Ministry, April 24, 1939, NS 10, vol. 49; Bahls to Propaganda Ministry, August 16, 1938, NS 10, vol. 45, Bundesarchiv.

4. Bahls to Propaganda Ministry, April 24, 1939; Bahls to Propaganda Ministry, August 16, 1938.

5. Bahls to Propaganda Ministry, April 24, 1939.

6. Ibid.; Hitler's agenda for Sunday, June 19, 1938, NS 10, vol. 125, Bundesarchiv; Bahls to Propaganda Ministry, August 16, 1938.

7. Bahls to Propaganda Ministry, April 24, 1939 (*sehr schlecht*, "*widerwärtig*"); Hitler's agenda for Sunday, June 19, 1938 (*Mist in höchster Potenz*).

8. Hitler's agenda for Saturday, November 19, 1938, NS 10, vol. 125; Max Wünsche to Propaganda Ministry, November 21, 1938, NS 10, vol. 45, Bundesarchiv.

9. Hitler's agenda for Wednesday, June 22, 1938, NS 10, vol. 125, Bundesarchiv.

10. SS-Untersturmführer to Propaganda Ministry, June 23, 1938, NS 10, vol. 44, Bundesarchiv; Wünsche to Propaganda Ministry, November 21, 1938.

11. Wünsche to Propaganda Ministry, November 21, 1938.

12. Hitler's agenda for Thursday, September 15, 1938, NS 10, vol. 125, Bundesarchiv.

13. Wiedemann, *Der Mann, der Feldherr werden wollte*, 78.

14. Hitler's agendas for Thursday, June 23, 1938, and Tuesday, June 21, 1938, NS 10, vol. 125; Bahls to Propaganda Ministry, April 24, 1939; Hitler's agendas for Thursday, June 30, 1938, Monday, July 4, 1938, and Sunday, June 19, 1938, NS 10, vol. 125, Bundesarchiv.

15. Disney movies were shown in Germany until 1935. For an account of Disney's business in Germany up to this point and Disney's anti-Nazi cartoons from the Second World War, see Carsten Laqua, *Wie Micky unter die Nazis fiel: Walt Disney und Deutschland* (Reinbek bei Hamburg: Rowohlt Taschenbuch Verlag, 1992).

16. Ernst Seeger to Wilhelm Brückner, July 27, 1937, NS 10, vol. 48, Bundesarchiv.

17. Elke Fröhlich et al., eds., *Die Tagebücher von Joseph Goebbels*, entry for December 22, 1937, pt. 1, vol. 5 (Munich: K. G. Saur Verlag, 2000), 64.

18. Fröhlich et al., eds., *Die Tagebücher von Joseph Goebbels*, entry for January 25, 1937, pt. 1, vol. 3/II, 344; *Camille*, directed by George Cukor (MGM, 1936).

19. Wünsche to Propaganda Ministry, November 21, 1938.

20. Werner Henske, "Amerikanischer und deutscher Humor," *Der Angriff*, October 23, 1937, 11.

21. Markus Spieker, *Hollywood unterm Hakenkreuz: Der amerikanische Spielfilm im Dritten Reich* (Trier: Wissenschaftlicher Verlag Trier, 1999), 344; *Block-Heads*, directed by John G. Blystone (MGM, 1938).

22. Martin Broszat, *The Hitler State* (Essex: Longman, 1981), 339; Bahls to Propaganda Ministry, July 4, 1938, NS 10, vol. 45, Bundesarchiv.

23. *Tip-Off Girls*, directed by Louis King (Paramount, 1938).

24. Hitler's agenda for Sunday, June 19, 1938.

25. Broszat, *The Hitler State*, 339; Hitler's agenda for Wednesday, June 22, 1938. Also see Kershaw, *Hitler 1936–1945*, 106.

26. Adolf Hitler, *Mein Kampf*, trans. Ralph Manheim [1925 and 1927] (New York: Houghton Mifflin, 1943), 107.

27. Reinhold Hanisch, "I Was Hitler's Buddy," *The New Republic* (April 5, 1939): 239–241.

28. Ibid., 242. Soon after Hanisch's account was published in German, Hitler had him tracked down and killed. See Joachim C. Fest, *Hitler* [1973] (New York: Penguin, 1982), 46.

29. *Der Tunnel*, directed by William Wauer (Imperator-Film GmbH, 1915). There is a copy of this film at the Munich Filmmuseum.

30. Kershaw, *Hitler 1889–1936*, 109–128.

31. Hitler, *Mein Kampf*, 106–107, 469, 471.

32. Ibid., 470.

33. Ibid., 470–471.

34. Ibid., 473–475.
35. Kershaw, *Hitler 1889–1936*, 241.
36. Hitler, *Mein Kampf*, 157; Kershaw, *Hitler 1889–1936*, 83.
37. Hitler, *Mein Kampf*, 163.
38. Ibid., 164.
39. Ibid., 164–165.
40. Ibid., 165.
41. Ibid., 188–190.
42. Ibid., 192–193.
43. Ibid., 191–194.
44. Thomas Weber, *Hitler's First War: Adolf Hitler, the Man of the List Regiment, and the First World War* (Oxford: Oxford University Press, 2010), 53, 214–215, 223.
45. Ibid., 173–174.
46. Hitler, *Mein Kampf*, 200, 190, 201–202. Hitler's blindness was in fact psychosomatic. See Weber, *Hitler's First War*, 221.
47. Hitler, *Mein Kampf*, 202–204.
48. Ibid., 206.
49. Ibid., 177–179, 181, 182.
50. Ibid., 180.
51. Ibid., 180–181, 179.
52. Ibid., 181–186.
53. Ibid., 188.
54. Michael T. Isenberg, *War on Film: The American Cinema and World War I, 1914–1941* (East Brunswick: Associated University Press, 1981), 147–151.
55. "Metro-Goldwyn-Film 'Mare Nostrum,'" *Licht Bild Bühne*, March 6, 1926, 12–13; *Mare Nostrum*, directed by Rex Ingram (MGM, 1926).
56. Erich Maria Remarque, *All Quiet on the Western Front* (Boston: Little, Brown and Company, 1929). For the reception of the novel in Germany, see Hubert Rüter, *Erich Maria Remarque: Im Westen nichts Neues: Ein Bestseller der Kriegsliteratur im Kontext* (Munich: Schöningh, 1980).
57. Oberprüfstelle report 1254, "Im Westen nichts Neues," December 11, 1930, Deutsches Filminstitut, Frankfurt (henceforth Deutsches Filminstitut), 3; Modris Eksteins, "War, Memory, and Politics: The Fate of the Film *All Quiet on the Western Front*," *Central European History* 13 (1980): 63.
58. Fröhlich et al., eds., *Die Tagebücher von Joseph Goebbels*, entry for September 2, 1929, pt. 1, vol. 1/III, 316.
59. *All Quiet on the Western Front*, directed by Lewis Milestone (Universal Pictures, 1930).
60. Hitler, *Mein Kampf*, 466, 468.
61. Eksteins, "War, Memory, and Politics," 63.
62. For use of the term "film war," see, for example, "Soll der Filmkrieg weitergehen? Schlachtfeld: Das deutsche Lichtspielhaus," *Licht Bild Bühne*, December 20, 1930, 1.
63. Eksteins, "War, Memory, and Politics," 71.

64. Ibid., 71–72; Jerold Simmons, "Film and International Politics: The Banning of *All Quiet on the Western Front* in Germany and Austria, 1930–1931," *Historian* 52, no. 1 (November 1989): 40–41. Leni Riefenstahl also mentions this episode in her autobiography: Leni Riefenstahl, *A Memoir* (New York: St. Martin's Press, 1993), 65–66. For a full account of the production and reception of *All Quiet on the Western Front*, see Andrew Kelly, *Filming All Quiet on the Western Front: "Brutal Cutting, Stupid Censors, Bigoted Politicians"* (New York: I.B. Tauris, 1998). For an account of the controversy surrounding the picture in Germany, see Peter Jelavich, *Berlin Alexanderplatz: Radio, Film, and the Death of Weimar Culture* (Berkeley: University of California Press, 2006), 156–190.

65. Eksteins, "War, Memory, and Politics," 72–75.

66. Oberprüfstelle report 1254, "Im Westen nichts Neues," December 11, 1930, 1–2; Eksteins, "War, Memory, and Politics," 75.

67. Oberprüfstelle report 1254, "Im Westen nichts Neues," December 11, 1930, 4–9.

68. *Reichsgesetzblatt*, May 12, 1920, 953.

69. Oberprüfstelle report 1254, "Im Westen nichts Neues," December 11, 1930, 9–13.

70. Ibid., 16–19.

71. Ibid., 22–25.

72. "Unser der Sieg!" *Der Angriff*, December 12, 1930, 1.

73. Oberprüfstelle report 1254, "Im Westen nichts Neues," December 11, 1930, 19.

74. Ibid., 13–14.

75. The conversation that follows is a direct translation from ibid., 14–16.

76. Results of Prohibition of "All Quiet on the Western Front," December 18, 1930, *All Quiet on the Western Front* file, Motion Picture Association of America (henceforth MPAA), Production Code Administration records, Margaret Herrick Library, Academy of Motion Picture Arts and Sciences, Beverly Hills (henceforth Margaret Herrick Library).

77. Carl Laemmle to Hearst, December 10, 1930, 9:10 AM, and December 10, 1930, 9:16 AM, William Randolph Hearst Papers, box 7, folder 17, Bancroft Library, Berkeley (henceforth Bancroft Library).

78. William Randolph Hearst, "Peace and Good Will," *San Francisco Examiner*, December 12, 1930, 1.

79. Filmprüfstelle report 29102, "Im Westen nichts Neues," June 8, 1931, Deutsches Filminstitut.

80. Deutsche Universal to Foreign Office, August 28, 1931, German legation in Lisbon, box 160: Filme, vol. 2, Politisches Archiv des Auswärtigen Amts, Berlin (henceforth PAAA).

81. "Germany Removes Its Ban Completely on 'All Quiet,' " *Film Daily*, September 3, 1931, 1.

82. Harold L. Smith to Frederick Herron, November 5, 1931, *All Quiet on the Western Front* file, MPAA, Production Code Administration records, Margaret Herrick Library.

83. Foreign Office to German legation in Lisbon, October 7, 1931, German legation in Lisbon, box 160: Filme, vol. 2, PAAA.

84. German embassy in Paris to Foreign Office, November 14, 1931, German embassy in Paris, 2281: Filme, vol. 3, PAAA.

85. Deutsche Universal to Foreign Office, November 27, 1931, German embassy in Paris, 2281: Filme, vol. 3, PAAA.

86. Resume, December 28, 1931, *All Quiet on the Western Front* file, MPAA, Production Code Administration records, Margaret Herrick Library.

87. G. A. Struve to John V. Wilson, December 29, 1931, *All Quiet on the Western Front* file, MPAA, Production Code Administration records, Margaret Herrick Library.

88. Frederick Herron to Jason Joy, January 11, 1932, *All Quiet on the Western Front* file, MPAA, Production Code Administration records, Margaret Herrick Library.

89. Carl Laemmle to Hearst, January 18, 1932, William Randolph Hearst Papers, box 7, folder 17, Bancroft Library.

90. Udo Bayer, "Laemmle's List: Carl Laemmle's Affidavits for Jewish Refugees," *Film History* 10 (1998): 501–521.

91. Deutsche Universal to Foreign Office, March 10, 1932, German embassy in Rome, 835a: deutschfeindliche Filmpropaganda, vol. 2, PAAA.

92. Hitler's agendas for Wednesday, June 22, 1938, and Saturday, November 19, 1938.

93. Hitler, *Mein Kampf*, 178.

94. David Welch, *Propaganda and the German Cinema 1933–1945* [1983] (New York: I.B. Tauris, 2001), 37.

95. *Triumph of the Will*, directed by Leni Riefenstahl (Leni Riefenstahl-Produktion/Reichspropagandaleitung der NSDAP, 1935).

96. Riefenstahl's strategy in *Triumph of the Will* also fit perfectly with Hitler's own abilities. "I must have a crowd when I speak," he once confided to a friend. "In a small intimate circle I never know what to say." Kershaw, *Hitler 1889–1936*, 133.

97. *Olympia*, directed by Leni Riefenstahl (Olympia Film, 1938). For a classic essay on Leni Riefenstahl, see Susan Sontag, "Fascinating Fascism," *New York Review of Books*, February 6, 1975, 23–30.

98. Hitler had recently orchestrated the murder of between 150 and 200 members of the SA on the Night of the Long Knives.

99. Six years later, Charlie Chaplin responded to Hitler in the anti-Nazi picture *The Great Dictator*. Early in the picture, he exploited his physical resemblance to Hitler to make fun of the dictator's oratorical methods. He looked at the crowd with an unwavering frown, he used carefully constructed hand gestures, and then, with the utmost seriousness, he picked up a jug of water and poured it down his pants. He was in such control of his emotions that he could express intense sadness and then announce that his emotional response was at an end. And when the crowd applauded, he appeared completely unmoved and silenced the applause in a flash. Chaplin was critiquing the emptiness of Hitler's performances in

*Triumph of the Will* by pointing out that Hitler's audience had not been listening at all.

But Chaplin wanted his audience to listen to *him*. He played two roles in *The Great Dictator*—not just the dictator "Hynkel" but also a Jewish barber—and as a result of mistaken identity, the barber gave the final speech. In setting up the scene, Chaplin revealed how much he had learned from Hitler. After a brief introduction by Herr "Garbage," he remained fixed to his seat, terrified of addressing the crowd.

"You must speak," his friend whispered.

"I can't," Chaplin replied.

"You must—it's our only hope."

"Hope," Chaplin muttered under his breath, and finally he got up to say something.

He started out quietly, almost apologizing to his audience. Then he erupted. He told his audience to think for themselves, to unite in the spirit of brotherhood, to put technology in the service of good rather than evil. "Even now my voice is reaching millions throughout the world," he said. He was following Hitler's methods, to the point of commenting on the film from within the film, only he was doing so to attack Hitler.

But then something went wrong. This gifted actor, who had studied Hitler's oratorical methods so carefully, suddenly became too emotional. As he told his audience what a wonderful world they could live in, he lost all control of his senses, and an involuntary body movement took over: his head started to twitch. For several uncomfortable minutes, the camera captured a speech by a man who was no orator. He was rambling, leaving no space between his words; he was expressionless, with his arms fixed by his side; and at the center of the screen was his twitching head. When at last he was done, he looked desperately at his audience, and the film cut to an entirely unconvincing shot of their applause. Not only did Chaplin lack Hitler's oratorical abilities; he also had none of Riefenstahl's technique in capturing oratory.

Years later a copy of *The Great Dictator* was found in the collection of the Propaganda Ministry. There is no record that Hitler actually watched it, but if he did, he probably would have laughed at the incompetence of that final scene. See Reichsfilmarchiv to Joseph Goebbels, August 15, 1944, R55, vol. 665, Bundesarchiv.

100. Ten years later, just when Hitler's last reserves were being deployed on the battlefield during the Second World War, he made another, far more misguided contribution to the German film industry. He ordered 187,000 inactive soldiers to serve as extras in the epic color film *Kolberg*, which showed German civilians rising up against the invading Napoleonic army. According to the director, Hitler was "convinced that such a film was more useful than a military victory." Kershaw, *Hitler 1936–1945*, 713.

101. My claim that Hitler personally supervised the production of German newsreels is based on materials in NS 10, the files of Hitler's adjutants, at the Bundesarchiv. The index for NS 10 notes that the collection contains

"screenings and judgments of newsreels and films with Hitler's recommended changes" (*Vorführungen und Beurteilungen von Wochenschauen und Spielfilmen mit Änderungsvorschlägen Hitlers*). This refers to Hitler's visible deletions and additions to the newsreel texts. Friedrich Kahlenberg, *Bestand NS 10: Persönliche Adjutantur des Führers und Reichskanzlers* (Koblenz: Bundesarchiv, 1970), 21. Studies of Nazi newsreels include Hilmar Hoffmann, *The Triumph of Propaganda: Film and National Socialism, 1933–1945* (Providence: Berghahn Books, 1996); Ulrike Bartels, *Die Wochenschau im Dritten Reich* (Frankfurt: Peter Lang, 2004).

102. Hitler's adjutant to Propaganda Ministry, June 2, 1938, NS 10, vol. 44, folio 72, Bundesarchiv. The original German text reads as follows: "Ich wünsche nicht, dass bei Veranstaltungen nur Aufnahmen von meiner Person gemacht werden. Die Veranstaltungen müssen in ihren Einzelheiten besser erfasst werden. Die Wochenschau muss über die Entstehung der neuen Bauten, technischer Werke, sportlicher Veranstaltungen mehr bringen. Der Bau der neuen Kongresshalle in Nürnberg ist z.B. noch nicht *einmal* erschienen. Die Wochenschau muss politisch witziger gestaltet werden, so z.B. jetzt Aufnahmen über die nervösen Vorbereitungen der Tschechoslowaken bringen. Zum Schluss muss dann eine Grossaufnahme des deutschen Soldaten zu sehen sein. Es darf keine Woche vergehen, in der nicht Aufnahmen der Marine, des Heeres und der Luftwaffe erscheinen. Die Jugend ist in erster Linie an solchen Dingen interessiert."

103. Newsreel 512, June 24, 1940, NS 10, vol. 49, folio 182, Bundesarchiv.

104. Unnumbered newsreel, NS 10, vol. 49, folio 278–282, Bundesarchiv.

105. Unnumbered newsreel, NS 10, vol. 49, folio 228, Bundesarchiv.

106. Unnumbered newsreel, NS 10, vol. 49, folio 146, Bundesarchiv.

107. Unnumbered newsreel, NS 10, vol. 49, folio 307–311, Bundesarchiv.

## 2. ENTER HOLLYWOOD

1. "Screen: Long Arm of Hitler Extends to Hollywood Studio," *Newsweek*, June 26, 1937, 22.

2. E. A. Dupont, "Die deutschfeindlichen 'Engel der Hölle,'" *B.Z. am Mittag*, November 20, 1930, 1–2. For discussions of Dupont's work, see Jürgen Bretschneider, ed., *Ewald Andre Dupont: Autor und Regisseur* (Munich: edition text+kritik, 1992); Paul Matthew St. Pierre, *E. A. Dupont and His Contribution to British Film: Variete, Moulin Rouge, Piccadilly, Atlantic, Two Worlds, Cape Forlorn* (Madison, NJ: Farleigh Dickinson University Press, 2010).

3. Dupont, "Die deutschfeindlichen 'Engel der Hölle.'" 1–2.

4. Ibid.

5. "'Hell's Angels': Why Germany Objects to the Film," *The Observer*, November 23, 1930, 10. For other commentary in the press, see "'Anti-German' War Film: Diplomatic Protest Likely," *Manchester Guardian*, November 21, 1930, 8; "'Hell's Angels': German Official Protest," *The Times*, November 21, 1930, 14; "Dupont Pans 'Hell's Angels,'" *Variety*, November 26, 1930, 6.

6. "Hetzfilme gegen Deutschland: Die Märchen von deutschen Kriegs-greuelen erreichen Rekordkassen am Broadway," *Der Film*, October 18, 1930, 2; "Intervention in London? Lebhafter Telegrammwechsel des Aus-wärtigen Amts mit London wegen 'Engel der Hölle,'" *Der Film*, November 22, 1930, 1; "No Reich Protest on Film: London Embassy Denies Diplo-matic Action on 'Hell's Angels,'" *New York Times*, November 21, 1930, 9.

7. "No Protest on War Film: Britain Says Germany Did Not Ask 'Hell's An-gels' Be Barred," *New York Times*, November 25, 1930, 34.

8. "'Engel der Hölle' in 20 Pariser Kinos," *Licht Bild Bühne*, September 21, 1931, 1; Frederick Herron to Jason Joy, November 17, 1931, *Hell's Angels* file, Motion Picture Association of America (henceforth MPAA), Production Code Administration records, Margaret Herrick Library, Academy of Mo-tion Picture Arts and Sciences, Beverly Hills (henceforth Margaret Herrick Library).

9. "Frankreich verbietet 'Engel der Hölle,'" *Licht Bild Bühne*, September 26, 1931, 1: Herron to Joy, November 17, 1931.

10. Lamar Trotti to Will Hays, September 13, 1930, *Hell's Angels* file, MPAA, Production Code Administration records, Margaret Herrick Library.

11. Frederick Herron to Jason Joy, June 7, 1932, *Hell's Angels* file, MPAA, Pro-duction Code Administration records, Margaret Herrick Library.

12. Jens Ulff-Møller, *Hollywood's Film Wars with France: Film Trade Diplomacy and the Emergence of the French Film Quota Policy* (Rochester, NY: University of Rochester Press, 2001), 69–74; Kristin Thompson, *Exporting Entertainment: America in the World Film Market, 1907–34* (London: BFI Publishing, 1985), 106.

13. "'One for One', Say Germans: Commerce Dept. Holds Valuable Informa-tion," *Variety*, November 19, 1924, 21.

14. Kristin Thompson, *Exporting Entertainment*, 106–107, 36, 128; Ulff-Møller, *Hollywood's Film Wars with France*, 74.

15. Modris Eksteins, "War, Memory, and Politics: The Fate of the Film *All Quiet on the Western Front*," *Central European History* 13 (1980): 66–67; George Canty, "Weekly Report 2," July 9, 1932, Commercial Attachés in Germany 1931–1940, RG 151, National Archives and Records Administration, Col-lege Park, Maryland (henceforth National Archives).

16. Frederick Herron to John V. Wilson, April 16, 1932, *The Lost Squadron* file, MPAA, Production Code Administration records, Margaret Herrick Li-brary; Canty, "Weekly Report 2," July 9, 1932.

17. Canty, "Weekly Report 3," July 16, 1932, Commercial Attachés in Ger-many 1931–1940, RG 151, National Archives.

18. German Interior Ministry, *Reichsministerialblatt*, July 2, 1932, 371. The translation here is from Georg Gyssling to Columbia Pictures, September 11, 1933, *Below the Sea* file, MPAA, Production Code Administration rec-ords, Margaret Herrick Library.

19. Auswärtiges Amt, Rundschreiben, August 27, 1932, German legation in Lisbon, box 160: Filme, vol. 2, Politisches Archiv des Auswärtigen Amts, Berlin (henceforth PAAA).

20. Paul Schwarz, "Warnungen wegen der Filme 'Hell's Angels', 'Casque de Cuir' und 'Mamba,'" December 10, 1932, Paris 2281: Filmwesen, vol. 4, PAAA.

21. Ibid.

22. Ibid.

23. Ibid.

24. Ibid.

25. Ibid.

26. "Keine United-Artists-Filme in Deutschland: 'LBB' Interview mit A. W. Kelly," *Licht Bild Bühne*, September 20, 1933, 2.

27. "United Artists Filme in Deutschland," *Film-Kurier*, March 8, 1934, 1; "UA Back into German Market After 4 Years," *Variety*, March 20, 1934, 15.

28. See the Filmprüfstelle lists for 1934 at the Deutsches Filminstitut, Frankfurt, which note the banning of the following United Artists films: *The Affairs of Cellini, Moulin Rouge, Roman Scandals*, and *Nana*. In the same year, United Artists' *Scarface* was banned by the highest censorship board: Oberprüfstelle report 7513, "Das Narbengesicht (Scarface)," November 22, 1934, Deutsches Filminstitut, Frankfurt. Two United Artists films, *Cynara* and *Our Daily Bread*, did get past the censors, but these were most likely distributed by a different company in Germany.

29. Frederick Herron to Jason Joy, March 21, 1932, *The Lost Squadron* file, MPAA, Production Code Administration records, Margaret Herrick Library.

30. Ruth Vasey, *The World According to Hollywood, 1918–1939* (Madison: University of Wisconsin Press, 1997), 80–84.

31. Referat des Gesandtschaftsrats Dr. Freudenthal, April 18, 1933, German embassy in Paris, 2282: Filmwesen, vol. 5, PAAA, 4–5, 2–3, 11.

32. Vasey, *The World According to Hollywood*, 82; Valentin Mandelstamm to Carl Laemmle Jr., March 31, 1930, *All Quiet on the Western Front* file, MPAA, Production Code Administration records, Margaret Herrick Library.

33. Referat des Gesandtschaftsrats Dr. Freudenthal, April 18, 1933, 1, 3.

34. Ibid., 3–4, 6–7.

35. Ibid., 7, 5.

36. *Wings*, directed by William A. Wellman (Paramount, 1927); Tony Thomas, *Howard Hughes in Hollywood* (Secaucus, NJ: Citadel Press, 1985), 42–43; Donald L. Barlett and James B. Steele, *Empire: The Life, Legend, and Madness of Howard Hughes* (New York: Norton, 1979), 64–66.

37. Dick Grace, *The Lost Squadron* (New York: Grosset & Dunlap, 1931), 15.

38. *The Lost Squadron*, directed by George Archainbaud (RKO, 1932).

39. Referat des Gesandtschaftsrats Dr. Freudenthal, April 18, 1933, 5, 13; "Diplomatische Schritte wegen 'Verlorener Schwadron,'" *Licht Bild Bühne*, April 4, 1932, 1.

40. Herron to Joy, March 21, 1932.

41. Herron to Wilson, April 16, 1932.

42. Frederick Herron to John V. Wilson, April 29, 1932, *The Lost Squadron* file, MPAA, Production Code Administration records, Margaret Herrick Library.

43. Referat des Gesandtschaftsrats Dr. Freudenthal, April 18, 1933, 10–11, 13.

44. Ibid., 6.

45. Ibid., 9–10.

46. "Aufzeichnung," April 18, 1933, Paris 2282, Filmwesen, vol. 5, PAAA.

47. Referat des Gesandtschaftsrats Dr. Freudenthal, April 18, 1933, 7–9.

48. Ibid., 9, 10.

49. Ibid., 12–14.

50. Canty, "Weekly Report 40," April 1, 1933, Commercial Attachés in Germany 1931–1940, RG 151, National Archives; Werner Freiherr von Grünau to Georg Gyssling, March 20, 1933, File 702.6211/663, 1930–39 Central Decimal File, RG 59, National Archives.

51. NSDAP to Reichskanzlei, undated, "General-Konsulat New-York," NS 43, vol. 47, folio 337, Bundesarchiv, Berlin.

52. *Captured!*, directed by Roy Del Ruth (Warner Brothers, 1933).

53. Resume, June 15, 1933, *Captured!* file, MPAA, Production Code Administration records, Margaret Herrick Library.

54. Gustav Müller, "Aufzeichnung," January 13, 1934, German embassy in Rome, 835a: deutschfeindliche Filmpropaganda, vol. 2, PAAA. This report contains all the cuts that Gyssling had requested seven months earlier.

55. Ibid.

56. Propaganda Ministry to consulates, embassies, and legations, January 25, 1934, German embassy in Rome, 835a: deutschfeindliche Filmpropaganda, vol. 2, PAAA.

57. This wording is from Gyssling's letter to Columbia Pictures about *Below the Sea*, which he sent at almost the same time. See Georg Gyssling to Columbia Pictures, September 11, 1933.

58. George Canty, "Economic and Trade Notes 237," May 17, 1933, Commercial Attachés in Germany 1931–1940, RG 151, National Archives.

59. "Ich bin ein entflohener Kettensträfling," *Völkischer Beobachter*, March 19–20, 1933, 5.

60. Frederick Herron to James Wingate, December 7, 1933, *The House of Rothschild* file, MPAA, Production Code Administration records, Margaret Herrick Library.

61. Müller, "Aufzeichnung," January 13, 1934; Frederick Herron to Gustav Müller, January 29, 1934, German embassy in Rome, 835a: deutschfeindliche Filmpropaganda, vol. 2, PAAA.

62. Herron to Wingate, December 7, 1933.

63. Gustav Müller to Frederick Herron, February 5, 1934, File 811.4061 Mad Dog of Europe/6, 1930–39 Central Decimal File, RG 59, National Archives; *Below the Sea*, directed by Albert Rogell (Columbia Pictures, 1933). Also see Gyssling to Columbia Pictures, September 11, 1933.

64. "2 U.S. Co.'s Bow to Nazi Stand," *Variety*, February 6, 1934, 11. Warner Brothers went even further in order not to get into trouble. In late 1933, the company released a picture entitled *Ever in My Heart*, which told the story of a German immigrant who experienced discrimination in America during the World War. He lost his job, his dog was stoned to death, and his

wife's family insisted that he change his name. "They let me be a citizen," he complained, "but they won't let me be an American." In other words, when the persecution of the Jews was beginning in Germany, Warner Brothers released a picture about the persecution of the German minority in the United States. *Ever in My Heart*, directed by Archie Mayo (Warner Brothers, 1933).

65. Propaganda Ministry to consulates, embassies, and legations, January 25, 1934.

66. "WB 1st U.S. Co. to Bow Out of Germany," *Variety*, July 17, 1934, 1.

67. Thompson, *Exporting Entertainment*, 36.

68. "Dept. of Com. Picture Dept.," *Variety*, December 17, 1924, 26.

69. Canty, "Weekly Report 1," July 2, 1932, Commercial Attachés in Germany 1931–1940, RG 151, National Archives; Canty, "Weekly Report 3," July 16, 1932.

70. Canty, "Weekly Report 35," February 25, 1933, and "Weekly Report 46," May 13, 1933, Commercial Attachés in Germany 1931–1940, RG 151, National Archives.

71. [Albert Sander], "Rassenfrage, Kontingent, u. Lizenzen. Das Raether–Interview in *The Era*," *Der Film*, July 16, 1932, 1–2.

72. Canty, "Weekly Report 41," April 8, 1933, Commercial Attachés in Germany 1931–1940, RG 151, National Archives.

73. Canty, "Weekly Report 44," April 29, 1933, Commercial Attachés in Germany 1931–1940, RG 151, National Archives; Canty, "Weekly Report 41," April 8, 1933.

74. "'Blocked' Marks Seen in Wider Use," *New York Times*, May 21, 1933, N7; "Schacht Loan Plan Faces Difficulties," *New York Times*, May 22, 1933, 23. Also see John Weitz, *Hitler's Banker: Hjalmar Horace Greeley Schacht* (Boston: Little, Brown and Company, 1997), 154–156.

75. Nearly two years after the Nazis came to power, Canty wrote: "Inasmuch as it is classified as a cultural product and not a commodity, the film was one of the last items to feel the full effects of the German exchange restrictions; and this only happened comparatively recently." Canty, "German Film Developments," December 27, 1934, Commercial Attachés in Germany 1931–1940, RG 151, National Archives. For the impact of the exchange restrictions on other American companies, see Edwin Black, *IBM and the Holocaust: The Strategic Alliance between Nazi Germany and America's Most Powerful Corporation* (New York: Crown, 2001), 67; Henry Ashby Turner Jr., *General Motors and the Nazis: The Struggle for Control of Opel, Europe's Biggest Carmaker* (New Haven: Yale University Press, 2005), 27.

76. Canty, "Weekly Report 38," March 18, 1933, Commercial Attachés in Germany 1931–1940, RG 151, National Archives. For the persecution of the Jews in the 1930s, see Saul Friedländer, *Nazi Germany and the Jews: The Years of Persecution, 1933–1939* (New York: HarperCollins, 1997). For the expulsion of Jews from the German culture industries, see Alan E. Steinweis, *Art, Ideology, and Economics in Nazi Germany: The Reich Chambers of*

*Music, Theater, and the Visual Arts* (Chapel Hill: University of North Carolina Press, 1993); Steinweis, "Hans Hinkel and German Jewry, 1933–1941," *Leo Baeck Institute Tearbook* 38 (1993): 209–219.

77. Klaus Kreimeier, *The Ufa Story* (Berkeley: University of California Press, 1996), 210–212.

78. Canty, "Weekly Report 41," April 8, 1933.

79. Canty, "Weekly Report 43," April 22, 1933, Commercial Attachés in Germany 1931–1940, RG 151, National Archives.

80. Ibid.

81. "U.S. Filmers Protest Restrictions In Germany, but Carry on Trade," *Variety*, April 25, 1933, 13. Jack Warner later gave an exaggerated account of what happened to his manager in Berlin and falsely cited it as the reason for his company's departure from Germany: "I went to Max Reinhardt's castle in Salzburg, Austria. There I got the sickening news that Joe Kauffman, our Warner Brothers man in Germany, had been murdered by Nazi killers in Berlin. Like many another outnumbered Jew, he was trapped in an alley. They hit him with fists and clubs, and kicked the life out of him with their boots, and left him lying there." In fact, Kauffman (whose actual name was Phil, not Joe) left Germany in 1934 after being beaten up by Nazi thugs, and he died peacefully in Stockholm later that year. Jack Warner, *My First Hundred Years in Hollywood* (New York: Random House, 1964), 248–249.

82. Canty, "Weekly Report 43," April 22, 1933.

83. Canty, "Weekly Report 44," April 29, 1933; Canty, "Weekly Report 41," April 8, 1933.

84. Canty, "Weekly Report 45," May 6, 1933, Commercial Attachés in Germany 1931–1940, RG 151, National Archives; Canty, "Weekly Report 46," May 13, 1933.

85. "U.S. Film Units Yield to Nazis On Race Issue," *Variety*, May 9, 1933, 13.

86. Canty, "Weekly Report 47," May 20, 1933, Commercial Attachés in Germany 1931–1940, RG 151, National Archives.

87. Douglas Miller, "Special Report 55: German Film Problems," December 23, 1935, Commercial Attachés in Germany 1931–1940, RG 151, National Archives. Miller added the following note to his report: "Director Kaelber . . . said that, now that all Non-Aryans have been eliminated from the German film industry, the next step . . . should be towards the destruction of the Jewish spirit. However, no details about this plan were announced by him."

88. Canty, "Weekly Report 49," June 3, 1933, Commercial Attachés in Germany 1931–1940, RG 151, National Archives. The Hollywood studios benefited greatly from the talents of a large number of Jewish filmmakers who left Berlin for Los Angeles. See "Hollywood to Give German Jews Work: Goldwyn Organizes Movement to Employ all the Able Film Figures Barred by Reich," *New York Times*, July 3, 1933, 14. Goldwyn's offer applied only to film specialists, not to film salesmen. For discussion of the émigrés, see John Russell Taylor, *Strangers in Paradise: The Hollywood Émigrés 1933–1950* (New York: Holt, Reinhart and Winston, 1983).

89. George Canty, "Special Report 4: German Film Law Extended for Three Years with Slight Modifications," August 1, 1933, and "Special Report 112: Outlook for the 1934/35 Season for German Films," June 26, 1934, Commercial Attachés in Germany 1931–1940, RG 151, National Archives.

90. Canty, "Motion Pictures Abroad: The German Film Industry During 1933," February 16, 1934, Commercial Attachés in Germany 1931–1940, RG 151, National Archives.

91. Canty, "Weekly Report 45," May 6, 1933.

92. Quoted in Neal Gabler, *An Empire of Their Own: How the Jews Invented Hollywood* (New York: Doubleday, 1988), 2.

93. A simple survey of American newspapers from the 1930s confirms this. In February and March 1933, there were approximately twenty articles that mentioned Hitler's persecution of the Jews in the *New York Times*. The same was true for the *Los Angeles Times* and the *Washington Post*.

94. Moshe R. Gottlieb, *American Anti-Nazi Resistance, 1933–1941: An Historical Analysis* (New York: KTAV Publishing House, 1982), 31–34. In addition to Gottlieb's book, which focuses heavily on the boycott movement, there is a general study of the response of the American Jewish community to the rise of Nazism: Gulie Ne'eman Arad, *America, Its Jews, and the Rise of Nazism* (Bloomington: Indiana University Press, 2000).

95. Gottlieb, *American Anti-Nazi Resistance*, 59–64, 83–85. The American Jewish Committee gave three reasons for its opposition to the boycott movement: (1) a fear of arousing domestic anti-Semitism, (2) a desire not to fight Hitlerism with Hitlerism, and (3) a growing tendency among Americans not to buy German goods anyway. The executive secretary of the committee, Morris Waldman, wrote, "A boycott is a two-edged sword which hurts innocent people, including Jews, both in Germany and in countries where boycotting is practiced."

96. "'Mank' To Produce Picture in East," *Hollywood Reporter*, June 6, 1933, 1; "Jaffe Leaves Radio to Go Independent," *Hollywood Reporter*, July 11, 1933, 1.

97. Sam Jaffe, "To The Entire Motion Picture Industry," *Hollywood Reporter*, July 12, 1933, 4.

98. "'Mank' Back At MGM," *Hollywood Reporter*, June 30, 1933, 1.

99. "Will Work on 'Mad Dog,'" *Hollywood Reporter*, July 19, 1933, 2; Leon Lewis to Richard Gutstadt, August 17, 1933, Jewish Federation Council of Greater Los Angeles, Community Relations Committee Collection (henceforth JFC), pt. 1, box 22, folder 14, Urban Archives Center, Oviatt Library, Northridge (henceforth Urban Archives Center).

100. Herman Mankiewicz and Lynn Root, "The Mad Dog of Europe," Copyright Records, box 158, reg. no. 25996, December 26, 1933, Manuscript Division, Library of Congress, Washington, DC (henceforth LC). Al Rosen sent the script to the Copyright Office in December 1933, and to my knowledge this is the only remaining copy. It was selected for preservation by Alice Birney. The names of people and places have been fictionalized in this version, but as my narrative explains, the original version used real names (Hitler, Goebbels, Göring, etc.).

101. Ibid., 41–42.
102. Ibid., 59.
103. Ibid., 60.
104. Ibid., 62–63.
105. Ibid., 82.
106. Ibid., 95–96.
107. Ibid., 92.
108. Ibid., 101.
109. Ibid., 108.
110. Ibid., 112, 114.
111. "Jaffe and Mankiewicz Flout Hays 'Mad Dog' Ban," *Hollywood Reporter*, July 18, 1933, 1.
112. "Hitler Regime Topic of 'Mad Dog of Europe,'" *Washington Post*, October 17, 1933, 11; Lewis to Gutstadt, July 21, 1933, JFC, pt. 1, box 22, folder 13, Urban Archives Center.
113. Joseph Breen to Sol Lesser, November 25, 1936, *The Mad Dog of Europe* file, MPAA, Production Code Administration records, Margaret Herrick Library. This is Breen's restatement of the argument he first made in mid-1933.
114. Lewis to Gutstadt, July 21, 1933.
115. Lewis to Gutstadt, August 17, 1933.
116. Lewis to Gutstadt, August 4, 1933, JFC, pt. 1, box 22, folder 14, Urban Archives Center.
117. Lewis to Gutstadt, August 17, 1933.
118. Ibid.
119. Ibid.
120. Ibid.
121. Gutstadt to Lewis, August 28, 1933, JFC, pt. 1, box 22, folder 14, Urban Archives Center.
122. For discussion of the German American Bund, see Sander A. Diamond, *The Nazi Movement in the United States 1924–1941* (Ithaca, NY: Cornell University Press, 1974). For discussion of the Silver Shirts, see Scott Beekman, *William Dudley Pelley: A Life in Right-Wing Extremism and the Occult* (Syracuse, NY: Syracuse University Press, 2005).
123. Gottlieb, *American Anti-Nazi Resistance*, 35–39, 66–67; Felicia Herman, "Hollywood, Nazism, and the Jews, 1933–41," *American Jewish History* 89, no. 1 (2001): 63–69; Leonard Dinnerstein, *Antisemitism in America* (New York: Oxford University Press, 1994), 105–127.
124. Gutstadt to Lewis, August 28, 1933.
125. Lewis to Gutstadt, November 1, 1933, JFC, pt. 1, box 22, folder 15, Urban Archives Center.
126. Lewis to Gutstadt, September 1, 1933, JFC, pt. 1, box 22, folder 15, Urban Archives Center.
127. "Rosen Wants Jaffe to Make 'Mad Dog,'" *Hollywood Reporter*, October 5, 1933, 3; "'Mad Dog' Starts Nov. 1 At Associated Studios," *Hollywood Reporter*, October 11, 1933, 6; Louella O. Parsons, "Coast Agent to Produce 'Mad

Dog of Europe'—Hitler Story is Purchased by Al Rosen—Picks Up Yarn after Sam Jaffe Abandons It," *Pittsburgh Post-Gazette*, October 9, 1933, 20; "Thalberg to Start Work in Fortnight—Notwithstanding Frown," *Los Angeles Times*, October 12, 1933, 11.

128. Alva Johnston, "Profiles: The Great Expurgator," *The New Yorker*, March 29, 1947, 43.

129. George Shaffer, "Teacher Tells Personal Life of Anna Sten," *Chicago Daily Tribune*, October 20, 1933, 21.

130. "Charges Nazis Here Using Threats to Halt Production of 'Mad Dog of Europe,'" *Jewish Daily Bulletin*, October 23, 1933, 3–4; "Plans Movie Based on Nazi War on Jews Despite Opposition," *Chicago Daily Tribune*, October 15, 1933, 2; Fred W. Beetson to Joseph Breen, May 4, 1939, *The Mad Dog of Europe* file, MPAA, Production Code Administration records, Margaret Herrick Library.

131. "Rosen to Film Hitler Story Despite Fears," *Washington Post*, October 15, 1933, 3; "Hitler Regime Topic of 'Mad Dog of Europe,'" 11; "Rosen Seeks Jewish Aid for His 'Mad Dog,'" *Variety*, October 24, 1933, 2; "Depicting the Times," *The New York Amsterdam News*, October 25, 1933, 6. Also see Gutstadt to Samuel Untermeyer, October 30, 1933, JFC, pt. 1, box 22, folder 15; Gutstadt to Lewis, October 30, 1933, JFC, pt. 1, box 22, folder 15; Lewis to Gutstadt, November 3, 1933, JFC, pt. 1, box 22, folder 16, Urban Archives Center.

132. "Hays Group Sued By Rosen on 'Mad Dog,'" *Hollywood Reporter*, October 24, 1933, 3; "Hays Group is Sued Over A Hitler Film," *New York Times*, October 25, 1933, 22; "Al Rosen's $1,022,000 Suit Over 'Mad Dog,'" *Variety*, October 31, 1933, 21.

133. "Charges Nazis Here Using Threats to Halt Production of 'Mad Dog of Europe,'" 3–4.

134. "Rosen Goes Ahead on Hitler Picture," *Hollywood Reporter*, February 9, 1934, 5.

135. "Al Rosen Returns," *Hollywood Reporter*, January 4, 1934, 2.

136. "Al Rosen Seeks Exhibitor Reaction Re 'Mad Dog,'" *Hollywood Reporter*, November 3, 1933, 4.

137. Rosen v. Loews's Inc., No. 263, Docket 20584 (2d Cir. July 23, 1947).

138. Propaganda Ministry to German embassy in Rome, June 9, 1934, German embassy in Rome, 835a: deutschfeindliche Filmpropaganda, vol. 2, PAAA. The *New York Times* reviewer wrote: "'Hitler's Reign of Terror,' a pictorial record of Nazi activities in Germany, which has reached the Mayfair screen, scarcely lives up to expectations, particularly after one listens to the florid introductory remarks. . . . In such a compilation it is always disappointing to find that part of the production has been staged, even though those responsible for the offering in this instance frankly admit that some of the scenes 'are reproduced from personal interviews and incidents witnessed by Mr. Vanderbilt during his tour of both Austria and Germany.'" Mordaunt Hall, "The Brown Shirts," *New York Times*, May 1, 1934, 26; *Hitler's Reign of Terror*, directed by Michael Mindlin (Jewel Productions, 1934).

139. Pierrepont Moffat, Memorandum, June 15, 1934, File 811.4061 Mad Dog of Europe/7, 1930–39 Central Decimal File, RG 59, National Archives.

140. Lester D. Friedman, *Hollywood's Image of the Jew* (New York: Frederick Ungar Publishing Co., 1982), 9–10.

141. Ben Hecht, *A Guide for the Bedevilled* (New York: Charles Scribner's Sons, 1944), 208.

142. *The Jazz Singer*, directed by Alan Krosland (Warner Brothers, 1927).

143. *Disraeli*, directed by Alfred E. Green (Warner Brothers, 1929).

144. Friedman, *Hollywood's Image of the Jew*, 12.

145. Leonard Mosley, *Zanuck: The Rise and Fall of Hollywood's Last Tycoon* (Boston: Little, Brown and Company, 1984), 125–127.

146. Ibid., 129–132.

147. Ibid., 134.

148. George Arliss, *My Ten Years in the Studios* (Boston: Little, Brown and Company, 1940), 222.

149. Arliss, *My Ten Years in the Studios*, 222–223; Tom Stempel, *Screenwriter: The Life and Times of Nunnally Johnson* (San Diego: A.S. Barnes & Company, 1980), 47–48; Harry M. Warner to Will Hays, June 9, 1933, in Rudy Behmler, ed., *Inside Warner Bros.* (New York: Viking, 1985), 12–13; "Arliss and 'Rothschild,'" *New York Times*, April 22, 1934, X4.

150. *Recollections of Nunnally Johnson: Oral History Transcript, interviewed by Tom Stempel*, Oral History Program, University of California, Los Angeles, 1969, Bancroft Library, Berkeley (henceforth Bancroft Library), 28.

151. *The House of Rothschild*, directed by Alfred L. Werker (Twentieth Century Pictures, 1934).

152. *Gentleman's Agreement*, directed by Elia Kazan (Twentieth Century-Fox, 1947).

153. Darryl Zanuck to James Wingate, December 4, 1933, *The House of Rothschild* file, MPAA, Production Code Administration records, Margaret Herrick Library.

154. Gabler, *An Empire of Their Own*, 187–189.

155. Michael E. Birdwell, *Celluloid Soldiers: The Warner Bros. Campaign against Nazism* (New York: New York University Press, 1999), 3.

156. Mosley, *Zanuck*, 130–131.

157. *Recollections of Nunnally Johnson*, 24.

158. Robert M. Fells, *George Arliss: The Man Who Played God* (Lanham, MD: Scarecrow Press, 2004), 135–136.

159. George Hembert Westley, "Rothschild," Twentieth Century-Fox Collection, USC Cinematic Arts Library, Los Angeles (henceforth Cinematic Arts Library).

160. Maude T. Howell and Sam Mintz, "Outline: Rothschild," July 27, 1933, Twentieth Century-Fox Collection, Cinematic Arts Library.

161. "A.H. Wiggin Sailing For Berlin Today: Strawn, Filene, Arliss and Mrs. H. F. Whitney Are Other Bremen Passengers," *New York Times*, May 20, 1933, 10; Arliss, *My Ten Years in the Studios*, 223–224; Fells, *George Arliss*, 136.

162. Arliss, *My Ten Years in the Studios*, 224–225; Fells, *George Arliss*, 135.

163. Count Egon Cæsar Corti, *The Rise of the House of Rothschild 1770–1830* (New York: Blue Ribbon Books, 1928), vii.

164. Ibid., 9, 51, 59, 75, 126–127.

165. Howell and Mintz, "Outline: Rothschild."

166. Arliss, *My Ten Years in the Studios*, 224–225; George Arliss, "Suggestions: Rothschild," September 5, 1933, Twentieth Century-Fox Collection, Cinematic Arts Library.

167. Maude T. Howell, "Outline: The Great 'Rothschild,'" September 11, 1933, Twentieth Century-Fox Collection, Cinematic Arts Library.

168. Maude T. Howell and Nunnally Johnson, "Rothschild," September 14, 1933, Twentieth Century-Fox Collection, Cinematic Arts Library.

169. Maude T. Howell and Nunnally Johnson, "The Great Rothschilds," September 23, 1933; Howell and Johnson, "First Temp.: The Great Rothschilds," October 28, 1933, Twentieth Century-Fox Collection, Cinematic Arts Library.

170. ROTHSCHILD conference, September 26, 1933, Twentieth Century-Fox Collection, Cinematic Arts Library.

171. Arliss, "Suggestions: Rothschild"; Corti, *Rise of the House of Rothschild*, 107–108.

172. Ibid., 103; Niall Ferguson, *The House of Rothschild: Money's Prophets, 1798–1848* (New York: Viking, 1998), 75–76.

173. Lewis to Gutstadt, December 7, 1933, JFC, pt. 1, box 22, folder 17, Urban Archives Center.

174. Gutstadt to Lewis, December 20, 1933, JFC, pt. 1, box 22, folder 18, Urban Archives Center.

175. Sigmund Livingston to ADL Representatives, Confidential Memo, March 20, 1934, JFC, pt. 1, box 22, folder 22, Urban Archives Center.

176. Ibid.

177. Lewis to Joseph Schenck, December 20, 1933, JFC, pt. 1, box 22, folder 18, Urban Archives Center.

178. Darryl Zanuck to Lewis, December 21, 1933, JFC, pt. 1, box 22, folder 18, Urban Archives Center.

179. Lewis to Gutstadt, December 23, 1933, JFC, pt. 1, box 22, folder 18, Urban Archives Center.

180. Lewis to Gutstadt, December 21, 1933, JFC, pt. 1, box 22, folder 18, Urban Archives Center; Will Hays to Darryl Zanuck, December 21, 1933, *The House of Rothschild* file, MPAA, Production Code Administration records, Margaret Herrick Library.

181. Joseph Breen to Will Hays, March 6, 1934, *The House of Rothschild* file, MPAA, Production Code Administration records; Joseph Jonah Cummins to Darryl Zanuck, March 16, 1934, *The House of Rothschild* file, MPAA, Production Code Administration records; Reverend C. F. Aked, "George Arliss in *The House of Rothschild*: A Joy and An Inspiration," *The House of Rothschild* file, MPAA, Production Code Administration records, Margaret Herrick Library.

182. Gutstadt to Lewis, March 16, 1934, JFC, pt. 1, box 22, folder 22; Lewis to Gutstadt, March 16, 1934, JFC, pt. 1, box 22, folder 22; Gutstadt to

Lewis, March 17, 1934, JFC, pt. 1, box 22, folder 22, Urban Archives Center.

183. Gutstadt to Mary G. Schonberg, March 23, 1934, JFC, pt. 1, box 22, folder 22, Urban Archives Center.

184. Lewis to Gutstadt, December 7, 1933; Sigmund Livingston to Louis B. Mayer, December 21, 1933, JFC, pt. 1, box 22, folder 17, Urban Archives Center.

185. Lewis to Gutstadt, December 23, 1933; Lewis to Gutstadt, December 21, 1933.

186. Lewis to Gutstadt, December 21, 1933.

187. Gutstadt to Lewis, December 14, 1933, JFC, pt. 1, box 22, folder 17, Urban Archives Center.

188. Lewis to Gutstadt, December 23, 1933.

189. Gutstadt to Lewis, December 22, 1933, JFC, pt. 1, box 22, folder 17, Urban Archives Center; Gutstadt to Lewis, December 14, 1933.

190. "Cinema: Up From Jew Street," *Time*, March 26, 1934, 22.

191. A lone dissenting review put the matter this way: "The traits held up for admiration are cunning, avarice, and revenge; and these are traits which are neither admirable nor peculiarly Jewish. If one may add a paradox of one's own to the many paradoxes with which this film is bristling, one would like to suggest that it really amounts to a libel on the race which it pretends to champion." William Troy, "Films: Bankers and Technicolor," *The Nation*, April 4, 1934, 398.

192. Darryl Zanuck to Joseph Breen, April 10, 1934, *The House of Rothschild* file, MPAA, Production Code Administration records, Margaret Herrick Library.

193. S. Y. Allen to Darryl Zanuck, April 11, 1934, *The House of Rothschild* file, MPAA, Production Code Administration records, Margaret Herrick Library; Gutstadt to Lewis, April 26, 1934, JFC, pt. 1, box 22, folder 23; Lewis to Gutstadt, April 30, 1934, JFC, pt. 1, box 22, folder 23, Urban Archives Center.

194. Fells, *George Arliss*, 143; Mosley, *Zanuck*, 142, 150–153.

195. Edward Zeisler to Lewis, March 22, 1934, JFC, pt. 1, box 22, folder 22, Urban Archives Center.

196. Lewis to Gutstadt, March 21, 1934, JFC, pt. 1, box 22, folder 22, Urban Archives Center.

197. Gutstadt to Lewis, March 9, 1934, JFC, pt. 1, box 22, folder 21, Urban Archives Center.

198. Lewis to Gutstadt, March 21, 1934.

199. Lewis to I. M. Golden, March 14, 1934, JFC, pt. 1, box 22, folder 21, Urban Archives Center.

200. "Breen to be Hays Group Code Chief: Appointment Marks First Important Step of Industry to Regulate Self," *Los Angeles Times*, July 7, 1934, A1; "Supreme Censorship Power Given to Hays," *Los Angeles Times*, July 8, 1934, A1; "Hays Plan Due Today: Self-Censorship Parley Called," *Los Angeles Times*, July 11, 1934, 1; "Hollywood Takes Step to Assure Clean Film," *Los Angeles Times*, July 12, 1934, 1.

201. Lewis to Sigmund Livingston, July 13, 1934, JFC, pt. 1, box 22, folder 25, Urban Archives Center.

202. Gutstadt to Lewis, August 1, 1934, JFC, pt. 1, box 22, folder 26; Lewis to Gutstadt, September 17, 1934, JFC, pt. 1, box 22, folder 26, Urban Archives Center.

203. Gutstadt to Lewis, March 23, 1934, JFC, pt. 1, box 22, folder 22; Gutstadt to Mary G. Schonberg, March 29, 1934, JFC, pt. 1, box 22, folder 22, Urban Archives Center.

204. Gutstadt to Lewis, June 25, 1934, JFC, pt. 1, box 22, folder 24, Urban Archives Center.

205. Gutstadt to Lewis, November 15, 1934, JFC, pt. 1, box 23, folder 1; Lewis to Gutstadt, November 19, 1934, JFC, pt. 1, box 23, folder 1; Lewis to Abraham W. Brussel, July 13, 1934, JFC, pt. 1, box 22, folder 25, Urban Archives Center.

206. Gutstadt to unknown recipient, November 1, 1934, JFC, pt. 1, box 23, folder 1, Urban Archives Center.

207. Gutstadt to Lewis, February 7, 1935, JFC, pt. 1, box 23 folder 4, Urban Archives Center. For examples of Gutstadt's many letters, see Gutstadt to Arthur Rosenblum, November 16, 1934, JFC, pt. 1, box 23, folder 1; Gutstadt to Lewis, December 18, 1934, JFC, pt. 1, box 23, folder 2; Gutstadt to Lewis, January 21, 1935, JFC, pt. 1, box 23, folder 3; Gutstadt to Lewis, February 4, 1935, JFC, pt. 1, box 23, folder 4; Gutstadt to Lewis, February 27, 1935, JFC, pt. 1, box 23, folder 4; Gutstadt to Lewis, March 15, 1935, JFC, pt. 1, box 23, folder 4; Gutstadt to Lewis, April 22, 1935, JFC, pt. 1, box 23, folder 5; Gutstadt to Mendel Silberberg, June 24, 1935, JFC, pt. 1, box 23, folder 5; Gutstadt to Lewis, July 29, 1935, JFC, pt. 1, box 23, folder 6; Gutstadt to Lewis, August 6, 1935, JFC, pt. 1, box 23, folder 6; Gutstadt to Lewis, August 20, 1935, JFC, pt. 1, box 23, folder 6; Gutstadt to Lewis, October 4, 1935, JFC, pt. 1, box 23, folder 7; Gutstadt to Lewis, November 5, 1935, JFC, pt. 1, box 23, folder 8; Gutstadt to Silberberg, March 3, 1936, JFC, pt. 1, box 23, folder 10, Urban Archives Center.

208. Henry Popkin, "The Vanishing Jew of Our Popular Culture," *Commentary* 14 (1952): 46–55.

209. Hecht, *A Guide for the Bedevilled*, 207, 209–210.

210. German embassy in London to Foreign Office, May 26, 1934, German embassy in Rome, 835a: deutschfeindliche Filmpropaganda, vol. 2, PAAA.

211. German consulate in Seattle to German embassy in Washington, DC, May 15, 1934, German embassy in Rome, 835a: deutschfeindliche Filmpropaganda, vol. 2, PAAA.

212. *Der ewige Jude*, directed by Fritz Hippler (Deutsche Filmherstellungs- und -Ververtungs- GmbH, 1940).

213. *Die Rothschilds*, directed by Erich Waschneck (Ufa, 1940).

1. "Here's one picture Germans spot as OK," *Variety*, March 27, 1934, 11.
2. Joachim C. Fest, *Hitler* [1973] (New York: Penguin, 1982), 406.
3. Kershaw, *Hitler 1889–1936: Hubris* (London: Penguin, 1998), 467; Fest, *Hitler*, 406–407.
4. Kershaw, *Hitler 1889–1936*, 467–468; Fest, *Hitler*, 407.
5. Fest, *Hitler*, 408.
6. Richard J. Evans, *The Coming of the Third Reich* (New York: Penguin Press, 2004), 353–354.
7. Ibid., 354.
8. Fest, *Hitler*, 408. I have replaced the awkward phrase "salutariness of criticism" in the English translation with the phrase "salutary nature of criticism."
9. Ibid., 408–409.
10. Kershaw, *Hitler 1889–1936*, 468.
11. Fest, *Hitler*, 409.
12. Kershaw, *Hitler 1889–1936*, 468; Fest, *Hitler*, 410.
13. "Hitler cabinet gets power to rule as a dictatorship; Reichstag quits *sine die*," *New York Times*, March 24, 1933, 1.
14. "A Moral Tribunal," *New York Times*, March 26, 1933, E4.
15. *Gabriel over the White House*, directed by Gregory La Cava (Cosmopolitan/MGM, 1933).
16. [Thomas F. Tweed], *Gabriel over the White House* (New York: Farrar & Rinehart, 1933), 134.
17. "Selfridge Declares Democracy a Failure; Predicts Its End within 100 or 200 Years," *New York Times*, June 22, 1932, 10.
18. Mordaunt Hall, "Gabriel over the White House," *New York Times*, April 9, 1933, X3.
19. [Tweed], *Gabriel over the White House*.
20. Perhaps Hearst obtained a copy of *Gabriel over the White House* from his friend Lloyd George.
21. James Wingate to Will Hays, February 11, 1933, *Gabriel over the White House* file, Motion Picture Association of America (henceforth MPAA), Production Code Administration records, Margaret Herrick Library, Academy of Motion Picture Arts and Sciences, Beverly Hills (henceforth Margaret Herrick Library); Bosley Crowther, *Hollywood Rajah: The Life and Times of Louis B. Mayer* (New York: Henry Holt and Company, 1960), 178; Matthew Bernstein, *Walter Wanger, Hollywood Independent* (Berkeley: University of California Press, 1994), 84; David Nasaw, *The Chief: The Life of William Randolph Hearst* (New York: Houghton Mifflin, 2000), 463–466; Louis Pizzitola, *Hearst over Hollywood: Power, Passion, and Propaganda in the Movies* (New York: Columbia University Press, 2002), 293–300.
22. Ben Proctor, *William Randolph Hearst: Final Edition, 1911–1951* (New York: Oxford University Press, 2007), 153–173.
23. Crowther, *Hollywood Rajah*, 179.

24. Louis B. Mayer to James Wingate, February 16, 1933, and James Wingate to Will Hays, February 23, 1933, *Gabriel over the White House* file, MPAA, Production Code Administration records, Margaret Herrick Library.

25. William Randolph Hearst to Walter Wanger, March 4, 1933, William Randolph Hearst Papers, box 38, folder 31, Bancroft Library, Berkeley (henceforth Bancroft Library); "'Gabriel' Film Sent Back to Hollywood," *New York Times*, March 17, 1933, 21. Also compare the scripts dated January 16, 1933, and February 7, 1933, which are available at the USC Cinematic Arts Library and Margaret Herrick Library. For an exact list of retakes, see "Notes on *Gabriel over the White House*," MGM Collection, USC Cinematic Arts Library, Los Angeles. A shorter summary of the retakes can be found in Howard Strickling to Howard Dietz, March 20, 1933, *Gabriel over the White House* file, MPAA, Production Code Administration records, Margaret Herrick Library.

26. Will Hays, Memorandum, March 7, 1933, *Gabriel over the White House* file, MPAA, Production Code Administration records, Margaret Herrick Library.

27. Stephen T. Early to N. M. Schenck, March 12, 1933, Motion Pictures File; Roosevelt to William Randolph Hearst, April 1, 1933, President's Personal File, Franklin D. Roosevelt Library, Hyde Park, New York.

28. Hearst to Louis B. Mayer, March 25, 1933, William Randolph Hearst Papers, box 38, folder 23, Bancroft Library.

29. Hays, Memorandum, March 7, 1933. Frederick Herron read the script and criticized it from a foreign policy perspective. He cited some particularly objectionable lines and then wrote: "We have a hell of a nerve to put anything like this in one of our pictures. . . . I just can't understand the type of mind that would put a thing like this into a scenario." F. L. Herron to Maurice McKenzie, February 27, 1933, *Gabriel over the White House* file, MPAA, Production Code Administration records, Margaret Herrick Library.

30. Hays, Memorandum, March 7, 1933.

31. [Tweed], *Gabriel over the White House*, 26. This scene was cut from the film.

32. Ibid., 40.

33. Raymond Gram Swing, *Forerunners of American Fascism* (New York: Books for Libraries Press, 1935).

34. "Metro optimistisch," *Licht Bild Bühne*, September 5, 1933, 1–2.

35. Ibid.

36. Douglas Miller, "Economic and Trade Notes 219," April 18, 1934, Commercial Attachés in Germany 1931–1940, RG 151, National Archives and Records Administration, College Park, Maryland (henceforth National Archives).

37. George Canty, "Special Report 56," December 27, 1934, and "Special Report 82," February 25, 1935, Commercial Attachés in Germany 1931–1940, RG 151; Douglas Miller, "Special Report 37," October 25, 1934, Commercial Attachés in Germany 1931–1940, RG 151, National Archives.

38. "Here's one picture Germans spot as OK," 11; "Zwischen heute und morgen," *Völkischer Beobachter*, March 2, 1934, 9.

39. H. Brant, "Zwischen heut und morgen," *Der Angriff*, March 1, 1934, 11.

40. Ibid.

41. Hall, "Gabriel over the White House," X3; Louella O. Parsons, "Walter Huston Impressive in Performance," *Los Angeles Examiner*, April 7, 1933, 13; "Flag Waves Smartly O'er 'Gabriel in White House,'" *Newsweek*, April 8, 1933, 25–26; "A President after Hollywood's Heart," *Literary Digest*, April 22, 1933, 13; "'Gabriel' a Sensation," *Hollywood Reporter*, March 2, 1933, 1. The exception was the review in *The Nation* entitled "Fascism over Hollywood," April 26, 1933, 482–483. For a full account of the reception of the picture in the United States, see Robert L. McConnell, "The Genesis and Ideology of *Gabriel over the White House*," *Cinema Journal* 15, no. 2 (Spring 1976): 7–26. For a perceptive analysis, see Andrew Bergman, *We're in the Money: Depression America and Its Films* (New York: New York University Press, 1971), 110–120. For an interpretation of the film that emphasizes American sympathy for the concept of dictatorship in the early 1930s, see Benjamin L. Alpers, *Dictators, Democracy, and American Public Culture: Envisioning the Totalitarian Enemy, 1920s–1950s* (Chapel Hill: University of North Carolina Press, 2003), 30–33.

42. Richard Evans, *The Third Reich in Power* (New York: Penguin Press, 2005), 328–336.

43. William Randolph Hearst, "Over-Capitalization, At Workers' Expense, Cause of Depression," *New York American*, October 9, 1930, 1; "Mr. Hearst Discusses Causes and Cure for the Depression," *New York American*, June 7, 1931, E1.

44. Brant, "Zwischen heut und morgen," 11.

45. *This Day and Age*, directed by Cecil B. DeMille (Paramount, 1933).

46. Censorship report for Holland, December 2, 1933, *This Day and Age* file, MPAA, Production Code Administration records, Margaret Herrick Library.

47. Advertisement for *This Day and Age (Revolution der Jugend)*, *Der Angriff*, January 4, 1934, 11; Douglas Miller, "Economic and Trade Notes 175," February 27, 1934, Commercial Attachés in Germany 1931–1940, RG 151, National Archives.

48. Benito Mussolini, "Highest-Placed Criminals Must Be Mercilessly Suppressed, Says Mussolini," *New York American*, October 23, 1932, L–13.

49. [Tweed], *Gabriel over the White House*, 186, 175, 195. Will Hays watched the scene in which the gangsters were executed and commented, "As to the racketeers, I have no suggestion. It is so absolutely right in everybody's opinion that it is what ought to be done." Hays, Memorandum, March 7, 1933.

50. Kershaw, *Hitler 1889–1936*, 492, 551, 555.

51. Brant, "Zwischen heut und morgen," 11.

52. Six months after *Gabriel over the White House* premiered in Germany, the real ending to this part of the story took place. From September 5 to September 10, 1934, Hearst attended the Nazi Party Congress in Nuremberg (which Leni Riefenstahl filmed in *Triumph of the Will*). He stayed at the same hotel as von Ribbentrop, Himmler, Heydrich, and Göring, and his oldest son attended several Nazi Party rallies. After the festivities, on September 17, he interviewed Hitler. "The question of whether I should see Hitler and what I should say to Hitler," he later said, "was discussed in

general with Mr. Louis B. Mayer before the interview took place." Mayer never verified Hearst's claim. See Pizzitola, *Hearst over Hollywood*, 304–325.

53. Markus Spieker, *Hollywood unterm Hakenkreuz: Der amerikanische Spielfilm im Dritten Reich* (Trier: Wissentschaftlicher Verlag Trier, 1999), 360. The two films were *Let Freedom Ring*, which premiered on February 27 and played for twenty-one days, and *Broadway Serenade*, which premiered on April 17 and played for fifty-six days.

54. R. M. Stephenson, "Special Report 9," July 21, 1936, Commercial Attachés in Germany 1931–1940, RG 151, National Archives; *Broadway Melody of 1936*, directed by Roy Del Ruth (MGM, 1935); Douglas Miller, "Special Report 7," August 2, 1938, Commercial Attachés in Germany 1931–1940, RG 151, National Archives; *Broadway Melody of 1938*, directed by Roy Del Ruth (MGM, 1937). According to the records of the commercial attachés, the most popular movie screened in the Third Reich was *Les Perles de la Couronne*, which played for 180 days in its first run in Berlin. See Miller, "Special Report 81," June 28, 1938, Commercial Attachés in Germany 1931–1940, RG 151, National Archives.

55. "When discussing the film year 1935, even the German press had to admit that foreign films had by far the greatest artistic and economic success in Germany, and it has repeatedly been regretted that the German film industry is unable to attain the light comedy touch which is so characteristic of the American feature film." Douglas Miller, "Special Report 62," January 22, 1936, Commercial Attachés in Germany 1931–1940, RG 151, National Archives.

56. Quoted in Spieker, *Hollywood unterm Hakenkreuz*, 129.

57. "Ein Herz ist zu verschenken," *Der Film*, August 3, 1935, 5.

58. "Sehnsucht," *Film-Kurier*, April 3, 1936, 2.

59. "Filmwirtschaftliche Aussenpolitik," *National-Zeitung* (Essen), January 3, 1935. For Hollywood's influence on German cinema in this period, see Spieker, *Hollywood unterm Hakenkreuz*, 149–157; Eric Rentschler, *The Ministry of Illusion: Nazi Cinema and Its Afterlife* (Cambridge, MA: Harvard University Press, 1996), 99–123.

60. Elke Fröhlich et al., eds., *Die Tagebücher von Joseph Goebbels*, entry for October 17, 1935, pt. 1, vol. 3/I, (Munich: K. G. Saur Verlag, 2005), 312–313.

61. Fröhlich et al., *Die Tagebücher von Joseph Goebbels*, entry for August 23, 1936, pt. 1, vol. 3/II, 165.

62. David Welch, *Propaganda and the German Cinema 1933–1945* [1983] (New York: I.B. Tauris, 2001), 37.

63. Ibid., 38.

64. Goebbels was wrong about this: the United States had a long and rich theatrical tradition.

65. "Dr. Goebbels vor den Filmschaffenden: Ein neues Bekenntnis zum Film," *Licht Bild Bühne*, December 16, 1935, 1–2. "Ein Held redet nicht immer heldisch daher, sondern er handle heldisch."

66. *It Happened One Night*, directed by Frank Capra (Columbia Pictures, 1934); Douglas Miller, "Special Report 55," December 23, 1935, Commercial Attachés in Germany 1931–1940, RG 151, National Archives.

67. *The Lives of a Bengal Lancer*, directed by Henry Hathaway (Paramount, 1935).

68. Douglas Miller, "Special Report 106," May 22, 1935, Commercial Attachés in Germany 1931–1940, RG 151, National Archives. *The Lives of a Bengal Lancer* first played at one theater for twenty-nine days, then at another for seven days, then at a third for seven days.

69. Ibid. My claim that *Triumph of the Will* was the most popular Nazi propaganda film of the 1930s derives from an exhaustive review of the American commercial attaché reports from the period. The only other film that was comparable was *S.A. Mann Brand* (1933), which played for fewer days but opened simultaneously at three theaters. The secondary literature on Nazi cinema does not include statistics on these run times. There is a table of box office earnings of German movies from 1940 to 1944 in Gerd Albrecht, *Nationalsozialistische Filmpolitik: Eine soziologische Untersuchung über die Spielfilm des Dritten Reichs* (Stuttgart: Ferdinand Enke Verlag, 1969), 430–431. For the term *Tendenzfilm*, see Welch, *Propaganda and the German Cinema*, 2.

70. Filmprüfstelle lists for 1935, Deutsches Filminstitut, Frankfurt (henceforth Deutsches Filminstitut); Welch, *Propaganda and the German Cinema*, 15, 18; Spieker, *Hollywood unterm Hakenkreuz*, 342.

71. R. M. Stephenson, "Special Report 101," May 26, 1936, Commercial Attachés in Germany 1931–1940, RG 151, National Archives.

72. "Angelsächsische Kameradschaft," *Der Angriff*, February 22, 1935, 4. "Eine Handvoll weißer Männer schützt ein Volk von 300 Millionen Indern vor dem Chaos."

73. Welch, *Propaganda and the German Cinema*, 149.

74. "A hero does not always speak heroically but he acts heroically": the phrase may even have been a subtle attack on *Triumph of the Will*, in which the hero's words were always received with the greatest applause.

75. "Bengali," *Berliner Tageblatt und Handels-Zeitung*, February 22, 1935, 6.

76. Ibid.

77. "Angelsächsische Kameradschaft," *Der Angriff*, February 22, 1935, 4.

78. Gerd Eckert, "Filmtendenz und Tendenzfilm," *Wille und Macht*, February 15, 1938, 22.

79. Leonhard Fürst, "Der deutsche Filmstil," *Jahrbuch der Reichsfilmkammer*, 1937, 32.

80. Statement by Reinhard Spitzy in *The Tramp and the Dictator*, directed by Kevin Brownlow and Michael Kloft (Photoplay Productions, 2002).

81. "Mit Gary Cooper in der Ufastadt," *Filmwelt*, December 2, 1938, [26]. Also see "Gary Cooper in Berlin," *Licht Bild Bühne*, November 23, 1938, 3.

82. *A Prelude to "Our Daily Bread,"* directed by David Shepard, 1983.

83. King Vidor, *A Tree Is a Tree* (New York: Harcourt, Brace and Company, 1952), 220–228. *Our Daily Bread* was generally well reviewed in the United States. See, for example, Andre Sennwald, "King Vidor and 'Our Daily Bread': His Fine Drama of a Cooperative Farm Is the Achievement of a Courageous Mind," *New York Times*, October 7, 1934, X4. Once again, *The Nation* was the exception, calling the film "a travesty." "Collectivism More or Less," *The Nation*, October 24, 1934, 488–490. Also see Bergman, *We're in the Money*, 71–82.

84. United Artists also organized a special screening of the film for President Roosevelt at the White House. "Show 'Daily Bread' at White House," *Film Daily*, October 2, 1934, 8.

85. Filmprüfstelle lists for 1936, Deutsches Filminstitut; R. M. Stephenson, "Special Report 49," November 14, 1936, Commercial Attachés in Germany 1931–1940, RG 151, National Archives.

86. "Der Letzte Alarm," *Völkischer Beobachter*, August 7, 1936, 13.

87. "Der Letzte Alarm," *Berliner Tageblatt und Handels-Zeitung*, August 6, 1936, 10.

88. *Triumph of the Will*, directed by Leni Riefenstahl (Leni Riefenstahl-Produktion/Reichspropagandaleitung der NSDAP, 1935).

89. *Our Daily Bread*, directed by King Vidor (Viking/United Artists, 1934).

90. "Die neuen Wunder," *Der Angriff*, August 7, 1936, 4.

91. Ibid.

92. Adolf Hitler, *Mein Kampf*, trans. Ralph Manheim [1925 and 1927] (New York: Houghton Mifflin, 1943), 466.

93. Kershaw, *Hitler 1889–1936*, 162, 344.

94. Ernst Hugo Correll, "Was bleibt der Autor dem deutschen Film schuldig?" *Jahrbuch der Reichsfilmkammer* (1937): 115–119. *Mr. Deeds* was not screened in Germany because of a technicality in the censorship process.

95. Pronouncement of the German Film Chamber, January 23, 1940, R109 I, vol. 1611, Bundesarchiv, Berlin (henceforth Bundesarchiv).

96. Correll, "Was bleibt der Autor dem deutschen Film schuldig?" 115–119.

97. *Friedrich Schiller (Der Triumph eines Genies)*, directed by Herbert Maisch (Tobis, 1940); *Der Grosse König*, directed by Veit Harlan (Tobis, 1942); *Bismarck*, directed by Wolfgang Liebeneiner (Tobis, 1940); *Die Entlassung*, directed by Liebeneiner (Tobis, 1942).

98. Welch, *Propaganda and the German Cinema*, 124, 154.

99. *Mutiny on the Bounty*, directed by Frank Lloyd (MGM, 1935); R. M. Stephenson, "Special Report 49," November 14, 1936, Commercial Attachés in Germany 1931–1940, RG 151, National Archives; "Die Kameradschaft der Seefahrer," *Der Angriff*, September 10, 1936, 13.

100. "Meuterei auf der Bounty," *Berliner Tageblatt und Handels-Zeitung*, September 9, 1936, 10.

101. Martin Bormann to Paul Wernicke, September 6, 1937, and Paul Wernicke to Martin Bormann, September 10, 1937, NS 10, vol. 48, Bundesarchiv.

102. "Metro optimistisch," 1; Filmprüfstelle lists for 1934, 1935, and 1937, Deutsches Filminstitut. *Looking Forward*, directed by Cedric Gibbons (MGM, 1933); *Queen Christina*, directed by Rouben Mamoulian (MGM, 1934); *Night Flight*, directed by Clarence Brown (MGM, 1933); *West Point of the Air* directed by Richard Rosson (MGM, 1935); *Souls at Sea*, directed by Henry Hathaway (Paramount, 1937); *Captains Courageous*, directed by Victor Fleming (MGM, 1937). The dates given in the main text indicate when the films were released in Germany.

1. E. Bahls to Propaganda Ministry, April 24, 1939, NS 10, vol. 49, Bundesarchiv, Berlin (henceforth Bundesarchiv).

2. George Canty, "Motion Pictures Abroad: The German Film Industry During 1933," February 16, 1934, Commercial Attachés in Germany 1931–1940, RG 151, National Archives and Records Administration, College Park, Maryland (henceforth National Archives). In determining the number of American films that were screened in Germany each year, I have examined the annual reports of the American commercial attachés stationed in Berlin, as well as their monthly statistics. Since these two sources have sometimes provided contradictory results, I have attempted to give the statistics most closely supported by all the available evidence. I have also taken into account the findings of Markus Spieker, who first used these statistics in *Hollywood unterm Hakenkreuz: Der amerikanische Spielfilm im Dritten Reich* (Trier: Wissenschaftlicher Verlag Trier, 1999).

3. [Albert Sander], "Rassenfrage, Kontingent, u. Lizenzen: Das Raether-Interview in *The Era*," *Der Film*, July 16, 1932, 1–2.

4. Oberprüfstelle report 7192, "Tarzan, der Herr des Urwaldes," March 2, 1934, Deutsches Filminstitut, Frankfurt (henceforth Deutsches Filminstitut).

5. George Canty, "Economic and Trade Notes 176," February 16, 1933, Commercial Attachés in Germany 1931–1940, RG 151, National Archives; *Tarzan the Ape Man*, directed by W. S. Van Dyke (MGM, 1932).

6. Oberprüfstelle report 6910, "King Kong," October 5, 1933; Oberprüfstelle report 6866, "Der Herr der Wildnis," August 3, 1933, Deutsches Filminstitut; *King of the Jungle*, directed by Max Marcin (Paramount, 1933). In my account of the censorship meetings in this chapter, I have sometimes turned the record of the discussion into direct speech. I have preserved the original meaning throughout.

7. *Reichsgesetzblatt*, May 12, 1920, 953.

8. *Reichsgesetzblatt*, February 19, 1934, 96.

9. Oberprüfstelle report 7192, "Tarzan, der Herr des Urwaldes," March 2, 1934, Deutsches Filminstitut.

10. Ibid.

11. Ibid.

12. Ibid.

13. Ibid.

14. Spieker, *Hollywood unterm Hakenkreuz*, 70.

15. Oberprüfstelle report 6759, "Die blonde Venus," July 4, 1933, Deutsches Filminstitut; *Blonde Venus*, directed by Josef von Sternberg (Paramount, 1932).

16. Oberprüfstelle report 7270, "Das hohe Lied," March 14, 1934, Deutsches Filminstitut. Not even Marlene Dietrich's $500 donation to the National Socialist film fund helped to overturn the decision. See Douglas Miller, "Special Report 89," April 26, 1934, Commercial Attachés in Germany 1931–1940, RG 151, National Archives.

17. Oberprüfstelle report 7513, "Das Narbengesicht (Scarface)," November 22, 1934, Deutsches Filminstitut; *Scarface*, directed by Howard Hawks (United Artists, 1932).

18. Oberprüfstelle report 6577, "Frisco Express-führerlos," April 22, 1933, Deutsches Filminstitut.

19. Oberprüfstelle report 4827, "Frankenstein," June 2, 1932; Filmprüfstelle lists for 1933 and 1934, Deutsches Filminstitut.

20. Oberprüfstelle report 7381, "Men in White," July 11, 1934, Deutsches Filminstitut; *Men in White*, directed by Richard Boleslavsky (MGM, 1934).

21. Douglas W. Churchill, "Hollywood's Censor Is All the World," *New York Times*, March 29, 1936, SM10; Frank S. Nugent, "New Censorial Swords Hang over Hollywood," *New York Times*, May 9, 1937, SM16. Also see John Eugene Harley, *World-Wide Influences of the Cinema: A Study of Official Censorship and the International Cultural Aspects of Motion Pictures* (Los Angeles: University of Southern California Press, 1940), 96–199.

22. For Hollywood's foreign dealings in this period, see Kristin Thompson, *Exporting Entertainment: America in the World Film Market 1907–34* (London: BFI Publishing, 1985); Ruth Vasey, *The World According to Hollywood, 1918–1939* (Madison: University of Wisconsin Press, 1997); John Trumpbour, *Selling Hollywood to the World: U.S. and European Struggles for Mastery of the Global Film Industry, 1920–1950* (Cambridge: Cambridge University Press, 2002).

23. The figure for 1934 is my own count based on the American commercial attaché reports, and it correlates with that in Spieker, *Hollywood unterm Hakenkreuz*, 337.

24. Max Schmeling, *An Autobiography* [1977] (Chicago: Bonus Books, 1998), 86–87.

25. Jeremy Schaap, *Cinderella Man: James J. Braddock, Max Baer, and the Greatest Upset in Boxing History* (New York: Houghton Mifflin Harcourt, 2005), 47, 144–146, 150; "Nazis Still Irked by Baer's Remark; Public Wants to See Champion Whose Gibe at Hitler Embarrasses Officials," *New York Times*, March 14, 1935, 26.

26. Joseph C. Nichols, "The Fight by Rounds," *New York Times*, June 9, 1933, 21; Schaap, *Cinderella Man*, 148–152.

27. Schaap, *Cinderella Man*, 153.

28. *The Prizefighter and the Lady*, directed by W. S. Van Dyke (MGM, 1933).

29. Frits Strengholt to Foreign Office, March 15, 1934, R 80310: Abteilung III, Politische und kulturelle Propaganda in den Vereinigten Staaten von Amerika, vol. 18; "Reich Bans American Film Because Max Baer is a Jew: 'The Prizefighter and the Lady' Halted by Goebbels after Successful Run; U.S. Reprisals Indicated," unidentified press clipping dated March 29, 1934, R 80310: Abteilung III, Politische und kulturelle Propaganda in den Vereinigten Staaten von Amerika, vol. 18, Politisches Archiv des Auswärtigen Amts, Berlin (henceforth PAAA).

30. R. M. Stephenson, "Special Report 101," May 26, 1936, Commercial Attachés in Germany 1931–1940, RG 151, National Archives. Also see the

Filmprüfstelle lists at the Deutsches Filminstitut, which indicate that American films were first subtitled and then dubbed.

31. Douglas Miller, "Economic and Trade Notes 219," April 18, 1934, and "Economic and Trade Notes 186," March 10, 1934, Commercial Attachés in Germany 1931–1940, RG 151, National Archives.

32. Miller, "Economic and Trade Notes 186," March 10, 1934.

33. J. C. White to Secretary of State, March 15, 1934, File 862.4061 Motion Pictures/83, 1930–39 Central Decimal File, RG 59, National Archives.

34. Miller, "Economic and Trade Notes 219," April 18, 1934; Strengholt to Foreign Office, March 15, 1934.

35. Strengholt to Foreign Office, March 15, 1934.

36. Ibid.

37. Ibid.

38. George Canty, Confidential Memorandum to Mr. White, Chargé D'Affaires, January 26, 1935, File Class 281: Germany 1930–1945, RG 151, National Archives.

39. Alexander Führ, "Aufzeichnung zu dem Schreiben der Metro-Goldwyn Mayer A.G.," March 16, 1934, R 80310: Abteilung III, Politische und kulturelle Propaganda in den Vereinigten Staaten von Amerika, vol. 18, PAAA.

40. Alexander Führ, "Aufzeichnung," April 5, 1934, R 80310: Abteilung III, Politische und kulturelle Propaganda in den Vereinigten Staaten von Amerika, vol. 18, PAAA.

41. Führ, "Aufzeichnung zu dem Schreiben der Metro-Goldwyn Mayer A.G.," March 16, 1934.

42. Ibid.

43. "Gegen unsinnige Gerüchte-macherei: Zur heutigen Uraufführung des Max-Baer-Films," *Der Angriff*, press clipping dated March 16, 1934, R 80310: Abteilung III, Politische und kulturelle Propaganda in den Vereinigten Staaten von Amerika, vol. 18, PAAA.

44. Führ, "Aufzeichnung zu dem Schreiben der Metro-Goldwyn Mayer A.G.," March 16, 1934.

45. H. Brant, "Männer um eine Frau," *Der Angriff*, March 19, 1934, 10. Also see "Männer um eine Frau: Capitol am Zoo," *Berliner Tageblatt und Handels-Zeitung*, March 17, 1934, 4; "Männer um eine Frau: Im Capitol," press clipping dated March 17, 1934, R 80310: Abteilung III, Politische und kulturelle Propaganda in den Vereinigten Staaten von Amerika, vol. 18, PAAA.

46. "Männer um eine Frau," *Völkischer Beobachter*, March 18–19, 1934, 6.

47. Miller, "Economic and Trade Notes 219," April 18, 1934; Miller, "Special Report 89," April 26, 1934; Führ, "Aufzeichnung zu dem Schreiben der Metro-Goldwyn Mayer A.G.," March 16, 1934.

48. Metro-Goldwyn-Mayer Film A.G., untitled memorandum, March 29, 1934, R 80310: Abteilung III, Politische und kulturelle Propaganda in den Vereinigten Staaten von Amerika, vol. 18, PAAA.

49. "Entscheidungsgründe für das Verbot der öffentlichen Vorführung des Films 'Männer um eine Frau,'" March 29, 1934, R 80310: Abteilung III, Politische und kulturelle Propaganda in den Vereinigten Staaten von Amerika, vol. 18, PAAA.

50. Ibid.

51. "Aufzeichnung betr. Verbot eines amerikanischen Films," March 30, 1934, R 80310: Abteilung III, Politische und kulturelle Propaganda in den Vereinigten Staaten von Amerika, vol. 18, PAAA.

52. Führ, "Aufzeichnung," April 5, 1934; "Aktenvermerk," April 6, 1934, R 80310: Abteilung III, Politische und kulturelle Propaganda in den Vereinigten Staaten von Amerika, vol. 18; Hans Heinrich Dieckhoff to Hans Ernst Posse, April 7, 1934, R 80310: Abteilung III, Politische und kulturelle Propaganda in den Vereinigten Staaten von Amerika, vol. 18; Alexander Führ, Untitled Memorandum, April 7, 1934, R 80310: Abteilung III, Politische und kulturelle Propaganda in den Vereinigten Staaten von Amerika, vol. 18, PAAA.

53. Konstantin von Neurath to Joseph Goebbels, April 1934, R 80310: Abteilung III, Politische und kulturelle Propaganda in den Vereinigten Staaten von Amerika, vol. 18, PAAA.

54. Oberprüfstelle report 7324, "Männer um eine Frau," April 21, 1934, Deutsches Filminstitut.

55. Ibid.

56. Ibid.

57. Ibid.

58. Ibid.

59. Arnold Bacmeister, *Bedeutung und Arbeitsweise der Filmprüfstelle in Berlin: Ein Rückblick auf die Jahre 1934–1945*, kleine Erweiterung, Bundesarchiv, 1–2.

60. Adolf Hitler, *Mein Kampf*, trans. Ralph Manheim [1925 and 1927] (New York: Houghton Mifflin, 1943), 177–178. "When the nations on this planet fight for existence—when the question of destiny, 'to be or not to be,' cries out for a solution—then all considerations of humanitarianism or aesthetics crumble into nothingness; for all these concepts do not float about in the ether, they arise from man's imagination and are bound up with man. . . . When people try to approach these questions with drivel about aesthetics, etc., really only one answer is possible: where the destiny and existence of a people are at stake, all obligation towards beauty ceases. . . . And since these criteria of humanitarianism and beauty must be eliminated from the struggle, they are also inapplicable to propaganda."

61. Dr. Kausch, ZSg. 101/9, folio 61, Bundesarchiv, Koblenz (henceforth BK).

62. George Canty, "Economic and Trade Notes 104," November 12, 1934, Commercial Attachés in Germany 1931–1940, RG 151, National Archives.

63. George Canty, "Memorandum to the Embassy," December 15, 1934, File Class 281: Germany 1930–1945, RG 151; Canty, "German Film Developments," January 26, 1935, Commercial Attachés in Germany 1931–1940, RG 151, National Archives.

64. R. M. Stephenson, "German Film Notes," January 15, 1937, Commercial Attachés in Germany 1931–1940, RG 151, National Archives.

65. *The Merry Widow*, directed by Ernst Lubitsch (MGM, 1934); "Memorandum of Conversation between Mr. Schoenfeld and Mr. William A. Orr," January 28, 1935, File 862.4061 Merry Widow/4, 1930–39 Central Decimal File, RG 59; Canty, "Confidential Memorandum to Mr. White, Chargé D'Affaires," January 26, 1935.

66. Douglas Miller, "Critical Situation of American Film Companies," May 14, 1936, File Class 281: Germany 1930–1945, RG 151; Miller, "New Film Contingent Decree," July 25, 1936, Commercial Attachés in Germany 1931–1940, RG 151, National Archives.

67. Miller, "Critical Situation of American Film Companies," May 14, 1936.

68. "Metro About Ready to Bow Out of Germany if Par-20th Will Likewise," *Variety*, July 22, 1936, 15.

69. "Paramount Claims '36 Was Okay In Reich—Company Only Lost $580," *Variety*, April 28, 1937, 25.

70. Miller, "Critical Situation of American Film Companies," May 14, 1936; R. M. Stephenson, "Special Report 92," June 5, 1937, Commercial Attachés in Germany 1931–1940, RG 151, National Archives. Also see "Par Moves German Headquarters to Paris, but Continues Nazi Biz," *Variety*, April 17, 1934, 15.

71. Douglas Miller, "New Film Contingent Decree," July 25, 1936, Commercial Attachés in Germany 1931–1940, RG 151; Miller, "German Film Situation at the Beginning of the Season 1936/37," August 14, 1936, Commercial Attachés in Germany 1931–1940, RG 151, National Archives.

72. Miller, "German Film Situation at the Beginning of the Season 1936/37," August 14, 1936.

73. Spieker, *Hollywood unterm Hakenkreuz*, 69; "U.S. Distribution Chiefs in the Capitals of War," *Motion Picture Herald*, September 9, 1939, 32–33.

74. Douglas Miller, "Difficulties of the Metro-Goldwyn-Mayer Film A.G.," April 23, 1936, File Class 281: Germany 1930–1945, RG 151, National Archives; Barbara Hall, *An Oral History with Robert M. W. Vogel*, Margaret Herrick Library, Academy of Motion Picture Arts and Sciences, Beverly Hills (henceforth Margaret Herrick Library), 1991, 120. According to Robert Vogel, who oversaw foreign publicity for MGM: "We were going to make this picture, THREE COMRADES, and we needed somebody to guide us on making the story, on making it correctly, so we brought in the MGM managing director in Germany, Fritz Strengholt. And Fritz showed up and I took him to Joe's office and he said he wanted to call his wife back in Berlin to tell her that he had arrived safely. And he put in the call and when he was finished, he said, 'That call was monitored and my wife is Jewish.' And he was scared to death. And when he finished his task here, he went back to Berlin, where the Nazis told him that if he didn't get rid of the wife he was going to be considered a Jew. And they pressured him to the point of him leaving the wife. She landed in a concentration camp."

75. G. P. Vallar to Hans Weidemann, October 15, 1936, R 56 VI, vol. 7, Bundesarchiv. For another letter from Paramount to the Nazi authorities,

see Leo J. Horster to Paul Wernicke, October 4, 1937, NS 10, vol. 48, Bundesarchiv.

76. R. M. Stephenson, "Special Report 11," August 9, 1937, Commercial Attachés in Germany 1931–1940, RG 151, National Archives.

77. Deutsche Fox-Film to Wilhelm Brückner, January 10, 1938, NS 10, vol. 48, Bundesarchiv.

78. Wilhelm Brückner to Deutsche Fox-Film, January 14, 1938, NS 10, vol. 48, Bundesarchiv.

79. For example, MGM slashed Ben Hecht's name from the credits of *Let Freedom Ring*, which was screened in Germany in 1940. See the censorship card for *Let Freedom Ring* (*Rivalen*), reg. no. 53290, Bundesarchiv-Filmarchiv, Berlin (henceforth BF).

80. R. M. Stephenson, "German Film Notes," February 28, 1939, Commercial Attachés in Germany 1931–1940, RG 151, National Archives. Stephenson claimed that the Americans sold only thirty-two movies to Germany in 1938, but in going through his own statistics for that year, I count forty-one. According to the Filmprüfstelle lists at the Deutsches Filminstitut, forty-five American movies were permitted in Germany in 1938.

81. Curt Belling, "Ein Drittel der Hollywood-Stars sind Juden," *Der Angriff*, November 22, 1938, 4.

82. The names on the blacklist (which contained numerous misspellings) were as follows: "Abner (Dunn & Abner); Anderson, Sherwood; Allan, Gracie; Arnold, Edward; Arthur, Jean; Bennet, Joan; Boland, John J.; Cagney, James; Carlisle, Mary; Carthy, B. McFranklin; Cobb, Humphrey; Crosby, Bing; Crawford, Joan; Dall, Virginia; Devine, Andy; Douglas, Melvyn; Dreiser, Theodore; Elridge, Florence; Fellowes, Edith; Fisher, Dorothy Conf.; Gach, Samuel B.; Gleason, Lucille; Green, Josef; Hall, Porter; Hemingway, Ernest; Herzbrun, Henry; Hopkins; Jaffee, Sam; Javens, Dorris; Kahane, B. B.; Jolson, Al; Kaufmann, Georg S.; Keating, Fred; Lang, Fritz; Lewis, Sinclair; Lubitsch, Ernest; Lunn & Abner; Mankiewicz, Herman J.; Mann, Evelin; March, Frederic; Martan, Alexander; Milestone, Lewis; Muni, Paul; Nichols, Dudley; O' Brien, Pat; Page, Charles; Rainer, Luise; [Gregory] Ratoff; Reinhardt, Hay; Rosen, Frederic J.; Rosenberg, Eugene Dr. (Rabbiner); Ross, Lanny; Sidney, Silvia; Sheehan; Shearer, Norma; Stander, Lionel; Stewart, Donald Ogden; Stuart, Gloria; Tone, Franchot; Vidor, King; Warner, Jack L.; Wray, John."

83. Douglas Miller, "Economic and Trade Notes 118: German 'Black List' of American Film Actors, Directors and Scenario Writers," November 23, 1938, Commercial Attachés in Germany 1931–1940, RG 151, National Archives. Throughout the Second World War, the Nazis continued to keep lists of Hollywood personalities who were Jewish or had participated in anti-German productions. See Hans Kolb to embassies and legations, April 24, 1941, German legation in Bern, 3368: Hetzfilme, PAAA.

84. This is my own count, as the American commercial attaché stationed in Berlin at the time did not prepare an annual report for 1939. He did claim

that the Americans had sold eighteen movies to the Germans in the first eleven months of 1939. See Paul H. Pearson, "Economic and Trade Notes 365," December 12, 1939, Commercial Attachés in Germany 1931–1940, RG 151, National Archives.

85. "'Blocked' Marks Seen in Wider Use," *New York Times*, May 21, 1933, N7; "Schacht Loan Plan Faces Difficulties," *New York Times*, May 22, 1933, 23. Also see John Weitz, *Hitler's Banker: Hjalmar Horace Greeley Schacht* (Boston: Little, Brown and Company, 1997), 154–156; Edwin Black, *IBM and the Holocaust: The Strategic Alliance between Nazi Germany and America's Most Powerful Corporation* (New York: Crown Publishers, 2001), 67; Gerhard Kümmel, *Transnational Economic Cooperation and the Nation State*, vol. 1 (New York: Columbia University Press, 2001), 41–44.

86. George Canty, "Outlook for the 1934/35 Season for German Films," June 26, 1934, Commercial Attachés in Germany 1931–1940, RG 151; Canty, "Special Report 56," December 27, 1934, Commercial Attachés in Germany 1931–1940, RG 151, National Archives.

87. Canty, "Outlook for the 1934/35 Season for German Films," June 26, 1934; Douglas Miller, "Special Report 12: New Film Contingent Decree," July 25, 1936, Commercial Attachés in Germany 1931–1940, RG 151, National Archives; "Metro About Ready to Bow Out of Germany if Par-20th Will Likewise," 15. On July 14, 1938, there was an unfortunate incident at Hitler's retreat near Berchtesgaden. Without any warning, a group of cameramen from the Fox newsreel company suddenly arrived to film the visit of a well-known general. According to one of Hitler's adjutants, "The Führer is very annoyed about this and orders them to leave immediately." Hitler's agenda for Thursday, July 14, 1938, NS 10, vol. 125, Bundesarchiv.

88. "Fox Toenende Wochenschau A.-G Berlin, Programm," July 5, 1934, German legation in Riga, box 104: Filmwesen, vol. 3, PAAA. Most studies of Nazi newsreels acknowledge that Paramount and Fox were active in this period but do not discuss the content of Paramount's and Fox's newsreels. See Hilmar Hoffmann, *The Triumph of Propaganda: Film and National Socialism, 1933–1945* (Providence, RI: Berghahn Books, 1996); Ulrike Bartels, *Die Wochenschau im Dritten Reich* (Frankfurt: Peter Lang, 2004); Klaus Kreimeier, *The Ufa Story: A History of Germany's Greatest Film Company, 1918–1945* (Berkeley: University of California Press, 1999).

89. "Fox Toenende Wochenschau A.-G Berlin, Programm," July 26, 1934, German legation in Riga, box 104: Filmwesen, vol. 3, PAAA.

90. "Fox Toenende Wochenschau A.-G Berlin, Programm," March 22, 1934, German legation in Riga, box 104: Filmwesen, vol. 2, PAAA.

91. "Fox Toenende Wochenschau A.-G Berlin, Programm," May 3, 1934, German legation in Riga, box 104: Filmwesen, vol. 2, PAAA.

92. Wolfe Kaufman, "Hitlerized Show Biz: Not Much Left of It in Reich," *Variety*, June 19, 1934, 1, 45; "Germany's Kontingent Boost to 8G Brings Talk of U.S. Quitting Reich," *Variety*, November 20, 1934, 13; "Para. Does Not Know How to Get Its German Money," *Variety*, February 5, 1935, 11; "Metro About Ready to Bow Out of Germany if Par-20th Will Likewise," 15.

93. Miller, "Critical Situation of American Film Companies," May 14, 1936, File Class 281: Germany 1930–1945, RG 151; R. M. Stephenson, "Special Report 53," December 30, 1938, Commercial Attachés in Germany 1931–1940, RG 151, National Archives.

94. Stephenson, "Special Report 53," December 30, 1938.

95. "Ich bin ein entflohener Kettensträfling," *Völkischer Beobachter*, March 19–20, 1933, 5.

96. "Wo ist das Kind der Madeleine F?" *Völkischer Beobachter*, May 5, 1934, 6; *Miss Fane's Baby Is Stolen*, directed by Alexander Hall (Paramount, 1934).

97. Spieker, *Hollywood unterm Hakenkreuz*, 238.

98. Zeitschriften-Dienst, nos. 1495 and 1218, BK.

99. "Ramona: Amerikanischer Farbenfilm im Capitol," *Völkischer Beobachter*, March 11, 1937, 6; "Bunte 'Ramona': Farbenfilm im Capitol am Zoo," *Der Angriff*, March 11, 1937, 4; "Der Erste Farben-Grosfilm: 'Ramona' im Capitol," *Berliner Tageblatt und Handels-Zeitung*, March 10, 1937, 8; "Kalifornische Romantik in Farben: Ramona," *Der Film*, March 13, 1937, 2; "Annabella in 'Zigeunerprinzessin': Neuer Farbfilm im Berliner Capitol am Zoo," *Völkischer Beobachter*, October 20, 1937, 7; "Landschaft und Lächeln—bunt: Capitol zeigte Annabella im Farbenfilm," *Der Angriff*, October 20, 1937, 4.

100. Wilhelm Frels, "Unsere Meinung," *Die neue Literatur* (April 1938): 213–214.

101. *Ramona*, directed by Henry King (Twentieth Century-Fox, 1936).

102. Frels, "Unsere Meinung," 214.

103. "Bunte 'Ramona': Farbenfilm im Capitol am Zoo," 4.

104. *Wings of the Morning*, directed by Harold D. Schuster (Twentieth Century-Fox, 1937).

105. Frels, "Unsere Meinung," 214.

106. Oberprüfstelle report 7819, "The Bohemian girl," June 13, 1936, Deutsches Filminstitut.

107. Hence titles like *The Jungle Princess, The Gypsy Princess*, etc.

108. *Shanghai*, directed by James Flood (Paramount, 1935).

109. Zsg. 110/11, folio 22, January 9, 1939, BK.

110. SS-Sturmbannführer to Herrn Ministerialdirektor Leichtenstern, July 16, 1938, NS 10, vol. 45, Bundesarchiv; "Das amerikanische Angebot," *Der deutsche Film* 3 (September 1938): 87. A few years earlier, Charles Boyer had starred in a Paramount picture called *Private Worlds*, which gave a humane portrait of life in a psychiatric institution. *Private Worlds* reached theaters in Germany at the same time as several notorious German films that advocated the extermination of the mentally ill. Despite the obvious contradiction, *Private Worlds* barely aroused comment in the German press. For the official approval of *Private Worlds*, see the Filmprüfstelle lists for 1935 at the Deutsches Filminstitut. For a discussion of the German films that advocated extermination (one of which was personally commissioned by Hitler), see Ian Kershaw, *Hitler 1936–1945: Nemesis* (London: Penguin, 2000), 257. *Private Worlds*, directed by La Cava (Paramount, 1935).

111. Elke Fröhlich et al., eds., *Die Tagebücher von Joseph Goebbels* (Munich: K. G. Saur Verlag, 2005), entry for January 13, 1936, pt. 1, vol. 3/I, 361.

112. Zeitschriften-Dienst, no. 1632, BK.

113. *Susannah of the Mounties*, directed by William A. Seiter (Twentieth Century-Fox, 1939); Censorship card for *Susannah of the Mounties* (*Fräulein Winnetou*), reg. no. 52619, BF. According to the German censorship card, "The 'little chief' and Sue [Shirley Temple] consummate blood brotherhood."

114. Heinz Boberach, ed., *Meldungen aus dem Reich: die geheimen Lageberichte des Sicherheitsdienstes der SS 1938–1945*, vol. 3 (Herrsching: Manfred Pawlak, 1984), 741.

115. Boberach, *Meldungen aus dem Reich*, vol. 4, 971.

116. Ben Hecht, *A Child of the Century* (New York: Simon and Schuster, 1954), 473.

117. *Let Freedom Ring*, directed by Jack Conway (MGM, 1939).

118. Censorship card for *Let Freedom Ring* (*Rivalen*), reg. no. 53290, BF; Censorship report for Germany, October 24, 1939, and June 10, 1940, *Let Freedom Ring* file, MPAA, Production Code Administration records, Margaret Herrick Library.

119. Censorship report for Germany, October 24, 1939, and June 10, 1940, *Let Freedom Ring* file.

120. Censorship card for *Let Freedom Ring* (*Rivalen*).

121. Spieker, *Hollywood unterm Hakenkreuz*, 293, 360; "Rivalen," *Film-Kurier*, February 28, 1940, 2.

122. Ernst Jerosch, "Rivalen," *Der Film*, March 2, 1940, 5.

## 5. "SWITCHED OFF"

1. "Lewis Says Hays Bans Film of Book," *New York Times*, February 16, 1936, 1.

2. Dorothy Thompson, *I Saw Hitler!* (New York: Farrar & Rinehart, 1932), 12–13.

3. For Hitler's difficulties with personal encounters, see Joachim C. Fest, *Hitler* [1973] (New York: Penguin, 1982), 511–538.

4. Thompson, *I Saw Hitler!*, 12–13.

5. Ibid., 5–6.

6. Ibid., 16.

7. Ibid., 6.

8. Ibid., 18. Hitler never actually abolished the Weimar constitution. He simply extended the emergency powers it granted the president for an indefinite period of time.

9. Ibid., 6.

10. Ibid., 19–20.

11. Ibid., 17.

12. Dorothy Thompson, "I Saw Hitler!" *Hearst's International-Cosmopolitan* (March 1932): 32.

13. Thompson, *I Saw Hitler!*, 13–14.

14. Ibid., 20–23, 15.

15. Peter Kurth, *American Cassandra: The Life of Dorothy Thompson* (Boston: Little, Brown and Company, 1990), 162.

16. Hans V. Kaltenborn, "An Interview with Hitler, August 17, 1932," *The Wisconsin Magazine of History* (Summer 1967): 284.

17. Bella Fromm, *Blood and Banquets: A Berlin Social Diary* (New York: Harper and Brothers, 1942), 169.

18. Frederick T. Birchall, "Dorothy Thompson Expelled by Reich for 'Slur' on Hitler," *New York Times*, August 26, 1934, 1.

19. Mark Schorer, *Sinclair Lewis: An American Life* (New York: McGraw Hill Book Company, 1961), 601.

20. Dorothy Thompson, "Good-By to Germany," *Harper's Monthly Magazine*, December 1934, 46

21. Ibid., 48–49.

22. Ibid., 51; Birchall, "Dorothy Thompson Expelled by Reich," 1.

23. Birchall, "Dorothy Thompson Expelled by Reich," 1.

24. "Dorothy Thompson Tells of Nazi Ban," *New York Times*, August 27, 1934, 8.

25. Kurth, *American Cassandra*, 204, 358, 232, 280.

26. Ibid., 242, 165–166; Vincent Sheean, *Dorothy and Red* (Boston: Houghton Mifflin Company, 1963), 263.

27. Thompson, *I Saw Hitler!*, 34–35.

28. Schorer, *Sinclair Lewis*, 355, 268, 560.

29. Raymond Gram Swing, *Forerunners of American Fascism* (New York: Books for Libraries Press, 1935).

30. Alan Brinkley, *Voices of Protest: Huey Long, Father Coughlin, and the Great Depression* (New York: Knopf, 1982), 24, 26, 28.

31. T. Harry Williams, *Huey Long* (New York: Knopf, 1969), 750.

32. Brinkley, *Voices of Protest*, 71–73.

33. Williams, *Huey Long*, 700–701, 818.

34. Swing, *Forerunners of American Fascism*, 78–79.

35. Schorer, *Sinclair Lewis*, 608–609.

36. Sinclair Lewis, *It Can't Happen Here* [1935] (New York: Signet Classics, 1970), 218–219, 203.

37. Most of the articles from *The Nation* are reprinted in Swing, *Forerunners of American Fascism*. There is a copy of Carey McWilliams' pamphlet "It CAN Happen Here: Active Anti-Semitism in America" at the Bancroft Library, Berkeley (henceforth Bancroft Library).

38. Lewis, *It Can't Happen Here*, 359.

39. Malcolm Cowley, *The Dream of the Golden Mountains: Remembering the 1930s* (New York: Viking Press, 1980), 296–297.

40. Schorer, *Sinclair Lewis*, 610.

41. Thompson, *I Saw Hitler!*, 29, vi.

42. Thompson, *I Saw Hitler!*, vii.

43. Adolf Hitler, *Mein Kampf*, trans. Ralph Manheim [1925 and 1927] (New York: Houghton Mifflin, 1943), 470. My emphasis.

44. Lewis, *It Can't Happen Here*, 49, 181.

45. Hitler, *Mein Kampf*, 474.

46. Sidney Howard to Ann Watkins, October 18, 1935, Sidney Coe Howard Papers, box 15, Bancroft Library.

47. Sidney Howard White, *Sidney Howard* (Boston: Twayne Publishers, 1977), 30–32.

48. Howard to Watkins, October 18, 1935.

49. Sidney Howard to Polly Damrosch, January 21, 1936, Sidney Coe Howard Papers, box 15, Bancroft Library.

50. Howard to Polly Damrosch, December 21, 1935, Sidney Coe Howard Papers, box 15, Bancroft Library.

51. Howard to Polly Damrosch, January 9, 1936, and Howard to Harold Freeman, January 19, 1936, Sidney Coe Howard Papers, box 15, Bancroft Library.

52. Sinclair Lewis and Sidney Howard, *Sinclair Lewis's* Dodsworth: *Dramatized by Sidney Howard* (New York: Harcourt, Brace and Company, 1933), xiii.

53. Howard to Robert Rubin, February 14, 1936, Sidney Coe Howard Papers, box 15, Bancroft Library.

54. Sidney Howard, "Preliminary Notes for A Motion Picture from It Can't Happen Here by Sinclair Lewis," October 28, 1935, MGM Collection, USC Cinematic Arts Library, Los Angeles (henceforth Cinematic Arts Library), 1.

55. Howard to Lucien Hubbard, December 5, 1935, Sidney Coe Howard Papers, box 15, Bancroft Library. Also see Howard to Sam Marx, October 23, 1936, Sidney Coe Howard Papers, box 15, Bancroft Library.

56. Howard, "Preliminary Notes for A Motion Picture from It Can't Happen Here by Sinclair Lewis," 1–3; Howard, "Preliminary notes for a motion picture treatment of: *It Can't Happen Here* by Sinclair Lewis," undated, Sidney Coe Howard Papers, carton 17, Bancroft Library, 1–3.

57. Howard to Damrosch, December 21, 1935; Howard to Helen Louise Coe Howard, January 26, 1936, Sidney Coe Howard Papers, box 15, Bancroft Library.

58. Howard to Polly Damrosch, December 30, 1935, Sidney Coe Howard Papers, box 15, Bancroft Library.

59. Howard to Polly Damrosch, December 31, 1935, Sidney Coe Howard Papers, box 15, Bancroft Library.

60. Howard to Damrosch, December 30, 1935.

61. Howard, "Preliminary Notes for A Motion Picture from It Can't Happen Here by Sinclair Lewis," 4; Howard, "Preliminary notes for a motion picture treatment of: *It Can't Happen Here* by Sinclair Lewis," 3.

62. Sidney Howard, "It Can't Happen Here: Temporary Complete," January 22, 1936, MGM Collection, Cinematic Arts Library, 17.

63. Ibid., 22, 32.

64. Ibid., 40, 50, 54.

65. Howard, "Preliminary notes for a motion picture treatment of: *It Can't Happen Here* by Sinclair Lewis," 11.

66. Howard, "It Can't Happen Here: Temporary Complete," January 22, 1936, 93–95.

67. Ibid., 95–103.

68. Howard, "Preliminary Notes for A Motion Picture from It Can't Happen Here by Sinclair Lewis," 8.

69. Howard, "It Can't Happen Here: Temporary Complete," January 22, 1936, 85–86. A few days earlier, Howard had admitted to a journalist that he was including no criticism of William Randolph Hearst in the picture. He felt guilty and wrote in his diary, "I disappointed [the journalist] a good deal being only a liberal. I suppose that a liberal really *is* a feeble article. He is a man who admits that he's sick but refuses to see the doctor." Howard, diary entry, January 13, 1936, Sidney Coe Howard Papers, carton 1, Bancroft Library.

70. Howard, "It Can't Happen Here: Temporary Complete," January 22, 1936, 110–114.

71. Ibid., 123.

72. Howard, "Preliminary Notes for A Motion Picture from It Can't Happen Here by Sinclair Lewis," 31.

73. Howard, "It Can't Happen Here: Temporary Complete," January 22, 1936, 133.

74. Howard, "Preliminary Notes for A Motion Picture from It Can't Happen Here by Sinclair Lewis," 28.

75. Howard, "It Can't Happen Here: Temporary Complete," January 22, 1936, 178, 183–184.

76. Howard to Polly Damrosch, December 19, 1935, Sidney Coe Howard Papers, box 15, Bancroft Library.

77. Howard to Damrosch, January 9, 1936.

78. Howard to Sinclair Lewis, January 23, 1936, Sidney Coe Howard Papers, box 15, Bancroft Library.

79. Sinclair Lewis to Howard, February 2, 1936, Sidney Coe Howard Papers, box 5, Bancroft Library.

80. Joseph Breen to Will Hays, December 18, 1935, *It Can't Happen Here* file, Motion Picture Association of America (henceforth MPAA), Production Code Administration records, Margaret Herrick Library, Academy of Motion Picture Arts and Sciences, Beverly Hills (henceforth Margaret Herrick Library).

81. Joseph Breen to Louis B. Mayer, December 18, 1935, *It Can't Happen Here* file, MPAA, Production Code Administration records, Margaret Herrick Library.

82. Howard to Damrosch, January 9, 1936.

83. Howard to Polly Damrosch, January 19, 1936, Sidney Coe Howard Papers, box 15, Bancroft Library.

84. Howard to Lewis, January 23, 1936.

85. Howard to Helen Louise Coe Howard, January 26, 1936.

86. Howard to Lewis, January 23, 1936; Howard to Luise Sillcox, January 23, 1936, Sidney Coe Howard Papers, box 15; Sinclair Lewis to Howard, February 3, 1936, Sidney Coe Howard Papers, box 5, Bancroft Library.

87. Howard to Damrosch, January 21, 1936; Howard to Helen Louise Coe Howard, January 26, 1936; Howard to Harold Freeman, February 11, 1936, Sidney Coe Howard Papers, box 15, Bancroft Library.

88. Joseph Breen to Louis B. Mayer, January 31, 1936, *It Can't Happen Here* file, MPAA, Production Code Administration records, Margaret Herrick Library.

89. Ibid.

90. Alvin M. Asher to Robert E. Kopp, MGM Corp, February 4, 1936, Sidney Coe Howard Papers, carton 17; Robert E. Kopp to Lucien Hubbard, February 6, 1936, Sidney Coe Howard Papers, carton 17, Bancroft Library.

91. Sam Eckman to Louis B. Mayer, February 5, 1936, Sidney Coe Howard Papers, carton 17, Bancroft Library.

92. Howard to Roger Baldwin, February 11, 1936, Sidney Coe Howard Papers, box 15, Bancroft Library.

93. Howard, diary entry, February 12, 1936, Sidney Coe Howard Papers, carton 1, Bancroft Library. Also see Maurice Revnes to Lucien Hubbard, February 1, 1936, Sidney Coe Howard Papers, box 17, Bancroft Library; Howard, "It Can't Happen Here: Temporary Complete," February 12, 1936, MGM Collection, Cinematic Arts Library.

94. Albert H. Lieberman to William H. Fineshriber, February 5, 1936, Papers of Rabbi William H. Fineshriber, folder B/6, Archives of Reform Congregation Keneseth Israel, Philadelphia (henceforth RCKI).

95. Felicia Herman, "American Jews and the Effort to Reform Motion Pictures, 1933–1935," *American Jewish Archives Journal* 103 (2001): 11–44.

96. William H. Fineshriber to Louis B. Mayer, February 7, 1936, Papers of Rabbi William H. Fineshriber, folder B/6, RCKI.

97. Fineshriber to Will Hays, February 7, 1936, Papers of Rabbi William H. Fineshriber, folder B/6, RCKI.

98. Fineshriber to Nicholas Schenck, February 7, 1936, Papers of Rabbi William H. Fineshriber, folder B/6, RCKI.

99. Howard, "Preliminary Notes for A Motion Picture from It Can't Happen Here by Sinclair Lewis," 10, 16, 18; Howard, "It Can't Happen Here: Temporary Complete," December 16, 1935, MGM Collection, Cinematic Arts Library, 34–35, 45.

100. Howard to Lewis, January 23, 1936.

101. Howard to Sinclair Lewis, February 13, 1936, Sidney Coe Howard Papers, box 15, Bancroft Library.

102. Will Hays to Fineshriber, February 14, 1936, Papers of Rabbi William H. Fineshriber, folder B/6, RCKI.

103. "Hollywood Tempest Breaks on 'It Can't Happen Here,'" *The Publishers' Weekly*, February 22, 1936, 900.

104. Howard to Rubin, February 14, 1936.

105. Howard, diary entry, February 14, 1936.

106. "Lewis Says Hays Bans Film of Book," 1.

107. "Hays Denies Order to Ban Lewis Film," *New York Times*, February 18, 1936, 27.

108. "The Nation," *New York Times*, February 23, 1936, E1.

109. "Denies Film Was Banned," *New York Times*, February 20, 1936, 15.

110. Quoted in Richard Lingeman, *Sinclair Lewis: Rebel from Main Street* (New York: Random House, 2002), 400. Dorothy Thompson had just interviewed Huey Long, and although she certainly believed that Long was dangerous, she also knew that he was radically different from Hitler. Long showed little respect for the institutions of democracy while he was governor of Louisiana, but he never sought to establish a totalitarian regime. He organized a campaign against the powerful moneyed interests, but he never made a scapegoat out of any religious or racial minority. The concept of a collective national destiny organized around submission to an all-knowing leader was entirely absent from Long's vision. See Kurth, *American Cassandra*, 208; Brinkley, *Voices of Protest*, 276–283.

111. Lingeman, *Sinclair Lewis*, 407. "Lewis refers to Long several times in the novel—his customary way of setting apart public figures from characters who might be identified with them, thus avoiding legal complaints. The problem of Long's demise was solved by merely adding 'the late' to all allusions to him."

112. "Berlin and Rome Hail 'Ban' on Lewis Film," *New York Times*, February 17, 1936, 21.

113. "It *is* Happening Here!" Advertisement, *New York Times*, February 17, 1936, 15.

114. Schorer, *Sinclair Lewis*, 623–625; Sinclair Lewis, *It Can't Happen Here: A New Version* (New York: Dramatists Play Service, 1938).

115. See, for example, Richard Aldrich to Howard, March 3, 1936, Sidney Coe Howard Papers, box 1; Howard to Richard Aldrich, March 20, 1936, Sidney Coe Howard Papers, box 15; Howard to Elmer Rice, March 28, 1936, Sidney Coe Howard Papers, box 15; Howard to Theresa Helburn, May 19, 1936, Sidney Coe Howard Papers, box 15; Tom Davin to Howard, May 20, 1936, Sidney Coe Howard Papers, box 6; Howard to Tom Davin, May 26, 1936, Sidney Coe Howard Papers, box 15, Bancroft Library. Also see Joseph Breen to Vincent Hart, February 19, 1936, Harry Rather to Joseph Breen, April 8, 1937, and Val Lewton to Joseph Breen, June 8, 1936, *It Can't Happen Here* file, MPAA, Production Code Administration records, Margaret Herrick Library.

116. "Sidney Howard Killed by Tractor on Estate: Playwright is Crushed in Berkshire Garage," *New York Times*, August 24, 1939, 1.

117. Dorothy Thompson wrote about the death of Sidney Howard and the signing of the German-Soviet Nonaggression Pact in her next column. See Thompson, "On the Record: To Sidney Howard," *New York Herald Tribune*, August 28, 1939, 13.

118. Auswärtiges Amt, Historischer Dienst, ed., *Biographisches Handbuchs des deutschen Auswärtigen Dienstes 1871–1945*, vol. 2 (G–K) (Paderborn: Ferdinand Schöningh, 2005).

119. For records of Gyssling's involvement with the Friends of the New Germany and the German American Bund, see numerous items in the Jewish Federation Council of Greater Los Angeles, Community Relations Committee Collection (henceforth JFC), pt. 1, box 16, folder 7; JFC, pt. 2, box 66, folder 24, Urban Archives Center, Oviatt Library, Northridge (henceforth Urban Archives Center).

120. "Interview with Vice Consul Grah, October 4, 1935," JFC, pt. 1, box 16, folder 7, Urban Archives Center.

121. Georg Gyssling to Joseph Breen, October 25, 1935, *Rendezvous* file, MPAA, Production Code Administration records, Margaret Herrick Library.

122. Joseph Breen to Georg Gyssling, October 26, 1935, *Rendezvous* file, MPAA, Production Code Administration Records, Margaret Herrick Library; *Rendezvous*, directed by William K. Howard (MGM, 1935). Both the Margaret Herrick Library and the Cinematic Arts Library hold multiple versions of the script of *Rendezvous*.

123. Referat des Gesandtschaftsrats Dr. Freudenthal, April 18, 1933, German embassy in Paris, 2282: Filmwesen, vol. 5, Politisches Archiv des Auswärtigen Amts, Berlin (henceforth PAAA), 13.

124. Henry Blanke to Hagemann, February 9, 1937, file on *The Life of Emile Zola*, folder 1019, USC Warner Bros. Archives, Los Angeles (henceforth WB).

125. Walter MacEwen to Hal Wallis, February 11, 1937, file on *The Life of Emile Zola*, folder 2297, WB.

126. Hal Wallis, Cutting Notes "Zola," May 10, 1937, file on *The Life of Emile Zola*, folder 2297, WB.

127. *The Life of Emile Zola*, directed by William Dieterle (Warner Brothers, 1937).

128. Referat des Gesandtschaftsrats Dr. Freudenthal, April 18, 1933, 8–9. Also see Jason Joy to Carl Laemmle, August 16, 1932, *The Road Back* file, MPAA, Production Code Administration records, Margaret Herrick Library.

129. Harry Zehner to Joseph Breen, October 13, 1936, *The Road Back* file, MPAA, Production Code Administration records, Margaret Herrick Library.

130. William E. Dodd to Secretary of State, February 8, 1937, File 862.4061 Motion Pictures/98, 1930–39 Central Decimal File, RG 59, National Archives and Records Administration, College Park, Maryland (henceforth National Archives).

131. "Deutschland protestiert.- Universal filmt 'Der Weg zurück' von Remarque," Undated memorandum, R 105011: Politische Abteilung, Referat Pol IX, Politische und kulturelle Propaganda in den Vereinigten Staaten von Amerika, vol. 1, PAAA.

132. Erich Maria Remarque, *The Road Back* (Boston: Little, Brown, and Company, 1931).

133. R. C. Sheriff, "The Road Back," December 11, 1936, General Script Collection, no. 1119, Cinematic Arts Library.

134. Georg Gyssling to Joseph Breen, November 5, 1936, *The Road Back* file, MPAA, Production Code Administration records, Margaret Herrick Library.

135. Joseph Breen to Will Hays, Re: The Road Back, February 12, 1937, *The Road Back* file, MPAA, Production Code Administration records, Margaret Herrick Library. For an account of Gyssling's actions that focuses on the experience of the director James Whale, see James Curtis, *James Whale: A New World of Gods and Monsters* (Boston: Faber and Faber, 1998), 291–309.

136. "Nazis Threaten U.S. Actors," *Hollywood Now*, April 10, 1937, 2.

137. Ibid.

138. Ibid. Also see Georg Gyssling to actors, April 1937, *The Road Back* file, MPAA, Production Code Administration records, Margaret Herrick Library. The State Department records at the National Archives contain many of Gyssling's original letters to the actors.

139. "Nazis Threaten U.S. Actors," 2.

140. Frederick Herron to Joseph Flack, April 16, 1937, File 811.4061 Road Back/15, 1930–39 Central Decimal File, RG 59, National Archives.

141. James Clement Dunn to Secretary of State, April 19, 1937, File 811.4061 Road Back/4, 1930–39 Central Decimal File, RG 59, National Archives.

142. "Universal Cuts 'Road' as a Sop to Germany," *Variety*, June 9, 1937, 6.

143. *The Road Back*, directed by James Whale (Universal Pictures, 1937). For the original ending, see Sheriff, "The Road Back," 154–158.

144. Hans Heinrich Dieckhoff to Under Secretary of State Sumner Welles, June 9, 1937, File 811.4061 Road Back/13, 1930–39 Central Decimal File, RG 59, National Archives.

145. Sumner Welles to Hans Heinrich Dieckhoff, June 10, 1937, File 811.4061 Road Back/24, 1930–39 Central Decimal File, RG 59, National Archives.

146. "German Consul Denies Rebuke Received in Actor-Warning Row," *Los Angeles Times*, June 16, 1937, 1.

147. Georg Gyssling to Joseph Breen, May 28, 1937, and June 6, 1937, *Lancer Spy* file, MPAA, Production Code Administration records, Margaret Herrick Library.

148. Georg Gyssling to German embassy in Washington, D.C., September 30, 1937, German embassy in Rome, 835a: politische Propaganda, vol. 2, PAAA. According to this report, the Hays Office told Gyssling that the producer and director of *Lancer Spy* were responsible for the film's worst features. "Both Jews!" Gyssling noted.

149. In early 1936, Gyssling was concerned about a minor independent film entitled *I Was a Captive of Nazi Germany*. He complained to Joseph Breen, who then tried to suppress the production. The producer's response to Breen was remarkable: "I am informed by competent authority that the German Consul exceeds his authority when he protests to your organization about the subject matter of pictures or the conduct of private individuals or firms in connection with a picture to be exhibited in the United States. The withdrawal of our application on account of this protest would be an admission on our part that the picture does not fairly represent Germany and its

people. . . . If the present regime in Germany did not win its popularity by inspiring the youth of Germany, if there was no Boycott of the Jews, if the Blood Purge and the burning of the books did not happen, if Minister of Propaganda Herr Goebbels did not suppress Herr Von Papen's speech on the necessity of the free press, if Isabel Steele was not arrested and charged with high treason, espionage and held for four months in solitary confinement at the Alexanderplatz and Moabit prison in Berlin, subjected to rigid cross examination and then deported without trial only after the United States Department of State demanded that she be given an immediate trial or freed, then the picture is unfair to the German Government. These facts are obviously true and must have been committed with the consent and approval of the German government. . . . In view of these facts, I must urgently insist that the picture be given your code approval or refusal. I regret the inconvenience, embarrassment and burden this matter may be to your office." Alfred T. Mannon to Joseph Breen, July 29, 1936, *I Was a Captive of Nazi Germany* file, MPAA, Production Code Administration records, Margaret Herrick Library. *I Was a Captive of Nazi Germany* was screened at a few independent theaters and received very poor reviews. See, for example, Frank S. Nugent, "The Globe's 'I Was a Captive of Nazi Germany' Dramatizes Isobel Steele's Adventures," *New York Times*, August 3, 1936, 11.

150. Propaganda Ministry to German consulates and embassies, "Betrifft: Hetzfilm 'Hitler, the mad dog of Europe,'" January 26, 1938, German embassy in Rome, 835a: deutschfeindliche Filmpropaganda, vol. 3, PAAA. The actor Sam Jaffe was not the producer of the same name who had initially embarked on *The Mad Dog of Europe* back in 1933.

151. Ibid.

152. Erich Maria Remarque, *Three Comrades* (Boston: Little, Brown, and Company, 1937).

153. "Metro Hesitant on Remarque's Story," *Variety*, June 30, 1937, 3.

154. Georg Gyssling to Joseph Breen, April 8, 1937, *Three Comrades* file, MPAA, Production Code Administration records, Margaret Herrick Library. Also see Gyssling to Breen, September 30, 1936, and May 28, 1937, *Three Comrades* file, MPAA, Production Code Administration records, Margaret Herrick Library.

155. Joseph Breen to Louis B. Mayer, May 11, 1937, *Three Comrades* file, MPAA, Production Code Administration records, Margaret Herrick Library.

156. "Erich Maria Remarque, the Celebrated Author of 'All Quiet on the Western Front,' Is in Paris," *Ce Soir*, press clipping dated September 11, 1937, *Three Comrades* file, MPAA, Production Code Administration records, Margaret Herrick Library.

157. F. Scott Fitzgerald had worked in Hollywood twice before but had never received a formal writing credit. Now was his chance to write a major feature starring four famous actors. Matthew J. Bruccoli, ed., *F. Scott Fitzgerald's Screenplay for* Three Comrades *by Erich Maria Remarque* (Carbondale: Southern Illinois University Press, 1978), 255.

158. F. Scott Fitzgerald, "Notes on 'Three Comrades,'" July 28, 1937, MGM Collection, Cinematic Arts Library.

159. Ibid.

160. See the full script in Bruccoli, *F. Scott Fitzgerald's Screenplay for* Three Comrades *by Erich Maria Remarque*. The USC Cinematic Arts Library holds many drafts of the script.

161. Ibid., 263.

162. Joseph Breen to Louis B. Mayer, January 22, 1938, *Three Comrades* file, MPAA, Production Code Administration records, Margaret Herrick Library.

163. Kevin Brownlow, interview with Budd Schulberg, "Chaplin and the Great Dictator," Photoplay Productions, roll 22. I am grateful to Kevin Brownlow for giving me the full transcript of his interview with Schulberg, a portion of which appears in his documentary *The Tramp and the Dictator*, directed by Brownlow and Michael Kloft (Photoplay Productions, 2002). I attempted to contact Budd Schulberg when I first embarked on this project in 2004. Schulberg died in 2009. According to an oral history at the Margaret Herrick Library, MGM also enlisted the help of the head of its German branch, Frits Strengholt, in the making of *Three Comrades*. Barbara Hall, *An Oral History with Robert M. W. Vogel*, Margaret Herrick Library, 1991, 120.

164. Three Comrades, Changes numbered 1 to 10, *Three Comrades* file, MPAA, Production Code Administration records, Margaret Herrick Library.

165. Joseph Breen to Louis B. Mayer, January 27, 1938, *Three Comrades* file, MPAA, Production Code Administration records, Margaret Herrick Library.

166. Ibid. For an account of the meeting, see "Off-Color Remarque," *New Masses*, February 15, 1938, *Three Comrades* file, MPAA, Production Code Administration records, Margaret Herrick Library.

167. F. Scott Fitzgerald and Edward E. Paramore, "Three Comrades: Temporary Complete," January 8, 1938, MGM Collection, Cinematic Arts Library, 4.

168. Three Comrades, Changes numbered 1 to 10.

169. F. Scott Fitzgerald and Edward E. Paramore Jr., "Script Revision [Three Comrades]," November 1, 1937, MGM Collection, Cinematic Arts Library.

170. Joseph Mankiewicz, F. Scott Fitzgerald, Edward E. Paramore Jr., Ed Hogan, "Conference Notes [Three Comrades]," December 20, 1937, MGM Collection, Cinematic Arts Library.

171. Fitzgerald and Paramore, "Three Comrades: Temporary Complete," January 8, 1938, 29.

172. Breen to Mayer, January 27, 1938.

173. F. Scott Fitzgerald and Edward E. Paramore Jr., "Three Comrades: Temporary Complete," February 4, 1938, MGM Collection, Cinematic Arts Library.

174. Breen to Mayer, January 27, 1938.

175. "Off-Color Remarque."

176. Bruccoli, *F. Scott Fitzgerald's Screenplay for* Three Comrades *by Erich Maria Remarque*, 266.

177. Three Comrades, Changes numbered 1 to 10; Breen to Mayer, January 27, 1938.

178. Joseph Breen to Georg Gyssling, May 16, 1938, *Three Comrades* file, MPAA, Production Code Administration records, Margaret Herrick Library; *Three Comrades*, directed by Frank Borzage (MGM, 1938).

179. Joseph Breen to Will Hays, June 18, 1938, *Foreign Correspondent* file, MPAA, Production Code Administration records, Margaret Herrick Library.

180. Vincent Sheean, *Personal History* (New York: Doubleday, Doran & Company, 1934).

181. "Wanger Postpones 'Personal History,'" June 29, 1938, press clipping, *Foreign Correspondent* file, MPAA, Production Code Administration records, Margaret Herrick Library. Walter Wanger also produced *Gabriel over the White House*.

182. John Howard Lawson, "Personal History," John Howard Lawson Papers, series 6, sub-series 2, box 75, folder 5, Special Collections, Southern Illinois University Carbondale (henceforth SIUC), 1–14. There is also an incomplete copy of the script in folder 56 of the James Wong Howe Collection at the Margaret Herrick Library, titled "Personal History—Changes—6/24/38."

183. Lawson, "Personal History," 51–54.

184. Ibid., 84–85.

185. Ibid., 108.

186. Ibid., 131–132.

187. Ibid., 129–130.

188. Breen to Hays, June 18, 1938.

189. Ibid.; Joseph Breen to Walter Wanger, June 21, 1938, *Foreign Correspondent* file, MPAA, Production Code Administration records, Margaret Herrick Library.

190. Breen to Hays, June 18, 1938.

191. Joseph Breen to Will Hays, June 21, 1938, and June 22, 1938, *Foreign Correspondent* file, MPAA, Production Code Administration records, Margaret Herrick Library.

192. "'Personal History' Shelved By Wanger; Fonda to RKO," press clipping dated June 29, 1938, *Foreign Correspondent* file, MPAA, Production Code Administration records; "Wanger Postpones 'Personal History,'" undated press clipping, *Foreign Correspondent* file, MPAA, Production Code Administration records, Margaret Herrick Library.

193. Joseph Breen to Will Hays, March 18, 1940, *Foreign Correspondent* file, MPAA, Production Code Administration records, Margaret Herrick Library.

194. *Foreign Correspondent*, directed by Alfred Hitchcock (United Artists, 1940).

195.  Lawson, "Personal History," 136.

196.  Ibid., 135.

197.  Five months after Walter Wanger postponed *Personal History*, the editor of a local journal, *Hollywood Spectator*, proposed his own idea for an anti-Nazi film. He urged the studio heads to expose the persecution of Jews in Germany, but his language, which was distinctly anti-Semitic, revealed that he had a less noble agenda: *"A Plea to the Jews Who Control Our Films To Use the Mighty Voice of the Screen on Behalf of the Jews Who Are Victims of Maniac of Germany....* There is one mighty voice in America which can be lifted in defense of your persecuted blood-brothers. You control that voice. It is the voice of the screen! You have controlled it from its inception. You have used it only as something to make money for you. You have your money. Will you now use it, if not to express your own feelings, at least to give expression to the feelings of Gentiles? . . . The world today is wondering what can be done. Make a picture showing what should be done. And be brave about it! Call a spade a spade. If Will Hays, your paid pussy-footer, stands in your way, brush him aside and keep going. Make a picture showing what Germany has done to Jews, and then showing what the world should do to Germany. Show a gathering of representatives from all the other countries in the world; have it declare that as long as Hitler reigns supreme in Germany, that country is not fit to associate with the other nations of the world. Isolate Germany and show what the effect would be when no nation would sell anything to it or buy anything from it, when its boundaries would be quarantine lines no decent person would cross. As an abstract theme, an entertaining picture could be based on the complete isolation of a major country. To my knowledge it is a theme which no book, play or picture has used. . . . Make your picture a Hebrew undertaking. Cast it with Jews until it itself is a demonstration of the heights to which members of your race have risen in screen art. But make it! Make it a Hollywood effort to protect the members of your race, and devote the big profits it would earn to the relief of those Jews who need it so badly." Welford Beaton, "From the Editor's Easy Chair: To the Jews Who Control the Films," *Hollywood Spectator*, November 26, 1938, 3–4.

198.  André Bazin, *What Is Cinema?* vol. 1 (Berkeley: University of California Press, 1967), 29.

199.  Lucien Hubbard, Outline [It Can't Happen Here], January 14, 1939, MGM Collection, Cinematic Arts Library.

200.  Lucien Hubbard, "It Can't Happen Here: Complete," May 29, 1939, MGM Collection, Cinematic Arts Library, 11, 125.

201.  Hubbard, Outline [It Can't Happen Here], January 14, 1939.

202.  Hubbard, "It Can't Happen Here: Complete," May 29, 1939.

203.  Hans Kolb to consulates, embassies, and legations, July 26, 1939, German embassy in Rome, 835a: politische Propaganda, vol. 2, PAAA.

204.  John Edgar Hoover to Secretary of State, December 23, 1937, File 701.6211/1015, 1930–39 Central Decimal File, RG 59, National Archives.

205. Joseph Breen to Louis B. Mayer, March 22, 1939, and June 2, 1939, *It Can't Happen Here* file, MPAA, Production Code Administration records, Margaret Herrick Library.

206. "Screen News Here and in Hollywood," *New York Times*, June 10, 1939, 14.

207. "Metro Studio Secretly Receives Nazi Editors,'" *Hollywood Now*, June 23, 1939, 1, 4.

208. Ibid.

209. "Mussolini, Senior, visits Hitler—Mussolini Jr., visits Hollywood," *Hollywood Now*, October 2, 1937, 1–2; "Hollywood Closes Doors to Hitler's Film Emissary," *Hollywood Now*, December 2, 1938, 1, 4; Neal Gabler, *Walt Disney: The Triumph of the American Imagination* (New York: Knopf, 2006), 449.

210. "Metro Studio Secretly Receives Nazi Editors," 1, 4; "Vogel Calls Visit 'Regular Matter of Business,'" *Hollywood Now*, June 23, 1939, 1.

211. "Vogel Calls Visit 'Regular Matter of Business,'" *Hollywood Now*, June 23, 1939, 1.

212. Harry Warner to Nicholas Schenck, Sam Katz, Al Lichtman, Eddie Mannix, and Mervyn LeRoy, June 27, 1939, Jack L. Warner Collection, box 93, Cinematic Arts Library.

213. "MGM Head Sharply Scored For Shelving Lewis Story," *Hollywood Now*, July 7, 1939, 1, 4.

214. "AFA Quiz Pursues Destiny Of 'It Can't Happen Here,'" *Hollywood Now*, July 14, 1939, 3.

## 6. SWITCHED ON

1. William C. DeMille, "Hollywood Thanks Hitler," *Liberty Magazine*, February 11, 1939, 16–17. © Liberty Library Corporation 2013.

2. Ian Kershaw, *Hitler 1936–1945: Nemesis* (London: Penguin Books, 2000), 166.

3. Elke Fröhlich et al., eds., *Die Tagebücher von Joseph Goebbels*, entry for January 8, 1939, pt. 1, vol. 6 (Munich: K. G. Saur Verlag, 1998), 228–229.

4. Ibid.; Zsg. 101/12, folio 10, January 9, 1939, Bundesarchiv, Koblenz (henceforth BK).

5. Zsg. 110/11, folio 23, January 9, 1939, BK.

6. Ibid., folio 22–23.

7. Zsg. 101/12, folio 3, January 3, 1939, BK.

8. "Man hört und liest: Chaplin als Hitler," *Film-Kurier*, December 7, 1938, 5.

9. Georg Gyssling to Joseph Breen, December 6, 1939, *Confessions of a Nazi Spy* file, Motion Picture Association of America (henceforth MPAA), Production Code Administration records, Margaret Herrick Library, Academy of Motion Picture Arts and Sciences, Beverly Hills (henceforth Margaret Herrick Library).

10. Zsg. 101/12, folio 3.

11. Ibid., folio 3–4.

12. Quoted in Kershaw, *Hitler 1936–1945*, 153.

13. Max Doramus, ed., *Hitler: Speeches and Proclamations, 1932–1945*, vol. 3 (London: I.B. Tauris, 1990), 1456.

14. "Die Filmhetze in USA: Wird die Warnung des Führers beachtet werden?" *Film-Kurier*, February 1, 1939, 2.

15. B. R. Crisler, "Film Notes and Comment," *New York Times*, December 11, 1938, 193; "Man hört und liest: Chaplin als Hitler," 5.

16. Luigi Luraschi to Joseph Breen, December 10, 1938, *Confessions of a Nazi Spy* file, MPAA, Production Code Administration records, Margaret Herrick Library.

17. Jack L. Warner to Charles Chaplin, March 23, 1939, Jack L. Warner Collection, box 58, folder 5, USC Cinematic Arts Library, Los Angeles (henceforth Cinematic Arts Library).

18. Charles Chaplin, signed statement to the press, March 18, 1939; "'Dictator' Foldup Denied By Chaplin," *Hollywood Reporter*, March 20, 1939, 1.

19. Christine Ann Colgan, "Warner Brothers' Crusade against the Third Reich: A Study of Anti-Nazi Activism and Film Production, 1933–1941," (unpublished dissertation, University of Southern California, 1985), 308–312. Also see Michael E. Birdwell, *Celluloid Soldiers: The Warner Bros. Campaign against Nazism* (New York: New York University Press, 1999).

20. Colgan, "Warner Brothers' Crusade against the Third Reich," 312–315. Also see "G-Man Turrou's Own Account of the Spy Situation," *Hollywood Spectator*, April 15, 1939, 18–19.

21. Joseph Breen to Jack L. Warner, December 30, 1938, *Confessions of a Nazi Spy* file, MPAA, Production Code Administration records, Margaret Herrick Library.

22. Joseph Breen to Will Hays, December 30, 1938, *Confessions of a Nazi Spy* file, MPAA, Production Code Administration records, Margaret Herrick Library.

23. Production Code Administration to Jack L. Warner, April 6, 1939, *Confessions of a Nazi Spy* file, MPAA, Production Code Administration records, Margaret Herrick Library.

24. Colgan, "Warner Brothers' Crusade against the Third Reich," 323–327.

25. *Confessions of a Nazi Spy*, directed by Anatole Litvak (Warner Brothers, 1939).

26. Colgan, "Warner Brothers' Crusade against the Third Reich," 405–414.

27. Hans Thomsen to Cordell Hull, May 8, 1939, File 811.4061 Confessions of a Nazi Spy/3, 1930–39 Central Decimal File, RG 59, National Archives and Records Administration, College Park, Maryland (henceforth National Archives); Thomsen [to Foreign Ministry], Telegram, May 8, 1939, Politische Abteilung, Referat Pol IX, Politische und kulturelle Propaganda in den Vereinigten Staaten von Amerika, vol. 4, Politisches Archiv des Auswärtigen Amts, Berlin (henceforth PAAA); Hans Kolb to consulates and embassies, October 12, 1939, German embassy in Rome, 822: Filme, vol. 6, PAAA. Also see "Objects to 'Spy' Film," *New York Times*, June 7, 1939, 30; Colgan, "Warner Brothers' Crusade against the Third Reich," 415.

28. Colgan, "Warner Brothers' Crusade against the Third Reich," 332.

29. Frank S. Nugent, "The Screen: The Warners Make Faces at Hitler in 'Confessions of a Nazi Spy,'" *New York Times*, April 29, 1939, 19.

30. Fröhlich et al., *Die Tagebücher von Joseph Goebbels*, entry for September 30, 1939, pt. 1, vol. 7, 131.

31. Douglas W. Churchill, "Hollywood Celebrates Itself," *New York Times*, June 18, 1939, 115.

32. Paul Holt, "Hollywood declares war on the Nazis," *Daily Express*, May 10, 1939, 12.

33. "M-G, Par, 20th Biz Safe in Reich," *Variety*, April 19, 1939, 19; Fröhlich et al., *Die Tagebücher von Joseph Goebbels*, entry for February 5, 1939, pt. 1, vol. 6, 249.

34. "Last Three U.S. Firms Still in Germany Read Handwriting," *Boxoffice*, April 22, 1939, 14.

35. Paul H. Pearson, "Berlin First Runs in July 1939," September 15, 1939, and "Berlin First Runs in August 1939," September 15, 1939, Commercial Attachés in Germany 1931–1940, RG 151, National Archives; Markus Spieker, *Hollywood unterm Hakenkreuz: Der amerikanische Spielfilm im Dritten Reich* (Trier: Wissenschaftlicher Verlag Trier, 1999), 359.

36. Reichsfilmkammer, "Rundschreiben Nr. 125," December 12, 1939, R 109I, vol. 1751, Bundesarchiv, Berlin (henceforth Bundesarchiv).

37. Will Hays to Ben M. Cherrington, October 6, 1939, File 811.4061 Motion Pictures/298, 1930–39 Central Decimal File, RG 59, National Archives.

38. R. M. Stephenson, "Special Report 53," December 30, 1938, Commercial Attachés in Germany 1931–1940, RG 151, National Archives; "Aufstellung der von den einzelnen Verleihfirmen zum kostenlosen Einsatz für das Kriegswinterhilfswerk zur Verfügung gestellten Filme," October 20, 1939, R 109I, vol. 751, Bundesarchiv.

39. Spieker, *Hollywood unterm Hakenkreuz*, 359–360.

40. Paul H. Pearson, "Economic and Trade Notes 414," January 6, 1940, Commercial Attachés in Germany 1931–1940, RG 151, National Archives; Karl Macht, "Clark Gable gibt an. Marmorhaus: 'Abenteuer in China'" *Der Angriff*, October 5, 1939, 5.

41. "Majors Economize to Offset War; Paramount News Gets Siege Films," *Motion Picture Herald*, September 23, 1939, 16; "19% U.S. Gross in Warland; Restrictions in 50 Places," *Motion Picture Herald*, October 7, 1939, 28.

42. DeMille, "Hollywood Thanks Hitler," 16–17.

43. Ivan Spear, "More Sociological, Political Film Meat for New Season," *Boxoffice*, June 15, 1940, 22. Also see "43 War or Related Subjects Now Available or are in Production," *Motion Picture Herald*, September 9, 1939, 23–24; "Rush Production on Pictures Dealing with European War," *Boxoffice*, June 8, 1940, 31.

44. Conference with Mr. Zanuck, "Four Sons," November 16, 1939, Twentieth Century-Fox Collection, Cinematic Arts Library.

45. Ibid.

46. *Four Sons*, directed by Archie Mayo (Twentieth Century-Fox, 1940).

47. "Rambling Reporter," *Hollywood Reporter*, April 24, 1940, 2.

48. Phyllis Bottome, *The Mortal Storm* (Boston: Little, Brown and Company, 1938).

49. Helen Corbaley, Comment [on "The Mortal Storm"], February 17, 1939, Turner/MGM Scripts, Margaret Herrick Library.

50. *The Mortal Storm*, directed by Frank Borzage (MGM, 1940).

51. John Goulder et al., "The Mortal Storm," December 11, 1939, Turner/MGM Scripts, Margaret Herrick Library, 48. In my account of this scene I have used passages from various versions of the script at the Margaret Herrick Library.

52. Andersen Ellis et al., "The Mortal Storm," February 2, 1940, Turner/MGM Scripts, Margaret Herrick Library, 44.

53. Ibid., 50.

54. Ibid., 52.

55. Goulder et al., "The Mortal Storm," 52.

56. Ellis et al., "Mortal Storm Changes," March 7, 1940, Turner/MGM Scripts, Margaret Herrick Library, 52.

57. Phyllis Bottome to Sidney Franklin [on "The Mortal Storm"], February 7, 1940, MGM Collection, Cinematic Arts Library.

58. See numerous letters from Breen in *The Mortal Storm* file, MPAA, Production Code Administration records, Margaret Herrick Library.

59. Hervé Dumont, *Frank Borzage: The Life and Films of a Hollywood Romantic* (Jefferson, NC: McFarland & Company, 2006), 289.

60. Victor Saville claimed to have directed *The Mortal Storm* himself, but all the evidence suggests that the director was Frank Borzage (as credited in the film). See Roy Moseley, *Evergreen: Victor Saville in His Own Words*, (Carbondale: Southern Illinois University Press, 2000), 140–142; Dumont, *Frank Borzage*, 291.

61. *The Wizard of Oz*, directed by Victor Fleming (MGM, 1939).

62. *Imaginary Witness: Hollywood and the Holocaust*, directed by Daniel Anker (Anker Productions, 2004).

63. Interview by the author, October 11, 2012.

64. Ibid.

65. Howard Strickling to Victor Saville, June 5, 1940, "Mortal Storm," MGM Collection, Cinematic Arts Library.

66. Wanda Darling to Jeanette Spooner, May 31, 1940, "Mortal Storm," MGM Collection, Cinematic Arts Library.

67. Neal Gabler, *An Empire of Their Own: How the Jews Invented Hollywood* (New York: Crown Publishers, 1988), 2. Also see Ben Hecht, *A Child of the Century* (New York: Simon and Schuster, 1954), 539–540.

68. *The Mortal Storm* was so similar to *The Mad Dog of Europe* that the owner of the rights to *The Mad Dog of Europe* later tried to sue MGM for stealing his idea. The judges noted the obvious resemblance between the two scripts and declared: "It was natural—whether or not it was commendable—for the defendant [MGM], because of its German business, not to wish to use the scenario in 1933; although it is of course conceivable that, later and in 1939 it might have turned to it and made use of the copies which we are to assume that it had in its library." Rosen v. Loews's Inc., No. 263, Docket 20584 (2d Cir. July 23, 1947).

69. *Escape*, directed by Mervyn LeRoy (MGM, 1940).

70. Conference with Mr. Zanuck, "I Married a Nazi," February 19, 1940, Twentieth Century-Fox Collection, Cinematic Arts Library; *The Man I Married*, directed by Irving Pichel (Twentieth Century-Fox, 1940).

71. Charles Spencer Chaplin, "The Dictator," Copyright Records, reg. no. D60332, November 10, 1938, Manuscript Division, Library of Congress, Washington, DC (henceforth LC), 33.

72. *The Great Dictator*, directed by Charles Chaplin (Charles Chaplin Film Corp, 1940).

73. Hans Thomsen [to Foreign Ministry], Telegram, February 13, 1940, Politische Abteilung, Referat Pol IX, Politische und kulturelle Propaganda in den Vereinigten Staaten von Amerika, vol. 4, PAAA; Thomsen to Cordell Hull, July 16, 1940, File 811.4061 Mortal Storm/1, 1940–44 Central Decimal File, RG 59, National Archives.

74. Henry F. Grady to Frederick Herron, July 25, 1940, File 811.4061 Mortal Storm/1, 1940–44 Central Decimal File, RG 59, National Archives.

75. Frederick Herron to Henry F. Grady, July 29, 1940, File 811.4061 Mortal Storm/2, 1940–44 Central Decimal File, RG 59, National Archives.

76. Reichsfilmkammer, "Sonder-Rundschreiben Nr. 133," June 27, 1940, R 109I, vol. 1751, Bundesarchiv; Kirk to Secretary of State, July 27, 1940, File 862.4061 Motion Pictures/132, 1940–44 Central Decimal File, RG 59, National Archives.

77. W. C. Michel to Cordell Hull, July 16, 1940, File 862.4061 Motion Pictures/131, 1940–44 Central Decimal File, RG 59, National Archives.

78. Paul H. Pearson, "Ban on Exhibition and Distribution of Fox Films in Germany," July 30, 1940, File 862.4061 Motion Pictures/136, 1940–44 Central Decimal File, RG 59, National Archives.

79. Reichsfilmkammer, "Rundschreiben Nr. 135," August 13, 1940, R 109I, vol. 1751, Bundesarchiv; Kirk to Secretary of State, August 20, 1940, File 862.4061 Motion Pictures/134, 1940–44 Central Decimal File, RG 59, National Archives; "Nazis Ban More U.S. Films: Metro-Goldwyn-Mayer is Barred as Anti-German Producer," *New York Times*, August 15, 1940, 2; "Amtliche Bekanntmachungen der Reichsfilmkammer: Verbot der amerikanischen Metro-Filme," *Film-Kurier*, August 10, 1940, 3.

80. "Nazis Oust Metro's Pix," *Film Daily*, August 15, 1940, 1, 6.

81. "MGM Dismissing 660 in Europe: Ban Forces Closing of All Offices of the Company in Nazi-Controlled Countries," *Hollywood Reporter*, August 14, 1940, 1.

82. Kirk to Secretary of State, August 23, 1940, File 862.4061 Motion Pictures/135, 1940–44 Central Decimal File, RG 59, National Archives.

83. Kirk to Secretary of State, August 20, 1940.

84. Kirk to Secretary of State, August 23, 1940.

85. "Lawrence (Metro) and Lange (Par) Want to Return to Europe Shortly; All Cos. Liquidating Foreign Biz," *Variety*, September 11, 1940, 12.

86. "Verbot der Filme der Metro-Goldwyn-Mayer, 20th Century Fox, Paramount im Reich und den besetzten Gebieten," October 31, 1940, German legation in Berne, 3368: Hetzfilme gegen Deutschland, PAAA.

87. *Man Hunt*, directed by Fritz Lang (Twentieth Century-Fox, 1940); *Underground*, directed by Vincent Sherman (Warner Brothers, 1941); *They Dare Not Love*, directed by James Whale (Columbia Pictures, 1941); *Foreign Correspondent*, directed by Alfred Hitchcock (United Artists, 1940).

88. For the isolationist movement in this period, see Wayne S. Cole, *Roosevelt and the Isolationists 1932–1945* (Lincoln: University of Nebraska Press, 1983), esp. 310–330.

89. For a compete transcript of the hearings, see *Propaganda in Moving Pictures: Hearings Before a Subcommittee of the Committee on Interstate Commerce, United States Senate on S. Res. 152, a Resolution Authorizing an Investigation of War Propaganda Disseminated by the Motion Picture Industry and of Any Monopoly in the Production, Distribution or Exhibition of Motion Pictures*, 77th Cong. (Sept. 9–26, 1941). Also see Clayton R. Koppes and Gregory D. Black, *Hollywood Goes to War: How Politics, Profits, and Propaganda Shaped World War II Movies* (New York: Free Press, 1987), 16–47.

90. *Propaganda in Moving Pictures*, 17, 36.

91. Ibid., 57–60. I have removed some redundant dialogue in this section for the purpose of clarity.

92. Barney Balaban, who appeared on behalf of Paramount, announced that his studio had not produced any of the films in question.

93. *Propaganda in Moving Pictures*, 423.

94. Ibid., 19–20.

95. Michael S. Shull and David Edward Wilt, *Hollywood War Films, 1937–1945: An Exhaustive Filmography of American Feature-Length Motion Pictures Relating to World War II* (Jefferson, NC: McFarland & Company, 1996), 291–294.

96. Clayton R. Koppes and Gregory D. Black, "What to Show the World: The Office of War Information and Hollywood, 1942–1945," *Journal of American History* 64, no. 1 (June 1977): 87, 93; Koppes and Black, *Hollywood Goes to War*, 66.

97. David Welch, *Propaganda and the German Cinema* [1983] (New York: I.B. Tauris, 2001), 38.

98. Koppes and Black, "What to Show the World," 88.

99. "Feature Review: Casablanca," October 28, 1942, Motion Picture Reviews and Analyses 1943–1945, RG 208, National Archives; *Casablanca*, directed by Michael Curtiz (Warner Brothers, 1942).

100. "Feature Review: Mrs. Miniver," August 4, 1943, Motion Picture Reviews and Analyses 1943–1945, RG 208, National Archives; *Mrs. Miniver*, directed by William Wyler (MGM, 1942).

101. Entry for *Mrs. Miniver*, American Film Institute Catalog.

102. Fröhlich et al., *Die Tagebücher von Joseph Goebbels*, entry for July 8, 1943, pt. 2, vol. 9, 64.

103. "Feature Review: Pied Piper," June 25, 1942, Motion Picture Reviews and Analyses 1943–1945, RG 208, National Archives; *The Pied Piper*, directed by Irving Pichel (Twentieth Century-Fox, 1942).

104. "Feature Review: Margin for Error," December 11, 1942, Motion Picture Reviews and Analyses 1943–1945, RG 208, National Archives; *Margin for Error*, directed by Otto Preminger (Twentieth Century-Fox, 1943).

105. *Once Upon a Honeymon*, directed by Leo McCarey (RKO, 1942). For a discussion of McCarey's contribution to the film, see Wes D. Gehring, *Leo McCarey: From Marx to McCarthy* (Lanham, MD: Scarecrow Press, 2005), 174–181.

106. "Feature Review: Once Upon a Honeymoon," October 30, 1942, Motion Picture Reviews and Analyses 1943–1945, RG 208, National Archives.

107. Ibid.

108. Ibid.

109. Sheridan Gibney, "Once Upon a Honeymoon: Cutting Continuity," undated, Core Collection Scripts, Margaret Herrick Library, 58–60.

110. Sheridan Gibney, "Once Upon a Honeymoon: Shooting Script," August 10, 1942 (Alexandria, VA: Alexander Street Press, 2007), 147–148.

111. Sheridan Gibney to Samuel Spewack [on "Once Upon a Honeymoon"], June 30, 1942, Motion Picture Reviews and Analyses 1943–1945, RG 208, National Archives.

112. "Feature Review: Once Upon a Honeymoon," October 30, 1942.

113. United Artists also released Ernst Lubitsch's *To Be or Not to Be*, which criticized the Nazis' persecution of the Jews without mentioning the Jews explicitly. This film opened in Poland before the war with a group of actors rehearsing a play that made fun of Hitler. Suddenly, a representative of the Foreign Office entered the theater and canceled the play, saying that "it might offend Hitler." In this scene, Lubitsch was probably alluding to Hollywood's dealings with Georg Gyssling throughout the 1930s. Lubitsch wanted to call the film *The Censor Forbids*, but the actors Jack Benny and Carole Lombard strongly objected. For the dispute, see Scott Eyman, *Ernst Lubitsch: Laughter in Paradise* (New York: Simon and Schuster, 1993), 297–298. *To Be or Not to Be*, directed by Ernst Lubitsch (United Artists, 1942).

    *To Be or Not to Be* was attacked by critics at the time for making fun of a serious situation. Lubitsch responded to them in the *New York Times*: "I admit that I have not resorted to methods usually employed in pictures, novels and plays to signify Nazi terror. No actual torture chamber is photographed, no flogging is shown, no close-up of excited Nazis using their whip and rolling their eyes in lust. My Nazis are different; they passed that stage long ago. Brutality, flogging and torturing have become their daily routine. They talk about it with the same ease as a salesman referring to the sale of a handbag. Their humor is built around concentration camps, around the sufferings of their victims." Lubitsch concluded by discussing a scene from the movie in which two German aviators immediately followed orders to jump out of a plane: "I am positive that that scene wouldn't draw a chuckle in Nazi Germany. It gets a big laugh in the United States of America. Let's be grateful that it does, and let's hope that it always will." Lubitsch, "Mr. Lubitsch Takes the Floor for Rebuttal," *New York Times*, March 29, 1942, X3.

114.  Hecht, *A Child of the Century*, 466.

115.  Hecht did not write *Gone with the Wind* from scratch but reworked an early version of the script by Sidney Howard.

116.  Hecht to Samuel Goldwyn, undated, Ben Hecht Papers, box 67, folder 1926, Newberry Library, Chicago (henceforth Newberry Library). In this letter, Hecht was complaining about changes to *Goldwyn Follies*; the following year, he wrote the script for Goldwyn's *Wuthering Heights*.

117.  Hecht, *A Child of the Century*, 517–518; Hecht, *A Guide for the Bedevilled* (New York: Charles Scribner's Sons, 1944), 7.

118.  Ben Hecht, *A Book of Miracles* (New York: Viking, 1939), 23–26.

119.  Ibid., 47.

120.  Ibid., 53.

121.  Hecht, *A Child of the Century*, 520; Ralph Ingersoll, Confidential memorandum to the staff of *PM*, April 22 1940. For the founding of *PM*, see the documents at the beginning of the microfilm edition.

122.  Ben Hecht, "A Diplomat Spikes a Cannon," *PM*, January 16, 1941, 11.

123.  Ben Hecht, "Run, Sheep—Run!" *PM*, March 26, 1941, 13.

124.  Hecht, "My Tribe Is Called Israel," *PM*, April 15, 1941, 14.

125.  Hecht, "These Were Once Conquerors," *PM*, August 24, 1941, 18; Peter Bergson to Hecht, August 28, 1941, Ben Hecht Papers, box 55, folder 1069b, Newberry Library.

126.  Peter Bergson to Hecht, September 12, 1941, Ben Hecht Papers, box 55, folder 1069b, Newberry Library; Hecht, *A Child of the Century*, 516, 533, 535–536.

127.  Hecht, *A Child of the Century*, 536, 537–545; "Orders Waited by Jewish Army: Palestine Organizer Says 100,000 Men Ready to Fight," *Los Angeles Times*, April 16, 1942, A2; "Group Will Honor Jewish Legion: Notables to Speak at Founding Celebration," *Los Angeles Times*, June 5, 1942, 6; "Committee Here to Push Drive for Formation of Jewish Army," *Los Angeles Times*, July 26, 1942, 14.

128.  "Himmler Program Kills Polish Jews," *New York Times*, November 25, 1942, 10; "Wise Gets Confirmations: Checks With State Department on Nazis' 'Extermination,'" *New York Times*, November 25, 1942, 10; "Half of Jews Ordered Slain, Poles Report," *Washington Post*, November 25, 1942, 6; "2 Million Jews Slain, Rabbi Wise Asserts," *Washington Post*, November 25, 1942, 6; "Slain Polish Jews Put at a Million," *New York Times*, November 26, 1942, 16. For the *New York Times'* coverage of the Holocaust, see Laurel Leff, *Buried by the Times: The Holocaust and America's Most Important Newspaper* (Cambridge: Cambridge University Press, 2005).

129.  David S. Wyman, *The Abandonment of the Jews: America and the Holocaust, 1941–1945* (New York: Free Press, 1984), 43–45, 58. Other books on this subject include Arthur D. Morse, *While Six Million Died: A Chronicle of American Apathy* (New York: Random House, 1968); Walter Laqueur, *The Terrible Secret: Suppression of the Truth about Hitler's "Final Solution"* (Boston, Little, Brown and Company, 1980).

130. Wyman, *Abandonment of the Jews*, 72–73.

131. Ibid., 77–78.

132. Ibid., 84–86. For an interview with Peter Bergson and Samuel Merlin that was not included in Claude Lanzmann's *Shoah* (1985), see the Claude Lanzmann Shoah Collection, Story RG-60.5020, Tape 3254–3258, November 15, 1978, United States Holocaust Memorial Museum, Washington, DC. For the activities of the Bergson group, see David S. Wyman and Rafael Medoff, *A Race against Death: Peter Bergson, America, and the Holocaust* (New York: New Press, 2002); Rafael Medoff, *Militant Zionism in America: The Rise and Impact of the Jabotinsky Movement in the United States, 1926–1948* (Tuscaloosa: University of Alabama Press, 2002); Judith Tydor Baumel-Schwartz, *The "Bergson Boys" and the Origins of Contemporary Zionist Militancy* (Syracuse, NY: Syracuse University Press, 2005).

133. "Advertisement: To the Conscience Of America," *New York Times*, December 5, 1942, 16.

134. "Advertisement: Action—Not Pity Can Save Millions Now!" *New York Times*, February 8, 1943, 8.

135. "Advertisement: FOR SALE to Humanity," *New York Times*, February 16, 1943, 11.

136. For the position of the State Department, see Wyman's *The Abandonment of the Jews*. Wyman discovered many disturbing State Department memos, such as the following, from spring 1943 (on page 99): "While in theory any approach to the German Government would have met with a blank refusal, there was always the danger that the German Government might agree to turn over to the United States and to Great Britain a large number of Jewish refugees at some designated place for immediate transportation to areas under the control of the United Nations."

137. Ibid., 87.

138. Ibid., 87–89.

139. Ibid., 90–91; Hecht, *A Child of the Century*, 557–558.

140. Ben Hecht, "We Will Never Die: National Pageant Memorializing the Two Million Murdered Jews of Europe," Copyright Records, reg. no. 84654, June 22, 1943, Manuscript Division, LC, 2.

141. While Hecht was working on *We Will Never Die*, he was in the middle of one of his fights with Samuel Goldwyn. He wrote to a friend: "I also got involved in the god-damnest sand-storm with Goldwyn and the Navy Department on a big Navy cavalcade picture. . . . I discovered that Goldwyn wanted to borrow the Navy to put on another kissing match between Gary Cooper and some new starlet. Rather than betray my country (again) I bowed out with the result that Goldwyn is hot-footing it East—to have me arrested, I think. He is going to corner me in Washington, D.C., where Billy Rose and I are engaged in throwing a big lobby at the State Department anent the massacre in Europe in the form of a Pageant. I shall be surrounded by 220 rabbis when Goldwyn arrives." Hecht to Gene

Fowler, April 8, 1943, Ben Hecht Papers, box 67, folder 1899, Newberry Library.

142. Wyman, *Abandonment of the Jews*, 92. "The Bergson group was anathema to most of the established American Jewish leadership. The Bergson organizations, opponents insisted, had no legitimate mandate to speak for American Jews, since they represented no constituency in American Jewish life. They were interlopers who had intruded into areas of action that were the province of the established Jewish organizations."

143. Ibid., 113, 114–115.

144. Ibid., 120–121, 157–177.

145. "Advertisement: To 5,000,000 Jews in the Nazi Death-Trap Bermuda Was a 'Cruel Mockery,'" *New York Times*, May 4, 1943, 17.

146. Wyman, *Abandonment of the Jews*, 144–146.

147. "Advertisement: Time Races Death," *New York Times*, December 17, 1943, 31; "Advertisement: They Are Driven To Death Daily, But They Can Be Saved," *New York Times*, August 12, 1943, 10; "Advertisement: We All Stand Before the Bar of Humanity, History and God," *New York Times*, August 30, 1943, 10; "Advertisement: How Well Are You Sleeping?" *New York Times*, November 24, 1943, 13.

148. "Advertisement: Ballad of the Doomed Jews of Europe, by Ben Hecht," *New York Times*, September 14, 1943, 12.

149. Wyman, *Abandonment of the Jews*, 148, 152–153, 154. For a more sympathetic assessment of Roosevelt's efforts, see Richard Breitman and Allan J. Lichtman, *FDR and the Jews* (Cambridge, MA: Harvard University Press, 2013).

150. "Advertisement: My Uncle Abraham Reports . . . By Ben Hecht," *New York Times*, November 5, 1943, 14.

151. Ibid.

152. Ibid.

153. Ibid.

154. Ibid.

155. Wyman, *Abandonment of the Jews*, 155–156, 200–201.

156. "Rabbi Wise Urges Palestine Action: Tells House Committee Rescue Resolution on Jews Does Not Go Far Enough," *New York Times*, December 3, 1943, 4.

157. Wyman, *Abandonment of the Jews*, 203.

158. Billy Rose to Hecht, January 30, 1944, Ben Hecht Papers, box 61, folder 1586, Newberry Library.

159. Samuel Merlin to Hecht, January 25, 1944, Ben Hecht Papers, box 60, folder 1472, Newberry Library.

160. Wyman, *Abandonment of the Jews*, 213, 285–287.

161. Peter Bergson to Franklin D. Roosevelt, January 23, 1944, *Palestine Statehood Committee Records, 1939–1949*, microfilm ed., Primary Source Media, roll 1.

162. Hecht to Rose Hecht, April 2, 1945, Ben Hecht Papers, box 73, folder 2257, Newberry Library.

163. Hecht, *A Child of the Century*, 578.

164. "I was aware that I was doing all these things as a Jew. My eloquence in behalf of democracy was inspired chiefly by my Jewish anger. I had been no partisan of democracy in my earlier years. Its sins had seemed to me more prominent than its virtues. But now that it was the potential enemy of the new German Police State I was its uncarping disciple. Thus, oddly, in addition to becoming a Jew in 1939 I became also an American—and remained one." Hecht, *A Child of the Century*, 518.

165. Hecht, *A Guide for the Bedevilled*, 202–203.

166. Ibid., 207–210.

167. Ibid., 213.

168. Ibid., 212–213.

169. *The Seventh Cross*, directed by Fred Zinnemann (MGM, 1944); Helen Deutsch, "The Seventh Cross: Outline," May 5, 1943, Turner/MGM Scripts, Margaret Herrick Library. The other pictures that mentioned the persecution of the Jews were *Address Unknown* directed by William Cameron Menzies (Columbia Pictures, 1944); *The Hitler Gang*, directed by John Farrow (Paramount, 1944); *Hotel Berlin*, directed by Peter Godfrey (Warner Brothers, 1945).

170. *None Shall Escape*, directed by Andre DeToth (Columbia Pictures, 1944).

171. Hecht, *A Guide for the Bedevilled*, 197–198.

172. Ibid., 198.

173. Ibid., 206–207.

EPILOGUE

1. Francis Harmon, "Western Europe in the Wake of World War II: As seen by a group of American motion picture industry executives visiting the European and Mediterranean Theaters of Operation as guests of the military authorities, June 17–July 18, 1945," Jack L. Warner Collection, scrapbook 2, European trip, box 81A, USC Cinematic Arts Library, Los Angeles (henceforth Cinematic Arts Library), 1; "U.S. Film Heads in London, Plan Study Tour of Reich," *New York Times*, June 19, 1945, 14. Harmon was also the vice chairman of the motion picture industry's War Activities Committee.

2. Harmon, "Western Europe in the Wake of World War II," 1.

3. Public Relations Division, Supreme Headquarters Allied Expeditionary Force, "Itinerary—Motion Picture Executives," June 17, 1945, Jack L. Warner Collection, scrapbook 1, European trip, box 81A, Cinematic Arts Library. A copy of the itinerary can also be found in the Records of the Information Control Division, Office of Military Government for Germany (U.S.), Records of United States Occupation Headquarters World War II, box 290, "Films—Technical Consultants," RG 260, National Archives and Records Administration, College Park, Maryland (henceforth National Archives).

4. J. J. McCloy to Harry Hopkins, January 8, 1944, File 862.4061 MP/1-1145, 1940–44 Central Decimal File, RG 59, National Archives. Zanuck was not

officially working for Twentieth Century-Fox when he made this proposal to Harry Hopkins. He had taken a leave of absence from the company and was serving as a colonel in the U.S. Army Signal Corps.

5. S. I. R., Memorandum for the President, February 8, 1945, Official File 73: Motion Pictures; Franklin D. Roosevelt to Harry Warner, March 3, 1945, Official File 73: Motion Pictures; Roosevelt to John G. Winant, March 3, 1945, Official File 73: Motion Pictures; Winant to Roosevelt, March 27, 1945, Official File 73: Motion Pictures, Franklin D. Roosevelt Library, Hyde Park, New York.

6. McCloy to Hopkins, January 8, 1944.

7. "Urges Films for Reich: Zanuck Tells Truman of Plan for Movies of Life in U.S.," *New York Times*, June 16, 1945, 10.

8. Harmon, "Western Europe in the Wake of World War II," 13–14.

9. Public Relations Division, Supreme Headquarters Allied Expeditionary Force, "Itinerary—Motion Picture Executives," June 17, 1945. The executives were meant to go to Nordhausen concentration camp, a subcamp of Buchenwald.

10. Harmon's notes no. 12, Jack L. Warner Collection, scrapbook 2, European trip, box 81A, Cinematic Arts Library.

11. Public Relations Division, Supreme Headquarters Allied Expeditionary Force, "Itinerary—Motion Picture Executives," June 17, 1945.

12. Harmon, "Western Europe in the Wake of World War II," 15; Photograph marked "1st Putsch Parade: Doorway Munich Adolph Ducked," Jack L. Warner Collection, scrapbook 2, European trip, box 81A, Cinematic Arts Library.

13. Harmon, "Western Europe in the Wake of World War II," 15–16.

14. Photographs marked "Dachau Death Boxes" and "Dachau Boxes," Jack L. Warner Collection, scrapbook 2, European trip, box 81A, Cinematic Arts Library.

15. Harmon, "Western Europe in the Wake of World War II," 15.

16. Ibid., 16–20; Harmon's notes no. 13, "Covering Discussions on Psychological Warfare and Information Control in Occupied Germany, July 4, 1945," Jack L. Warner Collection, scrapbook 2, European trip, box 81A, Cinematic Arts Library.

17. Harmon, "Western Europe in the Wake of World War II," 16, 18–19; Public Relations Division, Supreme Headquarters Allied Expeditionary Force, "Itinerary—Motion Picture Executives," June 17, 1945.

18. Francis Harmon et al., "Report Of Motion Picture Industry Executives to Major General A. D. Surles, Chief, Bureau of Public Relations of the War Department, Following their Tour of the European and Mediterranean Theatres of Operations as Guests of the Army," August 10, 1945, Jack L. Warner Collection, scrapbook 2, European trip, box 81A, Cinematic Arts Library, 5.

19. Jack Warner to Francis Harmon, August 9, 1945, Jack L. Warner Collection, scrapbook 2, European trip, box 81A, Cinematic Arts Library.

20. Francis Harmon to Jack Warner, August 10, 1945, Jack L. Warner Collection, scrapbook 2, European trip, box 81A, Cinematic Arts Library.

21. Jack Warner to Francis Harmon, August 10, 1945, Jack L. Warner Collection, scrapbook 2, European trip, box 81A; Harmon et al., "Report Of Motion Picture Executives to Major General A. D. Surles."

22. The U.S. Army Signal Corps had already captured images of the death camps on film. For a comprehensive record of this footage, see Charles Lawrence Gellert, "The Holocaust, Israel, and the Jews: Motion Pictures in the National Archives," National Archives and Records Administration, Washington, DC, 1989, 13–50.

23. The first Hollywood movies to mention the Holocaust were *The Diary of Anne Frank* (1959), *Judgment at Nuremberg* (1961), and *The Pawnbroker* (1965).

# ACKNOWLEDGMENTS

I would like to thank the staff of the following archives for helping me track down the materials on which this book is based: the Political Archive of the Foreign Office, the Bundesarchiv, and the Bundesarchiv-Filmarchiv in Berlin; the Bundesarchiv in Coblenz; the German Film Institute in Frankfurt; the Film Museum in Munich; the Margaret Herrick Library, the USC Cinematic Arts Library, the USC Warner Bros. Archives, and the Urban Archives Center in Los Angeles; the Bancroft Library in Berkeley; the Hoover Institution in Stanford; the Library of Congress and the United States Holocaust Memorial Museum in Washington; the National Archives in College Park; the Franklin D. Roosevelt Presidential Library in Hyde Park; the Newberry Library in Chicago; the Reform Congregation Keneseth Israel Archives in Elkins Park; and the Morris Library in Carbondale. I am especially grateful to Ned Comstock (USC Cinematic Arts Library), Gerhard Keiper (Political Archive of the Foreign Office), Jenny Romero (Margaret Herrick Library), and Alice Birney (Library of Congress).

I began writing this book while at the University of California, Berkeley, where I had the good fortune to work with three scholars who are sadly no longer with us: Michael Rogin, Lawrence Levine, and Norman Jacobson. I am also deeply grateful to Leon Litwack, who was wonderfully supportive; Martin Jay and Carol Clover, who provided excellent advice; and Kathleen Moran, Waldo Martin, and Anton Kaes, who went out of their way to help.

Over the past year and a half, I have benefited immensely from being a part of the Harvard Society of Fellows, and I am grateful to Bernard Bailyn, Walter Gilbert, Joseph Koerner, and Maria Tatar. I would especially like to thank Noah Feldman for his early belief in the project, and Elaine Scarry and David Armitage for reading the entire manuscript and giving extremely helpful suggestions.

I received assistance in hunting down archival materials from Kevin Brownlow, Julian Saltman, Rob Schwartz, Anthony Slide, Markus Spieker, David Thomson, and Andreas-Michael Velten. A Milton Fund Grant helped me to carry out much of the research. I learned a lot from an interview with Gene Reynolds. Daniel Bowles and Daniel Jütte helped with German translations. Shane White at the University of Sydney provided continuous encouragement.

This book found a home at Harvard University Press, and I am grateful to everyone there, especially my editor John Kulka, who has contributed keen insight over the past year. I would also like to thank Andrew Wylie and Kristina Moore for their unwavering support.

Greil Marcus has guided me from the moment I first stumbled upon materials in the archives. He has been unbelievably generous and constantly inspiring.

My greatest debt is to Melissa Fall. Without her, I would never have made it to the end.

# INDEX